"AN INVALUABLE ACCOUNT OF A SPIRITED FIGHTER FOR THE UNDERDOG ... IMMENSELY REVEALING. INDISPENSABLE TO THE GROWING BODY OF LITERATURE ON AMERICA'S TERRIFYING POSTWAR RED SCARE."—*Library Journal*

The National Best Seller

HOWARD FAST
BEING RED
A Memoir

"FAST'S AUTOBIOGRAPHY JOINS JACK LONDON'S *MARTIN EDEN* AS A CLASSIC STORY OF THE BIRTH OF A SELF-EDUCATED WRITER ... THE STORY OF HIS VILIFICATION, IMPRISONMENT, AND BLACKLISTING BY PUBLISHERS IS SEARING."—*Kirkus Reviews*

"OFTEN INTRIGUING AND ALWAYS WELL WRITTEN ... ALONG THE RED ROAD HE MET AND MINGLED WITH THE LIKES OF PETE SEEGER, PAUL ROBESON, JEAN-PAUL SARTRE, H. L. MENCKEN, JOHN HOWARD LAWSON, AND OTHERS ... A WELL-WROUGHT AND EVOCATIVE ACCOUNT."—*Booklist*

Books by Howard Fast

* Available from Dell

BEING
RED

Howard Fast

A LAUREL TRADE PAPERPACK
Published by
Dell Publishing
a division of
Bantam Doubleday Dell Publishing Group, Inc.
666 Fifth Avenue
New York, New York 10103

ISBN: 0-440-50412-0

Reprinted by arrangement with Houghton Mifflin Company, Boston, Massachusetts

Printed in the United States of America

Published simultaneously in Canada

November 1991

10 9 8 7 6 5 4 3 2 1

RRH

For you, Bette,
wife and partner in this long journey

BEING
RED

I

THERE IS NO WAY to tell the story of the curious life that happened to me without dealing with the fact that I was for many years what that old brute Senator Joseph McCarthy delighted in calling "a card-carrying member of the Communist Party." He had a way of saying it as if it were a spell to evoke Old Nick himself, and he shrouded each evocation of the devil in such nasty delight that you could fairly smell the smoke.

In my single encounter with the old monster, I tried vainly to instruct him in some of the more obvious truths of American history, in response to which McCarthy, in a towering rage, roared at me to go write a book. I wrote more than he asked for, but of that, later. At this point, I am trying to describe the circumstances that led me into the Communist movement, where I remained for twelve years, with a profound effect on all my life.

Pearl Harbor had happened, and the world was at war, and the United States joined the forces that faced Adolf Hitler and his fascist allies. It was 1942, and in the desperate rush by America to turn a peaceful nation into a war machine, many things were quickly if loosely put together. One of these was a propaganda and information center, something that the country had done well enough without in the past but was now a necessity in this era of radio. This propaganda and information center, so hastily thrown together, was called the Office of War Information, or OWI; and feeling that the only available pool of talent to man it was in New York City, the government took over the General Motors Building at Fifty-seventh Street and Broadway. In the first few months after Pearl Harbor, the government set to in a sort of frenzy to remake the building according to its needs, staff it, and somehow learn the art — if such it was — of war propaganda.

Howard Fast, meanwhile, was living the ultimate fulfillment of a poor boy's dream. Raised in bitter and unrelenting poverty, I had now plunged right into the American dream. Of the poverty, of the awful and painful years that I spent in what people call childhood, I will have more to say; at this point, 1942, I was sitting right on top of eighteen pots of honey. My third novel, *The Last Frontier,* published a year earlier, had been greeted as a "masterpiece," praised to the skies by Alexander Woollcott and Rex Stout, and chosen as a selection by the esteemed Readers Club, and my new novel, just published, called *The Unvanquished,* a story of the Continental Army's most desperate moment, had been called, by *Time* magazine who found in it a parallel for the grim present, "the best book about World War Two." I was twenty-seven years old, about to turn twenty-eight, and five years earlier I had married a wonderful blue-eyed, flaxen-haired girl, an artist by name of Bette, an artist by every right, and still my wife and companion, fifty-three years later. We had survived the first hard years nicely enough, and we had just put down $500 for an acre of land on the Old Sleepy Hollow Road near Tarrytown.

At Sears, Roebuck we purchased for twelve dollars a set of blueprints, and with a mortgage of $8000 and $1000 in cash, we built a small, lovely two-bedroom cottage. Bette became pregnant, we acquired a wonderful mongrel named Ginger, and I finished writing a book I would call *Citizen Tom Paine.* I cleared the land myself, Bette learned to bake and cook and sew small clothes, and I saw a rewarding, gentle future, in which we would have many children and Bette would paint and I would write my books and earn fame and fortune. And then the war came, and it all turned to dust.

In quick succession, my father died (my mother had died when I was eight and a half, and my father never remarried), my younger brother, close to me and my dearest friend, enlisted in the army, I drew a low draft number, and Bette miscarried our first child and sank into gloom. The future that we had planned so carefully was cast aside; Ginger was given to my older brother and promptly ran away and disappeared; the house was put up for sale; we moved into a one-room studio in New York; and Bette, convinced that my orders would be cut in a matter of weeks at the most, leaving her to face the possibility of years alone, joined the Signal Corps as a civilian artist, making animated training films.

Well, there it was, a pile of ashes but certainly not the worst such pile in those strange times. We were young, in good health, and I was successful and was looking forward to being in uniform. It is hard for us today, living with the horror of the atom bomb, remembering Korea and Vietnam, sick of war, and aware that the next war may finish the human race — hard indeed to think about a time when this country was knit together in a hatred of Nazism, wholly united in a conviction that we could not live in the same world as Adolf Hitler. But it was that way, and we knew that we would have to fight, and we accepted it — at least the great majority of us.

When I argued with my wife that it made more sense for me to enlist, as my brother had, than to wait around for a summons by the draft board, she objected strenuously and angrily, guided by the sensible feminine hope that the board would somehow miss me. I was bored and frustrated, and for two weeks I wandered the streets of New York, watched daytime movies, and looked with envy at every one of the thousands of uniformed men and women whom I passed. Then one midday, on West Fifty-seventh Street, I met Louis Untermeyer, and my life changed and nothing would ever again be what we had dreamed our lives might be. Whether it works that way, where a chance meeting can turn existence upside down, or whether what happened to me would have happened in any case, I don't know.

Louis Untermeyer, at that time in his middle fifties, had a national reputation as a poet and anthologist. His knowledge of poetry was encyclopedic, his critical sense wise and balanced, and his wit delightful. He would become a major figure in my life, a beloved friend as well as a surrogate father, but at that time I knew him only slightly, having met him once, a year before this chance meeting on Fifty-seventh Street. The previous meeting had been in Philadelphia, at the Academy of Music, where I was invited to make the first public speech of my life. In front of an audience of twelve hundred literary-minded

people, I read an address I had spent days preparing. I read it from
beginning to end, a matter of at least twenty minutes, but since I was
in a state of stark terror, no sound emerged from my lips. It was at
this moment of cold anguish and hopeless despair that Louis came
to my aid and saved me from some form of self-destruction by telling
me that the same thing had once happened to him, and that the
audience would not hold it against me but would cherish my platform terror as the stuff of an anecdote to tell their friends. (Let me
note that in due time I became an excellent speaker, one of the best
in the Communist movement.)

On this day in 1942 I greeted Louis Untermeyer as my savior and
eagerly accepted his invitation to lunch. Any meal with Louis was a
delight. He would bring a gourmet's appreciation to a boiled egg,
and his wit was so much a part of him that he had no existence
without it. During lunch I poured out my tale of boredom and frustration, and once again he offered a solution. The solution was the
Office of War Information, and it was located down the street, two
blocks from where we were eating.

Louis had shared my present feeling of impotence and frustration,
and he had offered his services to the OWI for whatever use it might
have for him. So he had been given a desk and was now writing a
propaganda pamphlet. Since at his age he could not bear arms, a
propaganda pamphlet was meaningful. He asked me to come back
with him, positive that the OWI would offer me the same thing.

To what end, I wondered. What on earth was the use of writing
propaganda pamphlets? Who would read them? What difference
would it make? What do you say — that Nazism is evil? Be of good
cheer, someday American troops will land on the European continent and destroy Adolf Hitler?

Louis calmly replied that since this was something the government
decided should be done, he was willing to do it. Possibly the pamphlets would be translated into the languages of occupied Europe;
possibly they would be dropped from planes. He did not convince
me that such a plan was other than useless, nor have I ever changed
my mind about that; at the time I was convinced that nothing I could
say would have the slightest meaning in occupied Europe. But I was
bored and discontented, and it was only a matter of weeks before I'd
be drafted, so I went along with Louis's suggestion and walked with

him back to the OWI, where I was welcomed with open arms, hired two days later, given a desk and a typewriter, and instructed to do a pamphlet on the American Revolution. Since my novel *The Unvanquished* was about the American Revolution, that was my thing. It made absolutely no sense to me. I had no notion of what use the pamphlet might be; I considered it a boondoggle. When I told Bette about it, I also informed her that I was ready to give the job back.

She thought otherwise, arguing that even if my pamphlet was some sort of boondoggle, the OWI needed time to give itself a direction. I had to agree with her. The desk where I did my writing was on the top floor of the building; on the floors below, Elmer Davis, newly appointed head of the Office of War Information, was trying to whip a massive short-wave radio operation into shape, setting up speaking and translation units for every country of occupied Europe — as well as for Spain, Portugal, and Sweden, still unoccupied by Nazi forces. Of this, at the time I was writing my pamphlet, I knew nothing. I took the elevator to my floor. Nobody had bothered to enlighten me about the problems of the floors below.

And they had their problems. Setting up the short-wave operation itself presented few difficulties, and though there were some hitches in putting together the translation desks — such as finding someone to man the Hungarian Desk other than cultural fascists — those were solved. Where the operation bogged down, curiously enough, was in setting up an operation called the American BBC. This had come into being because none of our medium-wave broadcasting units could reach the European continent. Medium wave was the normal radio transmission in the United States as well as in Europe, and though radio hams might have short-wave sets, ordinary households had the widely manufactured commercial medium-wave sets. There was only a sprinkling of the short-wave sets on the continent, and the Nazi SS worked assiduously to destroy them.

The feeling at the State Department and the War Department was that we must somehow reach the medium-wave receivers in European households, and since the only part of the European community that was both free and allied to us was Great Britain, our people cast their covetous eyes on the British Broadcasting Company. The British were none too happy at the thought of the Yanks putting their grubby fingers on the precious BBC, but their dependence on these same

Yanks was enormous, so there was no way they could shunt off our demands. Elmer Davis, a one-time correspondent for *The New York Times* and later a radio news commentator, was at that time the most respected man in the field of radio news transmission. Joseph Barnes, a veteran newspaperman, talented and respected, was brought in by Davis to work with him. Both of them understood the importance of medium wave as opposed to short wave, and they persuaded our government to lean on the British; the result was that the British agreed to turn over their BBC medium-wave transmitters to us for four hours a day, from two A.M. to six A.M. our time, which was seven A.M. to eleven A.M. London time. A T & T set up a triple transatlantic telephone transmission to London; it would take our voices across the ocean with practically no loss in quality.

So now we had it, a transmitting facility that would cover Europe with our propaganda and could be tuned in by every home on the continent. Now it remained only to find someone to prepare the basic fifteen-minute program that would be translated into eleven languages and repeated several times in French and German. My knowledge of what happened in this search came from John Houseman, who headed up part of the short-wave operation — dramatic radio propaganda — and whom I later came to know and like enormously. John — or Jack, as we called him — had given up his work as a successful producer to come to the OWI, and according to Houseman, three men were hired in succession to be the BBC anchor writer, and each of the three had served from a week to two weeks and was then fired. One was the head of the second largest ad agency in New York; the other two were newspapermen.

During a meeting with Houseman on another subject, Davis and Barnes raised the question of whom to hire for the BBC and where to find him. They told Houseman how desperate they were and what a letdown the three candidates had been, all of them highly recommended and men of experience. There were other men — it was before the time when they might have turned to women — whom they wanted, men in good positions who would not give up their careers even for the OWI. Houseman asked them exactly what they wanted, to which they answered someone who could write clean, straightforward prose, someone who was literate yet simple and direct.

To this, Houseman answered that he had just read the proofs of a

book called *Citizen Tom Paine,* clean, colorful political writing by a
kid name of Howard Fast. And how old was this kid? Twenty-seven
or twenty-eight. And how do they get in touch with him? He's right
here in this building, top floor, writing a pamphlet about the American Revolution. And what in hell was he or anyone else doing sitting
up there and writing a pamphlet about the American Revolution?
Didn't anyone up there understand that this was World War Two,
and not the American Revolution? A few minutes after this discussion, the head of the pamphlet department came to my desk and told
me that Elmer Davis, chief of the operation, wanted me downstairs
in the radio section.

I will never forget walking through the corridors where the short-
wave power packs were stacked floor to ceiling, seeing them for the
first time with a sense of awe, and realizing for the first time that this
building housed no boondoggle but rather was the heart of the Voice
of America. Suddenly, I felt that I was going to be fired, and for the
first time, I did not want to be fired; I wanted to be a part of this, the
tickers everywhere, the men in uniform, both army and navy, the
cubbyhole offices with their placards: FRENCH DESK, GERMAN
DESK, DANISH DESK, CROATIAN DESK — Croatians, where had
I heard of them, and who were they? — and inside each cubbyhole, different people, some bearded, some old, some of them young,
exotic women, scribbling, typing, all of them animated by fierce
energy. Were they refugees? I wondered. Refugees from Hitler were
romantic figures then. A dozen different tongues were competing
with the chatter of ticker tape machines and orders barked over a
loudspeaker system — and all of this going on in a building where
I had spent two quiet weeks working on a pamphlet about the
Revolution.

In Elmer Davis's office, Davis and Barnes and Houseman awaited
me. I walked into the room, and the three cold-eyed, hard-faced
men stared at me as if I were an insect on a pin, and then Elmer
Davis said, "Are you Fast?"

Of course, they were not hard-faced or cold-eyed, but I was
scared and unsure of myself and convinced that I was to be fired
for some awful foul-up in my pamphlet, which must have been
brought to them as proof of my culpability. I can recall the conversation that followed fairly well, by no means exactly after all

these years. Jack Houseman, my entry angel into this strange new world, began by spelling out the nature of what would be called from then on simply the BBC, how the deal with the British had come about, and what it was intended to do. Then Elmer Davis picked up and said to me, "That's why you're here, Fast. Jack says you can write."

They were all standing. Suddenly, they all sat down. No one asked me to sit down, so I remained standing. They kept looking at me as if I were distinctive in some way. I wasn't. I was five feet ten and a half inches, I still had plenty of hair, and I had round cheeks that embarrassed the hell out of me because they turned pink at my slightest unease. Brown eyes and heavy horn-rimmed glasses completed the picture.

"Do you follow me?" David asked.

I shook my head.

"What he means," Houseman said kindly, "is that he wants you to take over the BBC and write the fifteen-minute blueprint every day."

I shook my head again. If I had unclasped my hands, they would have been shaking like leaves. I was not being fired. This was worse.

"I can't do that," I said.

"Why not?"

"I just don't know how. I never wrote for radio. I never worked for a newspaper."

"We're not asking for reference," Barnes said. "Mr. Houseman here says you write simply and well and that you can think politically. We're asking you to write a fifteen-minute news program that will tell people in occupied Europe how the war goes, what our army has done, and what our hopes and intentions are. We want you to do it plainly and honestly, to tell the truth and not mince words. You are not to lie or invent. You will have a pool of some twenty actors available, and you will choose three each night to speak your words for the English section. Other actors will speak the foreign translations."

"It's no use," I pleaded. "I'm going to be drafted. I have a low number."

Elmer Davis came to me and lifted off my glasses. Staring at them, he said, "You're technically blind in your right eye, aren't you?"

"Oh, no," I said. "No. I see quite well out of that eye."

"You won't be drafted," Elmer Davis said.

"Suppose I botch the whole thing?"

"We'll give you a week, and if you botch it, we'll dump you."

"And if you are drafted," Barnes assured me, "you'll be back here in a uniform — unless we toss you out first."

There were no amenities; it took all of ten minutes, and then I was out of there with a guide to take me to my new office. My guide was a young woman whose name I have forgotten, and she led me to a large office, about fifteen feet square. A glass wall separated my room from the rest of the floor, where some twenty people were pecking away at typewriters. These were the newsmen, endlessly grinding out copy for the short-wave operation, a transmission that went on twenty-four hours a day. How often I would stare at that glass wall and its furious activity while the writers in short wave would occasionally stare back at the lonely writer, regarding his sheet of paper broodingly, pecking out a sentence and then studying it and studying it.

But right now, my guide was fitting the new writer into place, and she spelled out the nature of my operation. There were five teletype printers lined up against one wall — Associated Press, United Press, Reuters, Army Information Service, and the fifth some special Washington service that had been set up at the time. There was a direct telephone connection with staff headquarters in Washington — the Pentagon was being built but was not yet in operation — as well as two other outside telephones and an inside telephone for the various offices in the building. A large desk and typewriter for myself, and another for a special typist who would be assigned to me. I was informed by my guide that both army intelligence and naval intelligence would deliver material twice a day, and that I was to have absolute priority for anything I required anywhere in the United States, as long as the need connected with the BBC. Nothing was to take precedence over the four hours of the BBC.

My guide explained that this was a very special privilege and that it was not to be abused. She also informed me that my finished copy would be subject to "control," and that I should try to have it to control as soon as possible, before nine P.M. at the latest, so that there would be time for translation. Since we would start the triple telephone transmission to London with the English-language reading at two A.M., that would give the foreign-language desks only five hours for translation and mimeo. Today, they were transmitting selections from the short-wave copy desk; tomorrow, I would be expected to have my first fifteen-minute pilot script ready no later than nine, and from that point, I was to reduce my time if humanly possible.

While we were talking, the producer of the English-language fifteen minutes came in, and I was introduced to her. Helen Dunlop was an attractive young woman with bright eyes and curly hair who came from Pasadena, California. I was to see a good deal of Miss Dunlop during the coming months. She was to receive a carbon copy of the newscast as early as possible each day so that she could select available actors from the pool. Then my typist appeared, a good-looking Bennington graduate who had learned everything there was for her to learn at Bennington, except how to type. In her devotion to the war effort, she had taken a crash course, but her typing still left a great deal to be desired.

At dinner that night, I poured out to Bette the incredible changes that had come into my life. She mentioned my draft number, and I told her that Elmer Davis had assured me that if I was any good, I'd stay there, in uniform or not. "Which doesn't make me happy," I said. "I want to be a part of this war. Irwin Shaw says he won't write this war; he'll fight it."

"And you want to be equally stupid," Bette said. "There are only twenty-five million men in this country available to carry a gun, and how many can do what you're doing? Do you know what happened to you today? Do you have any idea what happened to you?"

The truth was, I didn't. The Voice of America had been dumped into my lap, and I was absolutely unable to comprehend what had happened. The whole face and image of the United States had been handed to me, and what I wrote would be most of what the dark pale that was occupied Europe would know of what we were planning and doing and what our reply to Nazism would be, and all I could make of it was that a man named Elmer Davis and another man named Joseph Barnes had ordered me to do something that I was obviously unfit to do. Well, unfit or not, I intended to do it and do it as well as I could.

They didn't fire me. The weeks stretched into months, and they didn't fire me. My number came up a few weeks after my BBC job began, and I was still of the belief that if you were going to fight fascism, the way to do it was with a gun in your hands. I wasn't worried about my bad right eye, because during the physical, standing on line to have my eyes examined, I simply memorized the chart. When my turn came and I handed my papers to the eye doctor, he studied them a bit longer than he had to, and then he consulted some notes on his desk.

"Fast?" He handed me a card to cover my right eye. No problem there. "The other eye now." I began to call off the chart, and the doctor grinned and held up three fingers. "Forget the chart. How many fingers?"

I guessed two.

"Actually, three. Come on, mister — go back to where you were."

"They set me up, didn't they? Who was it? Barnes? Davis?"

I stomped out of there in a fury and went back to the nightmare that they called the American BBC — and a nightmare it was. I had never driven myself like that before or since, and I was no stranger to hard work, physical or mental. I would get into my office at eight o'clock in the morning, usually to find someone from some branch of the government waiting for me. The White House wanted to stress the numbers of tank production because the Germans were saying that in no way could we ever match their numbers. Or Whitehall wanted us to play down the invasion of the continent. Or why wasn't I putting more emphasis on food production? This gentleman is from the Department of Agriculture. I could plead that he didn't have to come up from Washington in person and kill a precious hour of my morning. The secretary so instructed him. The secretary felt that I did not understand that a war was fought with food as well as bullets. The people on the continent were starving. Did I understand what it meant for them to know that there would be ample food? Nobody made appointments with me; they just poured in. The

Chamber of Commerce — how on earth did the U.S. Chamber of
Commerce know what I was writing? No one publicized that we had
four hours of BBC each morning, but everyone appeared to know.
Ordnance has this new carbine; eight o'clock in the morning, they're
there with the carbine. What in hell am I to do with a carbine? How
did I get here? I'm a kid, and I know practically nothing about anything. Ten P.M. I get back to my office, and a distinguished-looking
gentleman tells me that he has been waiting two hours. He represents
the shipyard owners of America. Do I know what shipyards mean in
this war? Do I understand that without ships we would lose the war?
I demand to know how he knows what I write, and he does a double
take and demands to know who I am. I'm Howard Fast. You? You're
Howard Fast? You? If it's not him, it's another. If I get my back up
about this kind of thing, going on day after day, then word gets to
Washington, and the State Department sends someone up to interview me. He wants two hours. I don't have two hours; I don't want
to be interviewed; just get out of here and let me work. The War
Department just interviewed me. What do you guys think I am —
some kind of German spy? Go back to Washington and tell them to
fire me. I don't give a damn. Fuck the whole lot of you, and if you
don't like my language, shove it.

Anyway, I had a way out. The public relations director of the
merchant marine walked into my office one day while I was trying
to deal with my five teleprinters, ticking away like mad, and at the
same time argue with naval intelligence and plead with my Bennington typist to cut her error factor to one a line. I remember that moment well because the spiffy young man from naval intelligence was
wrought up about Boise, which is either the capital of Idaho or a
warship named after the capital, and in both cases pronounced "Boy-
see," at least here in the United States. Speaking of the warship, I had
allowed my actors on the BBC of a few nights past to pronounce it
"Bwaz," which was also the pronunciation the French Desk gave it
in their translation, and someone attached to our embassy in London
had a wife or a mother-in-law or someone who had come from Boise,
Idaho, and was incensed at the ridiculous pronunciation of the name
of her hometown. That naval intelligence should have to bring this
nonsense to my attention was a part of the lunacy which surrounded
me, and I think at that moment it was the final straw. I don't remem-

ber what I said to the midshipman messenger, except that I used a number of four-letter words that reflected my gutter background.

He beat his retreat, and the man from the merchant marine asked me whether it was always like that around here, and when I replied that this was a quiet morning, he asked whether he could make me an offer. I told him that I was listening, and he informed me that at national quarters, the merchant marine, knowing they had suffered more casualties than the army and navy combined, felt their role in the war should be specified for posterity. With that in mind, they had riffled through the writers available, had come up with my name, and were prepared to offer me a commission in the merchant marine, at very decent pay, and with every perk possible. In return, I was to sail the merchant ships to every port they serviced. I would be given the best officer's quarters and every consideration. The notion that my life span would likely be shortened before the job was done didn't cross my mind. At twenty-six you are immortal. We talked, we shook hands, and I called Elmer Davis and informed him that I had to see him.

Mr. Davis greeted my announcement that I was prepared to embark on this wonderful adventure with two words: "Forget it." I asked him whether that meant I could not resign, and he said yes, it did; and when I wanted to know how he could stop me, he informed me that he had his ways, and he also told me that when I left his office, he would personally talk to the people at the merchant marine, and I could as of now understand that their offer no longer existed.

I told Bette later that they'd probably have me shot before they ever let me out of the place, but she was ready to embrace Elmer Davis. Intelligent women look on combat with a cold eye, and I was married to a loving and intelligent woman whom I saw less and less frequently. I went back to being the Voice of America, which was not without its rewards, grumble as I might. When I sat down at my typewriter, usually around two o'clock in the afternoon, after I had checked all the wire services, gone through the daily reports of army and naval intelligence, spoken to at least one colonel and one commander, not to mention the occasional general or naval captain, and began to write, I had a sense of great pride. If I could not be with my brother Julie, ready to go overseas and so proud of his sergeant stripes,

or with my friends, gone into the marines and the army, I nevertheless had something that no one else in America had, a voice into that
dark, sad land of occupied Europe, and each day as I tapped it out,
my skin would prickle:

"Good morning, this is the Voice of America."

"*Buon giorno* . . ."

"*Guten morgen* . . ."

"*Bonjour,*" and I knew that more than a million people in France,
their sets tuned low, would hear that: "Good morning, this is the
Voice of America, and here is the situation today . . ." Even today,
forty-eight years later, my eyes fill with tears at that wonderful line:
This is the Voice of America; this is the voice of mankind's hope and
salvation, the voice of my wonderful, beautiful country, which will
put an end to fascism and remake the world. We had no second
sight, and none of us could imagine the years that were to come. It
was a moment when our country was grand and splendid beyond
what I can make a reader imagine today, regardless of how eloquent
I may be.

On the other hand, I was far from being grand and splendid myself. Before taking this on, I had drunk very little; now I discovered
that at six o'clock, shaken by the day — as I was every day — if I
stepped out and down to the bar where the OWI people gathered
and had a martini, I would be braced to go back and face my problems, and to these problems, there was no end. For example, coming
up after this life-saving potion one day, I discovered that an under
secretary of state was on the phone from Washington to inform me
that Stalin had devoted his entire Order of the Day to the courage
and unselfishness of one Ivan Ivanovich, and that in light of this,
President Roosevelt felt that our whole BBC operation that day should
be a tribute to Ivan Ivanovich. It was six P.M.; it meant scrapping a
day's work and doing a new broadcast on Ivan Ivanovich. By seven
o'clock, the translation desks would be screaming for copy. By nine
o'clock, they would be in my office, cursing me in seven different
languages, ready to pull the copy out of the typewriter. On the other
hand, Roosevelt, the President of the United States, commander of
the armed forces, had made a request of me — and now onward and
upward. Of course, President Roosevelt knew that Ivan Ivanovich
was the common name for the Russian foot soldier, just as GI Joe

was ours, and I suppose he presumed that his under secretary of state would also know, and that the fifteen minutes would be a panegyric to the Russian infantryman, who well deserved it, having fought the Nazis to a standstill. But the under secretary did not know this and I did not know it, and when I pleaded with the under secretary to find out who Ivan Ivanovich was and what was his background, he pleaded busy. The minutes were ticking away. I grabbed my Bennington graduate, who couldn't type and who was on her way out, and told her to sit down and start calling the press, beginning with *The New York Times*. I went to the door of my office and yelled for the short-wave desk to go into the files and find what they could on Ivan Ivanovich, hero of the Soviet Union. I called the general staff offices in Washington and begged their public relations officer to get me the data on Ivan Ivanovich. Nothing. Absolutely nothing.

We may be sophisticated today, but then we were country boys, and we were all young, and twenty miles off shore the country and the world ended. I called the Russian embassy, and they said there was something missing before the patronymic, or perhaps after it, and that I had the name wrong. That may have been in transmission. The Bennington girl reported no luck with the newspapers. None of them had any notion of who Ivan Ivanovich might be, except that someone at *The Times* suggested that Ivanovich was a patronymic. I had the Bennington girl try to get back to the Soviet embassy, but they had closed down for the day. I couldn't believe that an embassy had closing hours, but she said that unless it was an emergency, they were closed. I called a Captain Barrett at army intelligence who had always impressed me with his ability to come up with answers, and he said why don't we call the Russian news agency here. Why didn't I or anyone else think about that? I called Tass and finally discovered that Ivan Ivanovich was the Soviet GI Joe; at eight o'clock I began to write my tribute to the Russian infantryman.

There were good days and bad days, but as far as my marriage was concerned, the bad days began to take over.

If we had not lost the first child through miscarriage, it might have been very different, and if I had not run into Louis Untermeyer on Fifty-seventh Street, it might have been different, but perhaps not. I don't think the outcome of World War Two would have been any different if Howard Fast's words had not blanketed the European continent every morning; but at the same time, Howard Fast would have had to be much wiser to understand that what he was doing was hardly the most important thing in the world. There had been nothing like World War Two. I think that every one of us involved in it felt a singular sense of duty and compulsion, which unfortunately was balanced by a woeful lack of responsibility. One of the lures of war is that it emancipates, and you drop everything but the clothes on your back and the gun in your hand. My own gun was four hours of powerful transmitters, and when I finally accepted the fact that my job was more important than writing a history of the merchant marine and that I could live my life without being a rifleman, I exalted my work. That sort of thing was endemic to the moment. Marriages were not undone but simply discarded. Careers were thrown on the scrap heap, especially by those dissatisfied with them; responsibility went down the drain — hey, I'm putting my life on the line, that's enough.

We were both surrounded by people who were convinced that they were at least part of the marrow of the anti-fascist struggle, Bette in the Signal Corps, I at the Office of War Information, each of us in a new world of fascinating people, all of them in one way or another rid of responsibility. We saw less and less of each other; we clung to each other and then let go. We were very young in a world that was tearing itself to pieces, and in spite of what we were able to do, neither of us knew very much about anything. My Bennington typist was tall, dark, beautiful, and rich — admiring and even more enchanted than I was with the silent masses of occupied Europe who heard my words; we were ripe for an affair. It didn't improve her typing, but she never complained about the long hours, and often at midnight, I found myself having dinner with her. I had never known anyone like her, and she had never known anyone like me.

Romance under stress makes good film sometimes, and if you're young and you love women and you're thrown together with a beautiful woman day after day, things happen. I had lunch with Louis Untermeyer and poured out my heart to him. He informed me that there were seven Bennington graduates working at the OWI, and he had mentioned Jack London once to one of them, and she had never heard the name and had no idea who Jack London was, and then he tried it with three more Bennington ladies and not one of them had ever heard of Jack London; but when it came to Marcel Proust and James Joyce, that was something else.

"So you see," Louis said, "if you left your lovely wife and married this lady, you might have a daughter and send her to Bennington, and then she wouldn't know who her father was, and the main point is that you're not Proust or Joyce and never will be, if you get my meaning?"

The Bennington lady went back to Bennington to do postgraduate work, and they sent around another typist who could type professionally. I returned to my senses, and Bette and I worked things out, and then she was pregnant again and I realized that we were married and intended to stay married. I was growing up, losing weight, and learning my job. Day after day, month after month, I wrote history and lived history — my life coming into focus every twenty-four hours when I sat down to my typewriter and spelled out "Good morning, this is the Voice of America."

I sat there laughing with pleasure at what I would write that day, and again I sat there with tears in my eyes. The news of the death camps and the crematoria was filtering through, but the news was unreal, confused, contradictory.

Now and again, I would lunch with John Houseman, and through these lunches I would meet, albeit fleetingly, a fascinating group of people, among them the director Nick Ray, Molly Thatcher, a lovely woman then separated from her husband, Elia Kazan, Orson Welles, Bessie Breuer, the wife of Henry Varnum Poore, Humphrey Cobb, Jerome Weidman, Philip Van Doren Stern, Carl Van Doren, and of course Louis Untermeyer, whose wit and charm never failed. I mention these people only to suggest the kind of talent that was assembled around the Office of War Information. I knew none of them well and saw none of them after I left the OWI, except for Carl Van Doren, one of the first of the modern historical revisionists. It was at his apartment a few years later that Bette and I spent an afternoon with Sinclair Lewis, a memorable afternoon because it erupted into a violent argument about anti-Semitism, based on a somewhat anti-Semitic article that had appeared in *The Saturday Evening Post*. Lewis took the part of the genteel anti-Semites, which shocked Bette and me, long-time admirers of the novelist. Aside from that, I can recall only his bitter diatribes against his ex-wife, Dorothy Thompson, among whose sins he included the theft of his library of detective stories.

Through all my months at the OWI, Jack Houseman maintained an avuncular attitude toward me. A heavy, handsome man, with a rich, somewhat English-accented voice, he was gentle and caring, and I suppose he felt a certain responsibility for my being where I was. Some three or four months into my job there, he asked me how it was going. I explained that my greatest problem was the selection and organization of the millions of words that poured onto me day after day. Elmer Davis had offered me additional staff, but that was not what I needed; the entire organization was in a sense my staff. I could have anything I wanted just by asking.

What I needed, Houseman decided, was a board of editors, who would work with the material all day and then put together a sort of front page — and at least fifty more writers to back them up. "None of which you'll get," he said. "On the other hand . . ." And then he laid out a scheme that would make life more tolerable. He said that, politics aside, *The New York Daily News* had the best news-gathering team in the country, considering that it dealt in short spots without the in-depth treatment of *The New York Times*. The paper had perhaps four hundred people putting it together, he told me, and when they pulled their first page-two and page-three proofs, they had a concise summation of the day's news that I could use. Of course, he added, it lacked the confidential intelligence material available to me, but I could blend that in. The main structure would be there, and I could rewrite it to suit my needs.

It was a brilliant notion. I called *The Daily News* immediately and found that the staff could pull a proof early enough for me to check it against my own layout, and then I could revamp if I had to. I must admit it gave me a sense of power to be able to ask for anything pertinent and get it. I called the transportation department and told them I wanted a motorcycle messenger waiting at *The Daily News* every day. It all worked out just as Houseman had suggested, and it made a difficult job less difficult.

In time I worked out most of the wrinkles. I lined up my sources in Washington, in San Diego, and in London. I established contact at the Soviet embassy with people who spoke English and were willing to feed me important bits and pieces from their side of the wire.

I had long ago, somewhat facetiously, suggested "Yankee Doodle" as our musical signal, and now that silly little jingle was a power cue, a note of hope everywhere on earth, conveyed by short wave as well as by our four-hour American BBC. When I sat down to write "Good morning, this is the Voice of America," I now had a grasp of things. I knew what I was doing instead of having to fight my way through each new situation.

Bette and I looked forward to the birth of our baby, praying that this time it would come to term. Reluctantly, Bette took her leave from the Signal Corps. We gave up our miserable one-room studio and rented a three-room apartment at 100 West Fifty-ninth Street, on the tenth floor with a marvelous view of Central Park, rent — $150 more money than we had ever dreamed of paying for an apartment. But by then, *Citizen Tom Paine* had been published and had received a front-page review in the *Herald Tribune*'s book section, a front-page place in *The New York Times Book Review,* and raves from every corner of the country. The State Department immediately signed a contract with me to publish it in pocket size in Serbo-Croatian, Slovene, Greek, Albanian, Hungarian, Bulgarian, Polish, Czech, Slovak, and Rumanian — as if *Citizen Tom Paine* were destined to be the face of America in every Middle European country. Other contracts were signed for occupied France. My day, never long enough, began to be interrupted by requests for interviews, and Dore Schary made a trip from California to talk about movie rights; but forty-five years would go by before *Citizen Tom Paine* could become a film. My ego enlarged itself dangerously, and if it didn't blow away what small store of wisdom I possessed, it was because of two remarkable people in my life, Bette and my publisher, Samuel Sloan.

I never knew a man whom I loved and valued more deeply than Sam Sloan. My first novel was published when I was eighteen years old, by Lincoln MacVeagh at the Dial Press, after which he became President Roosevelt's first ambassador to Greece. I received a $100 advance, and the book hardly sold enough to pay back the advance. My second novel, a romantic love story like the first, was published by Dodd, Mead and Company, my third by Harcourt, Brace and Company, where I met Sam Sloan as my editor. Sam Sloan was a wise, gentle, and compassionate man, and in all my life I never met another quite like him. He became my role model, my gentle hero figure, and, again, my notion of a true gentleman. I use the word again and again, because I know of no other that fits him so well, and it was his balance and his friendship that helped keep my feet firmly on the ground. As time passed, I was lashed and beaten enough to learn about humility, but in 1944, aged twenty-eight, I had small humility indeed.

Sam Sloan was a rudder, a balance in my life. I had written a book called *Place in the City* in 1936, published the following year, and Sam Sloan was the editor, and our friendship began. He left Harcourt, Brace soon after my novel was published, and my literary agent gave my next book, *Conceived in Liberty,* to Simon and Schuster. It sold about five thousand copies, which was a decent sale in 1938, and Simon and Schuster gave me a $1000 advance to write another book, a story I had in mind about the great trek of the Cheyenne Indians from their forced imprisonment in Oklahoma to their homelands in the Black Hills. In 1939 Bette and I drove to Oklahoma and other places in the West. We had never been west before, and it led to a feeling of admiration and compassion for the remarkable Cheyenne and Crow and Sioux Indians we met. But the book that came out of it was not much good, and the people at Simon and Schuster dismissed me and my manuscript out of hand.

Meanwhile, Sam Sloan, along with Charles Duell and Charles Pearce, had organized a new publishing house, Duell, Sloan and Pearce, and it was there that I brought my rejected manuscript. Sam Sloan read it and told me that I had a wonderful story. He said that if I tore up the manuscript and started fresh, he'd publish the book. I followed his advice then and later; instead of trying to fix what I had written when it was wrong, I threw it away and started again. I rewrote the story of the Cheyenne Indians. Sam published it in 1941 under the title *The Last Frontier,* and it was received with praise and enthusiasm. My head swelled, and Sam, thank God, provided a balance. I went on to write *The Unvanquished* and *Citizen Tom Paine,* which, as I said, was published during my tenure at the Office of War Information.

The balance of the war had changed. I wrote a newscast about Hans and Sophie Scholl, who had had the courage to distribute anti-Nazi pamphlets in the streets of Munich, and were caught and put to death.

American troops were fighting their way across the islands of the Pacific, and marine headquarters sent a captain to see me and explain with charts how the war was progressing in the South Pacific. Two nights a week I had to watch battlefield film clips so that my reports to occupied Europe would be realistic, and very often there would be captured German and Italian film as well. Morning, noon, and night, I lived the war and came to hate it, to hate war and every aspect of war. There were more and more discussions that began after the two A.M. transmissions, and the men and women who were the exiled voices from occupied Europe would join us, our actors, and technicians, and the talk would sometimes go on until daylight.

The change in me was for the most part marked by a growing sense of security. I knew what I had to do, and I was doing it well. Neither Barnes nor Davis had any complaints. In the position I had, I learned a great deal about the various theaters of war, and instead of endlessly seeking information, I began to be consulted, sometimes by people in the State Department, sometimes by people in army and navy headquarters, and more and more frequently by the foreign news departments of the newspapers, *The New York Times, The New York Herald Tribune, The Washington Post*. Actually, I was not supposed to give them hard news, but I was immensely flattered; it was only a decade earlier that I had trudged from paper to paper, pleading for a job, any kind of job.

Meanwhile, I had heard that we were constructing a medium-wave broadcasting system in North Africa, a station powerful enough to be heard on ordinary radios in most of occupied Europe, and of course I had no doubt but that I would be offered a position in North Africa like the one I had in New York. I even sounded out John Houseman on a job for Bette so that she could come with me; she had no objections to having our baby in an army hospital. There would be a pamphlet division, and she was an excellent artist and could turn her hand to anything — and once I was overseas, who knew where adventure might take me. My increasing hatred of war had not lessened my desire to be in the heart of the struggle.

As I recall, Elmer Davis had gone overseas to the North African establishment, and Louis G. Cowan had come in as chief of the radio program bureau. Cowan, a large, soft-voiced, and very decent man, was a long-time and respected radio executive and producer. As with so many of the top people at the OWI, he had given up a highly paid career to work for the insignificant wages paid by our office. One day, in early January 1944, he asked me to come to his office after I had done my draft of the day's BBC newscast.

When I got there, he shook my hand uneasily and asked me to sit down. I made some notes after the meeting, so it is possible for me to quote the dialogue more or less as it took place. He began by bringing me up to date on the progress of the North African operation. "We're ready to begin transmission in ten days," he said. "At that time, we will close down the American BBC; we'll return the four hours to the British with thanks and perhaps some small ceremony. Your present job will then be over, but not your job with the Office of War Information."

I smiled and nodded and asked him whether I would be doing the work in North Africa.

"You're not going to North Africa," he said.

"No?" I asked, trying to make something of that. "Then where?"

"Here," Cowan said unhappily. "Your job continues, of course."

"How can my job continue when we no longer have the BBC transmission?"

"We'll still be producing printed propaganda."

"Leaflets?"

"Leaflets, pamphlets."

"I can't do that," I said decisively. "I've been trained for medium wave, and that's where I belong. Do you know how much money and training you've put into me? How can you let that go down the drain? You know what I can do. You don't have to guess. Does Elmer Davis know about this?"

He nodded.

"And he's willing to dump me? I can't believe that."

"There's nothing he can do about it," Cowan said. "There's nothing I can do about it."

"What the devil are you talking about?"

"To go overseas as a civilian employee of this department, you need a passport. The State Department will not issue a passport for you."

"I can't believe that. I talk to them every week. They come to me for things. Why wouldn't they?"

Cowan swallowed each word as he spoke. He was acutely miserable as he informed me that the Federal Bureau of Investigation had instructed the State Department not to issue a passport to me, on the grounds that I was either a Communist or a Communist sympathizer with strong Communist Party connections.

"You know I'm not a Communist," I told him. "If you'll look in my files, you'll find a report from Moyer." (L. A. Moyer was the executive director and chief examiner for the United States Civil Service at that time.) "I've been thoroughly investigated and I have top clearance. You know that. I have top priority for all documents with army and naval intelligence."

"We know that," Cowan admitted.

"Then how the hell could I be a Communist?"

"Howard," Cowan begged me, "please calm down and listen to me. You are not being fired from this office. You still have your job. It is just that at this moment, the overseas assignment is too sensitive. Perhaps in time that will change. You are reassigned to the publications department —"

"Too sensitive after doing it all these months! And what in hell do I do in publications? Write one of those stupid pamphlets and rot here? You know how crazy this is. One moment I'm Roosevelt's fair-haired boy, and the next moment I'm a Communist spy. No, no — I'm not going along with this."

"Please, shut up and listen," Cowan said. He opened a file folder on his desk. "Listen! I don't make these accusations. Elmer Davis doesn't make them. They come from J. Edgar Hoover and the FBI." He read the names of four of our pool of actors, and then three more names from the Hungarian Desk, the German Desk, and the Spanish Desk, and then he informed me that according to J. Edgar Hoover they were all card-carrying members of the party.

I knew about the Hungarian. It was a joke around the place that we had had to choose between a Communist and a Nazi for the Hungarian Desk. I might have suspected the others, but my thinking didn't go in that direction. I just didn't care whether they were Communists or not; they talked sense, they understood the forces involved in the war, and their positions were always constructive. As for myself, during all of my tenure there I refused to go into anti-Soviet or anti-Communist propaganda. There was pressure on those

issues, not from Davis or Barnes or Houseman, but from a group in
the short-wave section, a group whose binding force was virulent
anti-Communism. Cliques were nourished by them; whispers, impli-
cations, and every so often a news item from one of the governments
in exile that had established themselves and had been given a home
and recognition in London were passed on to me. Since I could use
few if any of these offerings — they were mostly anti-Soviet — and
since I felt that, as our most powerful ally, the Soviet Union was
paying a terrible price for the defeat of the Nazis, I was not called on
to propagandize against the Russians to the people of occupied Europe, and this was noted and remembered.

I have mentioned my arrogance in my job; with a young fellow of
my age and background, nothing else could have been expected. To
so many of us, World War Two was a crusade against evil, and we
enlisted in it with a sort of religious dedication. At the OWI, I never
soft-pedaled my opinions. There was an evening young Arthur Miller
spent at our apartment, when he talked a great deal about historical
materialism being the only approach to truthful writing. At the time
I was impressed, and I raised the point at lunch the following day.
There were six of us at the table. An argument followed, and one of
the men present denounced both Miller and me as Communists. I
had no idea what Miller was or wasn't, but I said that if Miller was
a Communist, so was I and I didn't give a damn about it. It was
typical of my way of saying what I thought and never thinking twice
about the road my words traveled. To this day, when I write I will
sit and brood over a word or a sentence while the minutes tick by,
but my speech was something else.

Thus, I was not entirely surprised by what Cowan had said; I was
angered and indignant, but not totally surprised. I told him that either
I was sent to North Africa or I would resign.

"We don't want you to resign," Cowan said. "Davis made that
very plain. There is important work for you to do here."

"I don't want to write pamphlets. That's out."

"Last month," Cowan told me, "we dropped a million leaflets
over occupied Europe. That's no small thing."

"It's not my thing. If I can't go overseas for the OWI, I'll find
another way. I have to."

"You would do me a favor if you didn't resign — you would do

all of us a favor." He was pleading with me. I think that this was the
beginning of the witch hunt, not only in the Office of War Information, but in the Office of Strategic Services, William Donovan's precursor to the Central Intelligence Agency, and in army and naval
intelligence as well — a witch hunt that would slowly but surely mount
into the terror that overtook the country for the next ten years and
came to be known as the McCarthy period. I think that Cowan and
Davis were hoping to resist it in their organization. This would account for Cowan's plea that I remain with the OWI, but I was much
too angry to receive his request with an open mind.

A week later, I received the following letter:

United States of America
OFFICE OF WAR INFORMATION
224 West 57th Street
New York 19, N.Y.

January 21, 1944

Mr. Howard Fast
100 West 59th Street
New York, N.Y.

Dear Howard:

This is a most difficult letter to write. One of the unpleasant du-
ties related to my current assignment. Accepting your resignation is
pure compliance with your wish — not at all what we want.

It little behooves me, a latecomer as Bureau Chief, to tell you
what a fine job you have done for this country, the OWI, and the
Radio Bureau in particular.

It has been effective, intelligent and the output one would expect
from a writer of your talent. I recognize the many other demands
on your time, and your own deep desire to continue serving the
war effort until the war shall have been won and a just peace declared.

Please accept my own sincere thanks and with them the gratitude
of an organization and a cause well served. This goes for Mr. Davis,
Mr. Sherwood, Mr. Barnes, Mr. Houseman — and the many peo-

ple here who have been inspired by your sincerity and your achievement.

Sincerely,
Louis G. Cowan
Chief, Radio Program Bureau

Ten days later, I put together the handful of books and papers that
I intended to keep and walked out of my office for the last time. I
had come into this office first on the tenth of December 1942. I was
leaving it now on the first of February 1944.

2

I DON'T WANT to leave the impression that I worked in innocence all those months at the Office of War Information without realizing that there were Communist Party members working with me. It could not be otherwise, for this was almost the only available pool of men and women who had both a deep understanding of the political forces at work in the world and a consuming patriotism — a patriotism so totally embedded in them that it verged on the ridiculous. To write about the Communist Party and its struggles during those years of the thirties and forties and the fifties is perhaps the most difficult task a historian can face today, for starting with the end of World War Two, the American establishment was engaged in a gigantic campaign of anti-Communist hatred and slander, pouring untold millions into this campaign and employing an army of writers and publicists in an effort to reach every brain in America. Therefore to write objectively and truthfully about the American Communist movement poses a curious problem: Can one do this against a premise so widely held?

I don't know. Long ago, I lost my faith in anyone's objectivity, including my own. Five years after I left the OWI, when I was covering the trial of eleven Communist leaders for conspiring to overthrow the government by force and violence, I had an experience that went to the marrow of objectivity. I was standing in the big marble foyer of the U.S. Court House in Foley Square in New York, talking to one of the defense lawyers, a big, burly Irishman from Philadel-

phia, when Howard Rushmore walked by. Rushmore worked for
The New York Journal American and was probably the most important and energetic of the Hearst stable of red baiters and professional
anti-Communists.

I nodded to him and said to the lawyer, "There goes that sonofabitch Howard Rushmore."

To which the Philadelphia lawyer responded, "Come on, Howard,
you only hate him because he's their sonofabitch. If he were our
sonofabitch, you'd cover him with roses."

I can't remember a single line of dialogue in all my life that hit me
as hard and went as deep, and I am trying to keep it in mind through
all of these recollections.

So I plead no innocence about Communists in the OWI, but for
my part, I simply did not give a damn whether or not the people I
spoke to and worked with were Communists, nor were they a strange
apparition to me. I was born in 1914, and no one with a brain in his
head or a shred of social consciousness could have matured during
the two decades following my birth without being well aware of the
Communists and the Communist Party.

My father, Barney Fast, was a workingman all of his life. He was
born in 1869 in the town of Fastov in the Ukraine, and he was brought
to the United States in 1878, aged nine, by his older brother, Edward.
Immigration shortened Fastov to Fast, gave it to him as a last name,
and so it remained.

In 1897, working in a tin factory in Whitestone, Long Island, my
father made friends with a young man named Daniel Miller. Miller's
family had moved from Lithuania to London a generation before, and
Daniel, one of a family of five sons and two daughters, had made
his way to America alone. When the war with Spain began, Barney
and Dan and a few other Jewish boys working at the tin factory
organized a regiment to fight in Cuba and thereby revenge themselves for the expulsion of the Jews from Spain in 1492. They persuaded enough non-Jews to join up to make a regiment of three
hundred men, and one of the bookkeepers at the plant, a man in his
middle sixties named Charlie Hensen, who claimed to have been a
cavalry officer during the Civil War, offered to train the three hundred
as a cavalry regiment. That was not such a loony proposition as it

sounds, for the war in Cuba was disorganized, with all sorts of citizens getting into the act — as witness Theodore Roosevelt and his Rough Riders.

Hensen collected twenty-five percent of each man's pay, with which he proposed to buy uniforms, sabers, and horses. But after a few months, Hensen and the money disappeared, and Barney never did get to Cuba. He did, however, become bosom pals with Danny Miller, and Danny showed Barney a picture of his beautiful sister. My father fell in love with the picture, began to correspond with Ida Miller, saved his money, sent her a steamship ticket for passage to America, and in due time married her. In 1904 their first child, Rena, was born, and in 1906 they had a son named Arthur, a sensitive, beautiful boy that I know only from photographs. He died of diphtheria six years later. My brother Jerome was born in March of 1913, and I came in November of the following year. My mother's last child, Julius, was born in 1919. My mother died of pernicious anemia in the spring of 1923, when I was eight and a half years old.

We were always poor, but while my mother lived, we children never realized that we were poor. My father, at the age of fourteen, was an iron worker in the open-shed furnaces on the East River below Fourteenth Street. There the wrought iron that festooned the city was hammered into shape at open forges. As a kid, Barney had run beer for the big, heavy-muscled men who hammered out the iron at the blazing forges, and there was nothing else he wanted to do. But the iron sheds disappeared as fashions in building changed, and Barney went to work as a gripper man on one of the last cable cars in the city. From there to the tin factory, and finally to being a cutter in a dress factory. He never earned more than forty dollars a week during my mother's lifetime, yet with this forty dollars my mother made do. She was a wise woman, and if a wretched tenement was less than her dream of America, she would not surrender. She scrubbed and sewed and knitted. She made all the clothes for all of her children, cutting little suits out of velvet and fine wools and silks; she cooked and cleaned with a vengeance, and to me she seemed a sort of princess, with her stories of London and Kew and Kensington Gardens and the excitement and tumult of Petticoat Lane and Covent Garden. Memories of this beautiful lady, whose speech was so different from the speech of the others around me, were wiped out in the moment of her death. I remember my father coming into the tiny bedroom where I slept with Jerome, waking us gently, and saying, "Momma died last night." Although I was very young, I must have known what death meant — my mother had been sick for over a year — for at that moment my mind had to choose between memory and madness and forgetfulness and sanity. My mind chose forgetfulness so that I could remain sane. The process is not uncommon and is called infantile amnesia; it was not until years later that my memories of my mother began to return.

Because my memories of my mother were wiped out in a flash, the dark-haired woman who lay in the open coffin in our tiny living room — packed with family and curious neighbors — was strange to me. I wept dutifully. My mother's brother Gerry, a young physician and the only solvent member of her family, pressed a silver dollar into my hand, and it quieted my tears. I had never seen anything like it before.

All the dismal business of a death in poverty, of the tragedy of my poor father left with three small children and a nineteen-year-old girl who had been coddled and treasured by my mother to the point of becoming a spoiled child, shattered by her mother's death, does remain in my memory. For a few months after my mother's death, my sister tried to keep the family together; but more and more she saw herself trapped, doomed to spinsterhood by the responsibility of caring for the three little boys; and so acute was her fear that she plunged into marriage, compounding the tragedy and leaving my bewildered father to take care of the three small children. Jerome and I hated the man she married. His only virtue in our eyes was that he was British, somehow distantly related to us by marriage, but he was insensitive and stupid.

I loved my sister — and did so to the day of her death — but my father was shattered by her departure. My maternal grandmother — I never saw my father's parents — took my brother Julius to live with her in Long Island. He was only four years old, and there was no way my father could take care of him. Indeed, there was no way he could take care of Jerome and me.

My father was a dear and gentle man, a gentleman in every sense of the word, but his own mother had died when he was seven years old, and the death of his wife threw him into a deep depression. I know that several women loved him, but he never married again. If he had, possibly my life would have been different, but as it was, my brother and I were left from morning to night on our own, with no one to turn to, no one to care for or feed us — with a father who was depressed and disoriented and often did not come home until well past midnight, plunging Jerome and me into periods of terror that were to be repeated again and again.

The years that followed provided an experience in poverty and misery that was burned into my soul. In time, nothing much changed in the scheme of poverty; what did change was my ability to face and alter circumstances. I ceased to be wholly a victim. The place where we lived was a wretched slum apartment, made lovely by the wit and skill and determination of my mother; but after her death and the departure of my sister, the place simply disintegrated. Jerome and I, two small boys essentially on our own, had to be mother and father and brother to each other. Jerome cared for me; to the best of my ability, I cared for him. My father disappeared each morning at eight o'clock, and rarely did he return until after midnight; periodically, he was out of work. We made some efforts to keep the apartment clean, but that's not within the scope of small boys. The apartment became dirty; the cheap furniture began to come apart. Trash accumulated. In his depression, my father seemed unaware of what was happening. We had holes in our clothes, our shoes were coming apart, and Pop made only an occasional effort to rectify things.

In actuality, we had no childhood; it slipped away. When I was ten and Jerome was eleven, we decided to take things in hand. My brother was like a rock, and without him I surely would have perished. We needed money, and Jerry had heard somewhere that you could make money delivering newspapers, in particular, *The Bronx Home News,* which existed entirely on home delivery, with a system worked out by a man named Keneally. I don't recall his first name and there's no way I can find it, but I remember him with great fondness. He had an office in Washington Heights, and one day after school, Jerry and I made our way there and presented ourselves to Mr. Keneally, a tall, lean, long-faced man.

I can imagine how we appeared to him, two ragged kids with long, shaggy hair, holes in our shoes, holes in our stockings. "We can do it!" Jerry pleaded, and Keneally said OK, he'd give us a chance, even though we were too young to do a proper route. But one of his boys had left, and maybe the two of us together could do one route. He was very kind. He was of the generation of Irish who had fought their way up from the starkest poverty, and he understood. We were given a book of some ninety customers who took daily papers, including Saturday and Sunday, and each week we had to collect twelve cents from each customer. We paid a straight price for our bundle, and it amounted to about two out of every twelve cents — a price we paid whether we were able to collect or not.

So my working life began, at age ten, and from then until I was twenty-two years old I had one job or another, for three years delivering *The Bronx Home News,* then working for a cigar maker on Avenue B on the East Side, then a hat maker on West Thirty-eighth Street, then making deliveries and cleaning at an uptown butcher shop, and then at the 115th Street branch of the New York Public Library. When I left the library, I worked for a year in a dress factory, first as a shipping clerk and then as a presser — at least a presser in training. Meanwhile, I finished grade school, went to high school, got a scholarship to the old National Academy of Design, and worked there for a year. I gave it up when, at the age of seventeen, I sold a short story.

Jerry and I kept the household going, using our money to survive the periods when my father was on strike or out of work. How we did it, I don't know, for we had nothing going for us except each other; and when I was twelve, our younger brother, Julius, was returned by our grandmother to share our poverty. Here's a day of our youth: awake at seven, get Julie off to Public School 46, and then Jerry and myself off to George Washington High School on the streetcar, my father having already departed for work; cold cereal and milk for breakfast, find the nickel each that was our fare, and make something we could eat for lunch, a cheese or peanut butter sandwich on white store-bread, then school, then Jerry and I to our newspaper route while Julie did the best he could with his own door key, then stopping at the New York Public Library for a new pile of books, then home with our fervent hope that our small brother would be there. Or if not there, find him, usually at the local police station, where they kept a pen of lost children. We would have cake or candy when we could hit a *Bronx Home News* customer in arrears, sometimes a whole month of arrears, which would net us forty-eight cents, enough to buy us a couple of quarts of milk and a hand of bananas. If my father did turn up before ten o'clock, he would give us a dollar, and we'd go out to a late-night deli for a can of sardines and some tomatoes and lettuce and a loaf of bread. The long and short of it was that we survived. But looking back now over the spread of years to the time when I was ten years old, I'll be damned if I know what guardian angel protected us.

We huddled together; we clung to each other; and every evening, after an hour to do our homework, we read books from the blessed library. Books were our religion, our shining hope, our dreams, and our futures. Years later, Alexander Woollcott, the noted critic and wit and a member of the famous Hotel Algonquin Round Table, interviewed me, and in the course of the interview mentioned the British novelist Eden Phillpotts, bemoaning that no one read him anymore — although why they should have continued to read him, I have no idea — whereupon I declared that I had read at least three of Phillpotts's novels. Woollcott snorted in disbelief, and I explained that I read everything and anything from the shelves of the New York Public Library, having no guide to tell me what I should and what I should not read. (Radio was only beginning and of course there was no television.)

Saturday there was no school. Sunday, we finished our paper route by seven in the morning, and we had the whole day — at home if it rained or was too cold to be outside. The library was closed on Sunday, and on Saturday or any day, for that matter, you could take home only two novels, fiction being marked by a blue card. You were allowed two books of fiction, two of nonfiction — or of a different color time card. We soon discovered that the works of Mark Twain, Hawthorne, Poe, Melville, Cooper, Washington Irving, and a number of other early American writers of fiction were duplicated in a section called American Literature, marked with a yellow time card. That doubled the number of books we could take for a weekend, and since Jerry and I each had a library card, we could have eight books at our disposal for the weekend.

Outside was dangerous turf. My father, in his desire to leave the East Side ghetto where he had spent much of his boyhood, had taken an apartment at 159th Street, just west of Amsterdam Avenue, a street with Irish and Italians but no other Jewish family in calling distance. We were not tough kids; we were three very gentle little boys, cherished, spoiled, coddled by our wonderful mother — who had given us no equipment whatsoever with which to confront the world we inherited after her death. My brothers were content to avoid combat; I was not. Some wretchedly uncomfortable gene made it impossible for me to accept insults; I had to fight. There was a long list of provocations that plunged me into combat: being told that I had killed the God of practically every kid on the block, that I was a dirty Jew, a Jew bastard, a kike, a sheeny, the son of a whore, the son of a bitch — and I was always alone against two or three or five of them, and all the protective love of my brother Jerry never extended to street fighting. I learned street fighting the hard way, hated it, and after months of being beaten by overwhelming odds, I put the largest kitchen knife we had in my belt, walked down the stairs and into the street, and as four kids advanced on me, I presented the butcher knife and stated that I might get only one of them, but that one would be dead — quite a statement for a kid of eleven, and I meant it. Thank God that they were not up to it, or I might have spent the rest of my childhood in reform school. I bought an old hunting knife for sixty cents, and when I was not in school, I wore it strapped to my belt, and the result was that the attacks on me ceased.

The Jewish matter was doubly confusing, for until my mother died, I had no sense of being Jewish. We were not an Orthodox family; we belonged to no temple, observed none of the kosher laws; and since my father loved bacon and seafood, both forbidden to Orthodox Jews, I had only the vaguest notion that such laws existed. Also, the accusation that I was personally responsible for the death of Jesus Christ was not simply confusing but harrowing. To be accused of murder as a child is not a happy thing.

There was only one peculiar ray of sunlight in this nightmare of "childhood." My father's brother, Edward, some ten years older than Barney, had labored together with his wife, Jenny, in sweatshops at first and then in a small shirt business that he established and then sold. In the middle 1880s, he took what money he had and bought a small summer hotel near Hunter, New York, in Greene County, and with it about a thousand acres of woodland. His father had managed a sugar plantation on the banks of the Dnieper River near Kiev, and apparently both his father and my Uncle Edward possessed the Russian peasant's hunger for land. On part of these thousand acres, Edward discovered a rushing spring of pure, cold water, and he conceived the notion of bottling it and selling it in New York, thereby creating the Eagle Spring Water Company, one of the first bottled-water companies.

Edward and Jenny had only contempt for my father, whom they considered an irresponsible dreamer, guilty of the one sin they clearly recognized, having no money. They were both driven, compulsive people, but while my uncle was a hard but fair taskmaster, my Aunt Jenny was like no other woman I ever knew — greedy, cruel, selfish, without a shred of compassion, and filled with an unfailing hatred for Barney's three small boys. She was out of her time; she was truly a character from the Brothers Grimm's fairy tales. Edward reached out to Barney with an agreement to take the boys for the summer months, no great sacrifice, since his son, Sam, my cousin and fifteen years older than I, had established a summer camp on the property, and a few more children made no great difference.

But Aunt Jenny, forced to go along with this, managed to make our summers somewhat less than what they might have been to kids from a city slum. I know that my mother had feared and disliked Jenny, but I suspect that it was more than simple dislike, and that Jenny was avenging herself on Ida's children.

She was a small woman, but of extraordinary strength and energy. My cousin Sam, taking a tip from her, might pull us out of a game to pick up papers on the grounds or do some other chore; his mother, on the other hand, used direct methods. She would come searching for me — I was the culprit preferable to Jerry — with a stick of firewood in her hand. If she caught me, I'd get the wood over my head. If I ran, the wood would fly after me, and she always had a proper excuse, plain idleness, which she could not abide. My own tactic would be to take off into the woods between meals and stay there as long as I could. I got to know the kids of some of the old local families, poor people who scratched a living out of the mountain soil and worked for my Uncle Edward. The families had been in the mountains since Colonial times. They taught me things: how to catch

trout with my bare hands as the fish lay quietly under a rock — if a
fly fisherman caught you at it, he'd slap you around — how to skin
a garter snake and make a belt from the skin, how to make delicious
sassafras tea from tree bark, where to find wonderful blueberry
bushes — as distinct from bog blueberries — and other things too.

For all the cruelty of my aunt and my cousin, my summers became
the gyroscope, the steadying influence on my life. I think I lived for
the summer and in some sense I survived because of the summer. The
small stretch of the Catskill Mountains that reaches from Big Indian
to Lexington, in the center of the game preserve, was then one of the
most remarkable places in New York State: tall mountains, heavy
forests of hardwood and fir and balsam, teeming with animals, black
bear, deer, and wolf, and even — though rare — an occasional panther.
I came to love it, and even today, spoiled as it is, with the mountains
stripped clean for ski slopes and with ski shacks everywhere turning
the narrow valleys into a kind of rural slum, I feel a surge of joy at
the sight of those mountains.

The first toll that poverty takes is human dignity, and no family in
abject poverty lives like the Cratchits, in Charles Dickens's *A Christmas Carol.* He was faulted on that, and he wrote *The Chimes* to
show the other side of the coin; but he left out the sense that every
poverty-stricken family has of a world put together wrong. It was
particularly evident in New York, where the poor lived cheek by jowl
with the rich. The rich were always evident, a perpetual slap in the
face — yet they were not really rich, the people I so catalogued then,
those who lived on Riverside Drive and Fort Washington Avenue.
They were middle-class people, but we had nothing, and to us they
were wealthy in the only way we knew wealth. In those days of the
1920s, there was no safety net beneath the poor, no welfare, no
churches handing out free dinners. Survival in poverty was your own
affair. I have tried to explain this to people who expressed indignant
wonder at the fact that I joined the Communist Party. The absence
of unemployment insurance is educational in a way that nothing else
is.

One of the main reasons, perhaps, for our survival as a family unit
was the place where we lived. The anti-Semitism that prevailed was
maniacal; there is no other way to describe it. And this crazed Chris-

tian sickness forced Jerry and me at first, and then Julie with us, into
a closed, defensive unity. Aside from my uncle's family in the summer, no relative held out a hand to us. Some of them were well-to-
do; all of them lived comfortably, but my father's pride forbade his
asking for help, and none was offered. They were a lousy crew, and
I'll say no more about them.

We didn't complain, Jerry and I, and in a sense the challenge of
keeping the family alive was a game we played. We lived in two
worlds, the wretched world of reality and the marvelous, endlessly
exciting world of the books we read. In those days, bread, milk, and
cheese were delivered very early in the morning to the doors of the
prosperous. When we had no food, we'd be up at six in the morning
to find bread and milk and cheese that would keep us alive. We did
not consider it stealing; we never questioned our right to remain
alive. Once, we appropriated — a better word — an entire stalk of
bananas from a truck; some we kept for ourselves, eating bananas
until we could not face another. The rest we sold for a nickel a hand.
When we were utterly penniless and my father was unemployed, we
scoured the neighborhood for milk bottles, a nickel for each returned. We knew the back way into every house in the area; we knew
the rooftop area. We worked every small con we knew. We were
good-looking little boys, possessed of the same charm Jackie Coogan
and Jackie Cooper had as children, and always with holes in the toes
of our shoes, holes in the knees of our britches — kids did not wear
long pants then — our socks ragged to the edge of disintegration.
We lived only a half a mile or so from the old Polo Grounds, home
of the New York Giants, and we had worked out a con that never
failed.

We'd take up our position at the Polo Grounds entrance gate on
the Harlem River Speedway side, and we'd just stand there, two small,
wistful, ragged little boys, and we knew that the open-handed sport-
ing types going to the baseball game couldn't pass us by, especially if
they were making out with some long-legged beauty; and there was
never a time at a game when we didn't come away with ten or twelve
dollars — a dollar bill being the usual expression of sympathy. Quite
often, we'd be handed an extra pair of tickets, which we would then
hawk for a very nice price. There were two months, when I was
eleven, Jerry twelve, that we paid the rent with our Polo Grounds

money, and when I turned twelve, the same money bought me an excellent pair of roller skates. The skates meant freedom, the ability to move with decent speed anywhere in the city, time and money aside. Until I first turned the ignition key in an automobile, nothing equaled the mobility on the streets of New York that my skates gave me.

The infantile amnesia that had blacked out almost all memory of my mother at the moment I became aware of her death must have affected my brother too, for the wonderful, sun-drenched life that we had lived under her protecting arms soon had no existence whatsoever; and the memories of her and my life with her began to return only after I had passed my thirtieth year. The world of my childhood from age eight became my only world. I learned to survive against all odds; I learned the art of street fighting; I learned about sex in the tangled jungle of misinformation that made up the lore of the street; I learned the utter fatigue of work combined with rotten nutrition; and there were days when my brother and I fell asleep waiting for my father to turn up, unable to fight our fatigue any longer.

We loved Barney; we cherished him; he was a good, decent dreamer of a man who always had both feet planted firmly in midair; he was more our child than each of us was his; and the strikes and the periods of unemployment were cards fate dealt him. Life wasn't kind to him.

And there was yet another problem — I was born left-handed. In the 1920s there was no concept in the American educational system of the proper treatment and education of left-handed children. We were taught to write through a grotesque system of whole-arm movement called the Palmer method. For a right-handed child it was difficult enough; for a left-handed child forced to write with his right hand, it was impossible. My handwriting was a jumbled, unreadable scrawl, and the result was that during my first two years in grade school, I was regarded as just a trifle better than a moron. In those days, brain-damaged and retarded children were put in what was called "the ungraded class," from which I was spared only because I had learned to read at age five, my mother having instructed me so gently that when I entered the first grade, I was astonished that nobody else in the class could read. I soon learned to cheat my way around the insane Palmer method with a combination of block letters and lower case, and in due time I devised my own method of cursive writing, but only with my right hand — any use of the left hand, the devil's hand, as they called it, brought the teacher's ruler down across my knuckles — and I still write with my right hand today.

Although I began as one slightly better than a moron, the people at Public School 46 came to regard me as some sort of outstanding semigenius, the result being that at age eleven, instead of the proper age of fourteen, I was graduated and sent on to George Washington High School — another example of the errors in the educational theories of the twenties. I could read and write better than most fourteen-year-olds, but there the resemblance stopped. Although I measured five feet ten and a half as an adult, my full height came after puberty. I was half the size of the boys in my first high school class, and was totally unable to deal with certain subjects.

A word about Public School 46. It stood once, but stands no longer, at the corner of 156th Street and St. Nicholas Avenue, in upper Manhattan. It was an old Civil War hospital, made over as a primary school, and it was a place where no student ever talked back to a teacher and went unpunished. Its discipline was somewhat short of what prevails at West Point, and its methods of teaching were rigid and hopelessly old-fashioned. From the fourth grade on, students were forced to learn to spell ten words a day and to memorize a poem each week. We were taught American history and science, and we were given good books — The Adventures of Tom Sawyer, for example — to read and report on, and arithmetic up to algebra, and this in a primary school. Years later, as guest speaker at a convocation of English Teachers of Southern California, I suggested that elements of that kind of rigid education might be preferable to modern methods that fail to produce anything one could call education. I was practically hooted off the stand.

When I turned fourteen, in 1928, I reached an age of maturity, the difference between childhood and maturity being, to my mind, the difference between being a victim without recourse and a sort of adult with recourse. My brother and I had arrived at an age where we could change things. Filth was no longer a permanent part of our existence; it could be dealt with and done away with. We were work-

ing and Barney was working, making fifty dollars a week, the most
he had ever earned per week in all his life. Julie was living with us
now, nine years old, and both Jerry and I felt a sense of responsibility
toward him. We informed Barney that we were going to move out
of that miserable slum apartment, and when he put up a storm of
protest — he was incapable of altering his living place — we said
that we'd move without him. Jerry and I were both working for the
New York Public Library at that point, paid thirty-five cents an hour,
a sum that was reduced to twenty-five cents after the great stock
market crash; and with extra time on Wednesday and Saturday, I
took home nine dollars a week and Jerry eleven. Twenty dollars was
not to be sneezed at; indeed, it was in our world a princely sum, and
it bought us food and clothes. With Barney's fifty dollars added to
our twenty, there was an income of seventy dollars a week, unimag-
inable riches. It did not last very long, but long enough to get us out
of 159th Street and up to Inwood at the northern tip of Manhattan.

What a great day that was! We discarded everything we owned,
battling it out with Barney, keeping only the family pictures and a
few pieces of china. We moved into a spit-clean four-room apartment, which cost fifty-five dollars a month, twenty-five dollars more
than our previous slum dwelling. There were trees all around us,
parks, pleasant streets, a delightful place to live sixty years ago, though
it has become a crack-ridden slum today. Jerry and I were both at
George Washington High School, a mile walk up Fort George Hill,
and we both exulted that we had made it, that we had licked the
whole set of lousy circumstances that had dogged us over the six
years since our mother's death, that we had survived poverty and
hunger and fear and all the misery that life could throw at a couple
of children. Well, sort of. The crash came in October of 1929, the
company that had employed my father as a pattern maker folded,
and Barney never had a decent job again and very few rotten ones.

We were still poor; our net worth was nothing; but we were intelligent, educated, and strong. The worst part of poverty is ignorance
and hopelessness.

I began to think. From the time when the street became my life, I had
plotted, schemed, maneuvered, manipulated, cozened, and, when the
need arose, pleaded; and these are all mental activities, but by think-

ing I mean putting one fact against another and trying to measure the result. This kind of thinking is a very special thing.

The winter of 1929–1930, I worked at the public library in lower Harlem, at 203 West 115th Street. I was poorly paid — down to twenty-five cents an hour at that time — but I loved working in the library. The walls of books gave me a sense of history, of order, of meaning in this strange world, and I could very easily pick up two, three, sometimes four hours of overtime in a week. I worked from four to nine, closing time for five days, and on Saturday from nine to one. Since we did checking and arranging on Saturdays, I could pick up the overtime there, and I could always slip down to the closed reference shelves in the basement to get my homework done. My wages averaged between seven and eight dollars a week, but in the shattered prices of deflation, that was decent money. The important thing was the world of books around me. I read everything without discrimination — psychology, astronomy, physics, history, and more history — and some of it I understood and some of it I didn't.

And I began to think.

The subway ride I took to my home was a nickel. At the uptown end of the subway, where I left the train, out on the street, a man in a blue serge suit, jacket and vest and tie — a man of some fifty years — stood and sold apples for a nickel each. Every night, on my way home, I bought an apple, a large, shiny Washington State Delicious apple. I bought the apple because I was hungry, because the man touched something very deep inside of me, and because I had begun to think. This went on for several weeks. I was a kid with a job; he was a mature man, a businessman or an accountant or something of the sort to my guess. I thought of my father. Barney was a working-man; this was a middle-class educated man, and one night he stopped me.

"Hey, kid," he said, "what's your name?"

"Howard Fast."

"That's an odd name," he said. "Do they call you a fast worker?"

I stared at him without answering, and then I blurted out, "Do you have kids, mister?"

Now he stared at me, and then he began to cry. Tears — real tears. I don't know whether I had ever seen a grown man cry, and it remains in my memory as one of the most woeful moments of my life.

I grabbed my apple, pressed a nickel into his hand, and ran. I ran all the way home. He was gone the next day, and I never saw him again. There are theories that the level of consciousness varies from time to time, and that most of our lives are lived at a very low level of consciousness, almost like a walking sleep. Memory is sharpest when it recalls the highest moments of consciousness, and I believe this, and that moment seared my mind.

Other things were working out my personal mental schematic. I had seen my father on strike; I had seen him locked out; I had seen his head bloodied on the picket line. I had watched the economy of my country collapse; I had seen the packing-crate villages grow on the riverfront. I did not have to be instructed about poverty or hunger; I had lived them both. I had fought and been beaten innumerable times, not because of my religion — Barney never imposed religion on us, for which I am eternally grateful — but because I was Jewish; and all of it worked together to create in my mind a simple plea, that somewhere, somehow, there was in this world an explanation that made sense.

That was my way. I never faulted the other ways. I knew kids who were arrested, who turned into thieves or ran with the gangs — it was the time of Prohibition — and I understood this, and often enough I said to myself, There but for the grace of God goes Howard Fast. I was lucky. One of the kids ended up in the electric chair. Oh, I was damned lucky.

When I was twelve and we still lived on 159th Street, I tried, in an attempt to prove that I did not live in fear, to join the white gang in the Halloween War. Every Halloween, about fifty or sixty Irish and Italian kids who lived in the area would come together to fight the black kids from Harlem. The battleground was Macomb's Bluff, the ridge over the Polo Grounds, where there was a wide meadow stretching back from the cliffs that loomed over the Speedway. This vicious battle was traditional, and the police kept hands off — possibly because their hatred of the blacks was so intense — and usually, because the blacks could never muster as many kids as the whites, the blacks got the worst of it.

The favorite weapon of the white kids was a stocking they stuffed with pieces of broken glass, tying a knot above the stuffed end and using it as a swinging ball with deadly effect. I wanted to be a part of that gang and prove that I could be as tough and mean as the other kids — I was neither — but they drove me off as an unwanted Jew bastard. I was lucky. That day, they took one of the black kids prisoner, driving away the others, and in imitation of stories they had read in the tabloids and movies they had seen, they lynched the little boy — he was thirteen — putting a rope around his neck and pulling him up on a tree branch in the woods to the south of Macomb's Bluff.

That was the end of the Halloween Wars, and five of the white kids were sent to reform school. I was not there at the fight, but nevertheless it had a profound effect on me, and ten years later I wrote the story, which was published first in *Story* magazine — the magazine was banned in Boston for the first time in its history — and later by Duell, Sloan and Pearce as a book. It was the only time, in all my long life as a writer, that I wrote of my childhood, telling the story of this event exactly as it happened. In spite of all my efforts, I could not bring my childhood alive in terms of fiction except for this, and even in a dispassionate telling in my old age, I find that walls separate me from the intensity of the suffering of those three more or less abandoned children, myself and my brothers.

Jerry found a copy of *The Iron Heel* by Jack London. At that time, Jack London stood first among our literary heroes. Today, I find his prose flowery and too mannered, but our taste was less demanding then, and we read and reread every book of his on the library shelves — except for *The Iron Heel*. We could never find a copy in the library. The head librarian at 115th Street was a Mrs. Lindsay, a distant relative I think of the man who was to become our mayor, a very dignified and tall woman. I got up the courage to ask her why we didn't have *The Iron Heel,* and she informed me that it was considered a Bolshevik book. She had never read it, and she hoped I was not interested in such things.

How could I not be interested? *Bolshevik* was a wild word at that time; it was not so long before that the Bolsheviks had burst into history. You couldn't pick up a copy of *The Daily News, The Mirror,* or *The Graphic* without having the infamies of the Bolsheviks scream at you from the front page. The word, Russian for majority, has gone out of use today, but then it was the number one synonym for evil.

The Iron Heel was my first real contact with socialism; the book was passed around among the kids I knew at high school. If I had lived on the Lower East Side or in one of the Brooklyn immigrant enclaves, I would have had a taste of socialism with my mother's milk, but in this solidly Irish-Italian block there was no hint of it, and at that time George Washington High School was middle class, filled with well-dressed boys and girls who had allowances and money for a decent lunch in the school cafeteria. Against this background, *The Iron Heel* had a tremendous effect on me. London anticipated fascism as no other writer of the time did; indeed no historian or social scientist of the time had even an inkling of the blueprint Jack London laid out, which came into being a few decades after his death. In it, he drew the struggle against fascism by an underground socialist movement, and he did it so convincingly that we were not quite sure that what he wrote of had not already happened.

It was the beginning of my trying to understand why society was structured as I saw it to be structured. Communist bashing became so pervasive in the 1960s and 1970s that few people even attempted to understand or inquire into the forces that produced socialist thinking and, out of it, the Communist movement.

Homework for me was an indifferent matter. Sometimes I did it well, and sometimes poorly or not at all. My diet was bad and I was ridden with fatigue, and some of the subjects I simply could not relate to. In those times, bad students were not tolerated, any more than violence was tolerated, and I think I might well have been thrown out of school for indifference, and for the many days I preferred to remain in our wretched apartment and read, if not for two remarkable teachers whom I will never forget. If not for their intercession, I would have been expelled for truancy alone. Once, I got a job with a butcher, did two jobs a day, and spent the in-between hours in a movie house — admission ten cents — and this went on for seven weeks. Jerry joined me in our avoidance of the truant officer, and if they did nothing else, these two teachers prevailed on the school authorities to allow me to remain in school.

First, Mr. Orleans. He is long dead, and all my efforts to recall his first name have failed. He was the head of the department of mathematics and he had invented a mathematics aptitude test that was widely used and appeared to work. The school experimented with the test, and out of five thousand students, I ranked in the first twelve. Mr. Orleans organized these twelve students into a special class and took us through algebra, geometry, solid geometry, trigonometry, and calculus. He was a short, stocky, bald man who wore gold-rimmed spectacles, and he made it plain to us, his twelve students, that there would be no marks. As every problem could prove out, he wanted 100 percent on every paper.

The other remarkable teacher was my English teacher, Hallie Jamison: she was a tall, beautiful woman, white-haired, raised in Texas, at one time a friend of O. Henry (whose real name was William Sydney Porter). She had a romantic past, a lover who fell in France in 1918, and she knew all sorts of wonderful people who, for me, existed only in the pages of books. Among them were Apache Indians. I was a great American Indian buff and read everything on the subject that I could find, and I had a father whose proudest moment was when he went to Buffalo Bill Cody's Wild West show and actually shook hands with both Bill Cody and Sitting Bull — and had a picture postcard of Sitting Bull actually signed by the great chief. This was the meat of the first essay I wrote for Miss Jamison, the story passed on to me by Barney that Sitting Bull, when offered wages to be part of the show, refused and said that he would join Buffalo Bill only if he, Sitting Bull, had the right to sell picture postcards of himself at fifty cents each. Not only a great chief, but a brilliant businessman, he was held to be the only one who really profited from the show.

Miss Jamison loved Barney's story as related by me, and she told me I had an unusual gift for writing. She arranged to be my English teacher for my last two years in high school, and encouraged me to write. Together with Mr. Orleans, she prevented my expulsion from school for truancy and indifference. The charge of indifference arose when I handed in three French test papers unmarred by ink. My French teacher, whom I could not tolerate, called it a calculated insult and brought me up for expulsion, her charge backed up by other teachers who resented me. With reason, I am sure, for I took nothing for granted and challenged everything. But Miss Jamison put up a fight for me and won.

I learned well from Miss Jamison. I think she was fascinated by my background and the little I told her about how I had passed my childhood. I had a large store of words I had never heard said aloud, since in my very limited circle they were never spoken. Once I wrote something with the word *chameleon,* which I used improperly. When she pointed this out, I said, "You mean shamy leon." So with words, with ideas, with formulations. She had me read again — for I had read them all — the writings of Robert Louis Stevenson, not for the content, but to study usage and style. Whether I would have chosen Stevenson, I don't know, but she felt he was a great stylist of the time, and if she said so, that was enough. She suggested that I read the plays of Shakespeare and George Bernard Shaw. I had never read plays; it had never occurred to me to read a play; in my milieu, movies existed but not plays. I had seen amateur plays when I worked in resorts at summer jobs, but I had never thought of reading plays. Now I became engrossed with plays, reading Shakespeare and not always understanding what I read, but reading everything of Shaw's that I could get my hands on, enchanted by his prologues. And then, one day, arranging books in the library, I came upon Shaw's *The Intelligent Woman's Guide to Socialism and Capitalism,* and the die was cast.

I think I read somewhere that Shaw had so named his book to excite the curiosity of men, and I had also heard that he believed women to be more intelligent than men — a belief I share. In any case, *The Intelligent Woman's Guide to Socialism and Capitalism* is the clearest exposition of the subject I know of. I was then sixteen, and the book provided me with a new way of thinking about poverty, inequality, and injustice. Shaw had opened an enormous Pandora's box, and never in my lifetime would I be able to close it. The book also set me off in a new direction in my reading, and in quick succession I read Thorstein Veblen's *The Theory of the Leisure Class,* Bellamy's *Looking Backward,* and Engels's *The Origin of the Family.* My mind was exploding with ideas. I hurt dear Hallie Jamison by engaging her in a discussion as to whether any nation involved in World War One had been fighting a just war — her beloved having died on the Western Front — and I made a general nuisance of myself because of my obsession with knowing everything there was to know. In his novel *Martin Eden,* Jack London had stated unequivocally that a writer must have a total knowledge of science. I believed him and set out to gain just that, even reading a bit of Herbert Spen-

cer — recommended by London — in the process. Still in high school,
I found psychology, read the Watsonians and rejected them, read the
Gestalt theorists and liked them a little better, read the Binet-Simon
book on testing, gave intelligence tests to everyone I could corner,
and thereby washing myself out of the process, for when it came time
for me to be tested at school, I explained that I knew the tests forward and backward. Result — I never knew my own IQ and took
comfort in that.

How I did all this and managed to include the hours a day devoted
to thinking about girls, pretending that I was normal when actually
I lived in a state as horny as a large toad, made miserable and feeling
utterly deprived every time I encountered a pair of mammary glands
or dazzling buttocks on the other sex, salving myself with a set of
dreams that included women between fifteen and sixty and even my
beloved Hallie Jamison — well, I did it with an inexhaustible store
of energy.

Meanwhile, Jerry, sixteen months older than I, had graduated from
high school and enrolled at New York University. Julius was in the
eighth grade and would soon be moving to high school. New York
University was, and still is, a privately funded college. City College
then was a free school with very high scholarship standards. But
growing up as Jerry and I had, there was no way we could come up
as prize scholars. I had no marks in language, the French department
having marked me as a scholastic criminal, and Jerry had suffered
far more than I during the years that followed my mother's death.
He blocked things that I accepted and built a shell around himself.
He was smart and clear-headed, but filled with anger and very deep
hurts. At school, he got by with his native intelligence, but it was not
enough to give him grades for City College, and it wasn't until his
last year in high school that he even thought about college. Then he
decided he wanted to go to New York University's School of Business, to become either a certified public accountant or a lawyer. Since
I was not particularly interested in college, and since my younger
brother had four years of high school ahead of him, we made a family decision that Jerry would go to NYU. Tuition was $600 a year.
We decided to borrow the money from the Morris Plan, a private
bank and usury machine, and then somehow manage to pay it back
over the year.

My own plan was quite different. A year before, aged fifteen, I had decided to become a writer. There was no problem in making this decision. It was the only way of life I ever considered, from as far back as my memory goes. I decided to be a writer, to write stories and books, and to illustrate them myself. I had no desire to become an easel painter, only to be able to illustrate what I wrote — in the manner of Howard Pyle and N. C. Wyeth. They were my idols; the marvelous illustrations they did for books and magazines constituted my approach to art.

We had pulled the family together and out of the wretched morass of poverty and misery. Jerry and I were earning enough to keep the family going on a decent basis even when Barney was out of work. You didn't need much to get by in the early thirties. Jerry rooted jobs out of nowhere and everywhere, and when I graduated from high school in 1931, I was earning nine dollars a week as a page boy at the 115th Street library. The Morris Plan gave small loans on the strength of co-makers, without collateral. Their interest amounted to twenty-seven percent, but we somehow got Jerry through his first year of college and paid back the loan. I applied to both Cooper Union and the National Academy, then a sprawl of old-fashioned studio buildings at 110th Street, just east of the Cathedral of Saint John the Divine. The waiting list at Cooper Union was years in length; the National Academy accepted me for immediate entrance.

I enrolled at the National Academy. By God, I had done it. I was seventeen years old, and I was alive and healthy, when by all the odds I should have been either dead or hopelessly weak and sick. With my brothers and my father, I had a clean, proper home, a bed without bedbugs — as a kid they had made my life in bed a nightmare — books of my own, shoes without holes, a warm winter overcoat, and above all, I was a scholarship student at what was then the most prestigious art school in America. And as yet, I had done no time in jail, and that was not the least of my accomplishments, for I was not a quiet or contemplative kid, but one of those irritating, impossible, doubting, questioning mavericks, full of anger and invention and wild notions, accepting nothing, driving my peers to bitter arguments and driving my elders to annoyance, rage, and despair. I probably had some good points as well.

And I was innocent — not simply unsophisticated, but innocent in the sense that I was free of hate. That applied to both of my brothers too; we were without hate. As far as sophistication was concerned, that was a quality you had to pick up along the way.

I had become a writer and I would remain a writer. The question of ever being anything else never entered my mind; there was only one thing I could be in this life, and that was what I was. Each morning I arose at six and wrote. Two hours later, I left for the National Academy, where I practiced cast and figure drawing in the severe and tedious classical manner. I completed a story every few days and as promptly dispatched it to one magazine or another. It's hard to recall and believe in my own naïveté, for all of these first stories were handwritten in ink; and as I noted earlier, my altered handwriting was not easily read. After sending out about a dozen stories, I happened to mention to one of the librarians what I was doing, and to my dismay she informed me that no magazine would bother to read a handwritten story. Either I typed out my stories or forgot the whole matter.

We had a family discussion. After all, since I read each story aloud to my brothers once it was done, they had a sort of vested interest, and it was agreed that we would put out $1.75 to rent a typewriter for a month. I had to learn to use it, and while I made a few attempts at touch typing, I soon gave that up and settled into the two-finger method, which I continue to use. I kept the typewriter for a second and then for a third month, and then, incredibly, I sold a story.

Looking back, I find it astonishing; at the time, I felt it to be a miracle. It was not that I had no expectations of selling stories — I was supremely confident that one day I would — but that was a date in the indefinite future, and here, miracle of miracles, it had happened. The story was titled *Wrath of the Purple,* and the purchaser, for thirty-seven dollars in honest American money, was *Amazing Stories* magazine, the first of the science fiction magazines.

In 1931, thirty-seven dollars was a substantial sum of money — at least at my level of society. I was still working at the library, going there directly from the academy, but the best I could do at the library, even with all the overtime I could squeeze out of the job, was nine dollars a week, and here one story had brought me more than a month's pay. Now that I had reached my full height of five feet ten and a half inches, my work at the library changed. Rather than rearranging books, putting returned books back on the shelves, and seeing that all the reference numbers read in proper sequence, I was put to the business of tracking down overdue books, going to the apartments of the people who had borrowed them and reclaiming them — and if possible collecting the fines. The fine, as I recall, was two cents per day per book.

This took me into strange places indeed. The neighborhood around 115th Street and Seventh Avenue had changed. Only a few years earlier, the northern edge of Central Park had been a middle-class neighborhood; now it had gone down precipitously, much of it taken over by bootleggers and prostitutes. Only four blocks from the library, a six-story building had become the largest house of prostitution in New York and conceivably in the nation. I was told that over three hundred prostitutes worked out of that single building, and since most of their work was night work, they read books during the day. They made our branch of the library colorful and active, and the prim ladies who worked as librarians, themselves once so active in the drive for women's franchise, encouraged the prostitutes to read and tried with all good will to direct them to literature as a door out of sin.

But remembering to return the books they borrowed was not one of the better habits of the whores, and day after day I was sent into that vast whorehouse to reclaim overdue books. It was like stepping into an eighteenth-century fantasy, the world of Fanny Hill. I was the butt of the jokes and enticements of the whores and the threats, often ugly, of the pimps, for just as prostitutes abounded in that enormous whorehouse, so did pimps, and between being lured by the whores and occasionally smacked around by one or another of the pimps, I found that my job had become less than rewarding. It was the time before antibiotics, and while syphilis was slower in its destructive path and deadly conclusion than AIDS, it was also lethal, and street lore from the time I was ten held that to go to bed with a whore was to contract syphilis. I had no intention of tossing away my life for a roll in the hay with a delicious hooker. And some of them were just that, delicious and delightful, making a great game out of paying their library fines in kind. Along with this anthill of illicit pleasures, there were dozens of other smaller houses of delight where much the same situation prevailed.

After a few months of this, I informed Miss Lindsay that I no longer wished to collect overdue books and fines from delinquent "street ladies," as she called them. Since my former job had a new boy, I simply resigned and ended a very rewarding three-year association with the library. A friend of my father recommended me to a ladies' hat maker on West Thirty-ninth Street. It was a step upward, my wages now being fourteen dollars a week. I delivered hats to stores, packed hats, steamed felts, and did a number of other things that are somewhat vague in my memory today, but there was no way I could handle this job and my writing and attendance at the academy. After ten months, I decided that being both a writer and an artist was, in my circumstances, impossible. I had sold a short story; I left the academy.

I wrote my first novel when I was sixteen. I had never heard of anyone having a novel published at age sixteen, but I said to myself, Why not a first time? I finished it, read it through, and decided that it was so bad, the best thing I could do with it was to consign it to the trash can. The second novel dealt with my year at the academy. It was titled *To Be an Artist*. I brought it by hand to three publishers; each one asked me to come and get it — without comment. I was not deterred. I sold a story to a pulp magazine, and it brought me forty dollars.

I wrote my heart out every morning, and then I went to work for the hat maker. As the months passed, I discovered something that I had suspected for many years but had been unable to come to grips with, that the most wonderful, beautiful, and desirable of God's creations was called a woman. To a boy of seventeen, this phenomenon is shrouded in frustration and ineptitude. I learned about the bookstalls on lower Fourth Avenue (now Park Avenue South), hundreds of open stalls, thousands of books, and for forty cents I bought a battered copy of *Das Kapital* by one Karl Marx. Not too many years before, I had regarded books as things that existed only in the New York Public Library; now I was creating my own library, but as far as *Das Kapital* was concerned, I fought my way through two hundred pages or so and then surrendered. GBS did much better with explanation. *The Communist Manifesto,* which I bought for ten cents, a worn pamphlet, was full of brimstone and fire and much more to my taste. I fell in love with a girl named Thelma. I fell in love with a girl named Maxine. I fell in love passionately with a girl named Marjorie. The problem was that, what with working at a job, writing, trying to educate myself, and sharing in the housekeeping of our male ménage, cleaning, and cooking, I had no time to deal with young love.

Jerry, who was earning enough money to do some real dating, as opposed to my notion that a walk in Central Park was ample entertainment, invited me to come along with him one evening. He had met a young woman about six years older than his eighteen years and unlike any girl either of us had ever known. Her name was Sarah Kunitz, and together with her brother, Joshua, she had been to the Soviet Union several times. Her brother had written a book about Soviet Asia, entitled *Dawn Over Samarkand.* Those early thirties were years of our disastrous Depression — hunger and unemployment — and, at the same time, years when millions of people greeted the Soviet experiment in socialism as a beacon of hope for the world. Lincoln Steffens, a famous political economist and social commentator, had been to Russia, and he returned to say, "I have been over into the future, and it works." Ideological battles raged everywhere, pro and con, the Bolsheviks lauded and denounced. Myself, I was enthralled by the tales coming from the Soviet Union. I had read *Ten Days That Shook the World,* and John Reed stood along with Jack London and George Bernard Shaw as my literary heroes and role models. And now here, on this evening, my brother took me downtown to a restaurant called The Russian Bear, where I was introduced to Sarah Kunitz, Joshua Kunitz, Philip Rahv, and James T. Farrell.

It is impossible for me to convey satisfactorily an impression of that evening, much less what it meant to me. There was no college education in my life, and I had barely blundered through high school; my childhood had been work, and my smarts were street smarts, gutter smarts. I had never met such people — people who displayed a breadth of knowledge and understanding and fervor; I didn't know that such people existed. Sarah was wonderful. I fell in love with her immediately. I had not at that time read *Dawn Over Samarkand,* but here was the author, Joshua Kunitz, who talked about places out of the *Arabian Nights,* and here was James T. Farrell — another real, live author. I had never met an author before, and here was the author of *Young Lonigan,* here in the flesh.

I must interpolate a bit here and step forward in time. During the trials of Bukharin and other enemies of Stalin in the Soviet Union in the late thirties, the Communist Party of the United States split, the break-off faction being called Trotskyite. Both James T. Farrell and Philip Rahv, the editor of the left-wing magazine *Partisan Review,* broke with the CP and joined the Trotskyite movement. Years later, when I was invited to teach a semester at Indiana University, the English faculty gave a little party for me. They were a bit uneasy, since they couldn't decide whether I was a Communist Party member or not, whereupon one smartass member said he had a secret way of finding out. In the hearing of everyone, he asked me what I thought of the writing of James T. Farrell. When I replied that I consider Farrell one of the finest social realists of our time, the faculty member leaped to his feet and announced that I was not a Communist, since any party member would face expulsion if he dared to praise Farrell. This of course was arrant nonsense, but so was most of what was said about the Communist Party.

However, on this evening of my own young manhood, all of the above was in the future, and I sat at the table, completely enchanted, listening to the arguments and the counterarguments, the explanations, the endless river of ideas and notions and theories of this brilliant and — to me at the time — wonderful group of people. I didn't dare open my mouth, and when one of them asked me what school I was attending, I mumbled something unintelligible, not daring to say that I was, by my own definition, a writer.

Going uptown, Jerry and I discussed the evening. He was as awed as I was at meeting these people, but he felt that it was his duty, as my older and more sophisticated brother, to make light of it. I was utterly overwhelmed, and I made up my mind that I would join the Communist Party and become part of that tremendous struggle for a socialist world where there were no poor and oppressed, and where equity and compassion ruled.

On my own, I called Sarah Kunitz and asked her whether she would have lunch with me. She was delighted, and I chose a cafeteria on Seventh Avenue and Thirty-fifth Street. I told her something about my background, my education — or lack of it — and of my efforts to write, and then I came to the point and stated that I wanted to be a member of the Communist Party. I will be everlastingly grateful to her for talking me out of it.

She argued very firmly. I might be large and strong and competent, but I was still months short of my eighteenth birthday. A book by George Bernard Shaw was not enough for me to base my life on, and if I joined the party now, I might well regret it later. When I argued that she was a member of the party, she pointed out that this was something else entirely and that she was much older than I. That annoyed the very devil out of me, for I could see myself falling in love with her. I didn't think Jerry was too interested in her in that way, and I enjoyed the vision of a romantic liaison with this wise older woman.

"Listen," she said to me, "we have a writers' organization called the John Reed Club. It's very close to the party, but it's not the party. Nothing to sign, no cards — just go to the meetings and listen and talk when you want to, and you'll meet interesting writers and you'll learn."

I joined the John Reed Club and went to half a dozen meetings, but I could not connect with the people there. They were left wing and possibly some of them were Communists, but they were college people and college graduates, and they didn't have one damn notion of what was down there, in what Jack London called "the abyss." As for the lovely Sarah Kunitz, I would see her on and off over the next six years. She married and in time we drifted apart. I sent her my books and she gave me good advice and good criticism. When, twelve years later, I finally joined the Communist Party, she had become bitter about the party, not without reason, and our paths diverged. I don't know whether she still lives, but I remember her with warmth and love.

3

SUDDENLY, I WAS ANGRY with myself and rebelled against everything that was my life. I knew the streets and I knew what there was to know about the pain and filth and agony of the mean streets, and I could talk pig Latin as fluently as English — and beyond that was a world that didn't exist for me, barring the hills of Greene County, where I worked as a waiter and then as a camp counselor during most summers. Barney had a job, only thirty dollars a week, but that was a fortune and luck in the early thirties, and Julie was in school and Jerry had his two jobs and college, and I had to get out of there or burst. I talked it over with a friend, a young guy I had met during summer work, who also had ambitions as a writer, and we agreed to take off for the South and see what we could find. I'm not sure we knew what we were looking for, but it was something different from New York in the early thirties, and maybe all it amounted to was a need to get away.

Since we didn't know exactly where we were going, the idea was not sold easily to Barney, but he had long ago given up trying to talk me out of anything that I decided I must do. My friend's name was Devery Freeman, years later a television writer and executive in Hollywood, but at that time just another kid trying to find out what was over the horizon. He had twenty dollars and another ten that he kept under the inner sole of his shoe, which I learned about only many years later. He lived out on Manhattan Beach in a small house that was a very elegant structure by my lights. I never met any of his close family, nor did he ever speak about them, so I was never completely informed about his decision to accompany me, yet I was glad to have him along. I had only twelve dollars; the fact that he had twenty made him, in my eyes, a banker of sorts.

We took off on a fine morning in April, met at the Weehawken ferry with the purpose of catching a lift out of town while with the captured car audience on the ferry.

A Studebaker from the ferry took us to Philadelphia, and that was the last lift we had from a passenger car. If you had met up with us, you would have seen two skinny kids, brown trousers, shirt and sweater and jacket, both of us tow-headed, and neither of us very different from half a million other kids who were on the road, drifting north and south and east and west, always for a look beyond the horizon, where it might have been better but never was. It was an osmosis of sorts; if it had been fall, the greater flow would have been to the South and the West, but since it was spring, there was a flow to the North that might have been a trifle greater; and sometimes the flow was wherever the train or truck went.

We were picked up by a big fertilizer truck out of Philadelphia, and we rode through the streets of Washington in the early evening, the Capitol lit up, the white buildings ghostly and unreal, but a wonderful sight to two city kids. This was it then, this was Washington, the seat of everything, and it wasn't in a book but real and apparent. But when the truck dropped us outside Richmond, it was pouring rain, night, and we slogged through the outskirts of Richmond, soaked, tired, and hungry. A cop directed us to the Salvation Army shelter — not the last time I'd bed down in a shelter run by the Salvation Army, may they be cherished and rewarded — and we had coffee and doughnuts in the morning. It rained and rained that April. There was a night in Winston-Salem, North Carolina, when we crawled out of the rain into an old-fashioned office building, huddling under the stairs, and were asleep when it began to fill with the office workers in the morning. Someone called the cops, and they pointed us out of town instead of putting us in jail. Other cops were not that pleasant.

But there are other memories I have of hot, delicious sunshine, the live oaks and the Spanish moss and the magnolias, the South that one never forgets. There was one unforgettable day on a dirt road in the Pee Dee Swamp. We were picked up by two white kids who were riding the tailgate of an old wagon driven by an old black man and drawn by a lazy mule. For the next three hours we rode with them, no faster than a man walking, but lazy in the sunshine. We fought the Civil War again, all easy and laughing, the way kids are when they hold no animosity, and the Civil War was not so far away then, more than half a century ago. We made good friends with those boys, and I had some of the South and its feeling sink into me, a knowledge that stood me in good stead when I came to write a book called *Freedom Road*. I was always good with accents, and Devery and I picked up the local speech wherever we went. I knew all the accents and inflections of the city streets, but here was a whole world of speech, differing from place to place, and since we did so many miles on foot, we would find pockets of speech that appeared to have been forgotten by time.

Years later, trying to set the groundwork for a film in Wales, I was told by Welsh friends that one of the reasons the English resented them was their chameleonlike ability — not shared by poor Londoners — to speak like well-to-do Brits if they so desired. I must have been blessed with some such ability, and I armed my memory with every accent I encountered.

We walked through Savannah, excited by the beauty of that wonderful old city. We drifted aimlessly toward Tampa, riding trucks and walking for many miles. Outside Tampa, we stood on the side of a shadeless road an hour or so, trying to find a lift. We had walked about three miles from an orange-loading station, stuffed ourselves with oranges from a pile of rejects, and now here we were, the soles of our feet on fire, done in.

Across the road from where we stood there was a feed store, no different from a thousand other feed and seed stores in the South — shed to keep out the sun, side shed to shelter bags of feed, truck on the side, wife's washing on the other side, and to grace it, a typical Florida redneck sitting in the cool shade, chair tilted back, sucking on a grass straw. He had a long local face, burned red-brown by the sun, and blue eyes that studied us appraisingly. We must have stood there across the road from him for at least half an hour before he moved. Then he slowly tilted his chair forward, rose, and crossed the road to where we stood, and as he came I expected him to tell us to move on or he'd call the cops. Instead, he stopped a few feet from us and studied us again. Finally, he spoke one word, "Jews?," but with neither annoyance nor threat.

Devery remained silent; he was a Jew only by the faintest memory. I nodded. "We're Jews." After all, there was only one of him and two of us.

His whole demeanor changed. His face broke into a smile, and he explained to us that he had to make sure, because if it got around that he was Jewish, he'd be out of business in a week. That was new to me. Kids yelling what they learned at home or in church were one thing; a man unable to run a business in the United States because he was Jewish was something else entirely; but he explained very carefully that it was the nature and place of his business. He took us into his living quarters behind the store, fed us, watered us, and then sent us on our way. It was manna in the desert. Then the next day we found ourselves in Fort Lauderdale, walking. Fort Lauderdale was written on the ground, endless empty streets, blocks, cement sidewalks, but no buildings. The Depression had sliced away any hope of house or home or life, and in the empty square blocks weeds grew five feet high.

We were exhausted. We lay down in the weeds, and we were asleep almost instantly, and then were awakened in the black of the night by the beams of two powerful searchlights. Visible in the halo of light, the muzzles of two guns. Not the last time; in the South, the gun was out constantly in those days. This time, it was two Fort Lauderdale police officers who had noticed the two bodies in the weeds. We were scared to death, but the cops were decent enough, allowing that sleeping in the street was not encouraged in Fort Lauderdale, and since I had two dollars left and Devery had more, we were not booked as vagrants but were simply taken to the police station for the rest of the night. We looked harmless, and there were so many kids drifting around the country in 1933, that small-town cops just herded them on out of town. The cells at the police station were filled with vagrants, so the cops let us sleep on benches in the hall, free of bedbugs, as they pointed out, and then showed us out of town in the morning, with a warning not to return to Fort Lauderdale.

Walking, getting one more ride, we arrived finally at Miami Beach, were chased off the beach by cops, since we looked pretty ratty by then, and discovered that there was no more to cheer for in Miami than in New York. In Miami, Devery and I parted company at his insistence. I didn't think it was a good idea, and God knows I didn't want to be left alone there, but since Devery never mentioned anything that had happened to him on his way back to New York, my guess was that he had bus fare tucked away, enough for himself but not enough for two. Away with Devery. What the hell, I said to myself, I'm eighteen years old and I can take care of myself. I had eighty-five cents.

I hoarded that eighty-five cents. I can give no full accounting today, but I remember a loaf of bread that I bought for eight cents and ate over three days, together with oranges. You might not stay too healthy, but you could stay alive in Florida on oranges, and without stealing, for there was always fallen fruit lying by the roadside. There were no jobs. I would have taken anything to have a week's pay, even if only five dollars, because I figured that with five dollars I could make my way home. I gave up on Miami. I spent almost a whole day waiting for a lift, and then was picked up by a black man driving an ancient truck loaded with the carcasses of a dozen pigs with no refrigeration. The smell was horrendous. He was bound for Fort Lauderdale, and I had no desire ever again to be in Fort Lauderdale, so I had him drop me at Ojus. I met some kids on their way to the rail yards. I went with them, having just about given up on road lifts, and that evening I climbed onto an oil car. It was actually a string of slow-moving oil cars, and there must have been a thousand kids and older men crouched on the walks that ran alongside the oil tanks. At Boynton, the train pulled onto a holding track and the railroad police just about went crazy, chasing the riders, who scattered all over the yard, and swinging their billy clubs like men gone mad. In all those days in the South, I never saw anything as mean and brutal as the railroad cops.

I fell in with some men who were on their way to the bean farms in the Everglades, where the farmers were looking for pickers at two dollars a day. I figured that if I worked a week and made ten dollars, or maybe twelve if they did a six-day week, I could make out and go north with that, but they paid only after thirty days, and I had no intention of settling down there for thirty days. They charged twenty-five cents for a night in a filthy bunkhouse, and I guess that when I saw a bunkhouse, that decided me. I finished the bread and ate an orange and climbed onto a freight train, mostly cars filled with tomatoes. Those cars had a raised hood at each end, the front hood catching the air and driving it over the stacked crates of tomatoes, letting it out through the rear hood. There were other men on the train, but the railroad cop who rode with it had a reputation, so everyone kept down in the ventilation shafts. I picked up the train about noon, a beautiful, sunny day, and I sat myself down on top of the car, a box seat on my own observation deck. Above Palm Beach, the railroad tracks were on the edge of lagoon and ocean. Pink pelicans, palm trees, the lagoons, and the sea — the one lovely, untrammeled memory of Florida. I must have had two or three hours of this bliss, riding north toward my home, when I heard a scream, and looking around the lid I was sitting against, back toward the caboose, I saw the tough rail cop slapping his billy club against a rider's head, and the man in flight fell and rolled off the train. I went into the ventilation shaft like a squirrel into its burrow, and for the next few hours, until dark, I crouched there, breathing the smell of green tomatoes.

When the train stopped to water, I climbed out and fled the tomato train, but even the fear of the rail cops could not drive me back to the auto roads and the hours begging for lifts that never materialized. During the next twenty-four hours, I rode in an empty cement car or sand car that bounced so much that I thought my head would go to pieces, the cat walk of another oil tank train, and a string of empties. In the empty car, I met an old bindlestiff, who advised me that if I wanted to make it to New York in a hurry, I should seat myself in the blind front of a crack passenger train, on the step where the front car was coupled to the engine. He told me that if I remained awake, I'd make good time. If I fell asleep — well, it wasn't a good place to fall asleep.

At the railroad yard outside Savannah, I waited for the arrival of a north-bound passenger train and proceeded to put into effect the idea fed to me by the bindlestiff. I seated myself in the right position, and a moment later I was hauled out of my place by a railroad cop, put into a truck that was waiting and already filled with about twenty men, and was driven to a local lockup. The talk among the men in the truck was that we were destined for a Georgia chain gang, and that put a cold chill in my soul. I'm not sure at this point — it was night when we got there and night when I left — whether the police station was actually in Savannah. I remember better a sandwich with a thin slice of ham that we got and that I devoured hungrily. I was kept overnight in a cell, and the following evening, strangely enough, I was brought before a magistrate or justice of the peace or some such thing and asked a few questions. Most of the others had been dealt with already, and there were only a few men in the little courtroom with me. The magistrate asked me if I had any money. I shook my head. I noticed a Mason's ring on his finger, and I said that my father was a Mason, which he was not; but my condition at the moment was such that I would have told any kind of lie to get out of there a free man. My Uncle Edward, the one in Greene County, was a Mason, and I had heard enough about the power and brotherhood of Masons to hope it would work. It did. The magistrate asked whether, if I called home collect, my father would send bus fare. He allowed me to make the call at the police station, and I spoke to Barney, and the money for the ticket was sent. The only time I saw a real, uninhibited display of affection from my father was when I walked into our apartment in New York two days later.

Thus, when someone asks me how and why I became a socialist and a Communist, the answer is always inadequate. Intellectuals deal with ideas and abstractions. Never having had enough education to become a proper intellectual, I have spent my life dealing with facts and events, and this journey burned itself into my memory. I have tried to write these events as I experienced them, with no broader perspective than I had at the time and without giving them too much importance, yet I had journeyed through a society in disintegration, saved from inner destruction by World War Two, still six years in the future. And through all this, I had never whimpered or turned a thought against this land which I had come to love so, nor can I ever think of the South without recalling not the jails and the guns, but the wonderful slow wagon ride through the Pee Dee Swamp, arguing the Civil War with the southern kids. But I had reached an age where the innocence, born not of faith but of intolerable poverty, was beginning to crumble and where I began to understand that society could be planned and function in another way, called socialism; and because I came to believe that the only serious socialist party in America was the Communist Party, I was bitterly attacked and slandered for fifteen years of my life.

I have never intended this book to be an apologia, yet if it is to mean anything, it must be explicit. This particular incident in my growing was like a prolonged electric shock, to be driven through my mind over and over. Not that I dwelled on it. I went to work. I found work as a shipping clerk in a dress factory in the heart of the garment center, and I wrote, morning and evening, six, seven, eight hours a day. I had written three complete and more or less unpublishable novels before I took off for the South. I wrote two more in the few months after I returned, five novels, one a five-hundred-page opus. They are best unremembered. The sixth novel, which I called *Two Valleys,* found a publisher.

This first publisher, as I mentioned earlier, was the old original Dial Press, and the man who accepted the book was the editor in chief of that distinguished publishing house, a gentleman by the name of Grenville Vernon. I received a $100 advance, and the book was also sold to the British publishing house Michael Joseph. The fact that the author was not yet nineteen was made much of, and while the novel was no great work of art, it was a gentle and readable book, a love story set in Colonial times in the mountains of what is today West Virginia. The reviews were decent and kind, with many bows to my age, but sales were inconsequential because the owner of the company, Lincoln MacVeagh, had put the house up for sale. For all that, I was recognized as a bright new hope on the literary horizon. I was given a Bread Loaf Award, and I spent two weeks at that lovely spot in the Green Mountains, eating marvelous food, learning the finer points in the use of knives and forks, watching the critic John Mason Brown and his colleagues drink more martinis than I ever imagined human beings could consume and make sense, and falling moderately but romantically in love with Gladys Hasty Carroll, a very popular and beautiful writer of the time, and about ten years older than I. I actually gathered the courage to tell her I loved her before the session finished, but that was as far as it went, and I never saw her again. She was very kind to me.

Everyone praised my first success except Sarah Kunitz. By the time she read *Two Valleys,* I had finished another novel, *Strange Yesterday,* which also earned a mere $100 advance and was sold off by MacVeagh to Dodd, Mead and Company. She read both books, one still in manuscript, and she was neither kind nor restrained in her criticism. She pointed out to me that since Jack London, I was the first American writer to emerge from the working class (by no means the only one, I learned in time, yet there were very few), self-educated, and endowed with a God-given ear for human speech. By then, I had told her most of my background, including my southern adventure, and her point was that I had sold out and betrayed my background, my own suffering and experience, as well as my obligation to the working class, by writing two fairy tales. How was it, she demanded, that we could have dozens of middle-class writers writing about the poor in this time of a great Depression while the valid working-class writer Howard Fast spins fairy tales as historical novels? It was a furious argument, with my ego punctured in place after place, while I proclaimed hotly that I had no literary obligations to anyone, that I had gotten my own ass out of a sling without help from the working class or any other class, that nobody was going to tell me how or what to write, and that I wrote what I pleased and would continue to write what I pleased.

It took only a few weeks of mumbling to myself to realize that Sarah was right — well, perhaps not absolutely right, but certainly more right than wrong. This was in 1933, and ten years would go by before I could write truly about the South I saw and loved and hated, and that book was *Freedom Road*.

But she was right about the two books that had been published, and suddenly everything dried up and I stopped writing. Months went by and I wrote nothing. I worked in a garment factory, and I trundled trucks through the streets and packed cases and learned to use a pressing machine and a felling machine, and worked my way up to twelve and then fourteen dollars a week, and dated a beautiful girl who worked in a publishing house and then parted because beyond subway fare to work and back, a nickel each way, and fifteen cents more for lunch at the Automat, brown beans and coffee, I had nothing, not even a decent pair of pants. Jerry was in his third year of college — we managed that somehow — and Julius was in high school, and everybody worked, and our need to hold the family together, now that two of us were adults and my younger brother was pushing adulthood, became almost demonic. Barney could rarely get better than the lowest paid job, but we managed, with a kind of crazy pride that we took no welfare or outside help of any kind. Interest-

ingly, my father, a loyal Democrat and for years a county commit-
teeman who worshiped Al Smith, was always reminded by the local
Democratic boss that if worse came to worst, the party would step
in. I think of how many times he came around to check Pop's vote,
have a shot of bootleg gin, and say to him, "You know, Barney, that
the party will never let you or the kids go hungry." Well, there were
times when we were hungry, but we never dunned the party, and
Barney always rejected their annual turkey, with instructions that
they give it to some poor family.

And then I went back to writing. Up each morning at six, dress,
chew a sweet roll, drink a glass of milk, and write. Two more pulp
stories were sold, and I paid a semester of Jerry's tuition. On and off,
as I would hit a short story sale, I would pay tuition. I fought for my
writing now, so the two morning hours before I went to work were
a daily agony. More and more deeply aware of how right Sarah
Kunitz was, I struggled to write about myself. I put together a story
about a little boy, living on the street I lived on, whom I called Ishky.
I coined the name because it sounded very Jewish, and I had his
mother speak only the most broken English; but when his mother's
Yiddish was translated formally, it emerged as classical English, full
of *thee*'s and *thou*'s. I got the idea from Henry Roth's wonderful
book, *Call It Sleep*. Ishky had one friend, a little Italian boy, my
friend then, who played the fiddle and who, because he was a shoe-
maker's son, we called Shoemake. The body of the story concerned
the lynching of the black kid, the incident I referred to earlier. My
story would be called *The Children*, and I wrote and rewrote, and
tore up what I had and wrote it again, and drank coffee and smoked.
Drink had no allure for me; nicotine had.

But cigarettes cost money. The factory where I did my eight or
nine hours of survival work each day had a solidly Jewish immigrant
working force — cutters, machine operators, everyone — and the
chatter and gossip that never stopped were carried on in Yiddish. On
my first day there, when I had to have orders translated, they named
me the *goy*, Yiddish for Gentile. I had picked up the cigarette habit
from a waiter I worked with one summer. But brand cigarettes were
twelve cents a pack, and even the lowly Wings were eight or ten cents
a pack, depending on where you bought them — and this cut into
food money. Therefore I bought one pack a week, treasured it at

home as a crutch for writing, and depended on my bumming talents for daytime smoking. And since I never smoked more than two or three cigarettes during working time, and since practically everyone in the factory smoked, I could always find a butt. But only if I asked for it in Yiddish, and thereby my first Yiddish word was *pappyrus,* Yiddish for cigarette. Whatever my question, the workers would fling back at me, *"Freg mir in Yiddish"* (Ask me in Yiddish).

In due course, I learned twenty or thirty words of Yiddish, which enabled me to exist in the factory, bum cigarettes, and keep my reserve for writing. For months I played with the manuscript of *The Children,* adding to it, taking chapters out, giving it up, and then going back to it. There were weeks when my mind and body rebelled. I would be sleepless all night, fighting to be awake at six. I would get up at six and my mind would be mush. I would fall asleep over my typewriter. I would put the project out of sight and mind, resigning myself to life as a factory worker, full of self-pity and falling back on my lack of education in any normal sense as a lame excuse. Meanwhile, I began to read American history. It had absolutely no connection with *The Children,* but I decided that, since I had written two novels that Sarah Kunitz called fairy tales, I would try to find out what had actually happened in the time of the American Revolution.

Then a day came when I decided that *The Children* was as finished as it ever would be. My two published books and my handful of sold stories had persuaded a literary agency to accept me as one of its writers. The agency was McIntosh and Otis and was run by three pleasant ladies, Mavis McIntosh, Elizabeth Otis, and Mary Abbott. They were middle-class literary types, good agents, and to me characters out of an Edwardian novel. An additional attraction for me was that on the little table in their waiting room they kept a wooden box of cigarettes. I gave them *The Children* — forty-five thousand words of it — and washed my hands of it. I decided that I would continue as a writer, but let Sarah Kunitz say what she would — there would be no more about myself and my childhood. It was too close, too confusing, and too filled with pain.

Whit Burnett, publisher of *Story* magazine, bought *The Children* and published it. *Story* was the most distinguished magazine of the short story in America at a time when the short story was at its peak as an art form internationally and when American short stories were read and admired the world over — which says nothing for the finances of *Story*. Burnett paid fifty dollars for forty-five thousand words, by word count — still the practice at that time — one tenth of a cent per word. I was absolutely enraged when Mary Abbott telephoned to give me this offer, and I fumed and ranted until she convinced me that Whit Burnett published at a loss and that such was the reputation and distinction of *Story* that it could only profit me even if he paid me not one penny. Mary Abbot felt it was a very good thing for young writers to struggle and make do, but the young writers she knew came from proper middle-class families and good universities with fall-back. I had no fall-back whatsoever. Nevertheless, she convinced me that *Story* was the proper place for the short novel I had written. I told her to go ahead, but it would have to be $100. On and off, I had put a year into the book, and even as a newspaper delivery boy at age ten, I had not worked for two dollars a week. Also, since I had received an advance of $100 for each of my two published books, I might as well keep my price up. That's a joke; I would not want it misunderstood.

During the time when I was writing *The Children*, the most important event in my young life took place: I met my wife. It came about through a telephone call from Devery Freeman. I had not heard from him for months, and now he wanted a favor. A distant cousin of his had come to New York to study art at Pratt Institute and she was rooming with a girl who was studying art at Parsons School of Design. His cousin's name was Bea, and he was determined to get her into bed with him, a prospect not unlikely, now that she was here *sans* family; she came from Monticello, New York. What he needed was someone to take care of the roommate, whom he had never seen and about whom he knew absolutely nothing. I protested. I had met a left-wing dancer who was the present object of my adoration of women. He pleaded, and finally I agreed. Her name was Bette, and the girls had rented a basement-front room in an old town house turned rooming house in the Seventies on West End Avenue.

I met Devery, and we arrived together at West End Avenue at seven o'clock. Our plan was to take the girls out to dinner, and after dinner I would take Bette to a movie while Devery took Bea back to the furnished room to work out the details of his seduction. Dinner would be at an Italian restaurant on Seventy-second Street, between Broadway and West End Avenue. At Anselmo's, the tables had tablecloths, the napkins were of cloth and were white, and one could order a dinner as follows: tomato juice, small spaghetti or antipasto, veal cutlet with potato and a vegetable, spumoni, and coffee, all of it deliciously done and served for forty cents, whereby two could eat for eighty cents and leave twenty cents for the tip. Not only did Bette and I have our first meal there, but at least a hundred more in the same place over the next two years.

Once at the basement-front, down three steps from the street, I faced the girl of my dreams, a beautiful, shapely woman, five feet five inches, flaxen hair and blue eyes and a lovely smile. Bea was three inches taller, dark, attractive, but of no interest to me at that moment, and I breathed a sigh of relief when she was introduced as Bea, and the girl with the flaxen hair as Bette. I took her hand, studied her for a long moment, and then decided to marry her, which I did two years later. I am given to quick decisions, and very often I have regretted them; on the other hand, this was a good one. We took the girls to dinner, and then Bette and I left Devery to his own problems. We walked east to Central Park. It was a warm, lovely evening, and we walked to the Sheep Meadow, where we sprawled on the grass, along with two or three hundred other couples. We had no desire for a movie; that was a time when the word *mugging* did not exist and when most people in New York did not bother to lock their doors.

We talked and talked and talked. I told her my life and hopes, and she told me hers. She had grown up in Bayonne, New Jersey, and her living in New York was in the way of liberation. The fact that I had already published two books outweighed my present condition as a factory worker. We fell asleep there on the lawn, and it was four o'clock in the morning when I took her back to her room. I did not ask her to marry me until our second date. I turned twenty-one a few months later.

The Children was published a year and a half after Bette and I met, in the March 1937 issue of *Story*. Since it was so long a piece, it took practically all of the magazine. James J. Fee, the police inspector of Lynn, Massachusetts, was put onto it, and he read a copy of *Story,* the first copy he had ever read and possibly the first book he had ever read. He proclaimed that *The Children* was "the rottenest thing I ever read!" Only two copies of *Story* went to the local news dealer, and Inspector Fee immediately confiscated them. The next day it was banned in Waterbury, Connecticut, and an order for six hundred extra copies promptly came in from the newsdealers in that town. Whit Burnett danced with delight, and Mary Abbott called to congratulate me, telling me that I was so lucky, since having a work banned was the best thing that could happen to sales, and if only it was banned in Boston, sales would skyrocket. It was banned in Boston and in six other New England cities, and *Story* had the largest press run in all of its history. The book was hailed as a small masterpiece and lauded to the skies, and Whit Burnett said that *The Children* saved *Story,* at least for the time being. But saving Howard Fast was another matter, and when my agent suggested to Burnett that he let me share the prosperity by adding another $100 to the sum he had paid, he turned her down flat.

Sarah Kunitz embraced me, and the members of the John Reed Club saluted me and welcomed me into the literary fraternity. But as events unfolded, I was not so eager to be welcomed by the party. I took no part in the bitter arguments that raged on the left at that time, between the party people on one hand, loyal to Stalin, and the group loyal to Trotsky; but I listened and I heard and read of the events of 1936 with increasing bewilderment and horror. In August of that year, sixteen of the true old Bolsheviks, men who had participated nobly in the making of the revolution only twenty years earlier, including Kamenev and Zinoviev, were put on trial, forced to confess, and then executed. These were men I had heard spoken of again and again, and suddenly they were all traitors. There was no depth to my knowledge of the left; I had never been part of the Young Communist League, which flourished at City College and New York University. My whole contact with the left was through the John Reed Club, sitting at meetings and listening to lectures.

When the sixteen Bolsheviks were executed and the party began to split, I pulled back and away — and I had no more dealings or contacts with the Communist Party of the United States for the next eight years. During that time, I educated myself, went on with my task of learning to write, and married Bette Cohen.

We were married in June of 1937 in the tiny house of her parents. Her father was a wholesale newspaper distributor in Bayonne and

Jersey City, and while they were not poor, they barely managed, and there was absolutely nothing to alter our continuing poverty. They regarded me as some strange, feckless creature, hardly Jewish — behind my back they referred to me as "the goy," just as the workers at the factory did — and since they felt I was dooming their daughter to a life of poverty in the sinful abyss of New York, they had little affection for me. In time, their attitude changed.

On the other hand, my own poverty was lightened by heady moments of great wealth. Great wealth meant an advance of $500 from Harcourt, Brace and Company when it accepted *Place in the City* for publication, $700 from *The Saturday Evening Post* for a short story, $900 from *The Ladies' Home Companion*, $500 from *Elks* magazine. Such were the high points, but the high points dissolved almost instantly. In between there was poverty. The first time Bette and I reached a point where we had nothing, not a dollar in the bank, only thirty cents in our pockets, Bette began to panic. I explained patiently that this had always been, more or less, my financial condition, and that I had survived. I won five dollars in a crap game, and the following day, my dear Mary Abbott called to tell me I had sold two stories to *Elks* magazine for a sum of $900. I think that for a free-lance writer, the problem of survival is rarely entirely solved, but better to know what it is to be without money than to try to imagine the condition — and perhaps that is the case with most of the things one writes about.

Not only are marriages not made in heaven, but a fair amount must certainly originate in hell. On a scale of one to ten, ours was close to the top, underlined by a kind of desperate and relentless need for each other. We came from two worlds that could hardly have been farther apart, she from an Orthodox Jewish middle-class family, I from a region we have already explored; but she was already in revolt when we met, and the two years we were together before we married brought us close enough to fight through our problems. Perhaps there is no task presented to most human beings more difficult than marriage, especially in a world where the woman so rarely comes into the contract as an equal. Oh, I was lucky. Without her, I would have made a fine lot of impossible marriages; but she refused to allow my male idiocy to prevail, she helped me, fostered my writing, endured my depressions, my explosions, read everything I wrote, supported me firmly unless the product was worthless — and then criticized gently. She endured my propensity for finding too many women too wonderful, and she never gave up.

A writer is a strange creature. He is a delicate sheet of foil on which the world prints its impressions, and he is self-serving and self-oriented and yet utterly vulnerable, and when I say "he," I mean "she" as well, and for a woman it holds true even more painfully, for whatever a man suffers, a woman suffers more and feels more deeply; and though everyone may believe that he or she can write, in these United States of over two hundred and fifty million people, only a handful can claim the title of writer in its high sense. I married a gifted, beautiful woman who would one day be one of the finest sculptors we have, and she put aside her own need for my need. I don't know whether it was worth it, or how wise she was to follow me down the paths I took. If one grows old and a little bit wise, all the symbols of greatness and importance and glory shrivel to almost nothing.

By the time Bette and I married, I had finished *Place in the City* and the book had been published with less than earth-shaking results, selling perhaps five thousand copies; but now I was selling short stories for anywhere from $500 to $1000 each. Such sales every six months, though, did not pay the rent, and we filled in the low spots in every way we could. We wrote term papers for college students who had money and no brains; I did pulp stories for fifty dollars each — anything, since once I married, I gave up factory work to be a full-time writer.

Bette and I had invested in a 1931 Ford convertible, which cost us forty dollars. Not only did it run, but the clutch was so worn that no one else could start the car. A semimagical way of working clutch and gas pedal allowed me to put it into motion, and even though one of the tires had a hole the size of a fifty-cent piece, through which the inner tube protruded in a threatening bubble, we ran it for thousands of miles with no trouble. When something broke down, it never cost more than a dollar to replace it. We parked it on the street, and of course no thief in his right mind would have touched it.

We drove it everywhere, and on one of our journeys we went to Valley Forge in Pennsylvania, and spent the afternoon there, moved deeply by the reconstruction of the old Revolutionary War encampment. I decided then and there that I'd write a book about the army's winter in Valley Forge, and for the next six months I read American history and wrote the book I would call *Conceived in Liberty;* it became my first real breakthrough as a novelist.

With Sam Sloan, my editor, gone from Harcourt, Brace, and with his replacement there less than thrilled with the sales of *Place in the City,* Mary Abbott sent my new novel to Simon and Schuster. They accepted it immediately, published it, and sold about fifteen thousand copies, a decent record for my writing. The book, which dealt with the American Revolution somewhat in the realistic manner of Erich Maria Remarque's novel *All Quiet on the Western Front,* about World War One — a treatment never before applied to our revolt — was received with great enthusiasm by the critics. James T. Farrell reviewed it for *The New York Times,* kindly and constructively, and I was unusually thrilled by his guess that when I got the "lightning bugs," as he called them, out of my writing, I might become a very important writer indeed.

During the years between 1937, when I got married, and 1942, when I took over the Voice of America at the Office of War Information, I withdrew completely from active political involvement. For the first time in my life, I was tasting financial security, minimal but actual. Our first year was difficult. I had read bits and pieces, never a full story, of the magnificent running battle and flight to freedom of Chief Little Wolf and his Cheyenne Indians. I wanted desperately to write about it, but the only way I could do so would be to go to Oklahoma, where the old Cheyenne reservation had been, and talk to some of the old Cheyennes still there. Also, in Norman, Oklahoma, at the university, there were Indian students and, on the faculty, a man named Stanley Vestal, who knew more about the Cheyennes than any white man in America. I told the story to Simon and Schuster and talked them into paying me $100 a month for an entire year. We had $200 in our bank account. Ninety dollars bought us an ancient Pontiac to replace our Ford, and with $110 to live on, we set off for Oklahoma. It was a wonderful trip; the Pontiac was fine as long as one didn't push it too hard; and the world of the Great Plains was an incredible change for this survivor of the city streets. The country overwhelmed us, awed us. We spent a month in Norman, and then drove west to the Rockies and Arizona and New Mexico, at a time when there were only two decent cross-country roads, and then we turned back on a new road through the White Mountains of the Southwest to the Rio Grande and into Mexico — and all with the excitement and awe of great personal discovery.

But it was during our time at Norman that I tracked down the facts that became *The Last Frontier*. It was a wonderful adventure for two city kids, to sit through an evening with young Cheyenne and Crow students and listen to them play their ancient tribal music on wooden flutes, to talk to old, wrinkled Indians who remembered a childhood before the white man came, to watch Cheyenne athletes, tall, magnificently muscled men, playing football in their bare feet, and of course to meet Stanley Vestal. We spent hours with him, listening to his stories. So deeply was he a part of the Plains Indian culture that he believed that a proper playing of the tom-toms could bring rain. He had practiced, he told us, with some of the great tribal rain makers, and he knew that it could be done. That was a bitter, dry year in Oklahoma, and I asked him why he didn't bring rain now. He replied that when one upset the balance of natural forces, no one could anticipate the consequences. They might be, he held, much worse than drought.

On our way back to New York, hoarding our last few dollars, we stopped off at the Library of Congress in Washington to go through the single English-Cheyenne dictionary that existed, compiled by a Quaker missionary. It was available only in manuscript, an enormous scholarly work of almost 100,000 words. For the first time, I realized the complexity of tribal language and the difficulty of conveying facts without modern verb forms. Stanley Vestal had suggested that while in Washington we try to see and speak with the son of the great Apache chief Geronimo. He was painting a mural in one of the public buildings — Geronimo being an example of our practice of destroying those who oppose us and then honoring them. Vestal had told us in detail the story of Geronimo, who, with his band of twenty-one Apache warriors, had fought five regiments of the U.S. Cavalry for years, and we were eager to speak with his son and perhaps write about him. But he had no desire to talk to us or any other white writer.

Back in New York, we were dead broke once again, but with the guaranteed advance of $100 a month from Simon and Schuster, which would have been ample had not Sam Sloan invited Bette and me to his home in Yorktown Heights, where he had a pair of pure-bred

Great Danes; the bitch had just given birth. He presented us with one of the litter, and we named the puppy Yorick. Alas, indeed! For three months Yorick, who came from a royal line and was as stupid as most royalty, ate us out of house and home, a loaf of stale bread and half a pound of beef heart each day, until he developed meningitis and had to be put down. Bette and I wept like children and began to eat again.

It took nine months for me to write *The Last Frontier*, and when I had finished it, neither Bette nor I was particularly thrilled with the result. The editors at Simon and Schuster were less than thrilled, and they returned the manuscript with a note that canceled the unpaid $200 of my advance, and let me understand that prompt repayment of the ten months' stipend already spent would be expected. But none too soon, I assured them, since our next meal was the major problem.

Meanwhile, San Sloan's new publishing house, Duell, Sloan and Pearce, had begun to function, and when I told him that Simon and Schuster had dumped *The Last Frontier,* he asked to read the manuscript. He read it promptly and asked to see me, and the first thing he put to me was whether I knew how I went wrong. I didn't know, and then he explained, gently, that I had tried to tell the story from the Indians' point of view. "You can't," he said. "You can't get inside Little Wolf's head and you can't translate Indian speech into English and make it believable." Then what to do with what I had? That was when Sam told me to throw it away and begin again and tell the whole story from the white man's point of view. When I explained that I had carfare home and not much more, he immediately gave me a check for $2000 as an advance.

I started again from page one. I had the material, so the rewrite was easier, and some months later I brought Sam my new manuscript of *The Last Frontier*. I had spent a year and a half on the book, more time than I had ever given to a book before, and it was during that time that my father died. Through the last four years of his life, he had become the child and we, my brothers and I, the parents. Poor medicine had given him a bad infection in his bladder, and a botched operation in a badly run hospital had brought him, what with bleeding that went unattended, to the edge of death. He never fully recovered. Jerry and I cared for him as best we could, Jerry taking on most of the burden by having Barney with him and his wife. At the time Barney died, Bette and I were living in a tiny one-room apartment on West Eighty-fourth Street. No one in my family, on either my mother's or my father's side, reached out or visited us, or even offered anything in the way of condolence. Their "compassionate" wiping their hands of us after my mother's death continued in force, their lack of feeling for this plain, hard-working, gentle man who was my father, unchanged. My father had been a romantic, a man who dreamed good dreams, a man who worked bitterly hard all his life, and who gave me something invaluable, a sense of identity with the poor and oppressed of all the earth.

The publication of *The Last Frontier* marked the end of our time of poverty and intermittent small riches. Suddenly, Bette and I had enough money for all our modest desires, and, as I have related, I was hailed as a bright new star on the literary horizon. Carl Van Doren, writing a lead review of the book, said, "*The Last Frontier* is an amazing restoration and recreation. The characters breathe, the landscape is solid ground and sky, and the story runs flexibly along the zigzag trail of a people driven by a deep instinct to their ancient home. I do not know of any other episode of Western history that has been so truly and subtly perpetuated as this one. A great story has been found again, and as here told promises to live for generations."

Of course it was all too much. The literary world is never restrained in either its praise or its condemnation. There were no bad reviews, nor would there be any bad reviews for my next book, *The Unvanquished*, which I wrote and completed in the months between my giving the manuscript of *The Last Frontier* to Sam Sloan and its publication.

Years later, when I complained to my Zen teacher that my being a member of the Communist Party had thrust me into literary obscurity and made me the hate target of the literary elite who ruled the weekly book section of *The New York Times* and other such reviews, he looked at me with contempt and said, "You dare to complain of something that saved your own soul!"

Perhaps he was right.

As for my books — they were reviled once I became a Communist, but they were read and read, and at no time during the fifty-six years that followed the publication of my first novel did efforts to suppress them actually succeed.

4

DURING THE MONTHS at the Office of War Information, I conceived the notion of a book about black Reconstruction in the South, more specifically in South Carolina. A number of things led me in this direction. While at the OWI, I set my researchers to work on the problem of Negro (the word of the time) integration in the armed forces. Then there was the afternoon at Carl Van Doren's apartment, when Bette and I argued with Sinclair Lewis about anti-Semitism. Reports were beginning to filter out of Germany about the destruction of the Jews, and the question was sensitive indeed.

After that discussion about intolerance, all the notes and thinking that I had done for a novel about Reconstruction came together — and every moment I could steal from my work at the OWI was put to writing the new book. I would call it *Freedom Road*. At a party given by Charles Duell, one of my new publishers, I met his wife, Jo, who before her marriage had been Jo Pringle-Smith. If one accepts the idea, at least in a historic sense, that there was a true antebellum aristocracy in the South, and that the high domain of it was South Carolina, then the Pringle-Smiths occupied that upper tier. At the time I write of, they still maintained their old plantation as well as their mansion on the Charleston waterfront. Jo Duell was a beautiful, delightful woman, without the slightest pretense, and when I outlined the story I intended to tell, she became very interested and told me that to do it properly, I must spend a few days with her parents in Charleston. She said that she would arrange it as soon as I could go, and that while her mother and father were delightful and hospitable people — as I found them to be — they did nurse certain prejudices, and I was not to let drop that I was Jewish. I suppose that if they had asked me, I would have admitted it, but they were too well bred to ask a personal question. Their house was like a museum, and my few days with them were invaluable to me in my attempt to finish *Freedom Road.* The recognition that such gentle and kind people could harbor the prejudices they did was another step in my understanding of class position and racism, even as was Sinclair Lewis's anti-Semitism.

One day, trying to clarify her unfriendly attitude toward Mrs. Roosevelt, who, as she explained, could not be a dinner guest in her home, Jo's mother took me upstairs to the guest room and opened for my inspection an ancient leather trunk. The label inside the lid read DELANO TRUNKMAKER. I had thought the Delano to be on Franklin Roosevelt's side of the family, but my hostess said it did not really matter, both Franklin and Eleanor being the children of petty tradesmen. I can't imagine what would have happened had I told her of my own background.

All of this was in the few months after I left the Office of War Information. Bette was pregnant and still working for the Signal Corps. I worked night and day on *Freedom Road,* which I finished in April of 1944. Meanwhile, I was pleading with newspapers and magazines to hire me as a correspondent and send me overseas to where the war was being fought. In all of this, I was being slowly but surely drawn into a circle of Communist Party people very different from those I had known years earlier. These were what was known, in the party's order of organization, as the Cultural Section: writers, artists, dancers, actors, producers, editors, publishers, flaks, and advertising people.

One cannot write about this period without emphasizing that Harry Truman and the creation of what we know as the Cold War were still in the future. The Russians were our allies. The defeat of General von Paulus at Stalingrad and the Russian capture of his entire army doomed Nazi Germany, and while the end of the war was not on any timetable, defeat for the Allies was now unthinkable. Whatever anti-Communism had existed in America during the thirties and the war years, it was a formal matter in a world where the American Communist Party led the drive to organize the industrial workers and create the Congress of Industrial Organizations. Communists had laid down their lives in this struggle. They fought for the unemployed, for the hungry and the homeless and the oppressed, and it was their reputation for integrity and decency and honor that brought into the ranks of the party the leading cultural figures of the time.

And there is something else that is most important. A very substantial number of the best minds and talent in these United States were party members, and this has given me a set of almost insuperable problems. Do I want to name these people? Most of them are dead, but the curse of naming names that underlined the techniques of the congressmen on the House Committee on Un-American Activities still lies like a pall over the land. I can name Theodore Dreiser, because he was so proud of being a member of the party, and I can name Dr. W. E. B. Du Bois, the dean of black historians, for he and his wife, Shirley Graham, were also proud and open about it, as were Albert Maltz and John Howard Lawson and Dalton Trumbo, all of them dead, but there are dozens of others, a good many still alive and at the top of their professions, men and women who were secretly Communists and who left the party in due time, even as I did; and at this point, I have no right to name them. As my story goes on, there will be illustrated ample reason for my not naming them; yet I feel deprived that this galaxy of talent and national distinction and international fame cannot be called up to refute the uncounted slanders hurled against the Communist Party.

One thing, though: we were a party of the United States. Most of us had never been to the Soviet Union, and we knew little about it and less about Stalin. I don't believe our leadership lied to us; I think they knew as little as we did, and though ignorance is never an excuse, it has validity as an explanation.

As for Bette and me, we were drawn into this circle of New York City Communists who made up the Cultural Section of the party through people I met and worked with at the Office of War Information. We were not seduced; we did not have to be. The people we met were young and bright and sincere. Some were in uniform, waiting to be shipped out; others were stationed in New York, part of the Signal Corps and other units in the city. (Thirteen thousand members of the Communist Party were in the armed services during World War Two.) Still others worked in vital civilian jobs, and a good many had physical disabilities or families or were past military age. And, of course, there were the women — women whose intelligence, compassion, and understanding were beacons of the new feminism.

They invited us to their homes; they cherished us and informed us, and, one by one, admitted that they were in the party and that they wanted us to join them. We came to love them, but still we held back. We had a baby coming. I was moving heaven and earth to get overseas as a correspondent, convinced that the war would be over before I witnessed any part of it. Also, I had not entirely put my mind to rest about two things, the execution of the old Bolsheviks and the nonaggression pact between Stalin and Hitler. And there was *Freedom Road* to be completed.

Then Frank Tuttle, a fairly important Hollywood director, telephoned from the Coast. He wanted to take an option on *Citizen Tom Paine*. His friend John Bright was in New York. Bright would write the screenplay; we could travel to the Coast together, and I would stay with Tuttle for three days of discussion. Bette and I had run into the kind of trouble that was inevitable in a young marriage at that time. Nothing was stable, everything was of the moment, everyone was involved in a struggle that went on everywhere as well as on the battlefield, and nerves were tight and tension high. We felt that a few days of separation would be good for us and perhaps calm our irritation with each other, our anger and accusations. I went to the Coast alone.

It was my first time to California. In the course of my life, I would make at least thirty or forty round trips to California and eventually Bette and I would live there for six years, but this was the first time and it was a wonderland indeed. I stayed in the guest house at Frank Tuttle's mansion, set on a cliff edge under the big Hollywood sign. It was a time when, if one drove westward along the Sunset Strip, there were still barley fields sweeping down to the left and oil derricks among the fields. When we drove over Laurel Canyon into the San Fernando Valley to visit John Howard Lawson, Laurel Canyon Road was unsurfaced, a dirt road cutting through endless acres of orange and peach and pear and almond orchards and a scent so strong and delightful that one had visions of paradise. There was no smog, the ground was wet, and once in the fifty-acre spread that made up John Howard Lawson's place, I wondered that one could live in a place so damp. Today, the valley is a dry, smog-soaked patch of semidesert, criss-crossed by cement streets and thousands of little houses, a grim testimony to our efficiency in destroying the environment, root and branch.

All of the bright and fascinating people I met at Lawson's home were Communists. Some of the conversation that day was about F. Scott Fitzgerald and the long talks he had had with Lawson. At a low point in Fitzgerald's despair, Lawson had opened a new direction for his work, which led in time to the writing of *The Last Tycoon*. Fitzgerald had been ready to embrace the party, I was told, but whether he actually joined or not, I don't know. His last book was of course unfinished, but as he was another literary hero of mine, I was impressed. Lawson talked to me at great length, his main point being that the only truly conscious anti-fascist force during the war years was the Communist Party; but having just come from the Office of War Information, I argued against any position so all-inclusive. On the other hand, I had to admit that these guests of his, movie stars, film writers, directors, were clearer and more informed in their thinking than I had anticipated.

The following day, I was invited to lunch at the home of Herbert Biberman and his beautiful wife, Gale Sondergaard. During the McCarthy years, after the end of the war, Gale Sondergaard would be savagely attacked for her political beliefs and blacklisted for years, but at this time she was a working star, gifted and knowledgeable, a most remarkable woman. It was at their home in the Hollywood hills that I met Paul Robeson for the first time and began a friendship of many years with one of the most extraordinary human beings I have ever known. We talked at length then; his manner of taking one into a confidential conversation was very easy. I asked him many questions about the Soviet Union, a place he knew well and that I had never been to, and would not visit even to this writing. He in turn was impressed with what I told him of my work at the OWI. That flattered me enormously, and I asked his advice about all the pressure on me to join the Communist Party. He confessed to me that he was not a party member (not then or ever in his lifetime) and I say "confessed" because he asserted it with a sense of guilt. He admitted that he had asked for membership and then thought better of it, but he felt that in my case the circumstances were different, and that I would have to work it out for myself.

I told Robeson what I was trying to do in my book *Freedom Road,* and he said that someday, if it became a film, he would like to play the part of Gideon Jackson. But this was not to be. Along with me and almost every other person I met during that first trip to Hollywood, Paul was later blacklisted, and all our attempts to make a film with him playing the lead role, attempts during the next fifteen years, came to nothing. Eventually, *Freedom Road* was made into a hapless television film, with Muhammad Ali playing the lead.

The attempt by Frank Tuttle to make *Citizen Tom Paine* a film came to nothing, and the book was not to see film production for the next forty-five years. The entire relationship of my work to the film process has been inordinately strange. It began in 1939, with the publication of *Conceived in Liberty.* A man telephoned me, identified himself as the cousin of the movie mogul Harry Cohn, and told me that if I met him at the Columbia Pictures offices in New York the following day, he would sell my book to Columbia. He told me that Harry Cohn was in town, and that he would make the deal right there.

I met him at the Columbia offices, as he suggested, a small, sleazy man who talked so quickly that I had no time to digest his words. He said decisively, "Anything over thirty thousand, we split fifty-fifty. Right, kid?" Then before I could say yes or no, he plunged into Harry Cohn's office. Through the door muffled voices at first, and then a crescendo as the two men yelled at each other, Cohn, elegantly screaming something to the effect of "What the hell gives you the right to bring me this shit?" and his cousin yelling, "You owe me, you sonofabitch, you owe me." Evidently, the cousin was owed insufficiently, for there was no deal, yet Harry Cohn's description of my book echoed and re-echoed in my mind down the years as the ultimate critique. I returned from California with *Citizen Tom Paine* still unsold.

Just about that time, an odd incident happened concerning Sam Goldwyn. Irene Lee, Goldwyn's story editor and an old friend of

Bette's, telephoned us and said that Mr. Goldwyn was in New York, and he wanted to see me, and would I meet him at his suite in the Waldorf Towers. She said he was interested in the film rights to *Citizen Tom Paine,* and so I had another chapter in the ongoing story of film producers who decided that they would make the book into a film. I duly appeared at the Waldorf Towers suite as instructed, to face Mr. Sam Goldwyn, a big man, larger than life, dressed in green plaid pajamas, green plaid bathrobe, green plaid scarf, green plaid socks, and green plaid slippers, with a green plaid handkerchief hanging from his bathrobe pocket. Mouth open, I stared as Irene introduced us. Never had I seen anyone turned out like this, bright green matching plaids from head to foot, and instead of greeting him properly, I think I was wondering whether, if there was underwear under the pajamas, it was green plaid too.

Now what had happened was this. The playwright Sidney Howard had just opened his new play, *The Patriots,* on Broadway. He had an appointment with Goldwyn the same day. I was Howard Fast; he was Sidney Howard. Goldwyn confused the two names, so immediately after we were introduced he went into a long harangue about Thomas Jefferson and short pants, telling me that he did not hold it against Thomas Jefferson that he wore short pants, but short pants had always been death at the box office. Jefferson was a great American. Was it Goldwyn's fault that Jefferson wore short pants, which were death at the box office?

Not knowing about the Sidney Howard appointment, I came to the conclusion that Goldwyn was confusing Jefferson with Paine, and I mentioned this to him, stressing that I was the author of *Citizen Tom Paine.* He had no cross-references to fall back on, and when he heard *Citizen Tom Paine,* he immediately translated it into *Citizen Kane,* the title of Orson Welles's film about William Randolph Hearst, and he concluded that I was praising Welles. He launched a burst of fury toward Welles, declaring that he never wanted to hear that name again and that what Welles had done was an insult to the film industry and to everything American. When I tried once again to dissociate Paine from Kane, he cut me short, deciding it was time to rid himself of this strange man who insisted on talking about Orson Welles, and he delivered a short lecture on why I should remain with short pants and forget the movies and stay on Broadway. Then he said that so long as I understood three beautiful things, I would be successful: beautiful young love, beautiful sweet music, and beautiful laughter.

I wrote the story of the interview, calling it *Three Beautiful Things*, and it was printed and reprinted endlessly. This was an hour in the midst of the greatest and most awful war the world had ever seen, yet life went on with all of its inanities and non sequiturs. I had been part of the struggle, a key part of it, and now I felt that I had been cast adrift. I went back to the Office of War Information, pleading for an assignment overseas, only to be told that it was impossible. I had too many connections to "premature anti-fascists." I was being punished for being aware of the horror of Nazism before the United States declared itself of the same opinion. I was talked into a Signal Corps project, writing a screenplay of a piece of American history — attempting to teach GIs something of our history.

I was introduced to a young man named Lionel Berman, who was the Communist Party functionary in charge of the Cultural Section of the party. A slender, persuasive man, he spent hours talking to Bette and me. I learned in time that the people in the leadership of both the party and its Cultural Section considered bringing me into the party one of their prime tasks. The effort was headed up by Lionel Berman.

Meanwhile, *Freedom Road* had been published; Franklin Delano Roosevelt was gearing up for a third term; the battle of a handful of Jews against a German army in the Warsaw Ghetto had taken place and the resistance fighters of the ghetto had given the world a new measure of courage; and Allied troops marched into Paris. I was not living in a vacuum; I was living in the most exciting moment of history in my lifetime, and after creating the Voice of America — at least in good part — and giving whatever succor and hope to a Nazi-occupied continent that a voice of freedom could offer, I was locked away from the climax of the titanic struggle because I had spoken to and lunched with people the government called premature anti-fascists. That made no sense whatsoever, but the men and women I had come to know as Communists made a great deal of sense. I was no longer interested in the trials of the 1930s. I don't justify them; they were monstrous, but they were a part of the past, as was the pact between Hitler and Stalin. The plain fact of the matter was that Soviet troops, at a cost almost beyond measure, had destroyed Hitlerism and restored hope to mankind. I am not deprecating the enormous help from America, Lend-Lease as well as American armies, but it was the Russians who clawed out the belly of the beast. It is hard to recall today the terror of people in a world beset by the Nazi lunacy, but we lived with the knowledge that if Hitler triumphed, life, liberty, and the pursuit of happiness, as we knew them, would vanish from the face of the earth.

Thus, one day in August of 1944, Lionel Berman asked me whether I could be counted as one of their group, and I said that I would bring it to Bette and come back to him. Bette and I talked about it for hours. Of course, we had no second sight. We had no idea what the future held for those who called themselves Communists. We were part of a world, at that moment of history, in which the Russians were honored and admired, our allies, our companions in battle. We had a baby of four months, whom we had named Rachel Anne, and if we had known the hell and horror to which we would be subjected during the coming years, I don't think we would have joined the Communist movement. We were, I believe, decently courageous people, but we were neither suicidal nor stupid, and when younger people who have been subjected to decades of screaming anti-Communist propaganda, raised to the level of a religion, ask us how we came to join the party, simple answers do not suffice. The world changes.

So Bette and I discussed it and discussed it, all the pros and cons that we could see, and finally we came to the conclusion that if the anti-fascist struggle was the most important fact of our lives, then we owed it to our conscience to become part of the group that best knew how to conduct it. We joined the party. It was simply an act of assent: we are with you. We had no party cards, and in all my years in the party, I was never asked to do a dishonorable act or to take part in anything against the best interests of my country. Oh, I encountered stupidity aplenty in the leadership of the party, and rigidity in certain areas, criminal self-interest, gross ignorance, and unforgivable indifference — all of which I will write about in due time — but never was I asked to do anything that I could have construed as dishonorable.

And about this time, *Freedom Road* was published. Never in my life has a book of mine been accorded the avalanche of unrestrained praise that greeted *Freedom Road*. *The New York Herald Tribune*

called it "a stirring, passionate tale that will leave few readers un-
moved. It is a trumpet blast for freedom, equality, and justice."
Newsweek said, "No other novel about race relations carries the
strength of characterization, historical setting, and moving honesty
of *Freedom Road*. Howard Fast has written a terrifying book, as
timely as headlines describing our latter-day battle for freedom."

Perhaps it was the time. In the fire of war, the long hold of racism
was being bent and twisted by the precursor of the great civil rights
movement of twenty years later. The leading black newspaper of
Chicago, the *Defender,* wrote: *"Freedom Road* is a book that makes
history by rewriting it and telling the truth . . . a great novel, a great
story about a great man. It is an emotional experience never to be
forgotten . . . for the Negro people, *Freedom Road* is a potent, powerful, smashing weapon . . . a book to be hailed with hosannahs from
every church pulpit, to be read by kerosene lamps in southern shar-
ecroppers' shacks, to suckle Negro youngsters on the very food of
life, to be emblazoned indelibly on the memory of every black and
white American in these United States."

On the West Coast, in *The San Francisco Chronicle,* Joseph Henry
Jackson cried out, *"Freedom Road* is a powerful book, a persuasive
book, a nobly wrathful book." And across the country, in Boston,
The Herald, a newspaper that was to damn me incessantly once I
became a known Communist, declared that *Freedom Road* was
"powerful, simple, unbelievably real, and as dangerous to compla-
cency as a lighted match thrown into the dry undergrowth of a forest."

Eleanor Roosevelt devoted a column to it, dwelling on the importance of the book in terms of the day, and W. E. B. Du Bois said,
"His story is fiction, but his basic historical accuracy is indisputable;
its psychological insight is profound; and thousands of readers can
testify to its literary charm."

There is no way I can tell the story of my life without telling at
least part of the history of *Freedom Road*. It was not simply an
American book; it was a world book. A Soviet scholar doing a bibliography of *Freedom Road* traced its publication in eighty-two languages. An African scholar, a black man educated in England, wrote
to me that it was *Freedom Road* that spurred him to create a written
language for his tribe, and the first book ever translated into that
language was *Freedom Road*. Its pirated editions ran into the mil-

lions, and even now, forty-six years after the original publication of the book, I receive requests for publication from some part of the Third World. I have received at least half a hundred requests from India for new editions in Bengali and in Urdu by groups too poor to pay royalties, and never did I allow this to stand in the way of publication. Sometimes those seeking to publish would send gifts in lieu of royalties, and in this way my wife received a number of beautiful Indian saris.

When the Soviets were publishing and reading *Freedom Road*, in all the Warsaw Pact countries and in all parts of the Soviet Union, they estimated that *Freedom Road* was the most widely printed and read book of the twentieth century. I would amend that to the most widely read serious novel, but how many millions of copies were printed, I have no way of telling. The Soviets, who had raved about the book and possibly printed millions of copies, immediately halted publication and wiped my name from their literary courses and journals once I announced my resignation from the Communist Party, a procedure I was not unused to. Two years ago, a Russian journalist told me that my books in Russia were passed around and lent from person to person. Who knows — perhaps in time the Russians will once again allow *Freedom Road* into their bookstores and libraries.

At the time I went to my first party meeting, the Communist Party in New York State was structured as follows: under the national leadership, there was a state leadership, a party head for the state, a state committee around him composed of representatives from the various sections of the state organization. The organization was built in several layers in large industrial states like California, Illinois, Indiana, Pennsylvania, and New York. Each city in the state would have a party unit. Large factories would have factory units or shop units, and where a union covered several shops, there would be a trade union unit. Each county would have a county organization, and in New York City, Los Angeles, and Chicago, there were professional organizations, sections for physicians, including nurses, teachers, lawyers; and a large grab bag group of writers, editors, ad men, actors, directors, dancers, artists, and producers — the Cultural Section. When I joined the party, the New York Cultural Section numbered something over eleven hundred members.

The above sounds far more imposing than it was in real life. There were states in which there were no more than five or ten Communist Party members; there were cities without a Communist organization of any kind. The entire national organization of the party in its best year in the thirties never numbered 100,000. When Bette and I joined the party, the membership numbered about sixty thousand, which did not include the thirteen thousand party members who had joined the armed forces, and a great many of those, facing the repression that followed the end of the war, failed to renew their membership. William Z. Foster, the national party leader, told me that through the years since the organization in 1919 as the Workers' Party, at least half a million Americans had passed through membership in the party — joined and drifted out — and among them were enough illustrious names to make a small *Who's Who* of talent, intellect, and leadership in the United States. Yet it was not a party of the illustrious; they were a minority in the party. For the most part they held their membership in secret, and even today, as I have pointed out, the membership of famous people still living, with a few exceptions, remains secret. Among all the Western democracies, only the United States persecuted Communist Party members and made social outcasts of Communists. The average Communist in the thirties and forties was a decent, hard-working person who struggled for things he believed in, issues of the people's needs in his neighborhood and in his trade union, asking nothing and giving a great deal.

At this point, simply because the notion of Communism and Communists in recent years has been so maligned and distorted, it is necessary to recall something of the socialist movement in America. The roots go back to the founding of the country, to the Levelers, who were savagely persecuted by Oliver Cromwell for their belief in total equality, political and economic, and who fled here in the seventeenth century. From that point on, movements for social equality rose and dwindled in response to changing conditions, evolving eventually into the trade union movement. Concurrently a political movement arose, on the West Coast among the lumber workers of Oregon and Washington, and in the heart of the country among the workers in heavy industry. On the Coast, it was called the International Workers of the World, or the Wobblies, and in midcountry and in the East, it became the Socialist Party of Eugene V. Debs. The eastern movement was a historic growth from the Levelers to the experimental communities of Nauvoo, Brook Farm, and others. In due time, these movements coalesced into a group calling itself the Social Democratic Party and a more militant group called the Socialist Labor Party. In 1901, under the leadership of Eugene V. Debs and Victor Lewis Berger, the Socialist Party was formed from the Social Democratic Party and a group that split from the militant Socialist Labor Party; and Victor Berger went on to become, in 1911, the first Socialist to be elected to the United States Congress. During World War One, the Socialist Party split over the question of support for America's entrance into the war, which the left wing of the party denounced as a capitalist and imperialist slaughter. Out of this split, two left-wing parties emerged, the Communist Labor Party and the Communist Party of America. These two parties united in 1925 as the Workers' Party, and in 1929, under the leadership of William Z. Foster, they changed their name to the one we know today, the Communist Party.

It is not my purpose here to go into any sort of history of the Communist Party, but since this is a biography of a man who was for years a member of the party, some understanding of it and its work must be presented. As with the socialist movement, the Communist movement believes in socialism as its goal. In the nineteenth century, the means chosen was revolution; in the twentieth century, this gave way to the organization of the working people in their factories into trade unions and in their homes and neighborhoods into organizations that fought for lower rents, better living conditions, protection against landlords, better schools, and other neighborhood needs. In the factories, the Communist Party fought consistently for unions, organization of the unorganized, higher wages, better working conditions, medical care, and the shortening of the working day. And at the polls, the Communists worked to elect representatives who would fight for these ends. The workers joined the party out of need; the intellectuals, out of a sense of social justice.

So much for a bare statement about the party and its purpose. When World War One began, the Socialist Parties, here in the United States, in England, France, and Germany — bound in a pledge of international brotherhood to oppose war — abandoned this pledge and in each case supported the war efforts of its country. The left wing of each Socialist Party condemned this as a total betrayal of principles and split away to form a new kind of party, the Communist Party as defined by Lenin. It soon developed that public dissent from the party's platform and stand on issues was impossible. In this was the seed of the party's ultimate destruction.

Much of what follows is a prelude to that destruction which, in the United States, took place between 1956 and 1959. While a tiny group continued to exist, maintained for the most part by the memberships of FBI spies, and calling itself the Communist Party, the party in America was for all intents and purposes dead, and those of us who had been most active as members not only left the party, but made our position — namely, that the Communist Party as constituted in the United States had passed its time as a positive force in history — both public and specific.

I went to my first Communist Party meeting. Bette went to hers. We had discussed it endlessly and we had come to the conclusion that our marriage, already strained to the breaking point, would not survive my being a Communist and her being a non-Communist. As a painter, Bette was assigned to the artists' branch of the Cultural Section; I was assigned to the writers' branch.

The meetings of the writers' branch — indeed, of almost all branches or, as the professional anti-Communists called them, cells of the party — were held in the homes of the members. The first meeting I went to was typical enough to be a prototype of all the hundreds of meetings I attended. It was held in the apartment of a radio writer, Ronald Carter by name, a graduate of Williams College and a member of a leading family of the establishment. In that, he was one among a good many children of upper-class families who, in rebellion against the emptiness and coldness of their backgrounds, had joined the party, most of them to be disinherited. Ronald was charming, bright, and certain in his position. We had been introduced while I was at the OWI, and we had become friends before I knew that he was a Communist.

Ronald's place was in Greenwich Village, the whole ground floor of one of the brownstones. He was married to a lovely woman from a Virginia family of some standing, and I must say that he gave our small branch of the party a touch of class. I often thought to myself how odd it was that I should make my very first social contact with members of the East Coast upper classes in the Communist Party. Well, there were many things I had not anticipated.

At this first meeting, there were about twenty men and women out of a list of thirty, an average attendance. They were quite ordinary, pleasant people, half of them women, three of the men black. Some were radio writers, some magazine writers, some novelists, one or two editors. The women were attractive for the most part, bright, and well informed.

The meeting was called to order. The first business on the agenda was a report on the political situation at the moment and the condition of the war. The report was made by Paul Bernay, an old party member, middle-aged then and dead these many years. Most of the branch members were young; Paul was fifty-two, a radiologist by trade and assigned to our branch of the party to keep our thinking in line. That sounds like the very devil as I write it, but the fact of the matter is that Paul was a well-trained Marxist with thirty years of experience in the party and a deep fund of knowledge. His report on the war was brief and to the point. American forces had entered Germany. The Red Army was in Rumania and within miles of Germany. His conclusion was that the war would be over before the end of 1945. Politically, we as Communists were faced with a task of paramount importance — namely, the re-election of President Roosevelt to a fourth term. Paul insisted that Roosevelt must remain in office until the war was over and Nazism and fascism utterly destroyed.

To this end, the Cultural Section had organized a wide group of people into what we called the Committee of the Arts and Sciences for the Re-election of Franklin Delano Roosevelt. A long title, which we shortened to Arts and Sciences. Arts and Sciences was a broad group, by which I mean that it had a large roll of supporters who were not Communists, even though those who did the organizational work were party people. It held its meetings at the old Murray Hill Hotel. There was no question of deceit; the important and in some cases famous people who worked with the committee knew that Communists had created the committee; but we were still at a point of history when Communists were admired, at least by a good part of the population.

A hot discussion took over that first session. Why was this re-election of Roosevelt so important? Wasn't it a dangerous thing? Couldn't it lead to dictatorship? The party dealt in stepped logic; one thing was held to lead to another, and being able to think politically as a Marxist was supposed to give one the gift of specific prediction. Only it usually did not work the way the party decided it should, and history dealt harshly with Marxist prediction. There was much made of Roosevelt's famous statement that a soldier does not leave the battle in the middle. The party, as I was to learn, loved slogans.

Then the discussion turned, as it did in almost every meeting, to the role of the party. Some sat quietly. Some shouted angrily. Everything had to be related to the fact that we were giving our time and if need be our lives to the cause of socialism and that there could be no socialism or hope of it unless Hitler and Hirohito were destroyed; therefore, Roosevelt must remain in the saddle.

It sounds hopelessly mundane — and how much more mundane today, almost a half a century later! Is this the red menace that has been hammered into our minds for two generations, the enemy of all that is good and decent in our society? Alas, it is. *But these are dupes. These are not the real commies.* Alas, no; these are the real commies. If it were a trade union branch, they would have been discussing the no-strike pledge and ways to keep the shops working full blast. If it had been two years later in a trade union branch, they would have been discussing their role in a strike, now legitimate, since the war was over. If it had been a neighborhood branch, they would have been discussing price gouging and getting out the vote and holding election block parties. If it had been a Hollywood branch, they would have been discussing film for the war effort.

But never — and I write this thirty-six years after I left the party — never did I hear, at any Communist Party meeting, that pervasive and unending slander, the overthrow of the government by force and violence. Never did I hear it mentioned or discussed, and if it had been, it would have been put down immediately as brainless nonsense. I have no cause to defend, no banner to wave, simply a desire to set straight some facts that have been distorted beyond recognition.

The meeting finished with two programmatic goals. The first would be a reception for Harry S. Truman, the new vice presidential candidate, and the second would be a Roosevelt pre-election meeting in Madison Square Garden. Both of these would be run by the Cultural

Section. Just before the meeting finished, Lionel Berman appeared and said a few words about the importance of the election. He stressed that we knew very little about Thomas E. Dewey in terms of anti-fascist commitment, and spoke of the importance of keeping Roosevelt in command. Thomas E. Dewey, the governor of New York, had earned a national reputation as a racket buster during the thirties. As special prosecutor, he won seventy-two convictions out of seventy-three prosecutions. He was a decent, conservative governor, but the party mistrusted him and considered him a closet reactionary.

Over coffee after that initial meeting, Berman led me to believe that both of these projects, the reception for Truman and the Madison Square Garden rally, had been discussed with Roosevelt, who knew that they were Communist projects and who gave the go-ahead in spite of the feelings of some of his advisers that the party could not fill the Garden and it would turn into a fiasco. As with many other matters that I was privy to during my time in the party, I have written what Berman told me was true. I do not know whether there were party members in the government. Why not? The party was legal; the party was dedicated to the same ends of winning the war; and I know of no instance where a party member abused his trust. I do know of one party member, an attorney, who was in the executive then and who subsequently became an FBI informer and a double agent for the CIA, but his abuse of honor turned in another direction.

However, I am quite convinced that Truman knew, for I had a talk with him on the subject. Lionel Berman was still wooing me — he would have called it "developing" me — and during my conversation with him that evening he said that he would like to put me in charge of the Truman reception. I protested that I had never done anything quite like it, and he assured me that I would have ample help and that whatever funds were necessary would be forthcoming. There was no mystery about party funds. We paid dues and we raised money from sympathizers and we gave to fund drives, and so it went.

I discovered that I had talents as an organizer. We rented the big reception room — not the ballroom — on the main floor of the old Astor Hotel, that marvelous rococo building on Broadway and Forty-fourth Street, which, like so many wonderful New York buildings, has been torn down to be replaced with lifeless stone and glass. At least thirty people pitched in to help, and a group of very pretty young women of the theater organized themselves as hostesses. We invited every newspaperman of consequence, radio commentators, celebrities, magazine people, and local politicians, and most of them came. We had gallons of wine, hard liquor, and mixers for those who desired them, and a proper table of hors d'oeuvres; and everything was paid for out of our own pockets and not out of campaign money. The invitations said from five o'clock to eight so that we could catch people leaving their offices, but Truman turned up at four o'clock.

The others in our crew were busy with last-minute arrangements, no small matter, since we expected between five and six hundred people, and I happened to notice the man with metal-rimmed glasses and a gray double-breasted suit standing rather shyly at the door of the room. I walked over, asked whether he was Mr. Truman, and when he replied in the affirmative, I introduced myself and told him that I was one of the people who had organized the affair. He then asked whether I was affiliated with the local Democratic Party, and I replied that we were not affiliated but an independent group of writers and theater people. Left wing? he wanted to know, and I said yes, very left wing, and that led to some talk about the Communist Party and its support of him and Roosevelt. He never asked directly whether this was a Communist function, although he knew full well that we were what came to be called a Communist front organization. I will not pretend to reproduce any dialogue, but I have a keen memory of what was said. In any case, he was not in the slightest way troubled, and when our attractive theater ladies gathered around, he became very much at ease.

The larger affair, the election rally at Madison Square Garden, was sold out, again attesting to the efficiency of party people as organizers. I don't think any group of paid organizers could have worked so hard and so efficiently and so tirelessly. Bette and I discovered that active involvement in the Communist Party commanded the whole life process. One ate it and slept it — the meetings, the funds to be raised, the books to be read, and of course the fact that more and more one socialized with other Communists. At that time, with the war still going on, non-Communists were pleased to dine and visit with Communists. The heroism and sacrifice of the Abraham Lincoln Brigade in the Spanish Civil War were still bright in the American mind, and Communists were looked on as people of superior political knowledge whose dedication to democracy was a bit more than common sense might require. You will recall that when Louis Cowan at the Office of War Information told me sadly that my left connections barred me from being sent overseas, that would not have prevented my continuing to work in the domestic OWI had I so desired. Which helps to explain why, after the election, the Roosevelts invited the leading people in our Committee of the Arts and Sciences to join them for lunch at the White House.

It was to be the first, the last, the only time that I was invited to the White House, and I've been very grateful that my hostess was a wonderful woman, Eleanor Roosevelt. She had long been a heroine to me. Bette's excitement topped mine. There had to be a new dress, something very special. We had to find an all-day sitter for our seven-month-old Rachel, and of course I had to assure myself again and again that this was Barney Fast's kid who had made out with street smarts and not a hell of a lot else, and who now held in his hand a personal invitation to join the President of the United States and his wife for lunch at the White House. Had we made the wrong decision by joining the party? Or had it been the absolutely correct and inevitable path to follow? We were not overwhelmed by the importance of our contribution, but evidently Mr. Roosevelt did feel that it was important for us to be rewarded. Or, more realistically, his campaign manager felt that we were of some importance and responded to it.

Looked at through the eyes of Howard Fast, just turned thirty a few days before, it was a splendid and unforgettable day. I think that about thirty-five people had been invited to the luncheon. When we arrived, Mr. Roosevelt was not yet present, and Mrs. Roosevelt greeted us. The luncheon was a buffet, and when the food had been served, Mrs. Roosevelt drew me aside and we talked for about twenty minutes. She had already written about *Freedom Road* in her column, and when she saw from the guest list that I would be coming to the White House, she had read the book once again. She told me that both times she had wept like a child, and she prodded me for information about the book and how I had come to write it. I told her about my visit to the Pringle-Smiths and the trunk that her ancestor had built, and she burst out laughing and thought it was the most marvelous example of snobbery that she had ever heard of.

She asked me how I liked the lunch, and both Bette and I assured her that it was delicious, a small white lie. She was delighted with

our reaction. The lunch had consisted of green peas, mashed potatoes, and dried beef in a cream sauce (what the GIs inelegantly call
shit on a shingle), and ice cream and a cookie for dessert. Mrs. Roosevelt explained that she was determined that no lunch like this should
cost more than thirty cents a plate, and she asked how could one
dare serve expensive food when the boys in the armed forces were
eating cold C rations in muddy shell holes. Nothing was put on with
this woman; nothing was for effect; nothing was pretentious. Tall,
absolutely beautiful in her homeliness, wearing a plain brown dress,
she made you forget who she was. I would meet her again in the
months ahead, but that remains my best memory of her.

Just before the luncheon came to an end, the President was wheeled
into the room. There was none of the buoyant, cheerful, commanding presence that one saw in the newsreels. Time and sickness had
taken a bitter toll, and he sat bent over in his chair, shrunken, his
face a web of wrinkles. He shook hands weakly with each of us. It
was the only time I ever met him, and it's not a good memory. There
was something cold and chitinous about him, as if the life had already departed and in his agony only an iron will prevailed, and I
remember thinking of what a complex and tortured man this was
and wondering whether anyone, even his wife, ever knew him or
penetrated to the man himself. He was that very occasional person
in our history, a President of intelligence and commanding personality.

On our way out, we were given a tour of the historical White
House. Together with Dorothy Parker, Bette and I entered Lincoln's
bedroom, and suddenly Miss Parker burst into tears. Bette tried to
comfort her, and Miss Parker said that after meeting that wonderful
woman, this was too much. Curiously, she did not say that the emotion exploded after meeting that wonderful man. Later, someone else
remarked that she was drunk, but Dorothy Parker was not drinking
that day. She was responding to a kind of deep woe in Mrs. Roosevelt, a sense of tragedy that I was not aware of at that time. I was
much too full of myself and of Mrs. Roosevelt's having seen fit to
take me aside and talk to me.

The Franklin Delano Roosevelt I met and shook hands with at the
White House was a dying man. A few months later, he was dead,
and our world was shaken to its foundations — our world in both

the very large and very narrow sense, the narrow sense being New York and the people I worked with in the party. I was still very young and very prone to the belief that history was moved by great leaders, a curious non-Marxist notion to which the party clung and that, in the light of Stalin worship, did the party tragic harm.

Joe North, editor of *The New Masses,* the party's weekly magazine, asked me to write something on the death of Roosevelt. Joe was a brother of Alex North, the composer, who apparently was not close to the left and who would years later write the music for my film *Spartacus.* Joe was a heavyset, bright, lovable, shaggy, and irresponsible man — in some ways not unlike my father. Like Barney, he lived with both feet firmly planted in midair. His relationship to the party was a romantic affair that nothing could ever shake. We became good, close friends.

My interest in *The New Masses* had begun years before, back in the thirties, when it ran the series about the fascist Silver Shirts, and their attempt to reproduce in America an organization like Hitler's Brown Shirts. Then, in 1937, Bette and I were spending a weekend with James Reed, one of the editors at Harcourt, Brace, and his gracious wife, Helen Grace Carlyle, and one evening during that weekend, they took us to hear a *New Masses* investigative reporter talk about the Silver Shirts and other imitators of Hitler's Brown Shirts, right here in America; and after that we became readers of the magazine. At that time, *The New Masses* had a broad readership and it was specially brightened by the weekly presence of a writer who used the pen name Robert Forsyth; he later published his pieces as a book under the title *Redder Than the Rose.* At that point, *Collier's* magazine, where he was employed as a staff writer under his own name, Kyle Crichton, told him that he could be Forsyth or Crichton but not both. He decided to be Crichton.

The editors of *The New Masses,* particularly Joe North, became part of an effort that I learned about years later, a calculated effort to bring me into the party. Their first move was to reprint a chapter from *The Unvanquished,* for which they had only praise. Then came an invitation to be part of a symposium, then another symposium, then, after I left the OWI, a request for a piece on history in fiction, a few other pieces, and then the tribute to Roosevelt after his death.

Rereading it now, I find it fulsome and without any particular merit. When an icon perishes, it must be iconized, to coin a word, and many things are said that range from the ridiculous to the blatantly untrue. No one mentioned his rejection of the pleas of the eight hundred Jews on a ship offshore. He sent them back to die in Nazi murder camps. Wartime encourages neither truth nor good writing, and since the intrinsic nature of war is killing (or murder, if one sees it objectively), the accounts of the process must be gussied up enough to make the most lunatic of all men's institutions seem not only sane but reasonable. Tolstoy said flatly that every account of a battle is a lie, and I agree with him wholly. War itself is a lie.

The war went on, and the months went by, and our daughter, Rachel, would soon be a year old. The Allies were fighting their way across Europe and the Red Army was approaching Berlin from the East, and I was still locked up here in America. We were becoming impossibly cramped in our tiny apartment, and we decided to move. And then Oscar Dystel, editor in chief of *Coronet* magazine, telephoned and asked me to drop by his office. He had something important to discuss with me.

I liked Dystel enormously. He was easy to talk to and work with and he let me write about odd things that intrigued me and he never took the world too seriously. He printed a story of mine about a Jewish privateer (or pirate, if you will) during the War of 1812, who had patriotically sunk a slew of ships. His name was Johnny Ordronaux, and through the generations with various intermarriages, his descendants became Catholic. Some people raised merry hell with *Coronet* over my insensitivity, but since Johnny Ordronaux was long dead and being called Jewish was not yet slanderous, Dystel laughed the whole thing off. Like other editors I knew, he had been subjected to my pleading to be sent overseas as a war correspondent, and now he said he thought he had done it.

Done what? What?

He had put it through, and if I still wanted it, he'd send me overseas for the magazine. Did I want it? My mouth was watering.

Of course I wanted it. I would turn handsprings to demonstrate how much I wanted it. When do I leave? Mr. Dystel told me to cool down and listen. He had been unable to get me an accreditation to the European Theater of Operations, and anyway, as he put it to me, things were moving so fast in Europe that the war might well be over before I got there. Nor could he accredit me for the Pacific Theater. However, as of this moment, I was accredited to the China-Burma-India Theater, or, as they called it, the CBI. When I expressed my disappointment, Dystel very wisely explained that, as far as he was concerned as an editor, battles were less important than people and background. He underlined that writers don't take part in battles; they write about them, and battles were an explosive part of war but by no means all of it. He explained that I would go by Air Transport and that my route would take me across Africa, and that at any point before I arrived in India, my base destination, I could change my route or slow my passage, as long as I arrived at my destination. He suggested that, if possible, I should get into Palestine and do a story about the Zionist movement there. He also suggested that, once in India, I should try to interview Gandhi. His approach was via stories, not news dispatches, and I liked that. He told me that he'd try to get me off as soon as possible, but it depended on how soon they could get me fully processed and arrange my passage. It might be a week or five weeks.

Bette and I moved with all the speed we could muster. We found a large apartment on Central Park West. I hurriedly bought a uniform and had two extra pairs of glasses made. I was receiving no wages from *Coronet;* I would be paid for each piece; but since we were fat with the earnings of *Freedom Road,* money was no longer a problem. And then, in the midst of all this, I suffered a painful loss. Sam Sloan, my publisher and dear friend and teacher, died. That good, beautiful man was very slender and very frail, and his death came in a cruel and senseless manner. He was walking in New York, carrying a heavy briefcase of manuscripts, when he stumbled and fell, breaking a number of bones. He was taken to the hospital, where he developed an embolism and died. He left his wife, Peggy, a lovely woman, and two children. I often wondered how different my life might have been if he had lived. I could never replace him as a friend and as an editor.

5

I TOOK MY INJECTIONS — vaccines and such — and then I was instructed to report to Fort Totten on Long Island and wait for Air Transport. At Fort Totten, I was given a bunk in a barracks and told to remain there until transport was available. After three nights in Totten, I talked the CO into a deal: I would go home, and when my transport turned up, someone in the office would call me. Whereupon I returned to New York, arriving in time for breakfast, spent two hours with Bette and my little daughter, and then received a call to get back to Totten.

I returned just in time to pack my few things and run for the last seat on a C54 that was waiting at the airport. It was a hot day in late spring, and the plane sat on the fiery tarmac for two hours before it took off, and during that time we became soaked with sweat and were gasping for breath. A few hours later, we touched down in Gander, Newfoundland, the landing strip walled by snow piled eight feet high. It was a most incredible change of climate. We had an hour to walk around and use the exchange if we so desired. Shivering, our breath turning into clouds of frost, we prowled around the airport at Gander. Then, once again, we took off across the Atlantic to land in the Azores in a sort of summertime, and when we took off from the Azores, we flew straight through to North Africa and landed finally in Casablanca.

As we circled over Casablanca for landing, I saw below an enormous swimming pool or reservoir. I turned to the man sitting next to me, a grizzled old army colonel, and said to him, "That has to be the biggest swimming pool in the world."

"The second biggest," he said.

"And where's the biggest?"

"Sonny," he said to me, "whatever it is, wherever it is, there's something bigger or something better."

That stayed with me — one of several observations that cut into me and stayed — and I passed it on to my children as armor against superlatives. We landed, and I was driven into the city and quartered in an old French hotel. I stayed a day and a half in Casablanca, wandered through its streets, saw my first British regiment march by, and observed that the officers were a head taller than any of the enlisted men. Food and class. I went to a British-American social mixer and dance, but being a lousy dancer I only stood by and watched. I encountered a group of black troops from Senegal, handsome fellows who plied me with a hundred questions about Harlem. They all intended to live there. When I told them that I knew Paul Robeson, they fought to buy me beer. I drowned myself in beer, good French beer, and staggered back to my hotel, very drunk.

The following morning, I was awakened by a GI attached to public relations, or p.r., as I'll refer to it, and told that there was a request for me from p.r. in Tripoli. In order to explain this request, I have to say something about an old friend of mine, Philip Van Doren Stern.

I had met Phil Stern through Louis Untermeyer. Phil, who was a book designer — indeed, one of the best book designers in America — was in charge of design and manufacturing for Simon and Schuster. He owned one of those grand old brownstone mansions on Brooklyn Heights. When Untermeyer divorced his third wife — Louis was brilliant at many things but not marriage — he moved to Brooklyn and rented a floor in Phil Stern's house. Phil had a family and children and in any case was too old for the service, but like so many others, he was desperately eager to play some part in the struggle. General Sherman had said that war is hell, but Eisenhower observed that war is also boredom and that it was a pity that the endless hours of training and waiting for battle could not be put to some constructive use. Philip Van Doren Stern acted on this, took himself down to the War Department in Washington, and made a remarkable suggestion. He told them that he could manufacture, very inexpensively, a paper book of a size to fit in the blouse pocket of an enlisted man. He said that he would use good, exciting, and at least in part classic examples of great literature, readable books, rewarding books — and he sold the project to them. These books were called the Armed Services Editions, and Phil put hundreds of titles into print and printed millions of books — exactly how many I don't know, but millions. Wherever one went overseas, the Armed Services Editions were there. Phil had chosen four of my books, *The Last Frontier, The Unvanquished, Citizen Tom Paine,* and *Freedom Road.*

The fact that I had four titles on a list that went to the p.r. officer at Melleha Air Base in Tripoli had convinced him somehow that I was an expert on the plans and proposals for the United Nations, currently being discussed in San Francisco, and when my plane came down at Melleha, I discovered that overnight I had become a VIP and an authority on both the failed League of Nations that followed World War One and the United Nations being put together in San Francisco. At the Melleha installation, large posters announced that Howard Fast would talk on the United Nations, and the p.r. officer, a colonel who met me at the airport, informed me that this was no corporal's guard that I would be addressing but over two thousand GIs, since he had put out that every damn one of them was to turn up or he'd have their heads. He invited me to join him for dinner — in one of those magnificent officers' dining rooms that had been put up in every area the Americans took over. I was hungry, but I begged off, pretended that I had stuffed myself with lunch in Casablanca, and asked him to direct me to the officers' lounge. Once there, I grabbed anything I could find, *Yank, Stars and Stripes,* a three-day-old *New York Times* — anything that had some information about the United Nations. I had just three hours to become an expert, and while I never became that, I filled myself with facts and figures, and putting them together with my own beliefs in the possibility of a peaceful future, I carried off my lecture reasonably well. I had come a long way since that agonizing day in Philadelphia when all sound froze in my throat. I had spoken at meetings and at three universities on the subject of *Freedom Road,* and I was in the process of becoming a pretty good public speaker.

But my audience also read *Stars and Stripes* and *Yank,* and a hot discussion began on whether the Soviet American alliance was begin-

ning to crumble and whether Truman could make anything out of
the infant United Nations. I was also amazed at how many copies of
the Armed Services Editions of my books were presented to me for
autographing. The swelling of a writer's ego is an interesting if unhappy process: the very fact that someone will read words you have
written contributes to a rather meaningless glow of self-importance.

The p.r. officer couldn't do enough for me. He insisted that I join
a group of officers who were going to picnic and swim in the Medi-
terranean. I tried to get out of it, but he controlled my orders. I
pleaded that I was being sent to Burma to try to find the war with
Japan. You don't join the Communist Party without carrying a burden of morality — which is a burden, not a gift — and playing the
role of moralist. He countered that Burma was a long way off, and
even if I reached there tomorrow, there was no likelihood of a Japanese advance at this point in the war. In any case, I was the excuse
for the picnic. The beach was white and clean, the water was warm,
and the picnic baskets contained caviar and champagne and beer and
cold cuts. There was no talk of the war and no thought of the war.
World War Two was a vast enterprise, and years later a friend, a
professor of philosophy, Hyman Gordon by name, told me how he
and a handful of men in a machine gun company were at the point
that halted the fierce German counterattack at the Battle of the Bulge.
They had two million men behind them, but at that moment the war
was being fought by a single machine gun company. But here, there
was no thought or mention of war. These officers, who not too long
before had been bank clerks, insurance salesmen, bookkeepers, and
so on, were commissioned out of officers' training and now were
living high on the hog. Their dining room was baronial. It was only
slightly more than a year since I had been denied permission to continue my OWI work in North Africa, and here were the fruits of
conquest.

I learned and I changed. The next day, I flew to Benghazi, because
I had heard of something there called "the graveyard," which I thought
might make a good story. A young captain drove me out into the
desert in a jeep. About ten miles or so from Benghazi, if my memory
serves me, the road began to be hemmed in by wrecked and rusted
vehicles — tanks, half-tracks, jeeps, Bren gun carriers, sixteen wheel-
ers, command cars — every vehicle used in the process of warfare at

the time, including battered or exploded artillery and millions of shell casings. For perhaps two miles, the road ran between the walls of vehicles, and then the road climbed a hill to a height of perhaps two hundred feet, and there the captain stopped the jeep, smiled without humor, and said something to the effect of writing about war. Did I want to write about war? Here in this desert, in this terrible stillness under the burning Sahara sun, was the distilled essence of war. In every direction as far as the eye could see were vehicles, as if the desert itself had exchanged its substance of sand and stone for iron and rust, uncounted thousands of German and American and Italian pieces of war. Here was the graveyard of man's skill and genius, his highest achievement, the killing of other men.

I stood beside the jeep, staring at this monstrous scene until the captain became nervous and said that the sun was dropping and it would be dark and we had a long drive back. I had a longer journey than that back to the things I had once believed in, but there, totally and thoroughly, I understood war. I have never prided myself on intellectual brilliance nor have I ever believed that street smarts were a proper substitute for formal education, but I have been gifted with the ability to respond to a shaft of knowledge and to absorb it psychologically without chapter and verse. I think I became a pacifist at that moment, and I have been philosophically a pacifist ever since.

Most of this journey I made toward battles that ceased before I ever reached them was recorded in notes and letters and in the pieces I wrote, but one incident stands so vividly in my memory that I have not forgotten a single detail. It happened on the flight from Benghazi to Cairo. I was in a C46, a big, round-bellied cargo plane, designed to carry the instruments of war. It had no seats, and the dozen young GIs who shared the plane with me sprawled on the floor. They were a group of navigators and ground crew who were being shipped east as replacements for the Tenth Air Force. The plane was flying under blackout conditions. The war in Europe was practically finished, and though we were still bitterly at war with Japan, there was no possibility of a Japanese plane reaching North Africa, but it was one of those general orders that had not been contravened. As a result, the only light in the plane came from a small blue blackout bulb in the ceiling. It gave off only flickering radiance, so that those of us sprawled on the floor of the plane could hardly see one another; nevertheless, one of the GIs, a navigator named Charles Treston, was reading a book. Across the ceiling of the plane were two steel runners, long bars in clips, used to freight howitzers. Treston, a tall, skinny, sandy-haired boy, was clinging to one of these bars, holding the book he was reading up to the blue bulb, which gave him just enough light to make out the words.

I found it hard to take my eyes off him. It was not an uneventful flight. One of our motors caught fire, and the pilot had to put the plane into a dive to extinguish the flames. In this he succeeded, pulling out of the dive no more than a few hundred feet above the desert. It was an absolutely terrifying few minutes, a terror that every one of those on the floor of the plane shared — except Treston. Right through everything that happened, the fire and the dive, he clung to the rail and continued to read his book. I watched him and decided that this had to be the most gripping book ever written. I was wrong.

The moment we stepped out of the plane at Payne Field in Cairo I cornered Treston, told him I was a correspondent and that I wanted to talk to him. First, what book were you reading? He showed it to me. It was a novel called *Lady Into Fox,* the fanciful tale of a British lady who had the habit of turning herself into a fox. I had read the book and enjoyed it, but nothing in it suggested the grip it had exercised during the flight from Benghazi. I pressed him to tell me what there was about the book that had impressed him so, what kept him reading even when the engine caught fire.

"It's a book," he said, a statement he repeated again and again. What emerged from our talk was this. Treston had been born and educated in the hill country of Tennessee. Drafted right after high school, he had been trained by the air force as a navigator. Before he had encountered the Armed Services Editions, he had never read a book. Comic books, school texts, but never a novel. Now he had discovered the novel, and he lived for nothing else. In his present existence, there was a war and an air force, and neither was of any importance to him. Books were important; books were his life; and he existed from book to book, living in each new world that was opened to him.

I questioned him concerning titles. Had he read Hemingway? Yes, oh, yes. Tolstoy? Dreiser? London? Proust? Dickens? Fast? Remarque? Zane Grey? Yes, yes to all of them, but when it came down to which he preferred, he could frame no answer. In his new life, the wonder of books was their singularity. All writers were part of his marvelous new world, and this new world was, for all its strange people and places, within his ability to comprehend. The world of the war where he lived and worked defied comprehension.

I shared some of that. It defied my comprehension as well, for I was met at Payne Field by a cheerful young Captain Woodhill, who was a part of p.r. and who treated me as if I were visiting royalty. Who was I? Was this the nature of war? He took me to the VIP house, where I was presented with a magnificent room, polished woodwork, a bar, whiskey, soda — after which I was paraded around to meet various and sundry colonels and generals, Woodhill making sure I had their cards and background papers. I dined that evening in another baronial dining room, with a menu that would have put any New York wartime restaurant to shame — gourmet cooking, steaks, fresh fish, and the luscious fruits of Egypt. I had not yet seen Cairo and the indescribable poverty and filth and hunger and disease that were a major part of it. A box of cigars arrived at the table where I sat with Captain Woodhill and two colonels. I smoked a pipe but allowed myself to be talked into a wonderful Cuban Romeo and Juliet, here in an army — or so it was put — dining room five thousand miles from Cuba. Some other correspondents joined us and advised me to stay here. East of here was shit, all shit and malaria. The goddamn war is over, and if you got a brain in your head, you don't go to Burma, because in Burma the goddamn Japs don't know the war is over.

In bed that night, sleepless, I tried to put things in focus. When I wrote the Voice of America and sent my words and whatever hope and good cheer we could muster into every place on the continent where a radio was tuned in, I had added something to the struggle, perhaps not much but something. This assignment, which I had begged for and pleaded for, was a farce, a journey to nowhere. Each day, there would be p.r. handouts. You took the handout, rephrased it, and sent in your story. So far I had sent back nothing.

The next morning, my keeper-in-Egypt, Captain Woodhill, turned up bright and early, and cheerful, as well he might have been, because this was a lot more fun than the Ohio small town that gave birth to him.

He was full of news about Italian prisoners of war. There were still thousands of them in North Africa and about a thousand of them in a small compound nearby. We might as well see the prisoners of war, and then we could drive out to the Pyramids and the Sphinx. He meant that I didn't want to leave Egypt without seeing the Pyramids and the Sphinx. I told him that before I went on east of here, I would like to get into Palestine, and he replied that it was impossible, absolutely impossible. He explained that there had been a steady stream of GIs working passes into Palestine because Tel Aviv was the closest thing to New York out here and valid ice cream sodas could be had in Tel Aviv and nowhere else around here, and so much army stuff was being smuggled into Palestine, especially by English soldiers, that the British had closed the border. Jews, he said, they're everywhere, and they're all trying to push something into Palestine; they sell guns and trust a Jew to make a dollar out of anything. I told him that I was Jewish, and that ended any more talk about Palestine.

We went to see the prisoners of war instead. These Italians had been prisoners for more than three years, and if ever prisoners of war were content with their lot, you could say it of these men, browned by the sun, stripped to the waist as they worked, smiling with mouths full of white teeth — so different from the British soldiers with their semitoothless jaws and small stature — and more than ready to tell you how content they were to remain in North Africa until the war was decisively over. Woodhill offered that they had no will to fight for Mussolini and were worthless as soldiers; but it occurred to me that they were too intelligent to fight for Mussolini and perhaps too civilized to be much good as soldiers.

Then my tutor, the good captain, suggested that we return to the base, have lunch, and then have a tour of the Pyramids. This was Captain Woodhill's war, and I decided that it made sense to go along with it. We had lunch and went to the Pyramids. On our way, I saw something of Cairo, and never, not even in Calcutta a few weeks later, have I see such misery and human anguish — blind, diseased, pleading beggars without end, and defined by Captain Woodhill as hopeless, because it didn't matter what you tried to do for Wogs; it did no good, because they'd just as soon rot as lift a finger to help themselves. The opinion was widely held, and once you passed "east of Suez," the entire human race was defined by that word, Wog.

They were all Wogs; it did not matter what tongue they spoke, what color their skin happened to be, what nationality they were — they were Wogs, every last one of them. This deep racism, this fear of dark skin color, was so pervasive that a number of southern GIs surrendered their health to it. Once you entered Egypt and traveled east from Egypt as a part of the United States armed forces, you were supplied with Atabrine, a pill that was said to ward off malaria, even if one was bitten by the parasite-bearing mosquito. However, on a steady diet of Atabrine, one turned yellow. Under the normal tanning effect of the sun, the result was a sort of golden glow, which I always considered quite handsome and complimentary; but some southern GIs felt that it marked them with the stigma of a dark race, so they rejected the Atabrine and often fell victim to malaria.

We went to the Pyramids. I felt like a foolish tourist, but there were other soldiers at the place, British and American, trying the camel rides and appearing even sillier than I felt. I climbed to the top of the Great Pyramid and admired the marvelous view from there, and when I came down, I faced a huge Arab, who asked me whether I wanted a guide to lead me into a burial chamber of one of the pharaohs. The price was four shillings. I suggested to Woodhill that he go with me, but he said no, he'd wait for me outside; so I paid my four shillings and followed the large Arab into the Pyramid. Carrying a torch, he led me through the long black passageway to a spot where we could look down into the tomb, as a million other tourists had done, and there he lit a bit of phosphorescent paper and dropped it down to light the chamber below.

"Good enough, Johnny?" he said, or words to that effect, and then demanded five pounds, British, worth twenty-five dollars at that time. When I protested that the agreed-on price was four shillings, which I had paid, he took out a large curved knife and explained to me that the price had changed. He touched the edge of the knife with his finger and then touched his neck, and the change of price immediately made sense. I gave him the five pounds, and without further ado he led me back into the open, where Woodhill was waiting. A dozen yards from the base of the Pyramid, there was a pavilion about twenty by twenty, just a roof of canvas, and under this, a table and chairs where four men sat, large men in long white robes and red fezzes. Hanging from the roof was a sign with some Arabic printing and below it, in English, PYRAMID POLICE. Each of the four men had a large, heavy staff of wood with iron headings at both ends.

I told them what had happened. The large Arab was strolling off with an air of innocent indifference. When the four Egyptians heard my story, they leaped to their feet and raced after the Arab guide, caught up with him, and then beat him into a bloody, unconscious heap. They removed his money and returned my five pounds. I was utterly sickened by what had happened, threw the five pounds back at the policemen, said something in the way of rage at what they had done, and then stalked over to the jeep and got in and said to Wood-hill, who was sitting there and watching all this, that it was time to get the hell out of there. As he put the jeep in gear, one of the police ran after us with the five-pound note in his hand. The jeep was already in motion, but Woodhill began to brake it. I yelled at him to get us out of there, and as the policeman came abreast of us with the money, I shouted at him to shove it up his ass. We drove past the unconscious Arab guide, still lying in his blood, the police and the few army people, who were apparently indifferent to the unconscious Arab, and down the twisting sandy road that took us to the main highway. Woodhill was shaking, whimpering that you don't talk like that to the Pyramid police, because they'd remember the next time GIs were there. He wanted to know what the Arab had done, and I told him and explained that it was only a con, and I had seen cons pulled all my life, and you don't kill a man, you don't beat him to death for pulling a con. Woodhill didn't think he was dead, and perhaps he wasn't, and for my part I pitied anyone so stupid as to pull that one with the Pyramid police waiting outside.

Back at Payne Field, I was taken in hand by a Captain Phipps, public relations officer for the Air Transport Command. He fairly licked his lips as he greeted me, telling me that he had heard about my performance at Tripoli, and that he had set up a meeting for that night. I was to address at least a thousand GIs on the subject of the United Nations. Everyone was talking about the new organization and everyone was curious as hell. Since this was a central transshipping point for Air Transport, there would be no problem about an audience. Furthermore, he was changing my quarters at the VIP house, giving me the same suite of rooms that President Roosevelt had had

when he came through there. I could tell my kids, he said with delight, that I had slept in the same bed as FDR.

I liked Phipps immediately. Unlike gung-ho, straight-on Woodhill,
who was both direct and none too intelligent, Phipps was devious
and flattering. I liked that, being young enough to enjoy flattery. He
informed me, in response to my questions, they had had plans for
me and that they had discussed me at some length. "They" was the
public relations division of Air Transport. The Air Transport Command was in the process of setting up a vast network of airfields to
bring back thousands of troops a week from points overseas. Feeding
me a magnificent dinner in the also-magnificent officers' dining room,
congratulating me on my future, Phipps enlisted me as a chronicler
of Air Transport. He brushed aside the war with Japan; it was finished. The British had stopped the Japanese cold in Burma, and soon —
well, soon something would happen. The dropping of the atom bomb
was still seven weeks in the future, but already the whisper was around
that something enormous was going to hit the Japs.

I pinned him down to what they wanted of me. Air Transport, he
explained, wanted the following. After leaving Cairo, I would be
flown to the Negev in Palestine, the Sinai Peninsula, Iraq, Iran, Saudi
Arabia, Baluchistan, Karachi, Calcutta, Burma, Bombay, back to Cairo,
and then into Europe. Phipps smiled and dressed it up as the most
romantic adventure a man could desire. This is the big story, he assured me, and as for China — I would never get into China. They
had checked that out. I would absolutely never get into China. Would
I do it? I said I would do it. Saying yes to things thrust at me, without
stopping to find out what *yes* involved in its entirety, was one of
the continuing destructive habits of my life. Suddenly, I was the
fair-haired boy of Air Transport. I did my lecture on the United
Nations — better, I think, this second time. There were well over a
thousand GIs present, which was by no means bad, considering that
there was a USO performance that same night of Agatha Christie's
Ten Little Indians.

The next day, Phipps led me on a tour of Cairo, taking with him
an Assyrian-American GI who spoke Arabic. I remembered having
read Bill Saroyan's story about the handful of Assyrians who had
survived into modern times. They were so few that Pete, the Assyr-
ian, must have been related to the one Saroyan wrote about. He

agreed that he was, but distantly. We had dinner at Shepheard's Hotel, then saw *Ten Little Indians,* and then I was off on my Air Transport journey the following day. First the Negev, a tiny installation, then Sinai — called the "terrible wilderness" with good reason — then Iraq, Iran, Abadan, Bahrein Island. I saw Palestine — yet to become Israel — from three thousand feet, a bleak desert land, the only green patches those where the kibbutzim were, and all else that I saw were terrible mountains and desert, each place more unbearably hot than the previous place, great oil refineries where there was no other sign of civilization but the Bedouin tents, and then we were called down for landing at a British oasis called Habinya, because we had shown improper recognition signals. We were grateful they didn't shoot us down.

I was alone in the plane with the crew when the British brought us down. We had picked up some bomb handlers from the European Theater and had dropped them off here and there at the awful, lousy little Air Transport airstrips as ground crew, a heartbreaking process, since they had been away from home for better than two years, and when we were called down at Habinya, I was the only passenger in the big, empty, seatless C46. The British were not nice — very suspicious of me, very nasty to the crew, who had not the vaguest notion of what the recognition signals were there in the desert, nor did they care, since no American airstrip gave a damn about the signals or ever asked for them. Even in that unbelievable heat, the British did not refrigerate their beer. We drank warm beer and bedded down for the night naked in the hot plane, sprawled out on the floor, not allowed to depart until the British checked us out in the morning.

We lifted out of there in the morning and flew to a station in Saudi Arabia. My notes tell me that it was called Sharjah, but exactly where that is I don't know, since I can't find it on the map. I do know that, in making our approach before landing, we passed over a small walled and turreted city that might have served as an illustration for the *Arabian Nights,* but I saw no people in the city, and its walls were beginning to crumble. This place was not on the list of stations Phipps had given me as an itinerary, and I asked the captain why we were landing here. His unbelievable answer was that we were to pick up Coca-Cola empties.

Sharjah was the most dreadful place I have ever been to, before or

since. On a glazed white sand and salt desert, the small installation
shimmered in the implacable sunshine. We came to a stop about a
hundred feet from the installation, and when I got out of the plane,
I knew I would be dead before I crossed that hundred feet. I survived.
It was about eleven o'clock in the morning, almost at the peak of the
day's heat, and the ground crew refueling the plane wore gloves lest
their hands touch the metal and suffer burns; so did the GIs who
were carrying boxes of empty Coca-Cola bottles from the installation
and loading them onto the plane. When I climbed onto the veranda
of the installation, in the shade, I faced a huge thermometer, which
read 157 degrees Farenheit. Again and again since that time, I have
been told that human beings cannot live at 157 degrees, but there I
was and I was alive. Inside the installation, air conditioning kept the
heat down to 100 degrees, and it felt positively cool.

I told the pilot that I had been assured that these flights were for
me to hit the major airstrips of Air Transport. He nodded and said
that was so, but he had got a radio order to stop here for the bottles,
and, as he put it, you don't fuck with Coca-Cola, and he was too
close to going home to louse it up with a refusal to obey an order.
You're in the army, he explained. You don't disobey orders. He bought
me a beer; the rest of the crew had Coca-Cola.

We were at Sharjah less than an hour, but it was hard time, as the
local residents put it. In the winter it was 40 degrees better, but you
had the black flies. The GIs who were condemned to the place couldn't
say which was worse. The pilot signed the manifest and we staggered
out to the plane, which was now loaded with wooden crates of empty
Coca-Cola bottles, thousands of empty Coca-Cola bottles, there being
little else of comfort in Sharjah. They filled the C46 from floor to
ceiling, leaving only a narrow passage two feet wide on the side where
the doors had been. The C46 had two doors that would open wide
enough to admit a jeep or a howitzer; now, however, the doors were
missing, lost somewhere in the plane's wandering. This had not mat-
tered when the plane was empty, because I sat on the floor in the
pilot's compartment with the three-man crew. Now it was different,
as we discovered once we took off. Since I would be denied the comfort of stretching out on the floor of the plane, the crew stacked two
parachutes to make a seat for me, but we were hardly airborne when
the pilot sighed deeply and said something about the motherfucken

load and that he couldn't make altitude. I glanced out the window. We had left the white salt desert behind and were flying over sandhill desert. The sandhills were not very high, perhaps two or three hundred feet, but then neither were we very high, no more than a hundred feet higher than the sandhills.

My terror was interrupted by the pilot's announcement that he couldn't do a damn thing and unless we got some altitude we'd be up shit creek, as he put it. The navigator put in that we were out of balance, and the copilot began to cuss out the GIs who had loaded the plane. The pilot turned to me and very politely but deliberately suggested that I crawl back to the tail of the plane and see whether that would shift the balance. I did so, terrified, in the space left by the boxes, holding my breath as I crawled past the two missing doors, realizing that even an air bump could toss me out. As I looked out, we were so close to a sandhill that I felt I could reach down and touch it. A minute or two later, I was joined by the navigator. I asked him whether our move had helped, and he replied that it had not, not a blessed bit. It appeared that it was making things worse. Then what do we do? He told me to return with him to the pilot's compartment. When we got there, I told the pilot there was only one thing to do — start dumping the Coca-Cola bottles.

Was I crazy? Had I lost my mind completely? The navigator, maybe twenty years old, explained carefully and slowly, as one would to a child, Man, man, don't you know anything about war? I was just too stateside to understand. Guns they could dump, jeeps, ammo, even a howitzer, because nobody gave a fuck about jeeps or howitzers — but Coca-Cola bottles? No way. Not if you wanted to keep your points and not become a PFC again.

I didn't believe what I was hearing. When I yelled that we could be dead in five minutes, they shrugged. War is war. But war is not Coca-Cola bottles, and I ordered them to begin to dump the bottles. They were lieutenants and I had a sort of captain's rank, but they explained that I was only a civilian and I couldn't order them to do anything. Anyway, the pilot said, there's a strip only about fifty miles from here. He had radioed that we were coming in, and he felt sure he could make it, even if he couldn't get the plane up more than five or six hundred feet. Sure enough, we missed the sandhills and finally we saw the airfield up ahead, and as we approached for the landing,

I remembered something that the crew in their desperate tension had forgotten — that they had not dropped their wheels. When a C46 dropped its wheels, they came down with a crash that shook the whole plane. No crash, no wheels.

"No wheels!" I screamed at the top of my lungs. "No wheels!"

It was too late. The C46 hit the landing strip on its belly, screeched along, swaying from side to side, and finally came to a stop. The fire truck came racing to us, but there was no fire, just a ruined plane. After they had checked things — none of us was hurt — the crew told me that it was OK. Not a single bottle broken.

I wrote this up more or less exactly as it happened. I changed names because I didn't want anyone to get into trouble, and of course I called the story *Coca-Cola*. Neither *Coronet* nor *Esquire* would print the story, but it did get published and was eventually included in a book called *The Howard Fast Reader*. It has been reprinted many times, here and in Europe and India. I presume that most people reading it regard it as fiction. Not the case at all; it happened just as I tell it here.

Karachi was very hot, and most of the correspondents spent their time in the air-conditioned press building drinking cold drinks. American civilization had touched there, so they had not only Coca-Cola but ice cubes. Air Transport flew me up to Peshawar, and then I was driven to the Khyber Pass by a friendly British p.r. officer who had never been there. We had both read a lot of Kipling. He told me that the British vetted — his word — their young pilots by sending them into Afghanistan, where they would drop a few small bombs on annoying tribesmen, who would shoot at the planes with muzzle-loading rifles. There was no war with the Afghans at the moment.

There was nothing I liked about Karachi and a good deal that disgusted me, and as I moved through that jewel of the British Empire, the India of the Raj, I found more and more that disgusted me, for example, two British officers stepping out of the showers, naked, and being dried by two bearers, as servants were called. And as they talked, the bearers dried their penises and testicles, eliciting no reaction from them, since the bearers were that much less than human. But I get ahead of myself. I took Air Transport to Delhi, and there reported to Air Transport headquarters, presented my papers, and told them about my assignment to do the Air Transport story. They said they had had no word of my coming, and a Major Austin, in charge of p.r., told me that for the time being, Air Transport was closed to all correspondents — this in response to a thing aired in Congress about correspondents bumping soldiers who had been overseas for years. I argued that just a week ago, in Cairo, I had been talked into doing a p.r. job for Air Transport, flying all of its routes and doing a magic carpet story about it. Major Austin knew nothing about this — a typical army response — and had no authority to act on it. I asked him to call Cairo, which he did, and came back with the information that no one knew anything about it and that Captain Phipps had returned to stateside. His advice to me was to travel by train to Calcutta and try to enter China either by plane — there would be air passage in that direction — or over the Ledo Road.

All of this took five days, during which time I stayed in Delhi. I was given a room at the Curzon Barracks, in the very clean spit-and-polish city that the British had built to be the eternal center of India under colonial rule. But eternity, as Adolf Hitler and so many others have discovered, can be very short, and in India of 1945, British rule was already on the edge of a precipice. Nevertheless, New Delhi, the area the British had built, was quite grand, with splendid pink stone buildings and absolutely splendid quarters for the army people, British and American. It was hot as hell, and normally at this season the government and all its administrators would be up in the hills of Kashmir; with the war on, few of them dared leave. When my plane landed at the Delhi airport, the thermometer at the airport building registered 120 degrees; but even as I landed, a shower began and dropped the temperature to 105, which, compared with the heat I had already experienced, was quite comfortable. I recall two Red Cross nurses, starched and crisp, on the same flight, and apparently immune to the heat as they stepped out of the plane and walked to the installation, congratulating each other on how nice it was to be in Delhi again.

On my second day in New Delhi, I woke up to a comfortable 100 degrees, awakened by the sound of the bearers dousing the heavy rush shutters that separated the sleeping quarters from the veranda. They threw pail after pail of cold water against the shutters until they were soaked with water, and amazingly the room became cool and comfortable. The day before, I had wandered into an enlisted men's barracks, made the acquaintance of half a dozen GIs, and told them I would like to talk to them again. This morning, one of them, Ralph Loewe by name, came into the officers' dining room and told me that Mahatma Gandhi would be coming to Old Delhi late that afternoon, and since I had mentioned the night before that I would like to interview him, this might be the chance. I agreed — absolutely — but how do we get to Old Delhi? He said that it would be interesting to go by tonga cart.

At that time, and perhaps today for all I know, the tonga cart and the rickshaw were the major forms of transportation in India. Later, in Calcutta, I would see ancient Buick touring cars used as taxis, a great many of them, and in the front seat of each, two fierce-looking bearded Sikhs. But I noticed no taxis in Delhi as Ralph Loewe led me to a tonga cart. (I was never to see Loewe again after I left Delhi, but years later he wrote to me — by then he was a college professor — for permission to dramatize my novel *Spartacus*. I gave him permission, and his version was played in a midwestern college.) The tonga cart is a two-wheeled vehicle, much like the English dog cart, the driver facing forward, the passengers on the single seat facing backward. We started off for Old Delhi, then separated from New Delhi by a flat road across a brown, sun-baked plain. It was very hot that morning, and it became hotter, and the little beaten horse or pony that drew the tonga cart walked more and more slowly. Finally, well out on that sun-baked plain, Loewe burst out that he couldn't stand any more of this, he simply could not endure the suffering of the horse. Whereupon he paid off the tonga driver, let him drive his empty cart away, and decided that we would go the rest of the distance on foot. I must mention that Loewe each morning filled his pockets with pice, the smallest Indian coinage, about a tenth of a cent at that time, and then throughout the day gave some to every beggar who approached him — and in India their numbers were legion. But after a mile on the brown plain under the burning sun, I wished to hell that he had taken his sympathy for the horse and turned it toward us. Happily, two thirds of the way to Old Delhi, we were blessed with the sight of a Jain temple, standing in a little oasis of greenery, a tiny brook bubbling out of the ground and gracing the place with tropical plumage. A Jain priest motioned for us to enter, and, removing our shoes, we went into the delicious cool of the place, sat in the dark shadows of the temple walls, and then went on our way, renewed and refreshed, no questions having been asked of us. From what I could learn later of this sect, it is a gentle creed, not unlike Buddhism, with malice toward none.

Apparently, everyone in that part of India had heard that Gandhi was coming, for as we approached the railroad station, we became a part of a vast crowd that numbered in the tens of thousands and increased minute by minute. An English-speaking Indian, pressed up against us in the crowd, told us that Gandhi would be on the three o'clock train — or so they believed — and certainly he would say a few words to the crowd, but possibly not leave the train. When I said that I wanted to interview him, the people around us laughed. The man with the English said that he was a Muslim, but Gandhi was a saint, so it made no difference.

We saw the small, slender figure of Gandhi, but we could not get closer to him than fifty yards or so, and the few words he spoke were blown away on the wind. Then his train pulled out, but I was left with a deep feeling that something wonderful had happened.

As the crowd melted away, Ralph Loewe pointed to a lamppost at the edge of the platform. He said that once before, coming here, he had seen a group of people sitting under the lamppost in its flickering light while a Hindu taught them to read. He was so moved by the sight that he wrote a letter to the British High Commissioner at New Delhi, telling him of this condition and begging him to do something to alleviate the illiteracy. Which he did — by having a larger light bulb put into the lamppost.

That night, I sat in Loewe's barracks until about two o'clock in the morning. The GIs and I talked about war and peace, what was happening in San Francisco, where the United Nations was coming into being, whether the Russians had really found the body of Adolf Hitler in the ruins of Berlin, would we go on and fight Russia, was it true that the Japanese were begging for peace, and, most of all, what were the plans for the two million American and British and Australian troops in India? What was happening here in India? Why were they being kept here?

Word got around. The colonel in charge of U.S. Army p.r. in New Delhi sought me out and said that he heard I was in the enlisted men's barracks until early in the morning. He made his comments both accusatory and pejorative: I didn't belong there, I was an officer of company rank, and if I wanted to talk to enlisted men, there was a press room where that could be done. I had a much smaller hold on my temper in those days, and I snapped back that I was no god-damn officer — I had already learned to share the enlisted men's dis-gust with what they called "the fucken officer class" — and that he was not going to tell me whom to talk to or give me any other kind of orders, and that I'd damn well do as I pleased. The only power I had was the power to write about him, but then, overseas, that was very persuasive. He mellowed a bit. The top sergeant in Loewe's company had asked for permission to use the common room in the barracks for me to give a talk about the United Nations. The colonel said that he had refused, but now he'd changed his mind and would permit me to address the troops. About two hundred of them turned up for the talk, and when I finished, it turned into a discussion that went on for hours. The fact that a dozen or so British soldiers were there made it much more exciting.

My letter to Bette the next day was filled with bitterness and dis-gust. What was I doing here, traveling around and giving speeches on a subject about which I knew no more than the men who listened? There was no war here. Possibly in war there was some sort of de-mented integrity, but all I had seen since I first landed in North Africa was poverty and misery and thousands of American soldiers with nothing to do and officers living like pashas, most of them commis-sioned civilians and, as far as I could see, happy to be ten thousand miles from their wives and squalling kids — and what in God's name was I doing here? The truth was that I was doing something very important; I was doing what a writer does, watching and seeing and trying to understand.

I was, at least, curious. That's why I went to a Communist Party meeting the next day. After the discussion in the common room, one of the British soldiers asked whether he could speak to me privately. He took me aside and said bluntly, Fast, are you a Communist? That required some thinking, and while I was thinking about his question, he went on to say that a man named Bandar Sharim, who was the secretary or chief, as it might be put, of the Delhi section of the Communist Party of India, thought that I might be a member of the CP, and if I was, he wanted to talk to me.

I asked what made him think that, and the British soldier said that what he told this Sharim made him think that, and I asked what in hell the soldier knew about me, to which he replied, Only what he had heard. He was a big man for a British enlisted man, redheaded, with a pair of sharp blue eyes; and I looked him up and down and asked him how I could know that he wasn't part of British intelligence.

He snorted impatiently that he was fucken Irish and that the fucken Limeys knew he was a red, and I could ask around and even his stupid CO would tell me. And they had sent him into Burma twice the year before to get him dead and out of the way, and after listening to me, he decided that I was a Communist, and I agreed to meet with Bandar Sharim.

The meeting took place on the edge of New Delhi, in a small, neat, whitewashed house. I think there were two small rooms in the little cottage, and one room was crowded with Jack McClosky, the Irishman, Bandar Sharim, three other Indian Communists, and me. Sharim was tall and slender, a long head and an unsmiling face. The look of the others I hardly remember, except that one of them hobbled on two deformed legs. McClosky (the family name is an invention) told me an interesting story about the man with the deformed legs. It seemed that the British enlisted Indians as police spies, and every Communist had his spy attached to him. This man had made a friend of his police spy and organized a police spy union. For this, the British police punished him by breaking both his legs and preventing them from healing properly, a not uncommon practice under the Raj. It not only crippled a man for life but made him instantly identifiable.

The substance of the meeting was simple and direct. At that time, Gene Dennis was the general secretary of the Communist Party U.S.A. Sharim wanted to know how well I knew Dennis and how close to him I was. I had to tell him that I had never met Gene Dennis and knew him not at all. Could I get to him? I felt sure that I could. Certainly Joe North or Lionel Berman could arrange it.

Sharim then said that I was to tell Dennis that India stood at the edge of freedom, that surely in no more than twelve months British rule would come to an end. (This I remember very clearly.) Tell Gene Dennis, he said, that our four hundred million people have been wetting their mouths and learning to spit together. We will spit once together, and there will be such a wave of water that will wash the

British into the sea. But help us. Inform yourselves about our struggle, and let the American people know what we suffer and what we must do. We need your support desperately. Tell Gene Dennis how desperate we are.

I made one more appeal to the chief of Air Transport at Delhi, spelling out again the arrangements made at Cairo for me to be the historian-correspondent of the Air Transport Command, but he shrugged it off and made an interesting remark that I remember very well: "The company you keep, mister." I thought this to be a reference to the meeting I had had with the Delhi Communists, but when I pressed him, he admitted that it was something else entirely. When I had first put in for my passport to go overseas, there was a delay that had stretched into weeks. I finally wrote a note to Henry A. Wallace, asking him to help me, and a week later my passport appeared. Now this small favor that Wallace had done for me turned up on my record — with the addendum that my passport had been previously denied because of "reasonable suspicion of left leanings" and certain remarks I had made when speaking to the troops in Cairo. This officer impressed on me the fact that we were no longer allies of the Soviet Union.

The result was a three-day train trip from Delhi to Calcutta. If I had known how intriguing this long ride would be, I would never have asked to go by air. I left New Delhi early in the morning, driven to Old Delhi and the railroad station in one of the staff cars. During my previous visit to the station, it had been a carpet of white-clad people, packed shoulder to shoulder; this morning, the station was back to normal, crowds of men, women, and children, loaded with sacks and bags and baskets, goats, chickens; little fires where people were cooking food; an enormous, wonderful, horrible confusion through which I wandered hopelessly, picking up two GIs on the way, having bearers fight for the privilege of carrying our luggage — and then the three of us rescued by a Sergeant La Houd, who was from Minneapolis, of French-Canadian parentage. La Houd was marvelous, one of those talented staff sergeants who organize, command, and lead the United States Army — or did then — and who put up with and divert the stupidity of the officers.

He took us in hand, guided us to the mail car — he was the official army mail courier — ordered cold canned fruit juice for us to drink, and assigned us to the bunks that lined the side of the mail car. Then off we went on the Great Trunk Line of India. I have had many train rides in the course of my life, but none as wonderful, as remarkable as this one. It is hardly much more than a thousand miles, as the train goes, from Delhi to Calcutta, but this train stopped at every station on the line, and at times it stood for hours at a station, and at times it reversed its direction, and at times it chugged along at walking pace. Every stop along the way, there were bearers in fantastic costumes, with great feathered headdresses, who appeared at our car with tea trays, bread and butter and cucumber sandwiches, piles of cakes and cookies, steaming dark tea, which they deposited without asking whether we wanted them or not; and then at the next station, or the one after the next, a clone of the bearer would appear and say, Six rupees, sahib — or ten rupees or whatever — the mystery of how they communicated and collected without ever losing a tea tray remaining unsolved. All the wonders and horrors of India in 1945 were revealed to us as the train crept along.

When we reached Lucknow, we discovered that there was plague in the city. The train stood at the platform and we got out, and in front of me on the platform was a family of a man, woman, and five small children, all huddled in a tight group, the man with his head on his wife's lap, and as we looked at them, the man stiffened and died, his eyes open and turned up so that mostly the whites showed. His wife screamed, a wild, primeval scream, and all up and down the top of the train, which was thick with families clinging together, men, women, children, there sounded a haunting moan of sympathy. As the train rolled out of Lucknow, we saw a dirt road that paralleled the tracks, and all along this road were bodies of those who had died of the plague, bodies pushed off the road, with the buzzards tearing at the flesh and circling up with flesh hanging from their beaks.

We stopped at one station, and, informed that the train would be there for at least an hour, I got out and strolled around. About thirty yards from the station, a tribe of small people were huddled together on a bit of empty ground. I call them small people because the men were no taller than five feet, the women a few inches less. The men wore string loin clothes, the women some sort of bark skirts. The children were naked. The men carried spears with fire-hardened points

and small hide covered shields. Who were they? Two uniformed station attendants, who had appointed themselves as guards for this
strange tribe, told me that they had come down from the hills because the game was gone and somehow they had heard that there
was a thing (a train) that would take them somewhere, elsewhere —
all of this from signs. No one knew a word of their language; no one
knew who they were or where they came from or what their circumstances had been. It was all conjecture. No one had ever seen them
or their like before. They were rather beautiful people, with fine features, pale brownish-yellow skin, and on their faces expressions of
heartbreaking hopelessness, all of them pressed together, clinging to
one another. The Indian station attendants had found some rice and
fruit for them, but there was not enough to keep them alive.

The train moved on, and we left them there. It was a story without
beginning or end. I wrote it on the train, and called it *The Little Folk
from the Hills,* and I also did a story about the Communist whose
legs had been broken by the British, calling it *The Police Spy.* Both
stories were rejected by *Coronet* magazine, but they were eventually
printed elsewhere and reprinted all over India. Later, in Calcutta, I
found two of my books, *The Unvanquished* and *Freedom Road,* editions in English and editions in Urdu and in Bengali, all of them
pirated. But in that poverty-stricken land, I could not dream of asking for royalties.

Much of the rest of that endless train trip was across semidesert,
sometimes for miles with no living things in sight but the sacred cows
that were everywhere in Hindu India. I had dragged a portable typewriter with me from stateside, and most of the trip I sat and pounded
away on it, yet with a sense that nothing I wrote would be acceptable
to the prim little establishment magazine that had sent me here.

There is no way to describe Calcutta. It is a fact of nature that must
be felt, experienced, smelled, seen — and still there is no way to comprehend it. They said it had six million people — or eight or ten
million; no one actually knew. There was no way to take a census.
Starving peasants had poured into the city by the millions. They lived
on the streets, in shacks, under bits of corrugated tin, in back yards —
everywhere — to the point where the city had set aside whole streets
where the people from the countryside could live and sleep and die —

sleeping streets, dying streets. Was there ever such a thing in the world before?

I left the train at the main station, an exploding world of men and women and children, pushing, shouting, pleading, clawing onto the train, climbing onto the top of the train, falling off, being pushed off, bundles, baskets, women in saris, men in white shirts and trousers called dhotis, children everywhere, cows pushing the people aside, the sacred cows that were everywhere in Calcutta — and the people so gentle, so warm, so long-suffering. No one comes in contact with Indians without sensing that knowledge of suffering. I made my way through all of this, my orders in hand. I looked for a cab to take me to my destination, and there was the line of cabs outside the station, big, open, ancient touring cars, each driven, as I mentioned before, by a fierce, turbaned Sikh, with a second fierce Sikh sitting beside him, each with an enormous curved knife in his belt.

Off we went to find the press club where I would be quartered, and then, a few minutes later, the sky exploded. It was monsoon time. The Sikhs rushed to raise the roof of their open car, fastened it down, and drove on. The water fell, not in drops, but in great surging sheets, and ten minutes after the rain started, there was water up to the hubcaps of big wooden-spoked wheels. Another ten minutes, the rain stopped, and the six to eight inches of water in the streets began to recede. On the streets, the families who lived there sat in the water. It came and it went, like the day and the night. We drove on, trying to find the press club. The Sikhs asked questions, conferred, doubled around and back; the ancient taxi meter ticked away; we drove down one street and up another. We passed pools of water where men washed themselves and their clothes. The rain had dropped the temperature to about 90 degrees and the whole city was like a steaming bathhouse. And in time, we found the small palace that had been turned into a press club. The fare was still only twelve rupees, the rupee being then about forty-two cents.

I was billeted across the road from the U.S. Army general hospital, put together out of a long string of Quonset huts. I was given a small room. I cleaned up and was having some lunch in the dining room when an American soldier sat down at my table, introduced himself as Hal Levinthal, informed me that he had heard about me, and told me that if I was looking for stories, there was an officer in the hospital across the road who had won a field commission for unusual bravery. Levinthal stressed that field commissions are very rare. Would I like to talk to him? It might be a very good story.

And how did Levinthal know about me and where I was? He was vague about that. Word got around.

I was curious to see the inner workings of a field hospital the size of this one and I was curious about Levinthal and who he was and where he came from, so I went along with him, and we walked through the endless corridors of the hospital until finally we found our man. His name was Walter Neff. He was the son of my father's first cousin, which I suppose made him a second cousin or something of the sort — his father a physician who had treated my father during the last days of Barney's life — a strange coincidence, yet one of many strange coincidences that threaded through my life. I spoke to Neff, heard his story, and made my notes. I had never seen him before, and after that day, I never saw him again.

Levinthal intrigued me. He was a remarkable young man, formerly a Broadway press agent and one day to become a major producer on the national scene — but at this moment a top sergeant, one of those cool, knowledgeable enlisted men who ran the U.S. Army and fought World War Two to its conclusion under the façade of officer leadership. He had been in India for an eternity, and he knew every trick and wrinkle in the game. When Mao, fighting the Kuomintang and Chiang Kai-shek on the other side of the Himalayas, needed typewriters with Chinese fonts, Levinthal got them and conveyed them to the appropriate place. When they needed sulfa drugs and bandages, he did the same thing. He was monumental. He knew everyone and everything, and he knew more about Indian politics than anyone I had ever met.

He stayed with me that day, giving me a short course in life, horror, and what is indescribable and unspeakable. This was Calcutta at the tail end of a famine that took six million lives. Peasants, many of them Untouchables, poured into Calcutta from the countryside, thousands and thousands each day. There was no place for them, so the city government roped off certain streets and allowed the peasants to spend the nights on these streets. They were called the sleeping streets and they were still in use at this time, although the tragic back of the famine had been broken. Yet one morning when Levinthal took me to a sleeping street, I saw here and there, scattered over

the street, the bodies of those who had died during the night, skin
and bones, like the concentration camp survivors who had lived
through the Holocaust. A few months earlier, Levinthal told me, the
dead each morning would be so many that the British lacked sufficient trucks to carry the bodies out of town so that they could be
incinerated.

According to the account Levinthal gave me, when the Japanese
thrust through Burma toward Assam appeared to have some chance
of success, the British feared that the Assamese might welcome the
Japanese as liberators and go over to them. Accordingly, the British
made a deal with the Muslim rice dealers to corner the rice market —
I was subsequently shown an old airplane hangar piled thirty feet
high with thousands of pounds of rice — and thereby break the will
and strength of the Assamese and the Bengalese. I was told that the
rice reserves I saw were only a small part of what was withheld; and
during the next few days this story was backed up by a number of
witnesses. The British disclaimed responsibility, shifting the blame to
the rice dealers, who, the British claimed, raised their prices in response to the market; but one rice dealer I spoke to denied this and
held that the British controlled the price of rice. Certainly the British,
holding total power, could have seized the rice at their own price —
averting an enormous tragedy, the death by starvation of six million
human beings, men, women, and children.

In 1987, at a dinner party given by an Indian woman in New
York, I fell into a conversation with two Indian diplomats. I re-
counted the above experience to them, and they said that I was right
in every detail of my story and that there was abundant material in
the files of Calcutta University to prove the deliberate intent of the
British colonial administration in a crime so terrible that it rivaled
Hitler's Holocaust. I said that I thought they owed it to history and
civilization — if there was such a thing as civilization — to make this
tragic story public. They replied that during the first months of India's liberation, they had considered the publication of the facts and
circumstances that led to the great famine, but they needed England
too desperately to confront her or the world with this crime, and that
even today, the ties to England were of importance. And then, one
of them added, apologetically of course, that in 1945 and perhaps
today, life was cheap in Bengal and Assam.

That evening, Levinthal took me to the home of a Professor Chatterjee, who taught at the University of Calcutta. A sweet, soft-spoken man, married to a pretty and gentle woman, he made me feel at home immediately. I found that same quality of gentle courtesy and sweetness in many of the Bengalis I met. They lived in a little stucco cottage, halfway across Calcutta from where I was billeted. Professor Chatterjee had invited a local Communist leader to join us. That was still at a time when there was no public knowledge that I was a Communist, yet again and again I had found myself with Communists. Yet the question of was I or was I not did not come up, nor did I ever ask where Levinthal stood. It was a good and informative evening of talk, and I learned much about India and Calcutta. I noticed a curious thing: in the course of telling how, a few months earlier, a starving family of a man, woman, and three children were outside Professor Chatterjee's window, pleading for food, he without thinking removed gently from his dhoti insects brought down by the ceiling fan. He very gently brushed the insects off, not hurting them or stamping on them when they fell to the floor. Meanwhile, he was recounting how, that evening, he and his wife sat with their small bowl of rice, listening to the piteous pleading of the starving family.

He asked me what I would have done. Would I have given them my food? I answered that I would have. He shook his head and said that if I were to understand India's struggle, I must listen carefully and one day write of what he told me. He then went on to say that he and his wife had not given up their food. The peasant family would have died anyway. The small bowl of food could not have saved them. Six million people had died, and six million more would die unless India threw off the yoke of British rule. There are only a handful in this vast population who can lead the struggle for freedom, he said. We are not important, but unless people like us survive, the struggle will not be won. That was the gist of what he told me, yet I knew I could not think as he thought or react as he had reacted.

We left Professor Chatterjee's home at about eight o'clock. We knew he did not have enough food to feed us, and we spoke about another appointment. The local Communist organizer left with us, and Levinthal suggested that we dine at the Jewish restaurant. The press club had three jeeps and drivers to serve the correspondents, and tonight I had snagged one of them — fortunately, since the Jewish restaurant was miles away. I made no note of the Communist's name at the time, nor can I recall it, so I will simply refer to him as Sind.

We drove to the Jewish restaurant, which was like no Jewish restaurant I had ever seen, my references being the Jewish restaurants on the Lower East Side of New York City. This was a tall, stately white building, with a fine high-ceilinged interior, dark teak panels everywhere. Sind was reluctant to enter, but we talked him into it; his poverty was the poverty of the peasants and working people, but we convinced him that a single decent meal would not corrupt him; and indeed my own guilts were large enough after the discussion at Professor Chatterjee's home. Yet I had learned that if one was in India, one must accept the vast gulf between the rich and the poor; and the rich — not only the British but the princely and wealthy Indians — were rich beyond anything I had ever known. As for this splendid Indian restaurant, it was owned by a man who was a member of a Jewish community that had been established two hundred years before the birth of Jesus, since this community did not celebrate the feast of Chanukah, which recalls an event that took place in 165 B.C.

In the restaurant, there was a large round table reserved for American enlisted men. Some of the Jewish enlisted men appropriated potatoes and sour pickles from the commissary and taught the chef to make potato pancakes, so the meal would begin with platters of golden fried potato pancakes to precede the Indian food, which was excellent. The owner came out to be introduced, a handsome dark-skinned man, in no way distinguishable from other Bengalis. It appeared that this was a gathering place for enlisted men who were either intellectuals or in some way left of center, for one by one they drifted in until over a dozen men were packed around the table under a mantle of pipe, cigar, and cigarette smoke, with half a dozen discussions and arguments competing for listening time — and every so often a plea from someone at the table to keep it down and not have us thrown out. But they never were thrown out. The restaurant owner was too pleased to have them there, these strange American Jews in uniform eating their own barbaric food.

Before we dropped off Sind on our way back to the press club, he asked me whether I really desired to see Calcutta, and when I said that I did, he told me that he would pick me up the following morning at about seven o'clock. He had been educated at Oxford, and I remember only too well his remark to me as we parted, to the effect that I was more fortunate than Dante, who had had to create hell out of his imagination, whereas I could see it with my own eyes.

I lay in bed that night under my mosquito netting thinking about this strange first day in Calcutta. One of the soldiers at the table in the restaurant had remarked that after a certain amount of time in Calcutta, it was with you. Could you ever leave it again? He didn't think so. You retain it with a special kind of love and agony.

The following morning, at six forty-five, Sind was waiting for me outside the press club. He had brought our transportation with him, two ancient bicycles, which I stared at doubtfully. He was troubled. Was it possible that I did not ride a bicycle? Oh, yes, a bicycle. He told me to have faith; these were very good bicycles, and actually they did hold up. Mostly we walked them. Once we left them with a friend and took a rickshaw. When I protested that I felt degraded, sitting in a vehicle that was drawn by a man, Sind told me that the rickshaw man would feel much more degraded if he brought no money home to feed his children, and that when they rid themselves of the Raj, they would be able to rid themselves of rickshaws. (Whether or not that is the case, I don't know. I have not been back to Calcutta.) He also explained that we would be safer in the rickshaws, since we would go to places where there were bad men who would kill even for an old, patched bike but would have a respect of sorts for the rickshaw and its passengers.

I didn't question this. I questioned nothing Sind said as he took me deeper and deeper into the bowels of hell, the deep slums of Calcutta, where few Westerners ever go, the rotting houses, the people who had survived the famine, so thin they were like skeletons draped in tissue, the ankle-deep mud of the monsoon, in which people lived and slept, the sickness, the beseeching rotting eyes of the blind, the families crouched around small fires, which they fought for against the oppressive dampness, the open pit with eight or nine bodies waiting to be burned, but half full of water from the monsoon, the sacred cows wandering through this as if it were some verdant pasture, the smell of burning charcoal mixed with the sweet stink of death. I fought against crying out, Enough, enough, as if this were a punishment that I must undergo; I followed Sind meekly. People knew him. They greeted him. They wept to him, pleaded with him, listened to him — all of it in their own tongue, of which I understood not a word. Bengali is a strange, tantalizing language, cozening an English-speaking person with a feeling that he understands what is not understandable at all.

My day of knowledge came at last to an end. I had learned and graduated. Perhaps I had seen the full scale of human suffering; perhaps I had only scratched the surface. I would live with the memory all my life, yet it would fade and blur. I asked Sind how he lived in the company of such poverty. Who pays you? Who cares? I was a millionaire. I had over $200 in American money in my pocket. I was three times a millionaire in relative terms. Sind told me that party members pay dues, sometimes a few grains of rice, sometimes a few rupees a month if they were teachers or civil servants. Each week, the Communist Party published a one-page newspaper. Sind and other organizers would take the paper around, not to sell it but to read from it, going into the neighborhoods where I had been and into the villages around Calcutta. Each person listening would be asked to contribute a single grain of rice, if they had rice, and this provided most of the food on which Sind and the other organizers lived.

During the short time I had belonged to the Communist Party U.S.A., I had learned little of the ways and lives of the organizers. Afterward, I tried to relate this kind of self-denial and saintliness to conditions in the United States. It did not work. Where the conditions differ, everything differs.

At the press club that evening, I got to talking with a correspondent who worked for a New York newspaper. We spoke about the famine story, and he shrugged it off. He was a man in his fifties, comfortable in his place in Calcutta and not looking to make waves. He was an old newspaperman, not tough nor cruel nor indifferent. He said to me, That's the way it is, kid. That's the way it's going to be. Never knock yourself out with what nobody will print. Or words to that effect.

In bed that night, I lay for hours without sleep. I wept inside. I lived in a world bereft of sanity or justice. Even to the small boy who was Howard Fast, age ten, fighting his own battle for survival in the streets of New York, the world made a sort of crazy sense. But here —

well, what was here had been here, and it would continue to be here, and sooner or later Sind would be arrested and beaten to death or have his legs broken or stay in jail without trial or hearing, and any human being with a shred of common sense goes a different way.

I spent most of the night without sleep, trying to think about Bette and Rachel and how nice it would be to build another house like the cottage at Sleepy Hollow.

The atom bombs fell on Hiroshima and Nagasaki, and the war was over. I possibly could have arranged to go on a junket to Japan to look at what was left of those two tragic cities. I had no desire to; I wanted only to go home, and I shipped out of Calcutta on an armed Victory ship. The trip took six weeks, but finally one day we tied up at a pier on the Hudson River and I walked off the ship with my gear and hailed a taxi and rode home through a sunny, peaceful Manhattan and took my wife in my arms and held my little girl tight, and tried not to weep and tried to tell myself that God's in His heaven and all's right with the world.

6

I WAS HOME — in this beautiful, well-ordered, clean, and sanitary country that was like no other country on earth, in New York, my beloved, wonderful city. Here was my home and my wife and my lovely little girl, my daughter, Rachel, almost a year and a half by now. Here there was no war, no hunger, no desperate struggle for liberation.

For about a week, I communicated with no one, stayed with Bette morning, noon, and night, went to Central Park with her, the two of us sprawled on the grass, watching our little girl at play, took walks with her, went to the theater, came home, and made love.

During this lull in the storm that was beginning to take over my life, things were pleasant indeed. Before I went overseas, we had put an advertisement in *The New York Times* for a housekeeper, and the ad was answered by a young, open-faced Nisei woman. Before we could even begin to interview her, she blurted out that she was Japanese, that she was born in California but had been taken from her home and sent to a concentration camp in March of 1942, and that she had been in that camp up to a few weeks ago, and that if we felt she was an enemy, it was no use interviewing her at all. The thought of this pleasant girl as an enemy made us burst into laughter, and of course we hired Hana Masuda, and she remained with us for the next five years. She was a good, loving person, and she made our lives much easier.

But I reached a point where I decided that a week of home and happiness was enough, and I took myself down to the offices of *The New Masses* on East Twelfth Street. The offices were in a nine-story building between University Place and Broadway, a building that also housed *The Daily Worker* and the Communist Party leadership. The people in the top offices of the party, the general secretary and the members of the National Committee, were housed on the ninth floor, and in referring to them, one often spoke simply of "the ninth floor." The general secretary of the party at that time, Gene Dennis, was a tall, handsome man who had taken over the party leadership from Earl Browder. In 1944, Browder, the leader of the party through some of its most bitter struggles during the thirties, had attempted to change the party from a political party that offered candidates in elections to a sort of educational Marxist entity. His move, I believe, was based on the wartime and prewar influence of the party on Roosevelt's New Deal, and on the hope that it might continue. It is impossible here to go into the lengthy and frequently obtuse theoretical discussion on this point; much of it was almost as meaningless then as it would be today. Sufficient to say that Browder lost the struggle, was removed from leadership, and expelled from the party. Dennis was his successor.

I had never met Gene Dennis and I had never ventured to the sacrosanct heights of the ninth floor, and being in proper awe of the leaders of an organization I had come to respect and honor, I went first to Joe North in the more familiar offices of *The New Masses*. Would he set up a meeting for me with Gene Dennis? I had perhaps an exaggerated sense of the importance of carrying a message from the Communist Party of Northern India to the Communist Party of the United States, yet in all reality, a plea from one Communist Party to another was of importance and to be treated with respect. Joe agreed with me, picked up his phone, and was told that Dennis would see me. I took the elevator up to the ninth floor, was shown into Dennis's office. He sat behind his desk; he did not rise nor did he offer his hand. Nor did he smile. Nor did he ask me to sit down. Nor did he indicate that he was either pleased or displeased to meet me.

Now this is the national leader of the Communist Party of the United States. Here I am, one of the leading and — at that time — most honored writers in the country. The party busted its ass to get me into the movement. It showered me with praise, lured me with its most winning people, reprinted stuff from my books in *The New Masses,* and embraced me. But Dennis never asked me to meet him, and now that I was in his office, he looked at me as a judge might look at a prisoner before passing sentence.

Since he didn't ask why I was there, I delivered my message uninvited. Very briefly, I spoke of the crisis in India, and then I repeated to him what the Indian Communist leader had said. He listened, and then he nodded — a signal for me to go.

Am I crazy? I asked myself. Or is this some kind of joke? But Dennis was the last man on earth to exhibit humor. Wasn't he going to ask me what I had seen? Wasn't he going to ask me about the political situation? I had spoken about the largest colonial country in the world. Wasn't he interested? I waited. He told me I could go. I turned and left.

I then went from Dennis's office to Joe North and told him about Dennis's reaction to me and my message from India. Joe said that such was Dennis, and that Dennis was Dennis, and that he was not easy with people. It seemed to me that what a party leader dealt with most was people, and how the devil did he come to be the general secretary of the Communist Party? Joe admitted that Dennis was not the greatest, that it should have been Bill Foster, the grand old man of the left, but Foster had a bad heart and was too old. Since it was not much more than a year since I had joined the party, Joe felt that I should withhold judgment.

Joe North was to become, in the years ahead, one of my closest friends. He was a big, shaggy bear of a man, always unkempt even when he dressed with the greatest care, goodhearted, good-natured. He reminded me of Friar Tuck in the Robin Hood tales, a man without rancor or hostility, a man I loved and who became like a brother to me. With all that, he had given himself to orthodoxy, and that is a terrible curse — in a Communist Party or a religion or in politics or in any system of thinking.

A few weeks after my meeting with Dennis, I met with Joe North again and told him in great detail about the famine in Bengal, and I also told him that no one would touch the story with a ten-foot pole. I told him that I wanted to write it for *The New Masses.* He thought about it for a few moments, and then he shook his head. No, they could not print it.

Why? I demanded. Here was a story of gigantic proportions. Six million people had died. Was there to be no light on this, no blame, no call for justice? His answer was — war. War answered every question. It was a war that involved the whole world. The Japanese were then advancing through Burma. The British feared that they would enter India, and then they would have the unlimited resources of the subcontinent at their disposal. The British took what measures they could take.

I exploded over that. No other way to deal with it than to starve six million people to death? I would not have it. How could he say that? He soothed me, as he would many times in the future. We were fighting Nazism, the death of hope, the death of the future, and what was done was done by all of us. That was not the only injustice. War bred injustice.

The argument went on from there, but *The New Masses* would not run the story. Joe asked me to forget it, to put it away and perhaps at some future date we could examine it from another perspective. More than forty years later, I told the story in a novel called *The Pledge*. It created not even a ripple, no shock, no cries of disbelief. Thus it goes.

I reacted to Jean Paul Sartre much as I reacted to Joe North. I loved the man instantly, this wonderful little man with the heavy glasses who so strongly confirmed my feeling that I had not been wrong to join the Communist Party. "Today, how else can a man confirm his right to existence and his membership in the human race?" I noted that. He was brought to our apartment by Ronald Carter, who had been connected to the Office of War Information. It was still a time when a Communist could visit the United States and not be turned back by Immigration. Sartre had come to New York with a list of books that the French publisher Gallimard wished to translate and publish. Strangely, some literary agents and publishers refused his request, my own literary agents, McIntosh and Otis, among them. Ronald Carter informed me of this, telling me that, while Sartre was ready to accept the refusal of such works as Carl Sandburg's books on Lincoln and John Steinbeck's *Cannery Row* and a number of other titles, he could not accept the refusal on the part of my agents to release *Freedom Road*. Could he, Ronald, bring Sartre to see me?

I was furious with my agents, and I wrote out my own short agreement to the translation and gave it to Sartre when he arrived. Sartre's English was not of the best, and Ronald came with him to help with translation. Bette was at a meeting when they arrived. She hated meetings. She is not a chatterer, and she used to be irritated by the endless argument and bickering and repetition that went on at most Communist branch meetings. She came home that evening at about eleven or so, and when I tried to talk to her, she simply shook her head and said no, not one word. She had had enough talk that evening to last her the rest of her life and she would not listen to a word more, and off she stormed to bed. The following day, when I told her that I had sat until two o'clock in the morning talking to Sartre, she almost burst into tears. Why hadn't I told her? I don't think she ever completely forgave me.

We talked and talked. Sartre told me about his experiences in the French Resistance. He was with the philosophers' section of the Resistance, and while in most other sections of the Resistance there were traitors, there had never been a traitor in the philosophers' section. We talked about the party, about the Soviet Union, and what the future might bring. He was far more pessimistic about America than I was. He said he had the feeling here of night closing in. I knew what he meant. It was only the beginning of the six years of terror that overtook America, but already the smell of it was in the air.

When the truth about the Holocaust began to emerge, Clifton Fadiman made the suggestion in print that Germany be destroyed, root and branch, its population either executed for crimes or scattered across the earth, an iron fence built around Germany, and on the fence, signs proclaiming HERE LIES GERMANY, EXECUTED FOR CRIMES AGAINST THE HUMAN RACE. Sartre wanted to know whether a man of Fadiman's importance had actually made such a statement. Even in occupied France, such a thought would be inconceivable — or so he said. I told Sartre that a Red Army colonel who came to our apartment not long ago, and who had fought in the defense of Leningrad and lost his mother and two brothers in the battle for that city, exhibited the same disbelief of Fadiman's statement. Sartre was trying to understand America and Americans — and found it to be no easy task. I must say that I always found it equally difficult to understand the French.

We talked about the Russians and the Red Army colonel's reaction to Fadiman's statement. Sartre said that there were great depths of compassion in the Soviets, but also a streak of peasant cruelty. He didn't think that we in America understood the European or Russian peasant. Our farmers were not the equivalent, and perhaps that streak of peasant cruelty would cause great agony to the Soviet Union. At the same time he, like me, rejected the horror stories that were told against Russia, the stories of imprisonment and injustice and total disregard for the rights of anyone who opposed Stalin, stories unhappily proved true.

But Stalin was no great presence in our thoughts. I was far more interested in what was happening in America, and when the people at *The Daily Worker* asked me to go to Chicago, at my expense and without pay, to cover the strikes that had overwhelmed the city, I cheerfully agreed. Bette was hardly so cheerful. I had been working on a book about John Peter Altgeld, the governor of Illinois who, in the late nineteenth century, had freed the anarchists imprisoned after the disgraceful Haymarket affair; now I put it aside. She argued that I was being used unmercifully, and I agreed that I was being used, that I knew I was being used, and I felt it was entirely proper that I should be used. We still lived from month to month. We paid our bills, but we had no cushion of money put aside. I was a free-lance writer in a world that was building wall after wall against people of the left. Didn't I understand that?

I knew it and I understood it, but my fault was that I was a romantic. I had been one all my life; everything was an adventure. Even as a kid, in all the misery of my childhood, I found each day an adventure. One day, in the time before I stopped drinking, I was getting drunk with that wonderful woman and labor leader Elizabeth Gurley Flynn, and she told me how she used to wake up each morning saying to herself, "Today, perhaps, will be the day of the new world." I understood that. I was like that — expecting new wonders to unfold. That was why I could drop everything and take off for Chicago. A dozen times, if not for my wife's enduring patience and love, our marriage would have been shattered.

I spent a week in Chicago, covering strikes. It appeared that the whole country was on strike, thousands of steel workers and auto

workers — and workers in dozens of other industries — an explosion of all the pent-up restraint of the war years. I slept in homes of
left-wing workers, talked to them, ate with them; I had forgotten this
life. Oh, how easily one forgets how it is to be poor! How easily one
rationalizes! I had never worked in one of these great industrial plants;
I had worked since childhood, but not this kind of work. I roamed
around Chicago and I smelled Chicago and I tasted it, and maybe I
began to understand it somewhat. I learned a lot of things. It was
cold and bleak and miserable, and I walked in the picket lines and
wrote down what the workers faced and what they said; but always
I was the observer. This was still a time when steel was king and
America was the great steel maker of the world, and the struggles of
the men who made steel against Republic Steel and U.S. Steel and
Inland Steel and Bethlehem Steel were struggles against giants. I had
written the story of the great Republic Steel massacre for a book
Simon and Schuster was publishing, and here was history repeating
itself.

I came home and faced the fact that I had to earn a living. Bette
also pointed out to me that we had a large apartment, the rent of
which had to be paid, a small daughter, and that sooner or later the
world would know that I was a Communist and that every door
might well be closed to me. I must mention that during the years
before *The Last Frontier* and *Freedom Road* made me a sort of
household name among book readers, I had a pile of at least thirty
unsold short stories. After *Citizen Tom Paine* was published, there
was a constant demand for my stories. By now, every one of them
had been sold, but my new novel, *The American,* would soon be
ready for publication, and it was a choice of both the Literary Guild
and the Book Find Club. I had no fears about making a living, and
even if it did come out that I was a Communist, no publisher had
ever rejected a manuscript because the author was a Communist. If
publishers ever took that course, it would do away with so large a
chunk of current American literature that the notion was unthinkable.

I quieted Bette's fears, but she had better instincts about the unthinkable than I did, and only a couple of years later, Clark M. Clifford, special counsel to President Truman, found himself before a
congressional committee, pleading that when he purchased fifty copies

of *Citizen Tom Paine* and handed them out as gifts to his friends, he did not know that he was spreading Communist propaganda or that *Citizen Tom Paine* was a Communist book. This pitiful lunacy and self-degradation were just around the corner. How could I anticipate them?

Oh, no, none of that was conceivable yet. Now, we needed time out, time to think and to know each other again, and with Rachel and Hana Masuda, we took off for Maine. I had never touched base before with Maine or the Adirondacks or any of those places where the superrich resorts were located. But here we were in one of them, brought by a comrade whose very wealthy father had an interest in the place. We spent a month there, and it was a wonderful, peaceful interlude before the storm broke, the last such stretch of peace and quiet we were to know for many years. We had a little cottage to ourselves, we ate very good food at the central dining room, and we sat in front of a fire at night, talking sometimes and sometimes just staring at the flames. I knew just a very little then about sitting with quiet. It was something I had to learn. Years before, in the first year of our marriage, Bette and I had climbed Hunter Mountain in Greene County. On top of the mountain, a ranger manned a fire tower through the dry months, alone most of the time, and we asked him how he endured the solitude. He answered very simply that sometimes he would sit and think and other times he would just sit.

We canoed. Bette and I are a good canoe team, and we spent some of the happiest hours of our lives in a canoe, and a few years after this I ran a rocky stretch of the Delaware River that few had ever run before, a mile of hard rapids that simply lifted me up to the sky in my triumph over the white water. Now, here in Maine, we canoed almost every day, taking picnic lunches with us, exploring a river that ran into the lake, sitting quietly in the canoe, and watching moose and deer and black bear.

The party was determined that I should not go soft or be lured by the trappings of success. It was decided that I should be one of some ten party members to be sent to the party training school. The school was located in a small hotel on the shore of the Hudson River near Beacon, and the course was three weeks. I would be able to go home for weekends, but it still meant that I would be separated from my family once again.

With all that, I couldn't resist the thought of a Communist Party
training school, a title both ominous and enticing, depending on how
far to the left or the right you stood. There was study and discussion,
ten hours a day of lectures, seminars, and study. We studied economics, both capitalist economics and Marxist economics; American history, world history, philosophy, the history, structure, and function
of government, the origin of cities, classes, and nations, and of course
the forces that had led us into World War One and World War Two.
It was three weeks of study such as I never would have believed
possible. Some of the most famous college professors and scholars of
the time lectured to us. There was nothing secretive about the place.
People came and went quite openly, professors from Harvard, Yale,
Cornell, MIT. One came from the West Coast. Distinguished lawyers, economists who challenged us to poke holes in their thinking,
trade union leaders, and Communist Party organizers.

The students, two women, the rest men, were, with the exception
of myself, all involved in the trade union movement — most of them
workers in auto, meat packing, mining, and steel, all of them, except
the women and me, former enlisted men, all out of the army — no
navy — and all of them between twenty-six and thirty-two years old.
There were two black men, one of them, Abe Lewis, a veteran of
both the Spanish Civil War and World War Two. The other veteran
of both wars was a man named Irving Goff, who had led a detach-
ment of guerrillas behind the fascist lines in Spain, a handsome, remarkable man whose adventures would make a fascinating book.
He and I became close friends — a good friendship that lasted until
I left the party. The other close friend I made there was a handsome
Irishman, Jack White, an auto worker from Detroit. Like Goff, he
was an extraordinary and again a romantic figure. Together with
Abe Lewis, they were three of the most unusual men I have ever
known. Lewis had the kind of mind I had never encountered before.
He was illiterate, and he could not conquer his illiteracy, but his
memory was monumental. He remembered and could repeat every
word of every lecture. He knew whole books that had been read to
him, every word, every page, and we saw sufficient evidence of that.
He had been a political officer in the 15th Battalion of the International Brigades in Spain, and his Spanish was fluent.

The person in charge of the school was an old Communist whom
we called Pop Mendel. Whether that was his real name, I don't know,

nor did I ever learn his first name. He was in his seventies then, so his memory and experience went far back — back indeed to the day of Eugene Debs and the founding of the socialist movement in America. He lived and died secure in the knowledge that we would, to paraphrase the British hymn, build Jerusalem in our own sweet and pleasant land.

We were romantics; like a priesthood, we were dedicated to the brotherhood of man — as we saw it — with no knowledge and no prescience of what would be revealed about Stalin and the Soviet Union. The lies and slanders spread about us were so many, so vicious, and so patently untrue that we had no way of winnowing out the truth about Russia and Stalin from the mass of manufactured indictments of Communism. As far as the party was concerned, we were not deceived; we accepted its failings, just as many good and brave priests of the Catholic faith who had dedicated themselves to the struggle for freedom in Central and South America, not shaken in their faith by the safe priests who denounce them, have accepted the denunciation and brushed it aside for a higher truth.

Of course our position was tainted and flawed — and it became increasingly tainted and flawed. We were not educated to an open mind; we were drilled in facts as the party saw such facts, and while the party position was often brilliantly right, again and again it was brilliantly wrong; and ironclad obedience to the party position wreaked havoc in circles where the party had been respected and honored. I had become a sort of priest, and it would take a great deal of pain and suffering and some time in prison before I learned that you cannot buy freedom by constricting freedom. My writing would suffer, but this party to which I had pledged my wits and my energy would suffer even more, and throughout the world, millions would suffer.

All through those strange years I spent as a member of the party, a battle went on among writers, and looking back with whatever small wisdom age brings, I am filled with a kind of sadness. It should not have been. The division of these talented men and women of good will into Stalinists and Trotskyites was one of the great cultural tragedies of the time. For the very most part, writers are gentle and sensitive creatures, observers of a world that is, at least in part, alien.

They long for some kind of acceptance and approval so desperately that they allow themselves to be used by the left and the right, casting aside the knowledge that we are a brotherhood and a sisterhood without which this bloody and senseless world would be a good deal less civilized than it is. We are not our enemies, and when some writers defended the Soviet Union and the others castigated it we should have turned to discussion and argument, not to hatred and the destruction of one another — because in that mutual destruction were planted the seeds of ideological war and terror.

I remember Joe North telling me of meeting Theodore Dreiser on Fourth Avenue one day and, seeing tears in Dreiser's eyes, asked him what awful thing had happened. Dreiser replied that he was unaware of the tears; he had walked up from the Bowery and seen the wretched, the defeated, and the homeless, and he was simply thinking of man's cruelty to man. How could such a man be slandered and reduced in character because he was a member of the party?

Well, we were equally righteous, and nothing much good ever comes from righteousness and orthodoxy. My head was exploding with some sort of knowledge, and I was trying to live a normal life with my wife and my two-year-old daughter. And now, the new Rumanian ambassador, a diplomat of the new socialist Rumania, invited a group of us, party writers, most from the staff of *The New Masses,* to join him for lunch. He chose Berkowitz's Rumania, on Allen Street on the Lower East Side, as the place for the luncheon, and he asked us to meet him there. Six of us, led by Sam Sillen, a delightful long-time party member and then professor of English literature at New York University, assembled on the sidewalk in front of the restaurant, waiting for the ambassador to appear.

Promptly at half past twelve, a big black Cadillac drew up, and a smiling, pudgy man stepped out and greeted us. In a heavy accent but with a good command of the language, he introduced himself. It was one of those unusually hot spring days, and since the restaurant was air conditioned, he suggested that we go inside. Sam pointed to the driver, who sat in the car. As well as I can recall, the dialogue went somewhat like this:

SAM: You can park right here with your diplomatic plates. Tell the driver so that he can join us.

AMBASSADOR: Driver is all right.

SAM: Will he join us?

AMBASSADOR: He is driver. Why should he join us?

SAM: It's hot and miserable out here. Why can't he join us?

AMBASSADOR: He is just a driver.

SAM: He's a workingman. We're a party of the working class. How can we go in there and eat and leave him hungry here outside?

AMBASSADOR: I don't understand you. He's my chauffeur. What has he got to do with our discussion?

We all stood firm behind Sam in our own idea of democracy and equality, and finally the ambassador gave in and asked his bewildered chauffeur to join us for what became a very awkward luncheon. But the feeling that we had saved him from two hours in a black car in 85-degree heat sustained my sense of virtue — until I repeated the story to Bette that evening. She shook her head and said that she simply did not believe me. Nobody, she said, could be that witless. And not the ambassador — she meant our group.

By being democratic? I demanded. Rumania was now a Communist country. Was it too much to expect the ambassador of a Communist country to have some sense of democracy, equality?

She spelled out her answer. In the first place, the ambassador was a European. What we might think of as democracy did not even exist in European thinking — certainly not in Rumania, Communist or not. And if we had a chauffeur, would I take him to every luncheon meeting? Would I ask him to eat with me? Why doesn't Hana, our Nisei housekeeper, eat with us? And so forth and so on. I sulked and muttered my various arguments, none of them very substantial. I recalled a story I had sold to *The Saturday Evening Post* years before. In it, I had a farm wagon with two horses hitched in tandem. *The Saturday Evening Post* had a large rural circulation in those days and they must have received five hundred letters explaining that two horses were never hitched in tandem, but always side by side. Instead of admitting that I didn't know beans about how a two-horse wagon team should be hitched, I burrowed into the history of horse-drawn vehicles like a madman, trying to find some justification for tandem hitching in the nineteenth century. I found none, just as I found no arguments to convince Bette. Since I was married to her and very much in love with her, I swallowed my lesson in self-righteousness and then walked head on into my next one, the tables turned this time.

I had written a piece about a meeting I had addressed in Boston, and in it I described "a mixed group of boys and girls, white and Negro." The piece was for *The Daily Worker*. I had dropped it off but it was not printed that day nor the following day, and the day after that I was called downtown to face three of the editors and to undergo a process the party called "charges." I was being brought up on charges of "white chauvinism."

Why? Well, that was something I wanted to know. What had I done? I had no recollection of having written or done anything that smacked of white chauvinism. They hastened to enlighten me. I had referred to Negro boys and girls as boys and girls. Any reference to a Negro as a boy or a girl was chauvinist. The incredible reasoning — if one can call it that — behind this was that for generations of servitude, black slaves had been addressed as *boy* and as *girl*.

They wanted to know whether I understood this and realized what I had done. I said no. I said that it sounded to me like utter nonsense, and that for generations and even now, white servants were addressed as boy and girl, and I didn't see why a Negro could not be a boy or a girl. What are they?

Youths.

I dislike the word as a noun. Boys, girls, teenagers, kids, adolescents, high school kids, youngsters — there were enough words to describe the time between puberty and adulthood. Why youths?

It has dignity. It's a part of the search for dignity.

Bullshit. I told them that it was absolute bullshit, and that it made no sense, that *youth* did not pronounce easily and would never become a common word as a noun. I was slipping in deeper and deeper, and I was informed that this blank spot in my thinking demonstrated how poorly I understood white chauvinism, and if I could not accept the decision of the party on this usage, they would have to bring me up on charges for expulsion from the party.

I protested that they were kidding. They had to be kidding. To expel me from the party because of this silly disagreement on the use of a word?

Not the word. The failure to understand the depths of white chauvinism.

In retrospect, I ask myself why I didn't say "Expel me and the hell with it!" But retrospect has no validity, and this was 1946, not 1990, and as crazy as this moment might have been, this was the party of

Bill Foster and Big Bill Haywood and Elizabeth Gurley Flynn, the party that had organized the French Resistance and fought the Nazis to the death and taught the world a new lesson in courage and honor, the party that had created the Abraham Lincoln Brigade and never stinted at the price placed on freedom. No, damn it — let them be as loony as they wished about words — they were not going to expel me; and so I agreed that I would work on this problem and see the error of my ways.

And then it was May 1, 1946, and there had never been such a May Day for the left, not before then nor since. The veterans, recently discharged, wore their uniforms, thousands upon thousands of men and women in uniform, so many that the uniformed section of the parade marched like an Army Day parade, ranks of sailors, soldiers, marines, nurses. The group I was with, teachers, writers, artists, lawyers, and physicians, numbered over eleven thousand; and the number of paraders, as we counted them, was over 150,000, and when they packed Union Square, cheering left-wing and Communist leaders and speakers, one would have said that the future of the left in America was extremely bright.

And of course they would have been wrong.

7

IN DECEMBER OF 1945, I had received a letter from Dr. Edward K. Barsky, asking me to join the executive board of the Joint Anti-Fascist Refugee Committee. Since January 1939, when the combined forces of Francisco Franco, Adolf Hitler, and Benito Mussolini overthrew the legal Spanish government, bringing the Spanish Civil War to a finish, I had refused no requests for funds or speaking that might help either the survivors of the Abraham Lincoln Brigade or the Spanish Republican exiles. I was deeply involved emotionally in the Spanish struggle, and filled with guilt for not volunteering to serve in Spain. I considered Dr. Barsky's invitation an honor, and I replied enthusiastically that I would be honored to join his board.

Ed Barsky was a brilliant surgeon. He was, I think, forty-eight years old when I met him, a lean, hawklike man, handsome, commanding, evocative in appearance of Humphrey Bogart, a heroic figure who was already legend. When he was a young man, his skill was recognized, and he embarked on a glowing career, at the College of Physicians and Surgeons, an internship at Beth Israel Hospital, postgraduate year in Frankfurt and Vienna, pathology in Paris, and then a burgeoning practice in New York City. In 1937, he volunteered as a surgeon in Spain where, more than a decade before the United States Army followed his lead, he devised what amounted to the MASH unit, the mobile army surgical hospital. He based it on a truck, equipped with an operating room, that could be moved close to the front lines, and thereby deal with a wounded man almost minutes after he was struck. With this, Dr. Barsky reorganized the medical service of the Republican forces, set up an ambulance service, and managed to begin the organization of a flow of medical supplies from New York to Spain.

When Spain fell to Franco, Dr. Barsky returned to private practice in New York, but he could not and would not sever his connection with the Spanish Republicans, so many of whom had escaped Franco by crossing the Pyrenees into southern France, and as soon as the war in Europe ended, Dr. Barsky went to Toulouse and arranged for the purchase of an abandoned convent, which would then be turned into an excellent hospital. Arrangements were made with the Unitarian Universalist Service Committee to operate the hospital and to distribute food and medicine among the Spanish refugees. But the funds had to be raised here in America, and under the aegis of the Joint Anti-Fascist Refugee Committee, a fund-raising movement was begun, which we called the Spanish Refugee Appeal.

Thousands and thousands of Americans sympathized with the cause of Republican Spain. Alone, backed only by the volunteers of the International Brigades, the Spanish Republicans fought the armies of Hitler and Mussolini, as well as Franco's North African regiments. They fought in the cause of all mankind, as the world would soon discover when Hitler attacked Poland, but in 1937 and 1938, they fought alone. Neither Roosevelt nor Churchill would raise a hand to help them; then as now, the label of Communism was pasted onto Republican Spain, and since Hitler could have been stopped and hurled back in Spain, the world paid a terrible price for protecting fascism against the illusion of Communism.

But here in America, the hearts of thoughtful people went out to the Spanish cause, and when we asked for money, they gave us money. It was a unique fund-raising operation. Except for one woman, a remarkable and saintly woman named Helen R. Bryan, and a secretary, another fine woman named Rita Malone, no one who worked with the appeal took one penny from the funds that were raised; and these two women who ran the office were paid only a pittance. It was not hard to find the funds we needed. Eleanor Roosevelt gave us money; Mrs. Herbert Lehman, the wife of the governor of New York, gave us money; Lucille Ball, the brilliant comedienne, collected thousands of dollars for the appeal. Vincent Sheehan, the journalist and author, became a pillar of support to our appeal, as did John Mc-

Manus, president of the Newspaper Guild. The names of our supporters and contributors read like pages out of *Who's Who*. Olin Downes, Jose Ferrer, Ruth Gordon, Stella Adler, Fritz Mahler, Bishop Lewis O. Hartman, Elmer Rice, Moses Soyer, Raphael Soyer, Dr. Ernst P. Boas, Leonard Bernstein, Stewart Chaney, Donald Ogden Stewart, Mark Van Doren, Van Wyck Brooks — and I could go on and on. I say nothing about the political views of these people; I say simply that they gave money to the Spanish Refugee Appeal; and I make a point of this because it determined the next chapter in my life.

A process had begun in the United States as alien to our past history as Hitler's National Socialism. It began with President Truman's executive order requiring that all people working in the federal government in nonelective posts take a loyalty oath, swearing that they were not and had never been members of the Communist Party. Taking this oath opened one to the accusation that one was lying, and thereby subject to the severe federal punishment for perjury. Refusal to take the oath was tantamount to admission of membership in the party and thereby cause for dismissal. There has been endless speculation as to the reason for this action on Truman's part, the most frequent being his expectation, now that we had the bomb, of some sort of armed conflict with the Soviet Union, as one by one the bonds that had united us during the war crumbled.

Regardless of Truman's reasons, what followed during the next several years was directly the result of the loyalty oath procedure he had instituted. The process caught fire, and not to be outdone by the Feds, the state governments climbed onto the bandwagon, and then the city governments, and then the schools — hundreds of fine teachers were driven from their posts — and then public hospitals, public universities, and then the film industry and the publishing industry, and still there was no end to it. The punishment was not, as in Germany, death and the concentration camp; it was instead loss of one's job, blacklist in one's profession, and, very frequently, professional destruction and the inability ever to work again at one's profession; and the result was the kind of terror this country had never seen before or since those six years from 1946 to 1952.

Two of the instruments of this terror, but by no means the only instruments, were the House Committee on Un-American Activities, headed at that time by John S. Wood, and the Senate committee headed by Senator Joseph McCarthy. The House committee, set up in 1938, spent practically all of its postwar existence in a fraudulent, hysterical battle against the whole progressive left in America. Guilt by association had come into our legal system in 1940, with the Alien Registration Act, and following this piece of semilegality, in 1946 the United States Chamber of Commerce began publishing lists and reports that alleged Communist influence in various areas of American life. Lest one consider Truman's action small potatoes compared with what followed, it must be noted that his loyalty order covered two and a half million civil servants, and the Taft-Hartley Labor Act of 1947 required all trade union leaders to take oaths that they were not Communists.

It was within this situation that a process server sounded our doorbell and handed me a subpoena that read as follows:

BY AUTHORITY OF THE HOUSE OF REPRESENTATIVES OF
THE CONGRESS OF THE UNITED STATES OF
AMERICA

To the sergeant at arms or his special messenger:

You are hereby commanded to summon Mr. Howard Fast, a member of the executive board of the Joint Anti-Fascist Refugee Committee, to be and appear before the Un-American Activities Committee of the House of Representatives of the United States, of which the honorable John S. Wood is chairman, and to bring with you all books, ledgers, records, and papers relating to the receipt and disbursement of money by or on account of the Joint Anti-Fascist Refugee Committee or any subsidiary or subcommittee thereof, together with all correspondence and memoranda of communications by any means whatsoever with persons in foreign countries. The said books, papers, and records demanded herein are for the period from January 1, 1945, up to and including the date of this subpoena, in their chamber of the city of Washington on April 4, 1946, at the hour of 10 A.M., then and there to testify touching matters of inquiry committed to said committee; and he is not to depart without leave of said committee.

Herein fail not, and make return of this summons. Witness my hand and the seal of the House of Representatives of the United States at the City of Washington, this 29th day of March 1946.

John S. Wood, chairman

It was the first subpoena I had ever received, and I read it most carefully, noting with some amusement the curious language in which it was composed. I had not the slightest notion at that time what a congressional subpoena might imply, but I think I realized immediately that to subject the hundreds of good people who had given support and money to the Spanish Refugee Appeal to the questioning and vicious bullying of this hateful committee (it had already made its mark and reputation) was unthinkable, and to subject them to imprisonment — which, as I learned, a congressional committee can impose — was totally beyond the bounds of decency. There was not for a moment any question in my mind as to how I would respond to the subpoena; and I was even more irritated that they had chosen my wife's twenty-ninth birthday for their wretched hearing.

I called Dr. Barsky, and he told me that he was calling a board meeting immediately. Unfortunately, I had a speaking date for that evening that I could not break, so I told Ed Barsky that however the board voted, I would under no circumstances agree to turning over the records to the Wood-Rankin Committee, and he should record my vote in that manner. He said that there would have to be a discussion, and I told him that however the discussion went made no difference to me.

Bette, being a familial part of receiving the subpoena and listening to my telephone conversation with Ed Barsky, agreed completely with my position but was understandably nervous. What would it entail? What could the punishment amount to? I called Emanuel Bloch, who would one day be the attorney for the Rosenbergs and whom I knew, and Manny informed me that it could be anything from a fine to a year in prison. But, he hastened to assure me, no one goes to jail for contempt of Congress; it simply isn't done; and while we might get a whacking big fine, our people can certainly raise the money to pay it.

That was reassuring. Bette was and is indifferent to money. We had no notion as to how large the fine might be, but she said that she didn't care if we had to beg, borrow, and plead, so long as there was no question of prison. I hooted at the very notion. I was by no means indifferent to the heightened atmosphere of terror, but I felt that since no one employed me and since I lived by income from my books, for the moment I was at least economically safe.

My new novel, *The American,* the story of Governor Altgeld of Illinois, had just been published and was a selection of the Literary Guild and took its place on the best-seller lists. A flow of foreign translation contracts poured in, and my feeling of a sort of untouchability was marred only by a political cast to the local reviews. Was Fast writing as a Communist? I had never advertised my membership in the Communist Party. "Tendentious" began to appear in the reviews. On the other hand, the Book Find Club also selected it, and I assured Bette that regardless of this curious moment in history, the United States did not put its writers in prison. I was one of the leading writers of the time, my books had already sold millions of copies, and if my name was not a household word, it was widely known and respected. Clark Clifford had not yet whimpered to the committee that he did not know *Citizen Tom Paine* was Communist propaganda when he sent copies as gifts to fifty of his friends, but on the other hand, as Bette reminded me, Thoreau had gone to prison.

Very well, Bette decided, since we're not to worry, we'll take Rachel and Hana with us and make a sort of holiday out of it. Bette and I had not been to Washington since our invitation to the White House, and we felt it was time to see it again and to prowl around the Smithsonian and the art galleries. It was no surprise to me that the board of the Joint Anti-Fascist Refugee Committee agreed that the list of our contributors must never fall into the hands of the Wood-Rankin Committee, and to allow that to happen would be, on our part, a heinous and totally dishonorable action. The board concurred in this decision; the vote was unanimous; and we began to make reservations for April 4 at the Shoreham Hotel in Washington. There were seventeen of us, not including Dr. Barsky, who had already testified of his unwillingness to produce the records, and we were all in agreement on a number of points, namely, that the Wood-Rankin Committee was not a legitimate function of government, that is, of democratic government, that it existed only as a star chamber, that its essential function was thought control. No one was there under any other pressure than the subpoena. It's worth noting that John McManus was not subpoenaed, even though he was a member of the board. The committee was not yet prepared to tangle with the Newspaper Guild.

Seven of the people there that day were women, one of them Helen Bryan, the rest middle-aged housewives and teachers. We had three physicians, a comic book publisher by the name of Leverett Gleason, the head of New York University's department of Teutonic languages, Professor Lyman R. Bradley, the producer Herman Shumlin, a Spanish businessman, Manuel Mangana, and two labor leaders on the shop level. I don't know how many of them were Communists. I could guess that five of them were, but that's only a guess. All of them were courageous and principled people, warm and emotional.

A little of my own testimony, taken from the record, will indicate how the questioning went; it was not too different from the testimony of the others, and it agreed with the mechanical formula used by the committee. Sitting that day in the room in the House Office Building where we were examined were John S. Wood, the chairman of the committee, who was a representative from Georgia, John E. Rankin of Mississippi, Peterson of Florida, John Murdock from Arizona, and Herbert Bonner from North Carolina. J. Parnell Thomas of New Jersey distinguished himself later by having his investigator compile a file on J. Edgar Hoover, for which Hoover returned the favor by digging around J. Parnell's garden and coming up with enough dirty stuff to put the congressman in the slammer for two years. Thomas, along with another ferocious red hunter, Karl E. Mundt of South Dakota, and Gerald W. Landis of Indiana, desperate to make a name for himself and fighting Wood and Rankin for the limelight, completed the committee. Most of the questioning was done by the counsel to the committee, Ernest Adamson, a tall, lean man who gestured and posed and whispered and snapped harshly, imitating every film DA he had studied.

The hearing itself was a sort of limited star chamber affair, in which one entered the committee room alone and sat through the hearing alone, with the right to go outside and consult one's lawyer if one so desired. The attorney for the entire Spanish Refugee Appeal group was Benedict Wolf, of the firm of Wolf, Popper, Ross and Wolf. Either by intent or by his poverty of invention, he did not advise the use of the Fifth Amendment to the Constitution, the right not to incriminate oneself.

When my turn came, I entered the hearing room and faced the House committee. The members were seated around an oval table. Adamson, the counsel, stood throughout the hearing. They offered me a chair at the end of the table. After I had identified myself and given my place of residence, the questioning, sometimes childish, sometimes ridiculous, began:

CHAIRMAN: Now, you know what you have got with you here, don't you? You can tell this committee what's in your pockets, can't you?

FAST: I certainly can.

CHAIRMAN: Have you got the books that are called for in that subpoena? Or in your pockets, or with you here?

FAST: I will answer that question by —

CHAIRMAN (interposing): No; just answer it, yes or no. Have you got them here or not?

FAST: I will have to answer it in this fashion —

CHAIRMAN: No; I am not concerned about your reading your statement. You know whether you have got them with you or not.

FAST (reading): Mr. Chairman, I have been served —

CHAIRMAN (interposing): No; I just told you we don't want to hear a written statement. We have got the statement here on the desk, copies of it that you are fixing to read.

FAST: You are asking me a question. I want to answer that question in this way.

CHAIRMAN: We want you to answer it yes or no. That is the simple way to answer it. Have you got them?

FAST (reading): I have been served with a subpoena requiring me to appear —

CHAIRMAN (interposing): I didn't ask you about that. You have already told us that you have been served with a subpoena.

FAST: I have to answer the question this way.

MUNDT: You can answer the question yes or no.

FAST: You are asking me a question, and I have the right to answer that question as I see fit.

CHAIRMAN: You can answer the question and then make whatever explanation you want to make. Have you got the books and papers here?

FAST: Will you permit me to answer the question?

CHAIRMAN: Yes. Answer it yes or no.

FAST: I am going to answer the question —

CHAIRMAN (interposing): No; we don't want you to read the statement. We want you to answer the question. You are a man of average intelligence at least. Let us not try to evade or hedge —

Well, I had the accolade of average intelligence pinned on me by a representative of our government. The statement chewed over — for this line of questioning went on and on ad nauseam — was a joint response agreed upon by the appeal group, as follows:

> Mr. Chairman, I have been served with a subpoena requiring me to appear and testify and to produce certain books, records, and correspondence of the Joint Anti-Fascist Refugee Committee in my possession, custody, and control. I individually do not have possession, custody, or control over any of the material requested in the subpoena which was served upon me. The books, records, and correspondence of the Joint Anti-Fascist Refugee Committee are in the possession, custody, and control of Miss Helen R. Bryan, the executive secretary of our organization, and she is the legal custodian of this material. Since I do not have either in my possession, custody, or control the books, records, and documents described in the subpoena, I am unable to comply with your order to produce them.

The willingness on the part of Helen Bryan to assume the whole burden for the committee was typical of this remarkable and courageous woman — and at that time no one anticipated that she would pay for her moral purpose with a year in a federal prison. Indeed, I believe that if we had had any premonition that imprisonment would result from this, no one of us would have allowed Helen Bryan to take the fall. In fact, our attorney had assured us that this would not be the case, and that no one of us would go to prison. Perhaps what happened eased our conscience, for with a couple of exceptions, we all ended up in prison. But that still lay ahead of me.

However, the House Un-American Committee was by no means finished with me. When I had been with the Office of War Information, doing the Voice of America, bits and pieces of information concerning one Josip Broz, also known as Tito, began to filter in. I asked the various intelligence services I had access to to get me whatever they could on Tito and the campaign in Yugoslavia. All sorts of fragments of information came to me, but almost none of it could be pinned down. I did, however, make a file of these bits, and one day, speaking to Lev Gleason, one of the Spanish Refugee Appeal board members, I mentioned the Tito material. That was in 1943, before I joined the Joint Anti-Fascist Refugee Committee, and it was Gleason who told me about the Spanish Refugee Appeal. He thought that possibly the money he and Dr. Barsky were raising had helped to get Tito out of France, where, it was said, he had been a refugee, and back to Yugoslavia. This because he recalled the name of Josip Broz. But Josip Broz was a common name in Yugoslavia, and the Josip Broz whom Barsky had helped was not Tito. However, Lev Gleason became very excited about a book on Tito and his war against Hitler. He assured me that if I wrote something of perhaps twenty thousand words, he would publish it as a soft cover book.

Back at the OWI, I told Joseph Barnes about Gleason's offer, and I explained that neither Gleason nor I would take payment; the money would go to Spanish relief. The question was whether I could use the information put together by army intelligence. Barnes was enthusiastic about the project, and working during what free time I had, I managed to write the book. It was the first thing of any significance to cover Tito and his resistance, and it made a small sensation at the time, and everyone thought it was a good blow struck for the war effort.

However, the assertion that Tito was aided by money raised by the Barsky people was an error, but the Un-American Committee, forgetting that Tito and his partisans had fought several German divisions to a standstill and thereby rendered invaluable service to the United States, and thinking only that money we raised might have helped a Communist, proceeded to subpoena me again, with a summons to appear in Washington on October 23, 1946, at three P.M. Back to Washington and once more the star chamber, but this time I alone had been subpoenaed, and the committee, I felt, was somewhat short of a quorum. Only Representative Wood was present of the elected committee, and with him, Ernie Adamson, counsel for the committee, and of course a stenographer.

I was angry as hell this second time, and in my thirties — I was thirty-two then — I was not known for restraint of either tongue or temper. I blew my top and called Mr. Wood a number of unpleasant names, all of which he removed from the record. I indicated that he was a contemptible and disgusting little man, an enemy of not only human rights but human decency. I am amazed that he and Anderson took my outburst so calmly, but they did, and I went on to say that I had consulted respected legal authorities and they had assured me that an expression of contempt for men like himself could not be construed as contempt of Congress, and that since contempt of Congress consisted of refusing to answer questions, I was in the clear. I also pointed out the smallness and maliciousness of serving me a summons at seven P.M. one day and demanding that I appear by three P.M. the following day, and I mentioned that the summons was undated and unsigned and therefore invalid. Nevertheless, I had appeared, and I wanted them to make note that my appearance was voluntary.

Again, I was amazed at how calmly they accepted my anger and annoyance. I had expected them to throw me out of the hearing room, but of course if they had done so they would have lost any power over me, and thereby given the court to me. Instead, Adamson began the hearing by recalling my testimony of a few months earlier. Was I still a director of the Joint Anti-Fascist Refugee Committee?

I was.

And hadn't I testified, in the statement I had left with them, that the Spanish Refugee Appeal was engaged in no other activity than relief?

I agreed with that.

ADAMSON: You wrote a book called *The Incredible Mr. Tito* or something?

FAST: *The Incredible Tito*. Yes, I wrote it.

ADAMSON: And in it, on page 14, you say that the Joint Anti-Fascist Refugee Committee supplied funds for Tito to return to Yugoslavia. Is that so?

FAST: It is more than three years since I wrote that book. I don't recall what was on page 14. I haven't looked at it lately. Do you have a copy?

ADAMSON: I just told you what was on page 14.

FAST: I would rather look at what I wrote than rely on you. I haven't seen it lately. I don't know why you asked me down here. I didn't even know that you or that creature [pointing to Wood] knew how to read. I thought it was because of my new book, *The American*. I thought that perhaps you decided that no one else but you had a right to the word.

I must mention here that the record differed considerably from what went on in that room. Wood reacted with rage and did some

name calling of his own, using four-letter Anglo Saxon words with a
facility that matched my own gutter training. The record printed none
of that, nor did it print more than part of the following (out of the
record): "You miserable bastard, you think you've got us by the short
hairs. Let me tell you something. It's the other way around. We don't
have to cite you —" (and in the record): "There's a hotel strike on in
Washington. No room. Think about it. It means that you'd have to
go back to New York and come down here again. How would you
like that?" (and not in the record): "We don't have to cite you for
contempt, buster. We can serve you a subpoena every day of the
year."

I wasn't sure that they could, and afterward I was told that they
could not have gotten away with it, but I didn't know then, so I
spread my hands and said something to the effect of my answering
their questions and let's get on with it and get it over. I go by my
own notes, since I no longer have the record. I did my best, explaining slowly and carefully, to make them understand that the Josip
Broz in our records was not Tito, and that Tito had never been either
to Spain or to France. Wood was still boiling. I suppose no one had
ever spoken to him in such a way before, and here was this miserable
commie insulting him as he had never been insulted, and he was
powerless to do one damn thing about it. I don't look back on the
incident with any sort of pleasure, nor do I regret it. It came out that
neither of them had read the book, giving it to some underling who
had circled the passage on page 14. It read as follows: "An agent of
the Joint Anti-Fascist Refugee Committee contacted Tito, and the
Committee provided funds and means for Tito's return to Yugoslavia."

That bit had come from Lev Gleason, who had been told by Dave
White, a veteran of the Abraham Lincoln Brigade, that he had met a
man named Josip Broz in Spain. To put together any kind of a reasonable story about Tito in 1943, with the scraps and fragments of
information available to me, was nigh unto impossible. I did the best
I could, and now, pressed by Adamson to reveal the source of my
information, I was in something of a dilemma. If I said that it had
been collected at the Office of War Information with the permission
of Elmer Davis, they would call Davis before them. They loved important names and the publicity that came from those names, and

they would not hesitate to call Davis or anyone else from the OWI. So I fudged my answer, referring only to bits and pieces of information I had picked up by talking to people and by reading the newspapers. I suggested that if they had any doubts about the Josip Broz in France not being Tito, they should call the Yugoslav embassy and have it confirmed.

At that point, they appeared to realize that this inquisition would bring them nothing of consequence, and they dismissed me.

At the time of this second hearing, we had already been voted in contempt of Congress by the House of Representatives, and after being formally indicted by a grand jury, we learned that our trial date was set for June 13, 1947. The contempt charges were presented to the House on April 16, 1946, only nine days after the whole board had been questioned, and only a few brave voices in Congress spoke out against the Un-American Committee. Representative Vito Marcantonio led the movement in Congress in our defense, but I think Representative Emanuel Celler of New York put the situation in the best light. These are part of the congressman's remarks, as taken from *The Congressional Record* of April 16, 1946:

Mr. Speaker, we are making history, regrettable history, in finding innocent people guilty of contempt without trial, without jury, and without benefit of counsel. I believe we are turning our backs upon our glorious past if we pass this resolution. We thereby throw overboard the right of free speech, the right of security of one's property and person, and the right of castle.

If we pass this resolution, we pass up the American way of fair pla·· and embrace the way of unconstitutional procedure. I predict that our action will come back to plague us.

Why, if Tom Paine or Tom Jefferson or Andrew Jackson or Abe Lincoln were alive today, they would, I believe, run afoul of this Un-American Activities Committee. The radicalism of these patriots would not, I believe, sit well upon the stomachs of some of the members of this Committee.

Many years ago, Tom Paine, whose pen proved mightier than the sword during the American Revolution, said: "Prejudice, like a spider, makes everywhere its home, and lives where there seems nothing to live on."

The persons whose names you have heard read, who are subject to

this resolution, struck at these spiders that weave their webs of prejudice and intolerance for the unwary and the ignorant. For that and
that alone, they are to be punished.

Mr. Celler went on to spell out what was happening to our country, but the small terror had already begun, and in Congress, people
were being very cautious, very careful that the record of their past
should not strangle them in an uncertain future. Our attorneys assured us that we had a good chance to have the charges dismissed
when we were put on trial, and that even if we were found guilty,
we could appeal right up to the Supreme Court. I took it all lightly;
this was part of the game; this was part of what I had signed up for.
I was not to be punished for being a Communist, but my punishment
was a challenge to all liberals and to labor, as well as to the Communists.

We went on living, raising our daughter, writing, cooking, laughing,
being followed, having our telephone tapped, and bit by bit all that
became our normal lives. Bette is and was an unflappable, brave, and
wonderful woman. We never had a real disagreement about what I
should do and what path I should take. She shared completely my
old-fashioned sense of what is honorable and what is dishonorable,
and she never drew back from the threat of punishment. We met
Shirley Graham, the remarkable black woman who would later become the wife of Dr. W. E. B. Du Bois. His *Black Reconstruction*
was a book I had used and treasured. Shirley had come to us with
no place to go. She had two sons, and one of them fell ill with pneu-
monia. Desperate, she took this small boy to hospital after hospital
in New York City, and at each hospital they were turned away. The
little boy died. Shirley turned to us in her agony and we embraced
her and cherished her — something that she desperately needed at
that moment in her life. This was in America, less than fifty years
ago.

Our large apartment on Central Park West became a refuge and a
stopping place for a good many people. When my younger brother,
Julie, was discharged from the service, we were able to set aside part
of the apartment for him and his wife. We were not at that time
marked as Communists, although the accusations were building up

and Howard Fast provided both Westbrook Pegler and Howard Rushmore, the two leading red baiters of the time, with abundant copy. It was also at that time that we met Mike Todd. Actually, I have no memory of how we met him or who introduced him to us, but for some reason beyond my understanding, he fell in love with Bette and me. When he was in New York, he came to our place at least two or three times a week, appearing for breakfast, lunch, or dinner. He was generous to a fault, and absolutely charming, with his Damon Runyon speech, which he cultivated most carefully. When he heard that Julie and his new wife, Barbara, were living in a corner of our apartment, he immediately offered them a wonderful town house in the sixties. It was part of a great limestone mansion and stood behind it, with a garden between the two, a unique arrangement, which I never saw duplicated in New York. Mike had a lease on both houses, and for the moment they were empty.

In his apartment, Mike had a splendid Marin watercolor, and when Bette admired it, he took it down from the wall and offered it to us. It was worth thousands of dollars, and though he was quite earnest in pressing it on us, we refused to accept it. Another time, he walked into my office when I was working on a story I hoped to sell to *The Saturday Evening Post* or to *The Ladies' Home Journal*, where Stuart Rose, one of the editors, was still willing to print me. Mike, after reading what I had written, asked me how much they would pay me, and when I said $1000, he sat down and wrote me a check for twice that amount, telling me it would be his next film. When I protested that he couldn't afford it and reminded him that he owed the government a million dollars in back taxes, he said to me, "Howard, when I'm broke, I'm not poor." When I was about to go on trial for contempt, Mike pleaded with me to let one of his friends in Washington fix it and get me out of the case. I explained that it was a matter of honor, and this he understood very well indeed. Another time, when I was scheduled to debate Arthur M. Schlesinger, Jr., at Yale Law School on the proposition that civil liberties existed in force in the United States, Mike insisted that he drive Bette and me to New Haven. He bought us a royal dinner at Stonehenge on the way up, and he listened to the debate with great interest. The vote, I must say, was against me. I lost.

It was around this same time that I met Nat Goldstone, who would

later — years later, after the witch hunt — become my film agent
and would put together the deal with Kirk Douglas that produced
Spartacus. Nat was involved in the production of a delightful musical
called *Bloomer Girl.* The lyrics were by Yip Harburg, whom we knew
slightly then, and the book was by two dear friends of ours, Dan and
Lilith James. My own first venture into the theater had taken place
years before, when, together with a young friend, Ray Barr by name,
I wrote a light musical comedy called *Four Bachelor Brothers,* which
we produced first in a summer theater and subsequently in the Barrs'
living room for Peggy Wood, then a reigning musical comedy star
and so dazzling a beauty that Ray Barr and I fell totally in love with
her.

Nat Goldstone, a wonderful Hollywood original, had homage done
to him in the musical *Gypsy,* with the song "Have an Egg Roll, Mr.
Goldstone," and Dan James was a descendant of Jesse James. Inter-
estingly, I knew two descendants of Jesse James who were party
members.

Sitting in on the rehearsals of *Bloomer Girl* was sheer joy for Bette
and for me, in particular because my avocation was the theater — I
should say, my great love — and in between novels and newspaper
work, I wrote a dozen plays. Some were never produced. One, called
The Hammer, I will write about in these pages. In later years, two of
my plays were produced at the Williamstown summer theater. My
play about Tom Paine would do seven weeks at Kennedy Center, but
that is years ahead of the moment I write about now.

Yet I must mention a play I wrote at the height of the witch hunt.
It dealt with the betrayal, by a colleague, of a man who worked at
the White House as a staff member, and it was called *Thirty Pieces
of Silver.*

Denied production here in America, *Thirty Pieces of Silver* was
produced in five European countries and became a sort of staple in
Australia, where the play had long runs in both Brisbane and Sydney.
Curiously, during the writing of these memoirs, I wrote to the Federal Bureau of Investigation, asking under the Freedom of Information Act for the files they had kept on me through the ghastly years
of the repression. They sent me more than eleven hundred pages, and
in these pages, there was mention of *Thirty Pieces of Silver.* They had
become aware of the play — which was published in book form in

England — from a European "informant," as they put it, and they asked for a copy of the play. Even though it was then running in three European theaters, their informants could find neither a copy nor an abstract. The FBI, as their record in my file states, then handed the problem over to the Central Intelligence Agency. After several weeks, this brilliant organization, which eats up money faster than our taxes can be collected, sent their memo to the FBI, admitting that they were unsuccessful in obtaining a copy of the Howard Fast play. It had meanwhile been copyrighted and published in the United States, but neither of these organizations — on whom, we are told, our security depends — thought of going to the Library of Congress, where the play could be had simply for the asking. So much for intelligence.

The witch hunt, the small terror, was under way, growing each day. In California, Ronald Reagan, president of the Screen Actors Guild, was secretly giving names of those of his members whom he suspected of being communists to both the FBI and the House Un-American Committee, and the way was being paved for the infamous Hollywood inquisition. It had come home to me some months earlier, and curiously it was brought home most sharply when Ruth Field's two-and-a-half-year-old daughter got herself lost. The Fields lived in the apartment next to ours. Leonard Field, Ruth's husband, was in the service, fortunately working at the Signal Corps unit in New York, and when I went overseas, both he and Ruth rallied around Bette, and Ruth became a dear friend of Bette's and of mine too. She was a delightful woman, a Christian Scientist whose brimming health seemed to bear witness to her belief. John Cheever worked with Leonard, and he was a frequent dinner guest at our home as well as at the Fields'. We were further knit by the fact that Ruth's younger daughter Kathie — she had two girls — was about the same age as our Rachel. Ruth and Bette went to the park each day with the three girls.

One day while Mary Ruth, Ruth's older child, was at school, Ruth and Bette went to the grocery store with Rachel and Kathie. They took their eyes off the little girls for no more than half a minute, and when they turned around, Kathie had disappeared. The next hour was surely the most terrible that Ruth had ever endured and almost as awful for Bette and me. Someone had seen Kathie go out of the store, alone, but after that, every trace of her disappeared. Ruth be-

gan to race along the adjoining streets while Bette ran home to get
me to help. Fortunately, my car was downstairs, parked close to the
house, and I took off from street to street, looking, questioning, becoming increasingly desperate, pleading with people to try to remember whether they had seen a little girl lost. I passed Ruth and Bette
several times, but they preferred to stay on foot. And then the first
bright thought of the day struck me: Why don't I go to the local
precinct station?

Which I proceeded to do, and there, in the lost child pen, was a
dirty but quite happy Kathie Field. For the most part, Kathie was
inarticulate. You do not get much specific information from a child
of two and a half; but what we did manage to get out of her was
this. She left the store, lost her sense of direction, began to run, stopped,
began to cry, was picked up by a woman, who soothed her, talked
about the store where her mother was shopping; she was then taken
to another grocery store, and since there was no sign of her mother,
she was given over to a group of interested citizens, one of whom
was a city trash collector. They decided that the trash collector, going
in the right direction, should drop her off at the precinct house; being
high up on his driver's seat, he could toot his horn on occasion and
the mother might just notice. When I picked her up at the police
station, the pen contained at least six lost kids, dirty but happy. The
thing that impressed Kathie most was her ride on the garbage truck.

At dinner that evening, I said to Bette how sad it was that a child
lost should evoke such visions of fear. There was horror, but we were
blessed that there was less horror than human decency and compassion. She agreed. It was important to remember that, so why didn't I
write something about it? After dinner, I sat down at the typewriter,
and by two o'clock in the morning, I had eleven pages. It had simply
poured out, a mirror to what that day had been for the Fields and
for us. I called it *A Child Is Lost* and the following day I brought it
to my literary agent, Elizabeth Otis.

I had hardly returned home when the phone rang. It was Elizabeth. She had read the piece and was absolutely overwhelmed. She
said it was one of those pure things which happen on rare occasions,
and she could sell it anywhere. She suggested that we sell it to *This
Week,* the *Herald Tribune* insert, which was syndicated nationally
and would pay the most money. I agreed, and then she said, "Howard, do you have a name to put on it?"

"What do you mean, name?"

"I mean we can't sell anything to a national magazine under your own name."

"I just don't believe you."

Or words to that effect. I believed her, and she didn't have to remind me that my name had been all over the newspapers since the hearing before the House committee. I knew it was happening and I knew it was coming, but that didn't make it any less of a shock. I had felt that as a writer I was to a degree invulnerable, no boss to fire me or discipline me. I was learning. I told Elizabeth sourly that she should use any name she desired, and she chose the name Simon Kent. So it was, *A Child Is Lost* by Simon Kent. But Elizabeth Otis was absolutely right in her estimation of the piece. *This Week* bought it immediately at the preposterous price she asked, and no sooner had it appeared than reprint requests began to come in to my agent. It became a small money machine, reprinted not only all over America but in England as well, and to cap it, a film offer.

Annie Laurie Williams, an intriguing middle-aged woman with a face and figure like Mae West and a mind like a steel trap, was the motion picture end of the McIntosh and Otis agency. She telephoned and told me to hold on to my seat: she had an offer from Louis B. Mayer to buy *A Child Is Lost* for $25,000, not at all a bad price for a night's work. Bette and I had spent the money earned by *The American* and funds were getting very tight. This $25,000 was a bonanza indeed.

We celebrated properly with dinner and champagne and continued to congratulate ourselves for the next few days, and then Annie Laurie telephoned and informed me that she had just spoken to Mr. Mayer's legal department, and they knew that Simon Kent was a pseudonym, and contracts could not be made out to a nonexistent person. They had to know the name of the author.

Suppose you tell them my name?

She sighed and asked me whether I understood what was going on in Hollywood. A witch hunt was under way there, and the whole film community was utterly shaken. The film community was polarizing, and two actors, Ward Bond and Ronald Reagan, were leading the attack on the liberals. The community was saturated with fear, and everyone was lining up to take sides, and one of the leaders of the anti-red, anti-liberal faction was Louis B. Mayer. He was becoming a fanatic on the subject, and Annie Laurie assured me that if she revealed my name as the author, not only would Mayer dump the project, but he might very well dump her in the bargain.

I suggested something else. I said that I would give her the power of attorney for this project, and as my agent, she should make the contract in her own name. She tried that, but the M-G-M attorneys still demanded the name of the real author, and then Mayer telephoned Annie Laurie again, raging at her this time that she had tried to "slide under his nose," as he put it, a piece of work by a man he hated more than anyone else on earth, a man who would never set foot in his studio again.

Annie Laurie waited for the next shoe to fall. She was almost sure that I had never met Mr. Mayer — nor did I ever — but then, who knew?

Howard Koch! As Annie Laurie told it, the name exploded from Mayer's lips. Howard Koch! It would take a long time, Mayer went on to say, for him to forgive her for trying to pan off Howard Koch's work on him. She pleaded with him, saying that it was not Howard Koch, but he would not listen. Howard Koch it was, and the deal was over. I never met Howard Koch, before or since.

The ridiculous, the foolish, the idiotic always accompanies the exercise of terror, but a sense of humor is thrust aside. Power people have no humor; otherwise, they'd laugh at themselves and their antics. Power and terror and humor don't make an agreeable trio; otherwise, Hitler and Mussolini would have been laughed out of existence before they embarked on their murderous careers.

On the other hand, as ridiculous as it may appear, the net was closing. No national magazine, no film — but hold on. I had sold *The Last Frontier* to Sidney Buchman at Columbia Pictures. I put through a call to him. The project had been shelved. Forever, as it turned out. You see, John Ford, the great director of that time, had been pleading with me to talk Buchman into allowing him, Ford, to direct *The Last Frontier*. He said, to quote him, "I'll direct it right out of your book, your dialogue and nothing else. No fucken screenwriter — no, sir. Right from the book." And he would have too, and it would have been a splendid film.

But then Columbia Pictures, which had bought the book for Sidney Buchman, was told by J. Edgar Hoover that no film was to be made from my book, whereupon Columbia shelved it. John Ford, furious, frustrated by a blacklist he had only contempt for, went to Warner Brothers, told them that the story was in the public domain, and then slipped my book to a screenwriter and told him to go ahead and do the screenplay. Neither honest nor decent, but Ford was not strong on those virtues, and the project went ahead. Meanwhile, Columbia Pictures obtained a copy of the screenplay, gave it to their lawyers with my book, and then slapped a hold on the completed film, with the prospect of a large and disgraceful plagiarism suit against Warner Brothers. Warner settled out of court, paying Columbia a huge sum of money and giving them a large piece of the completed film, which was released under the title *Cheyenne Autumn*. As far as I was concerned, my share of the booty amounted to nothing. After all, Columbia owned the book.

On September 19, 1946, Professor Frédéric Joliot-Curie and his wife, Irène, arrived in New York, and two days later, Captain Cécile Segal, a physician with the French armed forces, gave a small reception for the Curies at the studio of Moise Kisling, the French painter, in his apartment on Central Park South. Since we knew Captain Segal and had entertained her frequently, she invited Bette and me to the reception to meet the Curies. Madame Curie's English was not up to her charm, but Frédéric was fluent in English, and he and I, sitting in a corner of the big studio, had a long and intimate discussion. He had been told by Captain Segal that I was a Communist, and since both he and his wife were members of the French Communist Party, he felt that he could talk freely to me. He was a romantic figure, tall, lean, handsome, a gifted physicist who had manufactured weapons for the French underground during the occupation. Without quotation marks, I put down the essence of our discussion. I asked him about Russia and the atom bomb.

FAST: Is there any expectation that Russia will be able to make an atom bomb?

JOLIOT-CURIE: Oh, but they have.

FAST: You mean they have the bomb?

JOLIOT-CURIE: Of course. They have two bombs now, and their present production is five a month — that is, by the end of September they will have seven bombs, and in six months they will be producing over a hundred bombs a month.

FAST: Are you sure?

JOLIOT-CURIE: I have worked with them. I have seen the bombs. How could I be more sure?

FAST: And isn't this top secret? Aren't you trusting me with something I shouldn't know?

JOLIOT-CURIE: Why not? I think it is very good that you should know it, that everyone should know it.

FAST: Then why don't you hold a news conference and give it to the press?

JOLIOT-CURIE: But how? I have no right to speak for the Soviets. I have no proof. I will say that I have seen this with my own eyes, that I helped, but who will believe me? You are all so convinced that the Russians are primitives.

FAST: Well, I write for *The Daily Worker* now and then. Suppose we were to print this in *The Worker?*

JOLIOT-CURIE: Why not?

The following day, I sat down with Milton Howard, the editorial writer of *The Worker,* and John Gates, then one of the editors and later to be editor in chief. I told them what Joliot-Curie and I had discussed the day before, and asked for their thoughts on what to do. Certainly, it had to be made known.

We talked about it for a good while. It was hard to believe that this could be the case without the knowledge of the much-touted new Central Intelligence Agency, but none of us had much respect for intelligence agencies that eliminated from their membership most of the intelligent people of the country. At the same time, we recognized that for this to become a shouting headline in *The Daily Worker* would be a mistake. Such an earth-shaking announcement should not come from *The Daily Worker.* On the other hand, we could not ignore it, and we had a most serious responsibility to our country. What to do?

Shortly before this, in an attempt to make the paper more readable, the editors had installed a Broadway gossip column. It was written by Barney Rubin, a Spanish vet, a veteran of World War Two, and an old Broadway hand. The decision was that Rubin would give an account in his column of the reception and of my conversation with Frédéric Joliot-Curie, and since *The Daily Worker* was avidly perused by the powers that be, the substance would become widely known, to the Justice Department, the CIA, and others.

So it was done. Now in the way of this happening, in the intimate conversation of Joliot-Curie and myself, in the way of my asking for the facts before he itemized them, in the way the whole thing developed, I do not for a moment doubt that he was telling me the truth. Why should he have lied? And if he intended to bear false witness, why with me? Why not to some important reporter, some famous magazine writer, or a press conference? He was a great figure of world importance, one of the leading scientists in the international community, but he was not a publicity-directed person nor did he have interests in that direction. He had simply conversed with me.

How then do we account for the fact that three years later, on September 23, 1949, President Truman announced to his cabinet that "we have evidence that within recent weeks an atomic explosion occurred in the USSR"? Secretary of State Dean Acheson said that this must mean that the Russians have the atom bomb. "The calmer the American people take this, the better," said General Omar Bradley, chairman of the Joint Chiefs of Staff. "We have anticipated it for four years, and it calls for no change in our defense plans."

What is one to make of this? Was Joliot-Curie lying? Did the powers that be stop reading *The Daily Worker*? Or was Truman lying for his own purposes? I don't know. I can only say, if such be intelligence, heaven help us.

8

BY NO MEANS was it all *Sturm und Drang,* and I don't know of anything in life so satisfying and nourishing as the sense that you are doing what you were put on earth to do, fighting for things you believe, for the poor and the oppressed and against racism. It gives one a feeling of being, of consciousness, and of connection. This connection is very important; if one is an isolated bit of matter on earth, without reason or explanation, then one exists with pain and sorrow. We were never sorrowful, and by and large we laughed more than we wept, always aware that we walked a path we had chosen on our own. Never, never was there the slightest danger of the Communists in America effecting any real change in government. If we perish as a nation — as we may do, blundering into atomic destruction — it will be stupidity, not an enemy, that will do us in.

The FBI played silly games with us, and during those years from 1945 to 1952, the worst seven years of the small terror, untold millions of the taxpayers' dollars were spent following us, tapping our telephones, bugging our homes — every foolish trick that one might glean from patterning life after the worst of television, all of it led by a little Hitler whose name was J. Edgar Hoover, who lived on the edge of his own nightmarish substitute for reality.

I have already mentioned my FBI file, which Natalie Robinson, a gifted investigative writer, had persuaded me to send away for. The eleven hundred pages detailed every — or almost every — decent act

I had performed in my life. If I were to seek some testament to leave to my grandchildren, proving that I had not lived a worthless existence but had done my best to help and nourish the poor and oppressed, I could not do better than to leave them this FBI report. In those pages, there is no crime, no breaking of the law, no report of an evil act, an un-American act, an indecent act — and I was no paragon of virtue, and I did enough that I regret — but the lousy bits and pieces of my life are nowhere in those pages, only the decent and positive acts: speaking at meetings for housing, for trade unionism, for better government, for libertarianism, for a free press, for the right to assemble, for higher minimum wages, for equal justice for black and white, against lynching, against the creation of an underclass, against injustice wherever injustice was found, and for peace, and walking picket lines, and collecting signatures. These are what make up that brainless report.

Yet no one, apart from the liberal left, ever questioned the function of a police in a democracy, a secret police, who tormented the decent and allowed the criminals to turn our country into the most crime-ridden and drug-ridden nation on the face of the earth. My own file must have cost the American taxpayers at least ten million dollars, as near as I can calculate, and when you multiply that by the thousands of leftists they tracked, spied on, and bugged, you get a very large piece of change indeed. A friend of mine, a screenwriter named Ed Anhalt, was in Russia working on a big TV project, *Peter the Great*. The KGB had a man on him, day and night, and Ed became quite friendly with his tails. He asked one of them why he was being tailed, since he was a writer working on a Russian-American project. It made no sense. The KGB man agreed, and he explained to Ed that if the KGB did not ask for more money each year, their budget would be cut. But when the money was forthcoming, they had to use it, and that meant more operatives, and having an American film crew here in Moscow was a golden opportunity to use up the excess flesh.

I imagine it's no different in the FBI. Bette and I gave an endless series of fund-raising parties. Not only did we have a huge apartment, living room thirty-five feet by twenty, dining room thirty by twenty, a huge apartment for which we paid $165 per month, but we never said no, and if it was not the Spanish Refugee Appeal, it was the Save Willie McGee fund, for a black man wrongly accused and sentenced, or for *The Daily Worker,* or Clothes for the French Resistance Fighters, or a strike fund, or the starving coal miners in Appalachia.

There must have been a sprinkling of decent men in the FBI. On one occasion, on the day before we gave a large fund-raising party, I received a drawing in the mail with the legend: "This bastard is FBI. He's crashing your party. Throw him out." It was a good drawing, and when the FBI man turned up, he was immediately recognized. He left quietly; if there was one thing you could give the FBI points for, it was politeness — except when they were dealing with left-wing homosexuals. Then they turned vicious, frequently beating the homosexuals savagely.

There were good people everywhere, but quiet. (If I am quiet, I won't be noticed and they won't remember that I was once on the side of the angels.) As the witch hunt broadened, as the Hollywood inquisition began, the small terror grew. It was not Hitler's Germany, but it was certainly a made-in-America small-time imitation. Bette and I, going into the King Cole Room one evening, came face to face with the actor Paul Stewart, a very fine actor and a quite important one, and though he was a dear old friend, he looked me straight in the eye and then turned away, afraid to recognize us in the presence of the people he was with. I've never faulted anyone for being afraid — only a lunatic is without fear — but the greatness in a human being is his ability to conquer fear, and there was a short market in greatness during those years. There were good people. Roger Butterfield, a staff writer on *Life* magazine in its glory days, telephoned me one day and asked me to meet him at a midtown bar.

When I got there, he pledged me to silence regarding my source, and then told me that he had been in Henry Luce's office when Senator McCarthy asked Luce whether a certain man was a member of the Communist Party. Luce said that he had his own contact in the National Committee of the Communist Party, one of the ten top men in the party. Luce then dialed a number on his private phone, and when the call was answered, Luce said, "Hello, Ben?"

We never pinned down Ben's identity, or whether Ben was a false name or not, but Butterfield risked a good deal to give me this information. He specified to me that he had no use for Communism, but was sickened by what was happening to his country, and of course the infiltration of the party by FBI agents was no secret to anyone.

None of this interfered with the use of our enormous apartment, nor was it possible to check among the people new to us who was or was not an FBI agent. In the eleven-hundred-page report, the names of the spies and the nature of the fund raisers they attended were blacked out, and the rumor among us had it that they always came through with a nice cash contribution to the party, courtesy of the taxpayers.

One day in 1947, Lionel Berman of the Cultural Section called and asked whether Bette and I could put together a reception for the Venerable Tung Pi-wu, who was the first president of Mao's liberated China. Chiang Kai-shek was still scrabbling to keep his foothold in China, but ninety percent of the subcontinent was under the control of Mao. The Venerable Tung Pi-wu was here to talk at the United Nations.

We said yes. We always said yes. And we got on the telephone and began to call everyone we could think of: newspapermen, columnists, editors, book publishers, writers. There was no time to send out invitations, but in response to our telephoning, over sixty people turned up. The reception was called for six o'clock, and the only refreshment we provided was white wine. The Venerable Tung Pi-wu, a most elegant Chinese gentleman, dressed in a beautiful robe, sparkling eyes in a wise old face, and a long mustache, at least six inches on each side of his chin, appeared fifteen minutes before the invited Americans, and he brought with him two young Chinese diplomats, slender, good-looking young men whose English was excellent and who informed me that Tung Pi-wu would answer questions in Chinese and that they would translate.

The apartment filled up with men and women who were bubbling with curiosity — the first meeting for most of them with any representative of the new Chinese Communist government, and most of them were more than impressed by this courtly old gentleman in his splendid embroidered silk robe. He was like something out of an old Chinese screen drawing, standing so simply with his hands folded in his wide sleeves. He answered question after question with quiet grace, even Max Lerner's rude observation about Communism in one country, to which he smilingly replied, "Correction. Two countries."

Leonard Lyons asked somewhat facetiously about the place of gossip, to which Tung Pi-wu replied that no one loved gossip more than the Chinese. They gossiped endlessly.

It was over by seven o'clock, and by then everyone had left except Tung Pi-wu and his two young translators, and six friends of ours, two couples and two single men, all in the party. One of the translators asked about those who stayed, and I replied that they were all party members and old friends, and with that, the Venerable Tung Pi-wu smiled and in faultless English said that now that the press had departed, we could relax and speak English.

I had to know why, when his English was perfect, he had insisted on speaking Chinese. He explained that his dignity and the dignity of his country demanded that he speak his native tongue, and also, it gave him time to think about the questions and his answers. Now we flooded him with questions, all our pent-up curiosity about China and what was happening and when Chiang would be driven off the mainland.

While this went on, Bette drew me aside and pointed out that it was eight o'clock and the Chinese showed no sign of departing, nor for that matter did anyone else, and told me to ask them all to stay to dinner.

But there were eleven of us, I told her. We'd made no preparations. How were we to feed eleven people?

That was to be left to her. I was just to tell them that they must stay for dinner, an invitation everyone readily accepted. In the kitchen, Bette emptied three huge cans of pork and beans into an oversized clay pot that had served us well on many occasions. She then cut up a dozen frankfurters that we had in our fridge, mixed the pieces into the beans, spread thick brown sugar over the top, and then topped the casserole with strips of bacon. When it came out of the oven half an hour later, the good odor filled the apartment; and when our Chinese guests ate it, they declared it to be the best food they had yet eaten in America, a marvelous culinary achievement, and comparable to Chinese cooking at its best. With it, Bette served hot corn bread and cold beer. I think that if I had eaten it for the first time as an adult, I would have concurred with the Venerable Tung Pu-wu's assessment.

Of course, being married to a good cook is part of it. We loved these incidents, and if there was fear in our lives, there was also wonderful joy, excitement, and dear friends, and we delighted in keeping our door always open. Once Jessica Smith, the wife of the lawyer John Abt, asked us on very short notice if we could give a dinner for the officers of a Russian merchant ship. Russian cargo ships were still docking at Manhattan slips, and when the officers of this ship turned up, it was another wonderful evening. How Jessica Smith came to invite them, I don't really recall, but anyone and everyone turned up at our home. My books had become a world product, and *Freedom Road* was practically a text in the Soviet Union. It could be Paul Robeson one night, lifting my little daughter in his hands, rocking her back and forth as he softly sang "Water Boy" to her, and the next day Ben Gold, the veteran leader of the Fur and Leather Workers' Union.

The Joint Anti-Fascist Refugee Committee had obtained for counsel O. John Rogge, one of the leading lawyers at the Nuremberg trials, a man who had spent weeks looking into the naked face of fascism, who had listened for hours and hours to an itemization of the crimes of Hitler and the SS, who had seen with his own eyes the horrors of the concentration camps. Now he was faced with a growth in his own country of the same disgusting vine. What happened to him was a symptom of that time, for when he stepped forward and took on our defense, he gave up his future. It was one thing to defend a gangster, a rapist, a murderer — that was part of an attorney's work and quite proper — but to defend a Communist was indefensible. After all, hadn't Roger Baldwin, the virtuous founder of the American Civil Liberties Union, instructed his young lawyers to defend any and all who required a fair trial, whose civil liberties might have been violated, even Nazis, but under no circumstances to defend a Communist? (I must mention that in time Rogge regretted his courage and went over to the other side.)

Rogge was a tall, handsome, pleasant man, gentle in all his approaches, a good lawyer who presented above all a picture of total integrity. He was cheerful about our future, and he foresaw no possible circumstances under which we might be found guilty. Then, on March 31, 1947, the grand jury indicted us, the board of the Joint Anti-Fascist Refugee Committee, not only on a single count of contempt of Congress, the sentence for which could be only a year in prison, but on a second count of conspiracy, the punishment for which could be five years in prison — a total of six years in prison if we were found guilty on both counts.

That came as a terrible shock. The thought that one could be sent to prison for six years, not for a crime, not for breaking any law of the United States, but simply for refusing to name good people, some of them leading citizens of this democracy, who had engaged in a compassionate gesture toward the sick and wounded of the Spanish Civil War, had never occurred to me. It sank home now. I was nearly thirty-three years old; I would be almost forty when I got out of prison if they gave me the maximum sentence. Talking with Bette, I laughed it off. After all, I was Howard Fast. My books were being printed by the millions all over the world. They didn't put people like me in prison — in other countries possibly, but not in the United States of America. I don't think I convinced Bette of anything. She is a gentle, soft-spoken woman who had come from a sheltered middle-class background, greatly talented, but shy. I had not swayed her into joining the Communist Party; she came to that conclusion on her own and joined the party separately. She saw very clearly what was happening to me and what was happening to the world.

The trial date was set for June 11, 1947, in Washington, D.C., with Judge Alexander Holtzoff presiding. But Judge Holtzoff was so blatant in his anti-Communism, spewing hatred both orally and in print, indicating, if one followed his remarks to their logical end, that all Communists should be put to death without trial, that we petitioned for him to remove himself from the case. When he refused and ordered the trial to proceed, Rogge drew up a writ of mandamus, and by virtue of this, the Court of Appeals halted the trial on the day it began and ordered Judge Holtzoff to proceed no further and to remove himself from the case. The Judge Holtzoff syndrome was by no means uncommon; people worked themselves into hysterical rages of hatred against the Communist Party and the Soviet Union — and this was only two years after the Soviet Red Army had destroyed Hitler's forces and together with the Allies had wiped Nazism from the face of the earth. During the May Day parades of the next few years, the parade streets were lined with parochial school teenagers, carrying huge signs — obviously created by professionals — that read KILL A COMMIE FOR CHRIST. That was the atmosphere in which we were tried — and not as Communists, for none of us, not even myself or Barsky, was accused of being a Communist. We were so indicted by the media, who, like dogs sniffing a trail of blood, cast restraint and decency to the wind and played every lie and slander that had ever been invented about Communists.

On June 13, two days after Holtzoff had been removed from presiding, our trial began again under Judge Richmond B. Keech. Judge Keech was icy cold, totally unsmiling, and reasonably objective. As we, the members of the committee on trial, sat in the courtroom waiting for the proceedings to begin, Mayor James Curley of Boston was wheeled into the chamber for sentencing. Curley, who, in his later years, had exceeded the limits to which even your run-of-the-mill crooked politician can go, was now in poor health and in a wheelchair, and as he was wheeled before Judge Keech, he broke into tears and wept over his crimes. With that, Keech suspended his sentence and told him to go and sin no more. There was whispering in our ranks, among the women of the committee, that Judge Keech had a heart. The cynical response from others and me was that the heart beat faster only for crooked politicians.

Before I tell the story of this rather extraordinary trial, I must say something about the defendants, for they were as unlikely a group as ever sat in a criminal courtroom. Originally, the Joint Committee consisted of sixteen men and women, but five of the defendants had purged themselves — as the legal term has it — meaning that, for one reason or another, they changed their minds and told the court that if it had been up to them they would have produced the lists of our contributors, but they had been unable to do so because the board voted otherwise. Having heard this, the judge suspended their sentences and discharged them. Many years have passed since then, and I see no reason to name them. These are the eleven who remained firm:

Marjorie Chodorov, a small woman, mother of a ten-year-old and a twelve-year-old, a housewife, simple and unshaken in her courage.

Ruth Leider, widow, attorney, supporting two children, twelve and fourteen — a woman of principle and courage.

Charlotte Stern, a graduate of Radcliffe, social worker, trade union leader, writer, economist — an extraordinary woman whose accomplishments would take pages if fully noted.

Jacob Auslander and Louis Miller, both of them gifted and compassionate physicians who, along with Dr. Edward K. Barsky, devoted themselves to the relief and health of the Spanish Republican veterans. Our closest association in the committee, speaking for Bette and me and my children, was with Dr. Louis Miller, since he was our family physician for the next fifteen years, a man we loved and cherished, totally devoted to his patients and his profession.

Lyman R. Bradley, of New York University, treasurer of the Modern Language Association, eligible for membership in the Sons of the American Revolution, had he ever desired it, was a wonderful, modest gentleman, whom I came to love as dearly as a brother. There were three men I knew less well, Harry M. Justiz, a lawyer, James Lustig, a labor leader, and Manuel Mangana, the Spanish businessman in Harlem, and of course myself. As different as we were, we were united in believing that no one of us could hand over to the Un-American Committee decent people who had trusted us. It would have been anathema.

This time I went alone to Washington. I had no idea how long the trial would take, and I did not want Bette and Rachel exposed to the summer heat of Washington, a city I was beginning to hate soundly. To imagine that marriage could be easy under these circumstances would be a mistake. Bette had to face the realization that our lives were changing once and forever. I was no longer the young genius of American literature. The day of the glowing reviews was over, and my novel *The American* was attacked savagely — as all of my books would be in the years that followed — and it was my own choice that had brought me here.

Each pain I faced, my good wife felt doubly. It hurt her beyond description, and while I could easily cope with the thought of prison, putting myself in the line of distinguished folk, tracing through such names as Thoreau and Tom Paine and Bunyan and a host of others stretching back to Socrates and romanticizing all of it, Bette could not cope with the thought that her husband and lover and partner and defender could be put away in a prison cell for six years. It was too cruel, too impossible, too senseless. Little rents were torn in our relationship; we were drawn together and driven apart at one and the same time. We clung to each other when I left for Washington to go on trial while my lovely little three-year-old daughter stared at us in bewilderment and tried to understand why her mother wept.

In Washington, the sixteen members of our committee — it was not until after the verdict that the five members who left us purged themselves — sat in the courtroom and watched the jury selection, a process that washed out my last bit of hope. Every single member selected and approved by the government worked for the government. I recall a large, stout black man, well dressed, a fine diamond ring on one of his fingers, and three cigars in his breast pocket. I had been watching him with a thin ray of hope, since he regarded the government attorney with no pleasure. He was asked his profession, and he replied, "Undertaker," a slight smile on his lips. He was immediately discharged for cause. Our twelve good men and women, all white, all worked for the United States government; in other words, the jury was totally employed by the prosecution.

It was not much of a trial. O. John Rogge's opening remarks to the jury were sincere, but hardly very inspiring. In part, he said:

What brought these people from different walks of life and with different backgrounds together? The facts will show that it certainly was not conspiracy, as the government charges. It was the same thing that might bring any group of Americans from different walks of life and from different backgrounds together. This group was brought together because they were all interested in providing relief for the anti-fascist refugees from Franco Spain — some of the oldest refugees from fascism — some of the first fighters against fascism . . .

Now, we are going to show that the House Committee on Un-American Activities would not recognize Un-American Activities if it saw them. We are going to show that thing which the House committee regarded as un-American other Americans regarded as very American.

We are going to show that the House committee, by its own standards, would regard such outstanding Americans as Thomas Jefferson, Tom Paine and Abraham Lincoln as un-American.

We are going to show that the House committee spent, and spends, nearly all of its time investigating and oppressing and harassing liberal groups and hardly any of its time investigating fascist groups.

We are further going to show that when the House committee investigates fascists, it treats them in an entirely different way. We are going to show that when the House committee has fascists before it, it treats them, believe it or not, with respect, but when it has liberals before it, it third-degrees them, it oppresses them, it harasses, abuses, and threatens them . . .

Mr. Rogge went on and on with his indictment of the House committee, but he seemed to me to have missed the main point of the trial: Had we or had we not been guilty of contempt? We had legally assigned our books to Helen Bryan, and therefore as a board we had no power to produce them. While this was a defensive maneuver, it was legally sound, and the argument should have been on whether we were indicted because we refused to guess what our actions would have been had we kept possession of the books. The conspiracy charge rested on the proposition that we had conspired to turn the books over to Helen Bryan, which was nonsense, since the action of a board of directors can hardly be regarded as a conspiracy. In any case, I had not been at the meeting where this occurred. But instead of arguing the legality of the charge, Rogge was engaging in a political attack against the committee. It left me bewildered, not only the defense Rogge put up, but the woeful mismanagement of the case by Benedict Wolf, an unimaginative, plodding man who encouraged Rogge in the path he took and also failed to advise us on the use of the Fifth Amendment, which would have obviated any trial. I think that O. John Rogge, still struggling with the nightmares he had experienced during the Nuremberg trials, could see the case only as a simple struggle between a fascist committee and a group dedicated to the cause of the men who had fought fascism in Spain, but the actions of Benedict Wolf never ceased to mystify me.

Set up in this manner, the trial proceeded to a foregone conclusion. We produced all sorts of witnesses, who swore under oath that we were honest, decent citizens; none of us had a criminal record; we were of good character; and one of my character witnesses, Mary Abbott of McIntosh and Otis, a motherly woman, testified that it was impossible to think of Howard Fast in terms of wrongdoing. (Even though she so bravely came to my defense, after the trial McIntosh and Otis suggested that I seek other representation, that is, a new literary agent.) Other witnesses, to the extent that the judge allowed, denounced the Un-American Committee, but none of it added up to anything decisive. The government attorney, on the other hand, held his argument and witnesses to the narrow point of whether or not we were guilty of contempt. In his closing argument, O. John Rogge continued his war against fascism.

In charging the jury, Judge Keech began by throwing out the conspiracy charge. On the second count, contempt, Judge Keech narrowed the point to the specific of contempt of Congress, explaining to the jury that refusal to answer a question or turn over pertinent records to a congressional committee was considered contempt. The jury then retired to consider the evidence.

Just to lighten things a bit, I suggested a pool of a dollar each on how long it would take for the jury to come in with a verdict. The guesses ranged from twenty minutes — my choice — to seven hours. Professor Bradley chose one hour, and since it took forty-nine minutes for the jury to bring in a verdict, he won the pool. Of course, the verdict was guilty. However, I was so lightheaded and delighted that the conspiracy charge had been thrown out that the guilty verdict bothered me not one bit. I knew that the top sentence for contempt was a year in prison, and after facing the idea of six years in jail and all the attendant horrors, a year in jail was a relief. Arrangements were made to post bond, and early that evening, most of us were on a train back to New York. A few weeks later, we were sentenced, ten of us to three months in prison, Dr. Barsky to six months. However, the case was appealed, first to the Federal Court of Appeals, where the appeal was rejected, and then to the Supreme Court, where we were denied certiorari, or the right to plead our case before the Supreme Court. We did not go to prison until the late spring of 1950, an event that I will deal with later.

If we discount that a jury draws its monthly paycheck from the prosecution, we were given a fair trial. The court was not corrupt, but the House Un-American Committee was so corrupt, so dishonorable, so blatantly vicious in its hatred of Communism and its embrace of fascism, that our hearing and trial as well as the hearings and trials that followed, in Hollywood and elsewhere, turned into international matters of enormous proportions. I had never anticipated anything like this or desired it. As much as I could, I have shunned publicity.

On the other hand, these prison sentences were something new in the land. It was almost unheard of that contempt of Congress should be punished with anything more than a fine. A committee of Congress was empowered to hold hearings about pending legislation; the notion of using such hearings as political weapons was the innovation of the House Un-American Committee, subsequently picked up by the Senate committee, a member of which was the infamous Senator Joseph McCarthy.

There were many explanations for what was happening in Amer-

ica, and more or less all of these explanations were based on illusion.
"We lost China to the Communists." Explanation: betrayal. But the
notion that China was ours to lose was so far from reality that from
there on arguments went crazy. The government and the press either
ignored or were unaware that the years of suffering in China led to
the Communist army's being formed and driving Chiang Kai-shek
out of the land. "We lost Shanghai." "We lost Canton." Who had
betrayed us? Who had taken China from us? Not the Chinese Communist army, but traitors in the State Department. Senator Mc-
Carthy, in a speech before the Republican Women's Club of Wheel-
ing, West Virginia, on February 9, 1950, finally defined the era by
holding up for the Republican women to see what he said was a list
of names of State Department people who were members of the
Communist Party. I believe that in those years there was little I did
not know about the Communist Party of the United States, and I
am ready to swear under oath — Alger Hiss had already been indicted — that there was no member of the Communist Party in the
State Department. The very thought, for anyone who knew the party,
was idiotic, but McCarthy was believed because he capped five years
of public paranoia. Here is the way Godfrey Hodgson, in his 1976
book *America in Our Time,* sums up the period:

> Long before McCarthy's speech at Wheeling, suspicion had begun to
> focus on the danger of Communist subversion. The House Un-Amer-
> ican Activities Committee was set up in 1938, and from the start de-
> voted about four fifths of its attention to investigating the left. The
> Alien Registration Act of 1940, in practice and in intention a sedition
> act, breached constitutional precedent by embracing guilt by associa-
> tion. The U.S. Chamber of Commerce began publishing, in 1946, a
> series of reports alleging clandestine communist influence in various
> areas of American life . . . In 1947, President Truman issued an exec-
> utive order requiring loyalty checks . . . for 2.5 million civil servants,
> several hundred of whom were dismissed as a result. Union leaders
> were required by the Taft-Hartley Act, of 1947, to take an oath that
> they were not communists, and in 1949 the leaders of the Communist
> Party themselves were tried and convicted for conspiring to advocate
> the overthrow of the U.S. government by force and violence. Well
> before the end of the 1940s numerous states and cities had passed

statutes and ordinances obliging teachers to take loyalty oaths, though these were subsequently struck down by the Supreme Court.

Hodgson presents a neat, objective summary of the situation; I, on the other hand, was in the middle of it, with no historical perspective or awareness of the future to guide me. What was happening was happening to me. My new book, *The American,* was being trashed mercilessly; I had been indicted and tried and sentenced to prison. My telephone was tapped. Featherbrained FBI agents were slipping into my apartment on occasions when I offered my place for fundraising affairs, and other agents were following me through the streets. We were beginning to live with fear and suspicion that in time became a rasp, abrading my relationship with Bette, cutting into our love, causing us to drink too much, to explode into anger at each other too often, and then to come together again and again.

There were friends who stood by, who were brave and unawed by the mini-terror. There was a great evening when the veterans of the Lincoln Brigade played host to the exiled mayor of Madrid. Or rather he played host to all of them, for he cooked the paella that topped off the evening. He called for a volunteer, a dishwasher and assistant, and since I was the only non-vet male present — he specified that he would subject no woman to his eccentricity — I volunteered and was accepted. I spent the next hour with him in the kitchen while he chatted away in Spanish to a stream of visitors. If anyone cares for the recipe, here it is: Peel and chop endless cloves of garlic, and put them into an enormous pan with several cups of olive oil. When the oil begins to bubble, throw in all the rice the pan can comfortably contain. Fry, mix, and turn the rice and add tiny bits of saffron, just a pinch at a time. When each grain of rice is well oiled and yellow, add four or five cans of clam juice. While the rice cooks, slice about two pounds of Spanish sausage and clean about thirty shrimp. Meanwhile, cook two cut-up chickens in another pot, boil a bit, and then fry. When the rice is finished, add the sausage and the chicken and hot sauce from a bottle. Then the shrimp. Then mix this whole concoction and transfer some to another pan if you need to. Cover both pans with a solid topping of Little Neck clams in the shell, and then place it all in the oven.

The odor, the taste, and the general joy of good food with heavy Zinfandel wine instructed us in the best and most civilized things in life and drew a curtain over the very peculiar history of 1947. At least for the moment. *A su salud,* spoken so many times, had a true and wonderful sound.

9

ON APRIL 13, 1948, my son, Jonathan, arrived in this curious and troubled world. He was beautiful, eight pounds and nine ounces, and in spite of his being two and a half pounds heavier than Rachel was at the time of her birth, the delivery was an easier one for Bette. We were completely delighted at exemplifying that obvious American middle-class statistic, two children, one boy, one girl. We had dreamed and talked at times of having four children, but the danger and tension that had come into our lives precluded that. In the months before Jonathan's birth, the terror had spread, one of the most newsworthy spreaders being an actor, name of Ronald Reagan. He had already been feeding to the FBI names of members of the Screen Actors Guild whom he suspected of being Communists, and since he was the president of the guild, one is at a loss to put a proper name to his conduct. However, this was not to become public knowledge until the last years of his presidency, and in October of 1947 he testified before the Committee on Un-American Activities that the guild was not controlled by Communists, although there were many Communist members. He named no names then, since to do so publicly would have undermined his position. Robert Taylor, a very important film star at that time, stepped into the gap, declaring manfully, "I personally believe the Communist Party should be outlawed. If I had my way, they'd all be sent back to Russia." He then proceeded to name names most generously.

For three days, the committee held its inquisition in Los Angeles,

claiming through the testimony of such woolly-headed creatures as
Ward Bond and Robert Taylor that the motion picture industry was
saturated with Communists and that the names of seventy-nine card-
carrying members of the party would be presented. That never happened, but ten leading gifted and important film workers were cited
for contempt. These included Albert Maltz, Dalton Trumbo, Ring
Lardner, Jr., Adrian Scott, Edward Dmytryk, Sam Ornitz, Lester Cole,
Herbert Biberman, Alvah Bessie, and John Howard Lawson, a group
better known as the Hollywood Ten. While they were by no means
the largest group to suffer, they were given the most publicity, as
Hollywood always is in America. The hearings resulted in an unprecedented move by the Motion Picture Association, a very powerful
force in filmmaking, to blacklist the ten indicted and to bar any Communist, proven or suspected, from working in any part of the industry. Fifty leaders in the film industry, top executives, meeting in New
York, issued the following statement: "We will forthwith discharge
or suspend without compensation those in our employ . . ." The sad-
dest part is that most of these fifty had no bias against the so-called
Communists, were open-minded on the civil rights issues the Communists fought for, and in many cases supported the same issues.
They acted out of terror — terror that these great institutions which
they had created would be invaded and taken from them, and that
was indeed a heartbreaking thing.

It was the progress of this spreading, creeping terror that began to
get to Bette and me. How far would it go and where would it end?
It was no comfort to know that the great majority of Americans was
indifferent to it and cared not a stick about what happened to Communists, left-liberals, and others like them. The great majority of
Germans had been more or less indifferent to the actions of Adolf
Hitler. The German people did not rise up in anger when Hitler put
500,000 members of the German Communist Party to death, and
why should we doubt that the same thing could happen here? As we
look back today, such thoughts may appear ludicrous. They were
not ludicrous then — not to people who were only four years away
from the Holocaust. I remember the black joke going around then:
Cohen meets Levy in Berlin in 1950. Levy asks what happened to
Goldberg. Levy replies, "He couldn't get out of America."

"What do we do?" I asked Bette. I would ask her that again and again. It had to be up to her, and she always said the same thing: "If you can live with it, I can live with it."

She was pregnant, heavy with the baby, and we bought a house. I don't know why we bought the house at that time of our lives. We invented reasons. It was hard to live in an apartment house, and harder for people as involved as we were in picket lines, demonstrations, fund-raising parties, and visits from people of every country and color. This was before the civil rights movement became a great national crusade. In 1948, no black could be seated in any first-class restaurant in New York; blacks went to black schools, whites to white schools. There were exceptions, but only to prove the case. One of the fine glories of the Communist Party of the United States was that we fought and often enough died for black freedom, and the truth that nobody much remembers is that in the very early years of the struggle for civil rights, we were at the side of the blacks, and precious few others who were not black were there with us. There is enough to be said against the party, but it's wrong to wipe out all the brave and wonderful things we did, not only in Spain, but here at home.

We lived in a good apartment house, 315 Central Park West, doorman and all, and one time Pearl Primus, the talented black dancer, came to see us and the doorman insisted she go around to the servant entrance. Of course, she would not, and she telephoned me, weeping, asking how this could happen at the home of Howard Fast. I told the doormen and elevator men that if it ever happened again, I'd kill them, and I was so furious I imagine they believed it.

But that didn't solve the problem. Blacks arrived there constantly: Paul Robeson again and again, Bill Patterson the civil rights leader, black dancers, fighters, musicians. Shirley Graham was practically living with us; and her brother Bill Graham, the largest beer and soda distributor in Harlem, and Dr. Du Bois and any number of others were frequently at our house; and I was always uneasy, fearing that something rotten would happen at the door again. So Bette and I offered this to ourselves as reason for buying the house; but I think that the ultimate truth was that we wanted to have our own wall around us — a kind of mythical protection: my home is my castle and all that — but perhaps not. It was simply that both of us wanted it, a place where anyone we asked in could come in.

City houses were cheap then. We could have bought a magnificent graystone mansion between Fifth and Madison avenues for $35,000 to $40,000, but being what we were at that time, as wedded to our beliefs as monks, we stayed on the West Side and finally settled on a charming three-story brownstone, with basement, at 43 West Ninety-fourth Street, which we bought for $19,000. It had never been a rooming house, and it still maintained its Victorian style and mood. We put about $10,000 more into fixing the heating and plumbing and painting, and there we were, searching for solid if symbolic refuge and security in a neighborhood that would in the next five years turn into a street of drugs and prostitutes, before being gentrified to the pleasant street it is today. We lived there for five years, and they were perhaps the most eventful and desperate years of our lives.

We stayed and we lived with it, and never did I hear from my wonderful wife a word of protest at the life we lived, never a word to tell me to get out of it all and give her some peace. There was no peace in our lives; joy and fun and rewards, but not peace.

We managed to get into the house before Jonathan came into this unruly world, and I should have been with Bette every hour of the first few weeks of the baby's life, but in many small ways we were being torn apart. The break would come and then we would heal it in each other's arms.

May Day came too soon after Jon's birth, and the May Day Committee delegated me, as its most prominent member, to go to the police for our permit. This time, we were challenged by a representative from Freedom House, who felt that to permit these enemies of all that was good to march downtown to Union Square was an insult to America. There was a large, wise old Polish cop who was chief of traffic, and he carefully explained to the Freedom House man that the May Day parade was a very normal part of the scene and had been for generations. "Look," he said, "on May Day, the left wing of labor marches. On Labor Day, the right wing of labor marches. Why do you want to make trouble?"

We got the permit, and Bette pleaded with me not to go. "Don't you see how fast things are changing?" she reasoned. I argued that on this May Day of 1948, the march would be larger than it had ever been. There wouldn't be any trouble. How many times I argued that with her! There wouldn't be any trouble. I was on the May Day

Visiting a farm in upstate New York, summer 1917

Barney Fast in Hunter, New York, 1935

Howard (*right*) and Jerome Fast, 1935

Julius Fast, 1935

Bette Fast, 1938

Author as war correspondent, 1945

Below: Street speech: New York City, 1948

William Z. Foster, Communist Party leader and labor organizer, 1947 (*UPI/Bettmann Newsphotos*)

Organized supporters of Paul Robeson form a line of defense against those protesting the second Peekskill concert, September 4, 1949. (*AP/Wide World Photos*)

Press conference after Peekskill. *Left to right:* Paul Robeson, holding a rock that had been thrown into one of the buses; Leon Strauss of the International Fur and Leather Workers' Union; Wilson McDowell, who was injured in one of the buses; the author. On the table is a shattered automobile window. (*AP/Wide World Photos*)

Mill Point prison (*Photo: Albert Maltz*)

Fast and fellow mason at the fountain of the *Prince of Essen*, Mill Point prison, summer 1950

Flier for *The Hammer*, which opened in New York City just after Fast's release from prison, September 1950

NEW PLAYWRIGHTS, INC.

PRODUCERS OF "LONGITUDE 49"

present

THE HAMMER

A NEW PLAY BY

HOWARD FAST

● America's outstanding novelist, author of "Citizen Tom Paine," "Freedom Road," "My Glorious Brothers," etc.

Directed by AL SAXE

● Director of the recent highly praised revivals of Sean O'Casey's "The Silver Tassie" and "The Plough and The Stars" and Odets' "Awake and Sing".

Opening SEPTEMBER 8th
at the CZECHOSLOVAK HOUSE
347 EAST 72nd STREET
(Between 1st and 2nd Avenues)

HOWARD FAST

Eugene Dennis, Secretary of the Communist Party of America, at a press conference after the Supreme Court's decision to uphold his conviction, June 1951 (*AP/Wide World Photos*)

The Fasts, 1952 (*Photo: Lotte Jacobi*)

American Labor Party candidate for Congress, 1952

The author (on sound truck in sleeveless sweater) on the campaign trail in the Bronx (*Photo: Cornell Capa*, Life *magazine, copyright © 1952 Time Warner Inc.*)

Paul Robeson presents the International Peace Prize to the author, 1953.
Seated, left to right: Essie Robeson, Mrs. Mellisk, Dr. W. E. B. Du Bois, Rachel
Fast, Howard Fast, Bette Fast (*Julius Lazarus/Courtesy of the Author*)

Bette Fast, 1956. Behind her is her
portrait of Rachel. (*Photo: Marvin P.
Lazarus*)

Howard and Bette Fast, California, 1976

Committee and in charge of the "culture block," as we called it, and the thought of missing the parade was out of the question. There was nothing but trouble, as it turned out.

On our block were almost eleven thousand teachers, lawyers, doctors, dentists, actors, writers, editors, publishers — an unbelievable crowd. The block, stretching from Broadway to Eighth Avenue, was a long one. The marchers began to assemble early, and by noon the block was packed. At that moment, at noon, the doors of a parochial school standing on the same street opened, and about a hundred screaming, cursing, teenage students, armed with everything from brass knuckles to pens, poured into the middle of our huge crowd, their fists flying, shouting their war cry: "Kill a commie for Christ!"

Suddenly, after twenty years of leading a more or less calm intellectual life, I was in a street fight again. It didn't last long, because the cops came swarming in, pushing the parochial kids back into the school and then turning on us. The first thing they wanted to know was who was in charge. I told them that I was. They then walked me over to the Broadway end of the block and ordered the lead group on the block to start marching. The parade had been moving for at least half an hour by now, but had not yet reached our street. Each block, starting at the most uptown block, had been emptying in turn, moving out into the avenue, trade union groups carrying their colorful old banners. If our block were to empty out and swing into the parade, it would have disrupted the entire parade. The banner passing at that moment stays in my mind: LADIES GARMENT WORKERS. BLACK AND WHITE TOGETHER. I kept thinking about that slogan all that day. The International Ladies Garment Workers' Union, led by David Dubinsky, shunned our parade. This was a rump group. When I had worked in a garment factory, some seventeen years before this, there were no black workers. Now there were a good many fighting for equality of pay and job. But that's out of this moment, when the cop yelled, "Start marching!"

"Stay where you are!" I shouted.

The cop walked over to me, put his face close to mine, and said quietly, "I said they should march."

I tried to be just as quiet and reasonable, and I explained to the officer that if we left the block now, we would interfere with the parade. He countered this with a few four-letter words that I took to mean that he didn't give a damn about the parade, and once again he ordered the block to begin to swing out into the avenue and march. I said, "Stay where you are."

By now, we had attracted a good deal of attention, and one of the trade union men stopped the parade, just in case our block had to empty. Down the block, the parochial school teenagers had started again their chant of "Kill a commie for Christ!" and the fight was on, and the cop gripped me by the arm and told me I was under arrest.

"For what?"

"March!" he shouted at the block. "Or you'll all be under arrest!"

The block began to march, and now the old Polish cop, the one I had spoken to about the permit, came over to see what the commotion was about, and he let out a howl, slapped his thigh, and chortled, "You got Howie."

"What do I do with him?"

"Take him to the wagon and lock him up."

The wagon was a detention truck, parked a few blocks away. As the cop started to walk me over there, Joe Derma turned up. Joe was an official of the Furniture Workers' Union, a man who looked like someone sent from central casting to play the part of a tough New York City cop. You only had to look at Joe, at his Irish face — he was Jewish — at his size and girth to know that this was a mean city cop, and on May Day, he was the appointed taker-away. He now appeared and said to the cop who was walking me to the wagon, "I'll take this sonofabitch. You get back to your post." If you're a cop in uniform, you don't argue with a detective, and Joe wasn't someone a cop would pick an argument with. He turned me over to Joe, went back to his post, and Joe told me to take off and catch up with the professionals. I had to run a few blocks, but I caught up, and there I was at the front of our block group again, until we came to the big wooden stand at Union Square where I was to be one of the speakers. As I mounted the stairs to the platform, the chief of traffic was standing and waiting, his gold shield glinting, his small blue eyes fixed on me.

"You were arrested, Howie," he said.

"They let me go."

"Just like that?"

"You didn't have any charge that would stick. What's the difference?"

"There's always a next time," he said.

But for two employees of the Fur and Leather Workers' Union, the time was now. They had argued too hard and resisted arrest, and the result was that they were taken away — before Joe Derma could get to them — and booked and charged with resisting arrest and with assault and battery. These were real charges and there was real hard jail time connected with the charges. Ben Gold, the head of the Fur and Leather Workers' Union, turned for help to a lawyer named Julie Trupin. Ben Gold was a sort of mythical figure in the labor movement, a great labor leader who had been one of the main organizing forces in the thirties, a man who had fought the mob face to face and driven them out of his union. The people in his union were among the best paid in the entire labor movement, and though the government tried to break the union again and again, Gold managed to fight back and hold the union together.

Julie Trupin was one of my dearest friends, a tall, handsome man, a head of golden curls that looked absolutely unreal, soft blue eyes, a will of iron, and a dedicated Communist. He was charming and engaging, and his acquaintance was wide and varied. Ben Gold turned to him, just as so many of us on the left turned to him, for legal advice, for help, for anything that needed someone like Trupin. It was pointless, Gold said, for two good and honest men to have to sit in jail for God knows how long. Gold asked Julie to put in the fix and get the two men back on the street. According to what Julie told me the following evening, the politics of it being what they were, the two union organizers would have gotten two to four — for a little scuffle with the cops.

In 1948, the brown building on Madison Avenue facing the back of Saint Patrick's Cathedral was shared by Random House and the local leadership of the church. It was known throughout the city as the Power House, and the man occupying it, Cardinal Spellman, was known as the Power. This was the same building that now serves as the Madison Avenue entrance to the Helmsley Palace Hotel; at that time the Power House peddled the fix.

(I must interpose at this point with a story about an incident that happened twelve years later, in 1960. I wrote a screenplay titled *The*

Hill. It was the story of the crucifixion according to Mark, to be shot in Harlem on Mount Morris Park, with a black cast and a black Jesus. We met a French p.r. lady at that time to whom a friend had given a copy of my screenplay. She was very thrilled by it, and asked me whether I would permit her to send it to Pope John XXIII. I said I would be delighted, and in due time I received a letter, not from the Pope but from the papal secretary, who wrote with the Pope's voice that he, Pope John, felt that nothing faced Christianity at this moment that was more important than the depiction of a black Jesus, that my depiction was splendid. He added, however, one caveat: if any question of Catholic faith or practice arose during the screening, I was under no circumstances to take the argument to Cardinal Spellman but, rather, to Cardinal Cushing in Boston. To this date, the film has not been made — many reasons — and I interpose this bit to underline that I was not alone in my opinion of Cardinal Spellman.)

Yes, the Power House on Madison Avenue peddled the fix. Julie Trupin said that he went to the house, made a few direct inquiries, and was introduced to a man with whom he had lunch. At lunch, the man said to Julie something to this effect: the price was the price. There was to be no dickering over price.

Having said that, he took out a mimeographed sheet with a list of almost every crime Julie had ever heard of, and next to each crime, a price. Julie asked Bette and me to guess what the price was for murder. Our guesses ran from $50,000 to $150,000.

Julie shook his head. "If it doesn't hit the papers first, the price is seven hundred and fifty dollars."

We refused to believe it. I knew as well as the next New Yorker how corrupt the city was in 1948, but this was beyond anything I could have anticipated. Going on with his story, Julie said that the price of assault and battery was $250, but when the cardinal's man heard that it was May Day, which translated "red," he upped the price to $2000. Julie had $5000 in hundred-dollar bills in his briefcase — cash having been specified — and he paid the price, and the two fur organizers walked. Apparently, it was all right to kill a commie for Christ, unless of course the commie paid off.

The Progressive movement in America has a long history — a socialist-labor splinter revolt against the corruption and social indifference manifest in the two major parties. Its first attempt at the polls came in 1912, with Theodore Roosevelt as its candidate. The effort came to nothing and marked Roosevelt's political eclipse. The second attempt came in 1924 and consisted of the remnants of the Farmer-Labor Party combined with the Socialist Party. Its major strength was in Montana, Minnesota, and Wisconsin. The candidate for President was Senator Robert La Follette of Wisconsin, and he polled over five million votes, a very respectable showing in a national population of under eighty million.

In 1948, convinced that Truman's politics had put us on a path that would inevitably lead to an atomic showdown with the Soviet Union, a left-liberal coalition of labor, middle class, small business, and intellectuals decided to attempt to revive the Progressive Party. Henry Wallace, the former Vice President, agreed to accept the presidential nomination. The party was inaugurated at a large meeting in Chicago and July 23 was set for a convention in Philadelphia.

Henry Wallace was then editor of *The New Republic*. Michael Straight, who later replaced Wallace as the editor, wrote in his book *After Long Silence* that "the executive committee of the P.C.A. met in December. Howard Fast, the novelist, moved a resolution calling on Wallace to lead a people's party . . ."

Perhaps, but I have no notes of this. I'm quite sure that Mr. Straight has notes covering that meeting, for he goes on to say that Helen Fuller fought the nomination bitterly, insisting that Wallace and the new party would be in the hands of the Communists. What a pity! The new Progressive Party was immediately denounced by much of the press and a good deal of the government as a Communist-front organization.

It was by no means a Communist-front organization, but it could not have come into being without the decision, the will, and the work of the Communist Party. By this time, the Communist Party had shrunk from its immediate postwar membership of sixty-five thousand, more or less, to about forty thousand in mid-1948. Nevertheless, most of those forty thousand were dedicated, hard-working people, and they supplied the initial energy that brought the Progressive Party into being. I was at both places, at the initial organizing meeting in Chicago and then at the national convention in Philadelphia; and I shared the illusion and the euphoria. The thought and act of bringing a new political party into being, of creating a new turning in American history, a party whose major platform would be peace, was so exciting that we put the real world out of our calculations. Suddenly, we saw ourselves as no longer hunted and tormented; now the American people in their millions would rise and embrace our program, peace on earth and a job for every man and woman who wanted to work. Coming out of the meeting in Chicago, we declared the new party to be now in existence.

The creation of the Progressive Party in 1948 was neither a conspiratorial nor an anti-American action. Perhaps it was an act of desperation without circumstances to support it, but it was neither a Communist conspiracy nor a Communist front. Men like Henry A. Wallace, Glen H. Taylor, Elmer A. Benson, and Clark Foreman were not fools or dupes of the Communists. In fact, the whole notion that Communists could manipulate people like puppets is sheer nonsense. The issues that Communists fought for were issues that people of good will believed in. I was not at that time known publicly as a Communist. The accusation was thrown at me, but I saw no reason to embrace the accusation. It was an odd moment in history, difficult to explain, difficult to understand even by the people living through it. Of course the FBI knew that I was a party member, but they had their own people in the party and they were not willing to risk them for the sake of labeling people like me. I imagine it was difficult even for the FBI to believe that so upright and socially conservative a citizen as I, author of the books I had written, was in all truth a party member. There were no lists; we carried no cards; but even if I had not been a Communist, I would have put all my energy at the disposal of the Progressive Party.

It became then, in 1948, the focal point of my existence. My own job was to rally writers to support the new party, but on July 20, three days before the Philadelphia convention, the federal government — read Harry Truman — dealt us a neat body blow: the Justice Department indicted twelve leaders of the Communist Party for conspiring to overthrow the government by force and violence. This was an act duplicated in modern times only by Franco, Hitler, and Mussolini, and such assorted dictators as Admiral Horthy of Hungary and his kind. It cast a chill of fear over every thoughtful liberal in America. It is amazing that certain people stood up to it, but a great many did. I went to fellow writers and asked their support for the Progressive Party. They gave it to us — not all of them; there was too much fear at that time — but a number of the very best. Norman Mailer, of course, flatly asserted that "Wallace is the only man in political life who is sincere in his desire for peace, and understands that a war with Soviet Russia will not leave enough of the world to satisfy the plans of even the meanest real estate operator." Others joined him, Charles A. Madison, Henry Pratt Fairchild, Stetson Kennedy, Agnes Smedley, Barbara Giles, W. E. B. Du Bois, Thomas Bell, Alfred Kreymborg — names half forgotten today, but of importance in shaping a good deal of the thinking at the time — and many others.

It was a heady experience for the thousands of men and women who attended the Philadelphia convention. A certain vibration comes into being at an American political convention, a sense of participating in an almost holy ritual that is as old as our country, a wonderful sense of togetherness, a heightened awareness; and in our convention this was combined with the belief (hope, dream, illusion, prayer) that America would be America again, that we would hurl the warmongers out of office, that a new age of equalitarianism would come into being, that black and white would walk hand in hand. We had all the trappings of a major party's convention, delegations from the states, inside deal making, fierce arguments over the platform — all the forms — and we who were in the middle of it actually believed.

We should not have been surprised, hurt, or bewildered by the result the following November — fewer than two million votes cast for the candidates of the Progressive Party. Considering the places where we had been ripped off the ballot, the manipulation, the orchestrated rage of the establishment against us, the screaming, endless red baiting that filled the newspapers and the new TV news programs, along with the steady stream of arrests of liberals and left-wingers, the fact that there were in America almost two million people who had maintained a balanced and independent point of view was, I think, nothing short of extraordinary. But we did not see it that way. Our dreams were shattered, and to a large degree that was the end, the final effort of the left-liberal-labor alliance that had been so vital and important a factor in American life since the days of Eugene V. Debs. In due time, there would be a new left, but it would be different and politically impotent, with no sense of party or platform in the traditional American manner.

It is also my feeling now, over forty years later, exercising hindsight, that the losses of the Progressive Party in 1948 in the miasma of terror and hatred that the administration had engendered, led by such vicious and utterly obsessive figures as Richard Nixon, Joseph McCarthy, Congressmen Wood and Rankin, and of course that shadow dictator of the United States, J. Edgar Hoover, marked the historical demise of the Communist Party of the United States. The party would continue to fight against this terror for the next ten years, but it would be a struggle that became increasingly lonely as other elements of the population, the people of good will, moved to the sidelines and waited silently, with hope that eventually sanity would return to America.

The Philadelphia convention was an important and colorful moment in my life. Not only did I learn a priceless lesson in practical politics, but I met one of my heroes — H. L. Mencken. During the first day of the convention, a newspaperman I knew told me that Mencken was looking for me. Mencken? H. L. Mencken? Yes, Henry Louis Mencken, you idiot.

Mencken found me a little later that day, pressed my hand in both of his, and told me immediately that if he had written *The American,* my novel about Altgeld, he would have put down his pen with pleasure. Fulsome, but I think he knew that I needed the praise, and it was just about the most wonderful thing that had ever been said to me, before or since. Mencken was a short, bright-eyed man, tousled, his suit wrinkled, wearing a skimmer, the straw hat of the time. He had come to the convention to cover it for his paper, but he told me he had really come to meet me. I don't believe that, but he was on the list of writers to whom I had sent my appeal, although he did not endorse the Progressive Party. Quite the contrary. He said to me, "Fast, what in hell's name are you doing with this gang?"

I tried to invent some clever reply, but all I could say was that it was a better place to be than at the Republican or Democratic convention. That was as far from a bright or witty rejoinder as one could get, but I was tongue tied, and the thought of preaching to Mencken or haranguing him was inconceivable. It was not just that I admired him and loved the way he wrote and thought, but he had just given me the best straightforward compliment I had ever received. I had no wish to challenge him. I owed him too much.

Mencken said, "There's a better place than that."

I guess I was grinning stupidly, waiting.

"With yourself," Mencken said.

I will remember that and our conversation to my dying day. It took a lot of years to find out what *with myself* meant, and I wonder sometimes whether Mencken said it casually or with a sense of the depth of the phrase.

"I can't put politics aside," I said.

"Put it aside? Hell, no. Henry Louis Mencken is a party of one. Do you understand me? You're a party of one. You don't put politics aside; you taste it, smell it, listen to it, and write it. You don't join it. If you do, these clowns will destroy you as surely as the sun rises and sets."

We talked for a good while, but there is no way I could put down the words of the rest of it. The brief exchange I quoted here, I remember word for word. The rest was about the Progressive Party and the Communist Party. I often hold that it is best not ever to meet a writer you admire or love; none of us comes up to our written words. We are human, frequently disgustingly so, but our words are the best part of us, the more so since they exist on paper and apart from us. But I was not disappointed with Mencken; and I don't think I would have been disappointed with Mark Twain had I met him.

I wrote a book about ancient Israel, and I called it *My Glorious Brothers.* It was not the best book I have written by any means, but it was the story of the fabled Maccabee brothers, written just months before the founding of the state of Israel, and read in Hebrew translation by practically every literate person in the new nation. The last book I wrote as a citizen of a normal time was *The American,* and it was published as the mini-terror began. As I have noted, for the first time since I began to publish, the reviews, with a few exceptions, were vicious and political. Norman Cousins held out against the crowd. He put my picture on the cover of *The Saturday Review* and he featured *The American* as the major review. Writing about the book, William S. Lynch said: "Fast has caught the great episodes [of John Peter Altgeld's life], made them moving and grand . . . Within the limiting framework of a fictionalized biography of an important but not well known American political figure, Howard Fast has produced another extremely satisfactory study." It was a sort of last hurrah.

When *My Glorious Brothers* appeared, in the first flush of Israeli

freedom, reviewers on both the left and the right were taken somewhat aback. To trash a novel about a Jewish struggle for freedom
was, in 1948, a little sticky. Israel was fighting for its life, and the
whole Western world had to admit to an exhibition of moral courage
hardly common in these times, so the reviewing community decided
either to ignore the book or to give it brief and noncommittal attention. With the cooperation of the bookstore chains — unwilling to
trifle with our new petty dictators — the sales of the book were reduced to one third of the sales of *The American*. At the same time,
Morris Schappes, one of the party's experts on Jewish affairs, suggested that I be brought up for expulsion on charges of Jewish nationalism. When this came to the attention of Jack Statchel, a member of the party's National Committee, he threw up his hands in
despair and told Schappes to forget it and said that any Jew who did
not feel sentiments of Jewish nationalism in 1948 had lost his soul.
Napping on the job, the Jewish Book Council of America gave me
its annual award, but after being taken to task by the FBI for so
doing, it removed my name from all subsequent lists of the award
and reference to it.

I don't want to leave the impression that I was the only one so
treated; this petty and disgusting lunacy was being repeated on every
level of American life. A list of those to be hunted down and persecuted was prepared by the owner of a supermarket; it was called *Red
Channels*, and in it were the names of hundreds of writers, actors,
directors, producers, educators whom this grocer, aided by investi-
gators he had hired, specified as Communists or fellow travelers (a
pejorative tag for anyone who might share a thought or an issue with
a Communist). *Red Channels* was picked up by every anti-liberal
force in America, reprinted again and again, and soon became as
omnipresent as Mao's little red book. It could be found in every
production office in the film industry, in book publishers' offices, in
newspaper offices, in practically every committee office in Congress.
It was a unique best seller. It drove innocent men and women from
their jobs and made them unemployable; it drove people to suicide;
and it helped to spread further terror. The fact that this filthy little
book became a standard by which to measure the guilt or innocence
of Americans in terms of betraying their country — a remarkable
fiction — is something that can only be noted. It cannot be explained.

But as far as Howard Fast was concerned, he made his own head-lines. December 17, 1947, *The New York Times,* CITY COLLEGE BARS RED SPEAKER AGAIN. December 18, *The New York Times,* HUNTER BARS FAST. N.Y.U. PERMITS TALK. December 5, *The New York Herald Tribune,* COLUMBIA BARS HOWARD FAST, FACING JAIL, FROM CAMPUS TALK.

And so it went, college after college, fifteen colleges in all, univer-sities that had opened their halls to Nazis, Italian fascists — only a decade before — now decided that Howard Fast represented too great a threat to American education to allow undergraduates to hear him.

They patently missed the fact that Howard Fast's largest dispen-sation of danger was to himself. I was steadily and sometimes obses-sively destroying a career that had started off only ten years earlier as one of the most promising of the time. In a sense I was also de-stroying my usefulness to the cause I felt most deeply. I had an inter-national career of fame and importance, but that meant little to me as against the unending calumny that I was subjected to in my own country. Again and again, I behaved stupidly, arrogantly, driving off people who wanted to be my friend and whose friendship I should have treasured — because they would not or could not agree with me — and all too often I had no other reason for my actions apart from the dictates of the party. I often reflect on my relationship with Moss Hart and his manager, Joe Hyman. I met Moss and Joe in 1940, after the publication of *Conceived in Liberty.* Moss loved the book and signed a contract with me to dramatize it. I was thrilled with this, because some seven months earlier Herman Shumlin had asked me to dramatize the book so that he could produce it. I found it too difficult at that time, and Moss too was defeated in his effort to turn it into a play. But Bette and I were still very young, in our mid-twenties, and we found Moss to be not only the most glamorous person we had ever known but an opener of many glamorous doors. He took Bette and me to dinner at the Colony, the classiest and possibly the most expensive restaurant in New York, and he invited us to his apartment, very wonderful for us at that time; and in all his giving, he was the gentlest and warmest person we knew apart from my publisher, Sam Sloan. He asked nothing from us, only that we take his gifts and listen to his fascinating stories about his family.

By our lights, he was very rich. He told us that he could not get by with less than $85,000 a year, a sum that in 1940 had a buying power of a million dollars today. Joe Hyman was as sweet and kind as Moss. We broke all connection with Moss when the red hunt began but remained always on the best of terms with Joe Hyman. He would not allow me to put him off and break our friendship with arrogance; he treated me as a kid who knew a great deal about some things and had to be forgiven his ignorance of other things. In 1948, having dinner with Bette and me, he asked us what we were doing about protecting our future.

"What future?" I demanded. "If I'm not dead in the next twelve months, it'll be a miracle."

"There it is," Bette said to Joe. "That's our boy."

"That's a silly way to talk," Joe said. "You have a four-year-old daughter and a new baby son, and you talk about not living another year."

"Well, I don't really mean it," I said, trying to placate a wife whose anger was increasing by the moment. "I don't mean it that way. But, Joe, they take away a piece of my future every day."

He asked me how much money I had. I was fortunate that no one employed me and no one could be persuaded to fire me. Something like that would come later, but my foreign sales were very large. There was never a month when I didn't get a royalty check from some foreign country. *Freedom Road* sold in the millions of copies, and close behind it came *Citizen Tom Paine. The Last Frontier* was reprinted everywhere. I told Joe we had about $15,000.

"Where do you keep it?" he wanted to know.

I told him it was in a savings bank. He persuaded me to give him $10,000, which he would invest for me, and with Bette's arguments overcoming my own street-smart suspicion, I gave it to him. With the money the next day, Joe bought me two stocks, IBM and Minnesota Mining. The certificates meant nothing to me. I knew little about Wall Street or the stock market except that they were instruments of capitalism and that during the Depression — the years that had shaped me — they were blamed for everything bad that happened in America. I had never heard of IBM or Minnesota Mining, and knew almost nothing about what they produced, and the possession of the certificates made me very uneasy. Also, I regretted taking most of our wealth and dumping it into those two pieces of paper. Unfortunately, Bette knew as little as I did. She trusted Joe more, but not enough to talk me out of selling the stock. I brought the certificates to my bank, and they said their broker would sell them and credit the money to our account. Having done that, I felt better, considering that it was certainly inconsistent for me, as a Communist, to own shares in capitalism. In the two weeks I had held the certificates, they had increased in value by over two hundred dollars, and if I had held them to the time I write this, they would probably be worth close to a quarter of a million dollars.

Peace and agreement have never been part of large organizations, and the Communist Party was no different. There was inner fighting, back biting, jealousy, and a fair amount of plain old-fashioned corruption. In my case, there were those who loved me and those who resented me and those who harbored a muted sort of hatred. I never took a penny of pay for all the hundreds of thousands of words I later wrote for *The Daily Worker,* and this put me in a very good position. Also, I was sick to death with the tired tricks the leaders of the party played with the English language. The word *little* became belittling. You could write of a white man with a *wolfish* expression, but never of a black man. And so forth. I refused to follow such dictates, and my decision provoked a partywide discussion. I was putting forth a non-party, non-Marxist position. I was rejecting the authority of the party. I replied that they had put their finger on it: I was asserting my own position. My belief in socialism was not waning, but my opinion of some of the arrogant, thickheaded people who were among the national leaders of the Communist Party was on a downhill course.

On the other hand, the leadership was under indictment, and their trial began on January 17, 1949. They had to be defended. I covered many days of the trial for *The Daily Worker,* so I saw it at first hand as it progressed. It was indeed the strangest trial that had ever taken place in the U.S. Court House at Foley Square in New York. The charge was that the leaders of the party had conspired to teach the overthrow of the government by force and violence. This meant that they were being tried for conspiracy. The fact that never in my time in the party, or in the time of any other member of the party, had the question of overthrow of the government by force and violence been raised or mentioned even in passing made no difference whatsoever. The thought that the handful of people who were still in the party — fewer than thirty-five thousand — could even contemplate the overthrow of the strongest power on the face of the earth was so ludicrous that it could be entertained only as a joke. And if one connects this with the realization that the majority of party members were gentle people whose central philosophy was the brotherhood of man, people of high principle and decency, the joke became even more macabre.

But when one sets this in the framework of hatred and terror that the Truman government had created — and in the framework of the drive to war that Truman led — it becomes more understandable. The government had already prepared a list of 300,000 people who would be immediately interned in case of war with Russia, and a number of large concentration camps had already been built (and are still in existence, for all I know).

The trial was not only bizarre but unique. It violated every protection of free speech and civil rights that the Constitution contained. The only precedents for such a trial had been in fascist Italy and in Nazi Germany. That the government did not have to prove that the party had ever advocated overthrow of the government by force and violence, but simply had to suggest conspiracy to do so someday, made the trial even more farcical. Since the party was threaded through with government agents, the prosecution had no problem in finding witnesses. The key to the charge lay in the party's reorganization in 1945; the government held that the conspiracy by the leadership had taken place during this reorganization.

The trial went on for months, and in the end there was no question in any thoughtful person's mind as to what the verdict would be. In his book *The Story of an American Communist*, John Gates, one of the defendants, describes its conclusion:

Our own case under the Smith Act went to the jury the afternoon of October 13, 1949. Federal court juries are notorious for being hand picked on a highly select blue ribbon basis. Acquittal by such juries was rare; where communists were involved, an acquittal was highly improbable. At best, some of the defendants hoped a juror or two might hold out, resulting in a hung jury and a new trial. The nature of the jury can be seen from the presence on it of Russell Janney,

author of the best seller *Miracle of the Bells*. Janney, a well-known
anti-communist, had declared in a speech shortly before the trial "We
must fight communism to the death."

The jury deliberated a few hours, had a good night's sleep, and
came in with its verdict shortly after eleven A.M. next morning.

That the jury made a mockery of the months of evidence and came
to its verdict of guilty almost instantly tells more about the nature of
this trial than a hundred pages of legal evidence. What fell to us —
and by us, I mean those of us in the arts — was the question of what
we could do in the new conditions of anti-Communist propaganda
created by the trial. It was not only the twelve defendants in Foley
Square who were under attack; in every trade union where the Communist Party had any influence, Communists and suspected Communists were being attacked and driven from their leadership positions, from the union, and from their jobs. In this, the anti-Communists
(many of them in their jobs because of the work and courage of the
Communist organizers) in the AFL and the CIO turned and led the
hunt against the Communists.

Where did that leave us? I had an idea that I put to some of the
leaders, but they brushed it aside. The party had no time or money
for what they certainly regarded as the high jinks of the intellectuals,
a group never too highly regarded by any Communist leaders at that
time. My idea was to organize a great meeting of the arts in the cause
of peace. My feeling was that the struggle for peace was paramount.
If the march to war could be halted, other matters could be solved
more easily. I laid out the details of what could be done to Lionel
Berman of the Cultural Section, and he agreed with me that it was
worth a try. The leadership of the party turned us down flat. They
felt that every resource had to be directed toward fighting the repression and winning the trial. They had little faith in what we might do,
and they had no money to spare for us.

What emerged finally was the Scientific and Cultural Conference
for World Peace. Subsequent histories and the newspapers of the
time indicate that it was Soviet-inspired and backed with Soviet money.
Let me put that to rest. It was my idea. I fought and argued for it
with all my strength and will and finally got the New York City party
organization to accept it. As the trial of the leadership began, so did

our own work begin, and believe me, the task was monumental. I had never worked so hard in my life, and with this, I continued my writing, and with all this damned nobility of purpose, I almost destroyed my marriage. When I look back at that curious, romantic, idealistic young man who was Howard Fast, arrogant, undefeatable, and very often intolerable, I am absolutely astounded that any woman could tolerate him. Somehow Bette did. We tore ourselves to pieces during that year of 1949, but somehow we survived as man and wife, and I hardly dare to contemplate what my life might have been without her.

The initial support for the conference was so overwhelming that it shook us out of our feeling of isolation and despair. Money and support poured in; before January was half over, we had enough support to reserve the grand ballroom at the Waldorf and with it enough adjacent feeder rooms. The beginning of the Communist trial had not sent the intellectuals running for cover; instead, they rallied to the cause of peace with the Soviet Union, reminding me of the story Sartre had told me about the Resistance movement of the philosophers. Almost six hundred of the leading creative people in the United States signed on to endorse the conference and support it with their presence and their pocketbooks. The newspapers denounced it as a Soviet ploy carried out with Soviet financing, but in this case I had my own position, and even if it seems immoderate boasting, I have lived long enough to blow my trumpet a bit. This great conference, the largest and most important gathering of intellectuals in the forties, was, as I said, my idea. I fought it through against the wishes of the leadership of the party. The Russians had no part in it, and though they opened their eyes at what was happening and sent delegates to the conference, such as the composer Dimitri Shostakovich (it was before the State Department got the neat idea of barring foreign radicals), they had absolutely no part in bringing the conference about.

The Hearst newspapers and *The New York Daily News* went absolutely crazy, and if you can imagine a newspaper frothing at the mouth, that describes their condition. Even *The New York Herald Tribune,* the best and most honest New York newspaper of that period, found it hard to accept that Shostakovich, recently harshly criticized by the Russian party, should have come to this peace confer-

ence. At the same time, the presence of the astronomer Harlow Shapley impressed them deeply. *The Daily Mirror,* perhaps the most scurrilous and dishonest member of the Hearst chain, had this to say:

> The Soviet propaganda conference to be held at the Waldorf-Astoria must not be confused with anything intellectual or cultural . . . When that conference in Poland ended, it was decided to hold another in the United States . . . in January . . .
>
> Now look at some of these names . . . They are the names of American citizens. The American citizens hired space in the Waldorf-Astoria Hotel. Of course this is a free country! Anybody can hire a place to make a speech! Anybody can hire out his house to be polluted by shame and treason!
>
> But look at these names: Harlow Shapley, professor of astronomy at Harvard University . . . Louis Untermeyer, poet, lecturer at women's clubs . . . Franklin P. Adams, the famed F.P.A. of the columns and of "Information Please" . . . One is not surprised to see the names of Howard Fast, Langston Hughes, John Lardner, Donald Ogden Stewart, Dalton Trumbo. But Thomas Mann, when you were a refugee from Hitler's wrath, this country let you in. You did not go to Soviet Russia for sanctuary. You came here . . . You plied your trade here in freedom. But we see your name on this list! Also, we see Dashiell Hammett, the "Who Dunit" writer . . . So among the composers, conductors, and musicians is Leonard Bernstein. Too bad! He's a talented guy and we hate to see him in such lousy company . . .
>
> What we say is that any guy can say what he wants to say and make any kind of music he wants to make. But do we have to listen, too? . . .
>
> For instance, the editor will keep this list as published in *The Daily Worker* and when he turns on the radio, or if he wants to go to a show or a movie or a concert, he will glance at this list and he will exercise his American right of patronizing somebody whose name is not on it . . .
>
> Isn't it glorious to live in a country where you still have the right not to listen?

If one is unable to believe that the above was published in a large circulation newspaper in New York, then I can only say, go to th files and look. And this idiocy was matched in a thousand oth newspapers. It is the kind of thing that the histories omit.

I have taken the credit for originating the idea of the Waldorf Conference and fighting it through the party leadership, but the actual creation and construction of the conference was the work of about a dozen dedicated men and women, helped, of course, by many others. I was only a small cog in that process. The rank-and-file members in the professional and arts section performed miracles of organization — and never were we more than a handful. My own role in the conference was to chair the literary section, and I was determined to keep it absolutely open. When Norman Mailer, at no time a Communist, denounced the Soviet Union as "state capitalism," I said fine — his point of view.

Mary McCarthy — anti-Communist — was neither a supporter nor was she invited, but she appeared, umbrella in hand, striding fiercely down the center aisle of the room where the literary panel was in session, accompanied by three friends, right up to the platform, where she declared loudly, "You wouldn't dare to let me speak!"

"Why not?" I wanted to know.

"Because I'll tell the truth."

I reached down and helped her up to the platform. "Go ahead, tell us the truth."

I think the unexpectedness of my action took a bit of the wind out of her sails, and nothing she said was very upsetting — certainly mild compared with what the Hearst papers were saying. That was the only time I ever met Mary McCarthy, and naturally I was soundly criticized for giving the platform to a Trotskyite, if, indeed, she was a Trotskyite.

However, the Waldorf Conference was a great success and a very important moment in that desperate struggle to prevent a third world war. It revealed that over five hundred of the nation's leading intellectuals were willing to put their careers and names on the line for a conference created by the Communist Party. At that point, in 1949, the lines were clearly drawn, and no one at the conference had any illusions as to who the organizers were. And I do believe that this brought home to the Truman administration that its carefully orchestrated campaign of terror had not yet reduced everyone to the point of abject cowardice and indifference.

A curious note in this curious year of 1949. On January 18, at a meeting of the New York School Librarians Association, an an-

nouncement was made instructing all school librarians to remove
any and all copies of *Citizen Tom Paine* from their shelves. At the
same time, J. Edgar Hoover, who had become the shadow dictator
of the United States, sent his G-men to the New York Public Library
and to the main libraries of other cities, instructing the librarians to
remove Howard Fast's books from the shelves and destroy them.
Not the books of Karl Marx or Lenin, but the historical novels of
Howard Fast. God only knows why.

Immediately, a committee of librarians of the New York Public
Library system invited me to speak to the librarians at the main building
at Fifth Avenue and Forty-second Street.

About two hundred librarians and library workers were at the
meeting, chaired by a lovely white-haired lady, who said words to
this effect: "An agent of the Justice Department came to me and told
me that, by orders of the director of the FBI, the books of Howard
Fast were to be destroyed. But this is not Nazi Germany and we do
not burn books. Mr. Fast, your books are safely stored in the basement, and when the time comes and this madness has passed, they
will be restored to the shelves. Now we would like to hear what you
think about this strange time we live in."

That was forty years ago, and she has passed away, but she taught
me a lesson in simple, quiet courage. She put her life and her career
on the line, for she was not young, and to be thrown out of her job
would have been like a death sentence. I don't remember her name.
God bless her.

10

A SCIENTIST WHO WAS PART of the team that developed the atom bomb dined with Bette and me during the Waldorf Conference. He was at the conference but was keeping a very low profile, and since he still lectures occasionally in his position as professor emeritus at an important university, I cannot name him even at this late date. The stink of those years has almost washed away, but not entirely.

The story he told us at dinner that evening was that he was one of a dozen or so physicists invited to Washington to meet separately with the Joint Chiefs of Staff. The question put to him — and to the others, he subsequently learned — was this: If a hundred atom bombs were exploded simultaneously in an area of two hundred square miles, would the heat engendered be sufficient to ignite the atmosphere and put an end to all life on earth? He replied that he had never done the calculations that would allow him even to guess at the answer, and that even if he had, no set of calculations could be depended on. It was a question of the size of the bombs, how they were dropped, how close to one another, and a number of other factors that would remain unknown until the hundred bombs were dropped. He said that even if the atmosphere did not ignite, the consequences in terms of radiation might be almost as devastating, and when asked to explain, he replied that such an attack on Moscow might create lethal radiation moved by the great wind currents across Russia and China and Japan and even to the West Coast of America.

His questioners had not mentioned Moscow or any other target, but the scientist felt it was plain that such was the direction of their queries. He said that they continued to question him with a desperation that was terrifying, but he maintained his position. In later discussions with five of the other scientists called to meet with the Joint Chiefs, he found that their experiences and their conclusions were more or less the same. I fully realize the importance of relating this incident, and I also know that I have no witnesses to this except my wife and the scientist himself. Still, it must be told. I don't know whether the testimony of these scientists remains valid, but it does suggest two things: first, that preparations for an atomic raid on the Soviet Union were under way, and second, that the use of atomic weapons in mass might well signal the end of any life on earth, human or otherwise. If the latter fact is true, we have witnessed forty years of madness in the production of thousands of atomic weapons that can never be used.

However, a few days after the Waldorf Conference had concluded, I received a cable from Frédéric Joliot-Curie, inviting me to a great international conference on peace to be held in Paris on April 20. I decided that a great international conference could do very well without Howard Fast, and I wired him my refusal. I had discussed the matter with Bette, and while she insisted that if I felt I had to go, I should go, I had grave doubts about leaving her alone with the children at this point. But Joliot-Curie would not have it, and his next cable said: INSIST ON YOUR PERSONAL PARTICIPATION ABSOLUTELY NECESSARY PEACE CONGRESS PARIS 20 APRIL. JOLIOT-CURIE.

Any telegram impresses me. It elicits the same sense of urgency that one gets from a lawyer's letter, and Bette shared my feeling. I don't want to, I told her, to which she replied that there was no way I could refuse.

I answered Joliot-Curie on April 1, 1949, writing: "I have your cablegram today and I am acting as speedily as possible to get a passport. Curiously enough, this time the difficulty is not with the State Department but with the federal judge who sentenced me to prison. He must grant me a release, that is, permission to leave the country before I can apply to the State Department for my passport."

My first efforts to get a passport were rejected, but when I agreed to do a series of pieces for *The Daily Worker,* neither the State Department nor Judge Keech stood in the way. My passport was issued for only thirty days, and it was the last passport I would hold for the next eleven years.

However, a good deal happened that is not in the files and has never been told before. Before I left for Paris, I was asked to meet with Paul Novick and Chaim Suller. These two men were important party functionaries, leaders of the Jewish Section of the party. At that time, in 1949, there were thousands of Yiddish-speaking workers in the garment industry, the cigar industry, and a number of other light industries. The party published its own Yiddish newspaper, the *Freiheit,* one of a number of foreign-language left-wing newspapers. As these foreign workers, Jews, Hungarians, Poles, Italians, grew old and died, their newspapers went out of existence, so ending a rich and vibrant part of American history that has been little noticed and, as far as I know, never recorded. The *Freiheit,* like the others, perished as its readers died, but in 1949 it was still a vital newspaper with a small but active readership. The Jewish Section was one of the foreign-language divisions in the party, and in New York City, it was the largest foreign-language group. Yiddish was then considered by the party to be the language of the European-born Jews. Novick was on the National Committee of the party, and as such he was able to speak for the entire leadership. Suller was his associate.

No one else was present at the meeting, and Paul Novick told me that he spoke with the full agreement of the National Committee. He said that the National Committee of the Communist Party of the United States, a member of the fraternal brotherhood of the Communist International, after full discussion, had decided to issue a charge of anti-Semitic practices against the Communist Party of the Soviet Union, and this charge held that the entire leadership of the Communist Party of the Soviet Union was ridden with anti-Semitism.

I listened to this, utterly dumfounded. I shook my head. This simply could not be. Nothing had led up to it, no signs, no indications. We were the party that fought anti-Semitism as we fought for the rights of the blacks and every other minority. We had died for these principles. We had never compromised.

"This can't be true," I pleaded. "This makes no sense."

"It is true," Novick said. "Can you imagine that we would make a charge like this if we didn't have proof? We have ample proof. We are not talking about our party or the French party or the Italian party — we are talking about the Soviets."

"But that's the center."

"No," Novick said sharply. "We're the center. We are responsible for our actions. If the Soviets lack the historical understanding to appreciate the consequences of what they are doing, then it is our duty to criticize them."

"How do I come into this?" I asked bleakly.

"You're going to Paris. The Soviets will send a large delegation to the Peace Congress. Find out who in the French party is in charge of their delegation and have him set up a meeting with whoever is in charge of the Soviet delegation. Then you are to state that as a formal representative of the National Committee of our party, you make this charge against the Communist Party of the Soviet Union — very formally, just as I put it to you: We accuse the leadership of the Communist Party of the Soviet Union of grievous acts of anti-Semitism and of a non-Leninist position. You must understand the gravity of these charges and the need for secrecy. If the press got hold of this, the consequences would be very bad."

At best, this sums up the sense of the conversation with Novick and Suller. They went on to specify some of the actions in Russia: the virtual abolition of all Yiddish-language institutions, the closing of Yiddish-language papers, the disappearance of certain important Jewish figures, and the indication — though without sufficient proof — that certain Jewish officers in the Red Army, men who had been highly decorated, had been summarily arrested and put to death. It was a shocking business and it would become more shocking in the years to come.

But then and again and again, I and others in the party were faced with what was for us a terrible choice: Do we regard these things as endemic to the structure and practice of the party, or were the incidents — of which we had only the vaguest proof — simply aberrations, diversions by error or misuse? Things limited to the Soviets and to be endured until they were set right? Hindsight is a weak attribute. I told Suller and Novick that I would deliver their message if it was possible to do so.

In those days, air travel across the Atlantic was still an uncertain novelty. I had flown the Atlantic once, and that was enough for the time being. I booked passage on the *Queen Mary*, where I shared a stateroom with Sir Victor Ellice Sassoon, the industrialist and philanthropist, the last of the great Jewish Anglo-Indian family. I had no idea of the background of the soft-spoken, handsome elderly gentleman who shared my cabin, nor did he know very much about the Communist writer with whom he was traveling. He was much too polite to inquire into my background, after my having told him that I was a novelist, nor did he tell me anything of himself except that his family had interests in the Far East.

However, no sooner had the ship cast off than I was sought out by a man named Melvin Johnson whom I had met overseas in 1945 and who now worked for some unspecified government bureau, which I guessed was the Central Intelligence Agency. He suggested that we share a table with Robert Conway, a correspondent for *The New York Daily News,* and thereby spare ourselves the fate of being stuck with some insufferable bores. Since this was my first trip on a luxury liner, I heeded his advice. Johnson was a pleasant, unobtrusive fellow, and having known him from a kinder past, I was not troubled by my suspicions. With Bob Conway, a big, easygoing Irishman, I struck up an immediate friendship. For five days, we ate all our meals together and we became very close and very fond of each other — even though after the crossing I never saw them again.

Our table was an endless seminar, Fast the Communist, Conway the older amiable newspaper man, open to anything and everything, and Johnson, who might have been anything and added a bit of zest to things. I must say here that during all those years of small terror — as compared to the large terror of an Adolf Hitler — I almost never encountered anger, antagonism, or accusation on a one-to-one basis. For the most part, people took it for granted that thousands of decent persons who were called Communists were simply liberals who had leaned too far to the left. A Communist did not exist in the flesh; he was a symbol, a semantic image, an idea, a trigger word — in fact, the only one-on-one vitriolic hatred ever directed at me came later, in prison, where a crazed professional criminal who was finishing a twenty-year sentence for murdering his wife, and who ran the prison garage, threatened to kill Albert Maltz and me because he hated Communists.

As Bob Conway and I became more at ease with each other, an

interesting notion occurred to me. Why couldn't the two of us, once
the Peace Congress was over, go on to the Soviet Union? We would
both report what we saw. *The Daily News* would run my story
alongside his, and *The Daily Worker* would run his story alongside
mine. I was sure I could get *The Worker* to agree. Could he get *The
Daily News* to agree? The notion excited Conway enough for him
to put through a radio telephone call to his editor, who answered
more or less in this fashion: "Are you absolutely crazy? Fast gives
you fifty thousand readers and you give him a million?"

So much for that. On our third day out, Bob Conway told me that
he'd run into a fellow he knew who was a partner in the House of
Morgan. There were three of the Morgan people on board, and Bob's
friend had asked whether he could talk Howard Fast into having a
drink with them.

That was by no means difficult, since I never dreamed that I would
have the pleasure of looking the "beast" in the face while he paid for
the refreshment. The beast consisted of three amiable and charming
fortyish gentlemen who could not conceal their delight at having Fast
at the table with them. Their curiosity was insatiable; they asked
endless questions. Did I think this American terror would continue
and become another Germany? How did it feel to be tried and sentenced to prison? Could the party survive? Would there be war with
Russia? Did I see any hope for democracy in America? Did I think it
would ever be as it was before the war? I didn't have answers any
more than they did, but what astonished me was that they shared
my fears. They were of the House of Morgan; they were the top
echelon of American finance — why were they so afraid?

"Because we can't survive fascism any better than you," one of
them said. But that was only four years after Hitler died in the bunker
in Berlin. These three men were perceptive, well-educated, and aware
of what was going on in Washington. They loathed Truman and put
him at the center of the situation. They exhibited no feelings of anti-
Communism; they had nothing to gain by being warm and friendly
toward me, yet they were. At one point, one of them said, "We read
your paper every day. Do you read ours?"

They meant *The Wall Street Journal,* and I had to admit that I read
it only occasionally. I doubted that they read *The Daily Worker* every
day, and I asked them why they would. Their answer was that only

two papers could be depended on to tell the truth, *The Wall Street Journal* and *The Daily Worker*.

As a novelist, I found the incident fascinating, and I thought about it many times since then, reflecting on the difference between these three cultured and charming men and the parochial school kids carrying their hate-filled cards. These men were far more deeply and fundamentally anti-Communist than the hoodlums on the street, or the Roy Cohns or the John Rankins. The hoodlums, high and low, were the functioning members of the inquisition; these men were on a level with Isabella of Spain. They would no more think of extending a hand to help me than Nixon would, but on a one-to-one basis, we could speak as civilized and cultured people. They saw me not as a ravening, bomb-throwing creature, but as a contender. They were not judgmental; they were interested in profit, and profit in the world of finance does not come from ignorance but from being able to assess the reality of things. They were interested and respectful; they left it to others to act as thugs.

Another incident on the trip underlined the attitude. In those days, the transatlantic liners made their European stop at Cherbourg, and from there one took the boat-train to Paris. Reservations for the boat-train were made on board ship on the last day of the passage. When I came for my ticket, there were an undue number of smiles from the ship's officers in the purser's office. Something amused them, but I had no notion as to what it might be. The ship docked, we went through customs, I said goodbye to Bob Conway and Melvin Johnson, and then found that I was in the same car as they were, and in that car were the three men from the House of Morgan and a couple of other people I had gotten to know on the ship. Well, why not? But the odd thing was that while their tickets put them in the main section of the car, mine put me in the single compartment at the front of the car. It was a compartment for six people, and apparently I was the first one to board the train. Since I had no intention of sitting there alone, I put my luggage on the rack and joined my friends in the main part of the car.

Smiles and a few giggles. I was not in on the joke and I was damned if I would ask them what it was. The train started. There were extra seats in the main part of the car, and I decided to take my luggage out of the compartment and keep it in sight. I went to the compartment, and now five people were seated there, a distinguished-looking older gentleman, a lady of his age who might well be his wife, a younger couple and a child. I opened the door and stepped in, and the gentleman asked, "What can I do for you?"

I pointed to the empty seat. "That's my seat."

"That is not your seat. This is our compartment."

"That's my seat," I said with annoyance. "I paid for it. Here is my ticket. I intend to occupy it."

"I shall call the conductor," the man said.

"No need to," I snapped. "I have established my right. I have no desire to make this trip in the company of ill-mannered people. You can have your damn compartment."

With that, I left the compartment and returned to the main part of the car, where everyone I knew was doubled over with laughter. Big joke, and I was the butt of it. I turned to Bob Conway, who stifled his laughter sufficiently to ask me whether I knew whose compartment that was.

"No, I don't."

"William Averell Harriman."

"My God, no!"

"Come on, come on, Harriman the multimillionaire and Fast the Communist —"

I couldn't laugh at it. Of all the men in government, Harriman was one of those I most respected, the man who had administered Lend-Lease, who was in part responsible for England's survival, who had been ambassador to the Soviet Union during the most trying months of the war — one of the few men in government whose honesty and integrity could never be doubted; and on the other hand, Fast, young, arrogant, big fat chip on his shoulder. As I walked back toward the compartment, I saw the conductor leaving. I entered gingerly this time, the words of my apology carefully worked out, but before I could say anything, Harriman was on his feet. "Our deepest apologies, Mr. Fast. You must forgive our rudeness, but we had no idea who you were, and in any case, I had no right to behave as I did —"

I tried to stop him, to make him understand that it was a tasteless joke, and both he and his wife insisted that I remain in the compartment. I refused as politely as I could, apologized on my own part, and left.

*

I had the key to a small apartment on the Quai de Passy, lent to me for the duration of the congress by a Dr. Maurice Segal, brother of Captain Cécile Segal, who had introduced me to Joliot-Curie. I should note that Frédéric Joliot-Curie was the chairman of the International Peace Congress, possibly the largest and most impressive meeting of the world's writers, artists, journalists, scientists, physicians, theater and film people, and leading political figures, elected and appointed, in all the history of mankind. While the United States was represented by only fifty-six notables, the public figures from England and the continent ran into the thousands. There was hardly a famous European name not present in Paris. The Americans on the organizing committee were Dr. Gene Weltfish, a professor at Columbia College, Dr. Du Bois, Donald Henderson, a trade union leader, Albert Kahn, a writer, A. W. Moulton, an Episcopal bishop, Paul Robeson, and myself; but the supporting delegation from the United States included fifty additional names. So much for those who dubbed this, with the usual contempt for anything that related to peace, as a Communist ploy. To me, it was a great outcry of humanity for peace.

Having deposited my luggage in the apartment and slept as well as I could in the excitement of being in Paris in April — the first time in my life — I set out in the morning to present my credentials and received my *carte d'identitée*, a piece of cardboard five by eight inches, my name and function on one side, blank on the other. I specify this because, in the course of the congress, I met Pablo Picasso. He threw his arms around me, kissed me full on the mouth — the only time I was ever kissed thus by a man — and said to me, "Come to my studio. I want you to have something. You must take whatever you desire." The poor demented creature who was Howard Fast, driven by an astonishing set of principles, scruples, and guilts, replied, "Oh, no. No. I couldn't do that. No, I couldn't take that kind of advantage of you. No — only if you would autograph my *carte d'identitée*."

I handed him my pen, and with a single motion he drew a lovely, perfect dove, and then signed his name to it. Arnold Zweig, the German novelist, and Pablo Neruda, the great Chilean poet and, later, Nobel Prize winner, were standing alongside Picasso, and each in turn asked me whether he could autograph the card under Picasso's little sketch. I was delighted, pleased, privileged. Neruda wrote a few words on the card, and Zweig did the same. Each signed it, and I would not have traded that card for all the works in Picasso's studio. At home, we put it in a beautiful velvet frame, glass on both sides, and then we lost it in a fire. Of such is the worth of possessions.

But to return to the moment I presented my credentials. I was told that the organizing committees would meet the press that afternoon at La Maison de Pensée on the Champs-Élysées, the Communist Party house of the arts. The difference then, in 1949, between the situation of the Communist Party of the United States and the Communist Party of France was enormous. The party in the United States had about thirty-five thousand members — an exact count is impossible — who had weathered the terror. The Communist Party of France, which had done so much in organizing the Resistance and fought the Germans through the occupation, had six million members and was the first party of France. It was, in 1949, at the height of its power and was still beloved by the majority of the French people.

At the press conference I met the other members of the organizing committee who had arrived separately from the States: Dr. Weltfish, Dr. Du Bois, Paul Robeson, and the others. The press conference took place in the garden of the house, and the press of the whole world was there. On that beautiful April day, I felt that I had magically been transported into another world, a world where Communists were honored, not hunted down and imprisoned, a world where people spoke reasonably of reasonable things.

I noticed that one of the press people kept watching me. She was a tall, dark-haired, slender woman, very handsome if not beautiful, and somehow vaguely familiar. When the press conference broke up, she approached me and introduced herself. "You don't know me, of course. You were seven years old the last time we met."

I found it then. "You're Rhoda Miller. I was eight years old. That was at my mother's funeral."

"Yes, yes, of course. And all these years I've seen your name and read about you."

We were first cousins. She was the daughter of Dan Miller, my father's best friend and my mother's brother. She was married to a man named Joseph de Silva, a citizen of Ceylon of Portuguese descent. Her husband was in Ceylon and would join her later, and they intended to live in Europe and write about postwar Europe. Meanwhile, she was covering the Peace Congress for a Communist paper

in Ceylon. She herself had been a member of the party for many
years.

Sam Sillen, editor of the American Communist publication *Main-
stream*, a party attempt at a classy quarterly, and I were dining with
part of the Italian delegation, across the width of Paris from the
apartment on the Quai de Passy. The Italian Communists were wonderful, the warmest, most delightful people imaginable. It was a fine
evening, and it broke up at midnight. The Italians told us that there
was a cab stand down the street, where one could easily find a cab,
even at this hour.

Sam and I found the cab stand easily enough. There were about
eight cabs parked in a little square, the drivers standing around talking and smoking. It was very late, and there didn't appear to be much
call for their services. Sam, whose French was excellent — mine was
primitive — told them where we wanted to go. Their response was
to shrug and make snorting remarks. I asked Sam what they were
saying.

"Assorted things," Sam said in English. "The nicest is for us to
walk. A free translation of the rest would be, bug off, take a shit —
a lot of *merde* — and assorted remarks about my mother and your
mother."

"Because we're Americans?"

"Exactly. They've got us by the short hairs and they're having a
ball watching us squirm."

I had an idea. I took out my *carte d'identitée* and handed it to the
nearest cab driver. He stared at it, turned it over, stared again, and
then passed it around to the others. The mood change was incredible.
Now they argued for the privilege of driving us, and the cab driver
who took me across Paris refused payment. I mention this because it
gave us a sense of what our presence in Paris meant, not as Communists, but as Americans at a peace conference.

In a dispatch to *The Daily Worker*, I sent an article about the Peace
Congress that I think gives a good picture of the event:

> I want to paint a picture of a day of the peace conference, at the Salle
> Pleyel in the Rue Mirabeau in Paris. We start in the morning at

nine o'clock, with the April sunshine warming the street — which is lovely, as what street in Paris is not — with the people of Paris finishing their morning coffee at the cafés, and then hurrying to work. Already the delegates are beginning to gather in the Pleyel, on the sidewalk in front and in the lobby, and already you can hear the rich mixture of the world's speech that was a part of the conference from beginning to end.

The Pleyel is a great music hall, somewhat larger than Carnegie Hall. On the sidewalk, *Humanité* is being hawked, the London *Daily Worker* and the Paris edition of *The Herald Tribune*. As the delegates arrive, the cameras begin to click and already the nerve-ending interviews for the press of twenty nations are being sought . . .

More and more of the delegates arrive, and now the big downstairs lobby is packed full . . . Here old friends meet who have not seen each other for twenty years; here people embrace, each discovering for the first time that the other lives. Here is the talk and the gossip and the professional and political exchange of the world . . . The French have a way of organizing things; it is not better or worse than our way, but different, a little more human, a little less rigid and dogmatic, yet wonderfully effective for all of that. You never expect things to happen, yet they do; order appears quickly, almost mysteriously . . .

The American delegation is on the left, to the extreme front. From there, you look back over the hall and read the names of the nations, some colonies, some possessions, some resistance movements, but all of them nations here, and their faces make a tapestry of humanity stretching up into the dim distance of the balconies.

Each day, a new president is chosen to preside. For this session, it may be Du Bois of America, or Fadeev of Russia, or Picasso of France . . . You look around and you discover that more than half the delegates wear earphones, listening with intense concentration. The system of simultaneous translation, installed by the French planners of the conference, is one of the most amazing features. All the translators are volunteers; some are French; some are Paris residents of other nationalities . . .

Then the break for lunch, with at least thirty various meetings to fill in the lunch interval. The American delegation meets at a restaurant nearby, and conducts their business while they eat — with the full cooperation of the management, waiters, etc., even though the restaurant is one of a great Paris chain. In fact, you learn early in your stay that your delegates card is the key to the city of Paris. Show it to a cab driver, and he will not only take you outside his regular terri-

tory, but he will reject a tip with indignation. Show it to a waiter, and
the restaurant is yours. Show it to a railway man, and you are his
personal charge.

The above is full beyond the call of a news story, but then my feet
rarely touched the ground during that time in Paris. These were the
heroes of the Resistance, the men who had lived through, not the
small terror that had taken over America but the great terror of
the Nazi occupation, men and women who had put their lives on
the line, who had seen their comrades tortured and murdered. Frédéric Joliot-Curie made ammunition and bombs in the basement of
the Louvre; he was the chairman of the congress. Louis Aragon, the
novelist and poet, was the co-chairman.

Aragon was a brilliant, delightful, and charming man. Like the
other French Communists at the meeting, he had been part of the
Resistance. I went with him to his apartment one afternoon, and
the moment we entered the street, greeting came from every side —
as if the street were a part of an adoring family — heads thrust out
of windows, hands waved. The small apartment he occupied with
his wife, the novelist Elsa Triolet, was filled with books, more of a
home for the books than the man and woman who lived there so
frugally.

Aragon sat at the podium with the other leaders of the conference,
and unless he was listening to some vital speaker, he never stopped
writing in an open notebook. I asked him one day, "Why, Louis?
Why must you take notes? Surely you have stenographers for that."

"Notes? What notes?"

"Well, you are writing constantly."

"Of course. I am writing my new novel. And if not now, when?"

And I was here, greeted, loved — not the political outcast I was in
America but a man admired for every step he had taken. The peace
meeting was to culminate in a giant soccer stadium on the outskirts
of Paris, and I was asked to make the address for the American delegation.

I had dinner one evening with Renaud de Jouvenel, a descendant
of one of the titled families of France, a Communist who still lived
in the old Paris mansion that his family had occupied for years. He
served a wonderful meal that began with goose livers, went on to an

entrecôte, and finished with remarkable tarts. He offered to translate my remarks at Buffalo Stadium and to correct my pronunciation. I then rewrote the short speech phonetically and it came off as if I knew a bit of French. He also told me that Laurent Casanova was the person in the French Communist Party to see about my assignment on anti-Semitism from our National Committee; the next day, he introduced me to Casanova, a tall, handsome, solidly built man who listened to my problem with an impassive face. Fortunately, Jouvenel was there to speak for me, since Casanova either had no English or was unwilling to use it.

The head of the Soviet delegation to the Peace Congress was Alexander Fadeev, a Russian writer. I said that I wanted an unbugged room and asked Mr. Fadeev to bring a translator. This was the first time I had been involved in something of this nature, and I was surprised at how seriously both Jouvenel and Casanova considered it. "We regard Communist Parties as equals," Jouvenel told me later, "and Casanova thinks well of you." Why, I don't know. I ate a large dose of humility among these men and women who had put their lives on the line when Paris was occupied by the Nazis. Casanova arranged the meeting with Fadeev for the following afternoon. I felt somewhat peculiar about that because the day before I was to meet with Fadeev, the Russians gave a splendid dinner for the American delegation. It took place in a wonderful restaurant established in Paris by White Russians after the 1917 revolution. The walls were tiled with niches for icons, an interior as grand as any I had seen in Paris. I was also surprised to see the warmth the White and Red Russians displayed toward one another. There was much drinking and toasting, several of the toasts by Fadeev, the man I was to meet on the following day. He was a very large, very handsome man, a great shock of white hair on a head that appeared to be carved of stone, and piercing blue eyes.

The next day Jouvenel appeared to take me to the meeting with Fadeev. It was held in a small basement room in the Salle Pleyel, and I was assured that the room was not bugged. Jouvenel left. I was there alone with Fadeev and the translator. I was not nervous but was certainly unsure of myself and somewhat tentative. I began by saying that I had been instructed to bring formal charges against the Central Committee of the Soviet Union. That was a mouthful, and I had to pinch myself figuratively to believe that I said what I had said.

It was translated, and then Fadeev thought about it for a while and then he nodded and told me to go ahead.

"Do you want to take notes?" I asked him.

"Do you have notes?" he wanted to know.

"Under these circumstances, no, of course."

"Then I don't need notes. Do any of the French comrades know what this is about?"

"No. It's absolutely secret. I was instructed that it must be absolutely secret."

"Very well. Go ahead." He was neither friendly nor unfriendly. He was absolutely calm and passive.

I plunged right in. "Our National Committee charges the leadership of the Soviet Union with anti-Semitism, the violation of a basic socialist ethic and a grave threat to the world Communist movement."

I had worked that one out for myself, and when I finished, I reserved the right to be nervous and a little scared. It was my own decision to put a little elegance into the charge, to give it at least a minimum of literary flavor, and while I had heard about the respect one Communist Party has for another, I was not very certain that it worked in practice. Fadeev, I had been told, was a member of the Supreme Soviet of the Soviet Union.

He worked on what I had said, his eyes half closed, humming softly to himself, a nervous habit, I felt; and then he said, simply, "There is no anti-Semitism in the Soviet Union."

"No more than that?"

The translator put the question to him.

"There is no anti-Semitism in the Soviet Union."

As I look back, I am amazed by my anger and irritation. Before I left, I had been well briefed in New York on the evidence our party had. There was evidence that at least eight leading Jewish figures in the Red Army and in government had been arrested on what appeared to be trumped-up charges. Yiddish-language newspapers had been suppressed. Schools that taught Hebrew had been closed. There was more of this, and I had committed it to memory then, though I can't remember the full details of it today. Yet what amazes me is that I did not back down before his bland response. I had the most enormous respect for the Soviet Union; like thousands of other

Americans, I believed it to be the bastion of world socialism. That
was another time.

"What are you telling me?" I asked Fadeev. "I am told by very
responsible comrades to bring a most serious charge against your
leadership — a charge that is underlined by the murder of six million
Jews by the Nazis — and your response is that there is no anti-Semitism in the Soviet Union? Am I supposed to go back and say there
is no anti-Semitism in the Soviet Union? We have evidence." I spelled
out all the details. "If some of these charges are untrue, we know
that the closing of the schools is true. We know that other things are
true. Why can't you discuss these things?"

"Because there is no anti-Semitism in the Soviet Union." A slight
show of annoyance now.

I realized that I was getting nowhere, that he had fixed on his
response and that he would not elaborate on it. I would return to the
leadership of the Jewish Section of the party, Paul Novick and Chaim
Suller, two very gentle people; Fadeev, on the other hand, would
return to — what? I did not know. Also, it might well be that Fadeev
knew nothing about anti-Semitism in Russia. Seven years later, at the
Twentieth Congress of the Communist Party of the Soviet Union,
after Khrushchev's revelations of Stalin's monstrous deeds, Fadeev
put a pistol in his mouth and blew his brains out.

But now, in April of 1949, I was left with a reply that was no
reply, and after I came away from the meeting, my own doubts grew.
Few Russians known to the West had the reputation of Alexander
Fadeev, for integrity, for bravery in the struggle against the Nazis,
and for his calm, warm attitude as a representative of his country.
Could it be that Suller and Novick were wrong? Only a few years
earlier, Russia had paid a price of twenty million human lives to
destroy the Nazis and wipe out fascism. I also knew the details of a
half-forgotten story, that Russia had, in the midst of her struggle
against the Nazis, moved three million Polish and Ukrainian Jews
eastward beyond the reach of the Nazis and their death camps, and
thereby saved their lives. So what was the truth of it? Had I brought
a valid accusation to Paris, or had I put my foot in my mouth, a
practice not entirely strange to me?

The meeting at Buffalo Stadium helped to wipe out the doubts and
frustration engendered by Fadeev. The massive crowd, a hundred

thousand in the stadium and thousands more marching through it, was a sight unlike any I had ever witnessed. The brigade of French troops who in World War One had refused to act as a firing squad and execute their comrades who had been unable to leave their trenches in the face of withering German fire came marching into the arena. The crowd went wild. Here were these men in their fifties and sixties, in their old World War One uniforms, heroes in an action I had never even heard about, symbols of the human need to retain compassion above all orders of army commanders — and they evoked a roar from the crowd that was like a prayer thundered against all the oppression of man by man.

Quiet fell as I rose to deliver my small speech. I was introduced as the American writer who would not be silenced and who now faced prison. I read the French words of Jouvenel's translation slowly and carefully, trying to remember his instructions on pronunciation, and the very fact that I was speaking French, if poorly, brought the crowd to their feet. It was a great moment for me, and a great deal more than I deserved.

But my pretense at French betrayed me. The organizing committee asked that a few people from each delegation travel to other French cities where local meetings would be held. I volunteered for Toulouse, thinking that this would be a good opportunity to see the hospital that had been created with the help and the funds supplied by Dr. Barsky's Joint Anti-Fascist Refugee Committee, and for which I was going to jail. I left Paris on a Monday morning, taking the sleeper to Toulouse and suffering all the misery of travel in France by someone who has not one word of French. If I had only pleaded this, the organizing committee would have sent a translator with me. However, in Toulouse this difficulty disappeared. At the station, I was met by a large delegation of the French Resistance, along with a group of Spanish Republicans. Anticipating my lack of knowledge of French, they had enlisted Madame Étiennette Benichou, a small, bright-eyed, alert woman, to be my guide and translator. She had been one of the leaders of the Resistance, and her home had been a pivot and center of the Resistance.

She gave me a fine tour of Toulouse, that old and lovely city that nestles under the slopes of the Pyrenees. I was greatly impressed by the hospital. Our committee had purchased an ancient, broken-down château, and in a very short time, along with Spanish physicians and volunteers, had turned it into a spotless, beautifully run modern hospital.

After we left the hospital, Madame Benichou asked me whether it would be an imposition to request that I autograph some of my books at a bookstore. I assured her that nothing warms a writer's heart more than autographing his books, whereupon I was taken to a bookstore jammed with men and women waiting for the author to appear. I suppose they realized that I could not refuse their request and had prepared for me in advance, and for the next three hours I autographed French translations of *Freedom Road* and *The American*.

I had written a small speech for the big peace meeting that evening, and Madame Benichou was kind enough to do what Jouvenel had done, translating it into French and rehearsing me in the pronunciation. That went off well enough, but the people at Toulouse, feeling that they could not send Howard Fast, poor ignorant sod, back alone to face the terrors of France without a word of French, assigned a translator to ride with me.

A week later, I was back in New York, out of the romantic dream where I was not a despised Communist waiting to be sent to prison, but a hero to some of the leading minds on earth — and the one was as off-base as the other; for my persecution in America was senseless and stupid and my elevation to heroic stature in France was equally unfounded in any kind of reality. I had been selected because the field was thin, but such selection influences a person as much as other things.

HANA MASUDA, the young Nisei woman who had come to us straight from one of the "relocation centers," was unable to cope with what was happening to Bette and me. During the five years she had been with us, watching circumstances tear at us, watching us turn on each other, and then hearing that I must go to prison, she had grown increasingly upset. She had become part of our family. Bette and I were two people totally in love; Hana agonized over the tension and quarrels she witnessed. We were the same two people. What was happening to us? She tried to understand why I was going to prison. She said to me once, "You and Bette are the most generous and honorable people I ever knew. It makes no sense. It's like the thing that happened when they put us in the concentration camp." And then one night, it was clear that she could no longer stand the tension in the household. We called her family on the Coast, and her brother came east for her and took her back to California. We had met her brother while he was still in uniform, a part of the Nisei battalion that fought so gallantly in Italy and Germany.

Bette had begun to paint seriously, and she was making good progress. She is a brilliant artist, and in later years, when she turned to sculpture, she began to be recognized as one of the fine sculptors of our time. I was working intermittently without pay as a reporter and columnist for *The Daily Worker*, and we had two very young children to care for. I saw that the relationship was tottering, and I told Bette that she had had the short end of the stick long enough. I had been off anywhere and everywhere, and the weight of running the family fell on her. "You know, I could die and never see Europe or any place other than right here," she said to me. I agreed with her almost desperate feeling. It came of too much strain, too much being alone, and the constant terror. "You have to get away," I told her.

And then the third subpoena was served. I was awakened from my sleep at midnight by the ringing of the doorbell. Our house on Ninety-fourth Street had big wooden doors that we locked at night. I went downstairs and asked who was there. The man identified himself as a process server. I told him, in some choice street talk, to get out of here and if he wanted to serve some damn process on me, to return in the morning. He demanded that I open the doors. I told him I'd see him in hell first. By now he was yelling at the top of his lungs, and I was matching him. Upstairs, Bette had the children — both of them terror-stricken — Rachel five, Jon a little more than a year old, clutched in her arms in bed. I think if I had opened the doors, I might have killed that man; but fortunately I had enough sense to pick up the phone and call the cops. A few minutes later, the cops arrived and grabbed him. I heard him arguing with them that he was a process server for a committee of the United States Congress, and that I had to take service. A cop called out to me, "Mr. Fast, do you want to open the door and take service?"

"In the morning. Not now."

"I don't blame you," the cop said, and then he turned to the process server and said, "You heard him. Now get out of here or I'll put you under arrest."

During those years, I had my ups and downs with the New York police, but on balance I'll give them all the points in the book over the strange specimens who staffed the Federal Bureau of Investigation.

But that incident clinched it, and I told Bette, "Get away from it for a while." They had taken my passport when I returned from France, but she still had hers. "Go to Europe. Take a few weeks," I told her. "I'll take care of the kids."

She protested that we couldn't afford it, and to leave me with two small children would be too cruel. I assured her that we'd find a way to afford it. We decided to repeat the process that had brought Hana to us, and we put an advertisement in *The Times*. It brought to us a black woman named Juliette Brown, in her late fifties. She had been a registered nurse and now wanted a less demanding job. That was one part done in the plan for Bette to have some time off. Then there was the committee, where I stood on the Fifth Amendment to the Constitution and refused to speak at all. I was learning the ins and outs of being a common criminal.

Bette tried to back out of the trip. I insisted. Finally, we agreed that she would go during the month of August and that while she was away, I'd find a place in the country for myself, Juliette, and the children. Fortunately, Juliette had no ties to prevent her leaving New York for a month, and she had found the job with our family to be what she was looking for — and of course her experience as a nurse gave me a great deal of reassurance. Asking around, we found that a couple named Milvey had a house on Mount Airy in Croton and were willing to rent it for the month of August. August came, and Bette and I had a tearful parting, and I packed Juliette and the two kids and appropriate luggage into a rented car and took off for Croton.

Mount Airy, in Croton Township, was an absolutely fascinating place and deserves a spot in American history. In elevation, it is something between a large hill and a small mountain, and since a few years after the turn of the century, it has been called Red Hill. John Reed had a cottage there, as did Robert Minor and the artist William Gropper and Sam Sillen and Joseph North, a rich mixture of Communists, socialists, people who were neither but loved the beauty of the place, and even here and there an anti-Communist who had long since surrendered his beliefs but would not surrender his home on Mount Airy. The Milvey house was a comfortable modern home in a splendid grove of old oaks, fairly isolated except for one house on the other side of the grove, which belonged to a psychiatrist, whose name, if my memory serves me, was Dr. Wechsler.

The first three weeks of August were restful and without any great incident. I luxuriated in our being alone, in not having the telephone ring — I had given only a few people my number — and in having nothing demanded of me or imposed on me. Bette kept in constant touch, so I had no worries in that direction. I was then finishing the manuscript that became *The Proud and the Free,* about the great revolt of the Pennsylvania Line during the American Revolution, and I was also trying to write an essay about literature. I worked and I played with my children, and our very simple meals were prepared by Juliette. The three weeks were like a sunny dream interposed in my normal life. The ground in the grove was littered with acorns, and I explained to the children that from these small acorns, the mighty oak trees grew. They loved the notion, and they decided to gather acorns for a grove of their own. In the entranceway of the house, there was one of those huge copper fifty-gallon kettles that institutions used to use. Rachel suggested that if we filled the kettle with acorns, we could have the biggest oak forest in the world.

I fell in with the idea because it made for an endless game. For two weeks we gathered acorns every day and stowed them in the kettle. It was one of those hazy, easy summers when time stretches out, and the game went on, and at the end of two weeks, the kettle was almost full of heaven knows how many acorns.

Then, one afternoon, there was one of those crashing thunderstorms and all the lights went out. I had been taking a nap in an armchair, and whenever I fell asleep reading, Rachel and Jonathan embarked on another game, stealing my moccasins and hiding them. Now on this afternoon of the thunderstorm, Dr. Wechsler, whom we had not met, came through the grove that separated us to see whether we needed help. He knew there was a man living here without a wife and with two children, and since we never locked the door, he entered without knocking. He stood at the door watching me. I was crawling around on the living room floor, looking under couch and chairs, trying to find out where Rachel had hidden my shoes, while Rachel was gurgling with laughter. Jonathan, frightened by the thunder and lightning, was upstairs, being soothed by Juliette. The good doctor watched me and then his eye fixed on the kettle of acorns.

"Have you lost something?" he asked me.

"My shoes."

"And how did you lose them?"

"When I doze off, the little folk take them away."

"Oh?" Now he was staring at the acorns again. "That kettle was empty," he said, thinking, I'm sure, of the last time he had been at the Milveys.

"We filled it," Rachel said proudly.

"Oh? And why?"

"We're going to grow an oak forest."

He looked at Rachel and then he looked at me. I was still hunting for my moccasins.

"An oak forest?"

"That's right."

He turned and fled. Occasionally, in the years that followed, whispers of my strange behavior reached me.

That was the only incident of any consequence that troubled those lazy three weeks. The fourth week of August was different. Pete Seeger had someone in his singing group call me and tell me that a great peace meeting would be held here in Westchester County. Would I be the chairman? I said no, I was not interested; I did not want to chair anything. I was writing, and the writing was coming fine, and that was that.

Then Pete Seeger called. It was going to be a wonderful summer concert. Paul Robeson headed the list of singers, and Pete would be there with the Weavers, and there would be other folk singers, and I, Howard Fast, had just returned from Paris —

"Pete," I pleaded, "I can't have any trouble. Bette's in Europe. I'm here with my kids."

"Bring the kids," Pete said. "There'll be a thousand kids there. Everyone's bringing their kids. And it makes a continuity with Paris. No one can speak for peace the way you can." He went on and on, and finally I agreed. I would do it. It was to be on August 27, 1949.

But when I told Juliette what I had in mind, she shook her head and said, "You will not take Rachel and Jonathan."

"Why not?"

"Because your wife told me to take care of the kids, and I promised that I would."

"But it's a summer concert, that's all. Nothing will happen."

"It will happen, all right," she said grimly. "You listen to me. I been a long time colored."

I gave it up and agreed not to take the kids. What follows is part of a report I wrote for the Civil Rights Congress soon after the concert:

That golden evening of August 27th remains in my mind most clearly, most softly; it was such a soft and gentle evening as one finds on the canvas of George Inness, and even he could create that dewy nostalgia only when he painted one part or another of the wonderful Hudson River valley. By choice, I took the little back roads twisting among the low hills and narrow valleys. I avoided the business section of Peekskill, and found the state highway north of the town. I had never been to the Lakeland picnic grounds before, and I drove slowly looking for the entrance — which is on Division Street, a three-mile stretch of country road that connects Peekskill with the Bronx River Parkway.

Yet I couldn't have missed the entrance. Hundreds of yards before I reached it, I found cars parked solidly on either side of the highway, which made me wonder, since it was more than an hour before the concert was scheduled to begin; and at the entrance itself there was an already unruly crowd of men. Just inside the grounds I stopped my car. There, a few yards from the road, a handful of teenage boys and girls had gathered. There were not more than five of them and they were trying to hide their nervousness at the jeering, hooting crowd on the road. They had come up from New York to be ushers at the concert.

"What shall we do?" they asked.

"Who's running things?"

They didn't know, they said. It was so early — they didn't think anyone had come yet. But maybe there was someone down below.

"Well," I told them, "don't let anyone in who isn't here for the concert. Just keep cool and be calm and nothing will happen."

That seemed to be a refrain of mine, that nothing would happen, that nothing could happen. "I'll park my car and see if I can't find someone to take things in hand."

The entrance to the Lakeland picnic grounds is a left turn off the main road as you drive from Peekskill; the entrance is double, coming together in a Y shape to a narrow dirt road. About eighty feet after the entrance, the road is embanked, with sharp dirt sides dropping about twenty feet to shallow pits of water. About forty feet of the road are embanked in this fashion, and then for a quarter of a mile or so it sweeps down into a valley — all of this private road and a part of the picnic grounds. At the end of this road, there is a sheltered hollow with a broad, meadowgrass bottom, a sort of natural arena, hidden by low hills from the sight of anyone above on the public highway. It was in this hollow that the paraphernalia for the concert had been set up; a large platform, two thousand wooden folding chairs, and a number of spotlights powered by a portable generator. I looked at my watch before I drove down to the hollow and it was just ten minutes to seven. As I came in, a large bus had just discharged its passengers, boys and girls, Negroes for the most part, who had come early to be ushers. About a hundred and twenty other people were already on the scene, most of them women and small children. A party of boys and girls from Golden's Bridge, a summer colony, sat on the platform, their legs dangling. None of them were over fifteen; most of them were much younger. The children from Golden's Bridge had come down in a large truck which was parked now next to my car — and which was destined to play an interesting role that night. Just by the good grace of fortune, half a dozen merchant seamen who were vacationing in the neighborhood had decided to come early; I had good reason to be grateful for them and for four trade unionists who happened to be present. But none of these, I discovered, knew who was in charge of the concert.

A boy running. I watched him as he came in sight around the bend of the road, running frantically, and then we crowded around him and he told us that there was trouble and would some of us come — because the trouble looked bad; and he was frightened too.

We started back with him. There were twenty-five or thirty of us, I suppose; you don't count at a moment like that, although I did count later. There were men and boys, almost all the men and boys. I thought that this would be no more than foul names and fouler insults. So we ran on up to the entrance, and as we appeared, they poured onto us from the road, at least a hundred of them with billies and brass knuckles and rocks and clenched fists, and American Legion caps, and suddenly my disbelief was washed away in a wild melee. Such fights don't last long; there were three or four minutes of this, and because the road was narrow and embanked, we were able to beat them back, but the mass of them filled the entranceway, and behind them were hundreds more, and up and down the road, still more.

I said that we beat them back and held the road for the moment, panting, hot with sweat and dust, bleeding only a little now; but they would have come at us again had not three deputy sheriffs appeared. They hefted their holstered guns, and they turned and spread their arms benignly at the mob. "Now, boys," they said, "now take it easy, because we can do this just as well legal, and it always pays to do it legal."

"Give us five minutes and we'll murder the white niggers," the boys answered.

"Just take it easy — just take it slow and easy, boys, because it don't pay to have trouble when you don't have to have no trouble."

And then the three deputy sheriffs turned to us and wanted to know what we were doing there making all this kind of trouble.

I kept glancing at my watch. It was ten minutes after seven then. The interruption helped us to survive. Not that the deputies intended that; but it was a beginning and there was no precedent for this kind of thing in Westchester County in New York State, and the three sheriffs with the polished gold-plated badges were uncertain as how to play their own role. For that reason they held back the "boys" and asked us why we were provoking them.

I became the spokesman then, and a good many of the things I did afterward were the result of this — chiefly because I was older than most of our handful and because the merchant seamen and the trade unionists nodded for me to talk. Anyway, I had agreed to be chairman and it seemed that this was the kind of concert we would have, not with Paul Robeson and Pete Seeger singing their lovely tunes of America, but with a special music that had played its melody out in Germany and Italy. So I said that we were not looking for any trouble, but were here to hold a concert, and why didn't they clear the road so that our people could come in and listen to the concert in peace?

"You give me a pain in the ass with that kind of talk," said one of the deputies delicately. "Just cut out the trouble. We don't want no trouble and we don't want no troublemakers."

I explained it again. I explained to them carefully that we were not making trouble, that we had not lured these innocent patriots to attack us, and that all we desired was for them to clear the road so that people could come to the concert.

"How the hell can we clear the road? Just look up there," they told me.

"Tell them to get out and they'll get out," I said.

"Don't tell me what to tell them!"

"Look, mister," I said, "we hold you responsible for whatever happens here."

"Up your ass," said the guardian of the law.

"We'll talk to the boys," another said.

And then they talked to the boys, and we had five minutes. I didn't listen to what they said to the boys. I was beginning to realize that they had no intention of doing anything about them, and when I looked up at the road and saw the roadblocks and the solid mass of men, I began to realize that not only was it extremely unlikely that anyone else on our side would get in, but quite unlikely that any of us already here would get out. Just as the sheriffs turned back to talk to the mob, a man came walking through. This man was in his middle twenties. He was tall; he wore a beard, a beret, and loose, brightly colored slacks. I asked him who he was and what he was doing here. "I'm a music lover," he said.

No self-respecting writer dares to invent such things; but they happen. "Can you fight, Music Lover?" I asked him.

"I can't and I won't." There was indignation and disgust in his voice.

"But you can and you will," I pointed out. "Otherwise, go back up there. This time they'll tear you to pieces."

Later that evening, I spoke to the music lover again. I never learned his name; he will always be Music Lover to me, but when I spoke to him again he had lost his beret, his slacks were torn, and there was blood all over him — and a wild glint in his eyes.

The men and boys had clustered around me in the little respite. "We're in a very bad place," I told them, "but we'll keep our heads and in a little while some real cops will come and put an end to all this insanity. Meanwhile, we have to keep the mob here where the road is narrow and high, and it's a good place to defend in any case. We keep them here because there's a lot of kids and women down below. That's our whole tactic. Agreed?"

They agreed.

"All right. Just two things. Let me do the talking and let me decide when there's a quick decision, because there won't be time to talk it over."

They agreed again, and our time was running out. A compression of incident and event began. First I told the girls to run back down the road, get all the women and children onto the platform, keep them there for the time being, and send every able-bodied man and boy up to us. Then I asked for a volunteer.

"I want someone to crawl through those bushes, reach the road, find a telephone, and call the troopers — call *The New York Times* and *The Daily Worker,* call Albany and get through to the governor — I want someone who can do that."

I got him. I don't know what I can say about him, except that he had great inventiveness and lots of guts. We pooled our nickels and gave them to him. He was small and bright-eyed, and I have never seen him since that night. Three times he went back and forth and he did what he was supposed to do.

Now the remaining men from below appeared and I counted what we had. All told, including myself, there were forty-two men and boys. I divided them into seven groups of six, three lines of two groups each — in other words, three lines of twelve — formed across the road where the embankment began, each line anchored on a wooden fence, our flanks protected by the ditch and the water below. The seventh group was held in reserve in our rear.

I looked at my watch again. It was seven-thirty. The three deputy sheriffs had disappeared. The mob was rolling toward us for the second attack. This was, in a way, the worst of that night. For one thing, it was still daylight; later, when night fell, our own sense of organization helped us much more, but this was daylight and they poured down the road and into us, swinging broken fenceposts, billies, bottles, and wielding knives. Their leaders had been drinking from pocket flasks and bottles right up to the moment of the attack, and now as they beat and clawed at our line, they poured out a torrent of obscene words and slogans. "We'll finish Hitler's job! Fuck you white niggers! Give us Robeson! We'll string that big nigger up!" and more and more of the same.

I'm not certain how long that second fight lasted. It seemed forever, yet it couldn't have been more than a few minutes. In that time, the sun sank below the hills to the west of us, and the shadow of twilight came. We concentrated on holding our lines. The first line took the brunt of the fighting, the brunt of the rocks and the clubs. The second line linked arms, as did the third, forming a human wall to the mob. In that fight, four of our first line were badly injured. When they went down, we pulled them back, and men in the second line moved into their places. Here were forty-two men and boys who had never seen each other before, and they were fighting like a well-oiled machine, and the full weight of the screaming madmen did not panic them or cause them to break. By sheer weight, we were forced back foot by foot, but they never broke the line. And then they pulled back. For the moment, they had enough. They drew off, leaving about twenty feet between the front of their mob and our line of defense.

On our part, we were hurt, but not so badly that every man couldn't stand on his feet. We linked arms and waited. As it darkened, change came into the ranks of the mob, a sense of organization. Three men appeared as their leaders, one a dapper, slim, well-dressed middle-aged man who was subsequently identified as a prosperous Peekskill real estate broker. A fourth man joined them, and a heated discussion in whispers started. At the same time, cars up the road were swinging

around so that their headlights covered us. Though the police and
state troopers were remarkably, conspicuously absent, the press were
on the scene. Newspaper photographers were everywhere, taking picture after picture, and reporters crouched in the headlights, taking
notes of all that went on. In particular, my attention was drawn to
three quiet, well-dressed, good-looking men who stood just to one
side at the entrance; two of them had notebooks in which they wrote
methodically and steadily. When I first saw them I decided that they
were newspapermen and dismissed them from my mind. But I saw
them again and again, and later talked to them, as you will see. Subsequently, I discovered they were agents of the Department of Justice.
Whether they were assigned to a left-wing concert or to an attempted
mass murder, I don't know. They were polite, aloof, neutral, and at
one point decently helpful. They were always neutral — even though
what they saw was attempted murder, a strangely brutal terrible attempt.

The four men in front of the mob broke off their discussion now,
and one of them, a good-looking man of thirty or so, came toward
us. He wore a white shirt, sleeves rolled up; his hands were in his
pockets; he walked to our line and in a not unfriendly manner said,
"Who's running this?"

"I'll talk to you," I said.

He told me he was a railroad worker, a Peekskill resident, and had
been drawn into this because he belonged to the local Legion post. He
underlined the fact that he liked commies no better than the next man,
but that this kind of thing turned his stomach. "I'm on the wrong
side," he said. "What I want to know is this — will you call it off if
we do?"

I told him that we had never called it on, and that if he could get
them to empty the road, we'd leave. He said he'd try. He went back
and resumed his whispered argument with the three leaders of the
mob, and now behind us our truck appeared. That did it. The mob
saw it coming and they attacked again. I had not fought this way in
twenty years, not since my days in the slums where I was raised, not
since the gang fights of a kid in the New York streets; but now it was
for our lives, for all that the cameras were flashing and the newspapermen taking it down blow by blow, so you could read in your
morning papers how a few reds in Westchester County were lynched.

It was night now, and now for the first time I understood our situation completely and could guess what the odds were that we would
all die in this way, so uselessly and stupidly.

And the FBI men watched calmly and took notes.

I looked at my watch — still less than two hours since I had kissed my little daughter.

And then we were fighting again, and then we beat them off again. Their courage was so small that when we turned and came at them, cursing them and telling them that we'd kill a few of them, they fell back until some thirty feet of the embanked road were clear in front of us. But three of us had been hurt very badly, and we helped them into the truck, where they could lie down. We had no bandages except handkerchiefs and shirts, which we used to stop bleeding. And at that moment, something very curious happened. As they came at us again, we began to sing, "Just like a tree that's standing by the water, we shall not be moved." It stopped them cold. They saw a line of bloody, ragged men, standing with their arms locked, standing calmly and singing in a kind of inspired chorus, and they stopped. They couldn't understand us.

They didn't want to touch us now, or they couldn't, so they turned to the rocks. First a rock here and there, then more, and then there was the heavy music as they beat a tattoo against the metal side of the truck. The man on my left was struck in the temple and collapsed without a sound. You didn't have to look; when you heard the fleshy thud, the sound of bone and skin breaking, you knew that someone was hit and that there was one fewer to stand on his feet and face the mob. First I counted how many of us were hit, and then I stopped counting and dropped back to the truck and put my head together with one of the seamen.

"Five minutes more of this," he said, "and we'll be finished." I suggested that we use the truck as a moving shield while the driver took it down to the hollow in low gear. Suddenly, the motor roared.

"All right, let's go!"

There were about twenty of us still on our feet. We dashed around the truck as it lurched forward, and then because the driver had forgotten to switch on his lights, he drove off the road, missed it completely, and sent his truck lurching and careening across the meadow into the night.

Now we ran down into the hollow, and we held together as we ran. As we swung around the curve of the road below, I saw the amphitheater for the first time since I had driven down there earlier in the evening: the platform with the women and children on it and huddled close, the two thousand chairs standing empty, the table of songbooks and pamphlets — and all of it bright as day in the brilliant glare of floodlights. These lit the whole of the meadow, and as we swung around at the bottom, we saw the mob of screaming, swearing patriots, chanting their new war cry, "Kill a commie for Christ," and their lust to kill the "white niggers," break over the hillside and pour down into the light.

For just a moment we stood there, trying to catch our breath, and then we drove into them because there was nothing else to do. At this point, we were half crazy, as full of hate as they were, and so violent was our fury and our own screams that they broke and ran. They turned at forty or fifty yards, formed a wide circle, and stared at us and swore at us with every filthy word they could remember. We, on the other hand, climbed onto the platform and made a line in front of the women and kids. Here, at least, we could use our feet to kick. The children, half frozen with terror, watched all this. The women began to sing the "Star-Spangled Banner," urging the children, most of them in tears, to join in. A few of the braver hoodlums ran at the platform. We beat them back.

And then the lights went out. Someone had cut the line from the generator, and now the mob, in utter frustration at finding a handful of "commies" so hard to kill, seemed to go absolutely crazy. They attacked the chairs. We couldn't see them, but through the darkness we heard them raging among the folding chairs, throwing them around, splintering and splashing them. It was not only senseless, it was sick — horrible and pathological. Then one of them lit a fire, about thirty or forty yards from the platform. A chair went on the fire, and then another and another, and then a whole pile of the chairs, which belonged not to us but to a Peekskill businessman from whom we had rented them. Then they discovered our table of books and pamphlets, and then, to properly crown the evening, they reenacted the Nuremberg book burning, which had become a world symbol of fascism. Standing there, arms linked, we watched the Nuremberg memory come alive again. The fire roared up and the defenders of the "American way of life" seized piles of our books and danced around the blaze, flinging the books into the fire as they danced. Suddenly, up in the direction of the road, an army flare arched into the sky, made a balloon of bright light, hung there, and then swept slowly and gracefully to earth. I looked at my watch. It was a quarter to ten.

Silence, broken only by the half-hysterical sobbing of women and the whimpering cries of little children. It was not easy to sit there in the dark. We had to be firm and sometimes harsh with them, but we had decided that no one would leave the platform until some civil or military force from the outside came through to us.

And then we saw a pair of headlights. Slowly, searchingly, the car drove down into the hollow and toward us, stopping only a few feet away. Three men got out. They walked toward us, leaving the head-lights of the car on to light their way. A few feet from me they stopped, nodded at me, and stood quietly for a moment. I recognized them now; they were the well-dressed men with the notebooks who had watched the fighting on the road up above and taken notes as they watched, the FBI.

"You did all right," one of them said suddenly.

"You did a damn good piece of work up there," from another. "It was damn fine discipline all the way through."

"What in hell do you want?" I demanded. I was in no mood to be polite to anyone now.

"We thought we might help you out. You got some badly hurt people, so if you want us to, we'll take them to the hospital."

"Go to hell!" I said, and then one of our men was plucking my sleeve and pulled me back and whispered that he knew them, that they were FBI and that I could trust them.

"Why?"

"Because right now they got no stake in this either way. Didn't you see them before? They're neutral. This is just a big experiment to them and they're neutral. Some of the kids are bleeding badly and I think one of them has a fractured skull. If they say they'll take them to the hospital, they will."

I asked him how he knew who they were, and he replied that he had been working in Westchester County long enough to know. "Anyway, the kids are hurt. We'll take a chance." We selected the three worst hurt. They got into the car, and the FBI men drove off. We were again in the quiet darkness.

The fire burned down. In the dark, we waited the minutes through, one after another, and then suddenly the silence in the hollow erupted into noise and action.

First an ambulance, which came roaring down into the hollow, si-ren wide open and red headlights throwing a ghostly glare. Then car after car of troopers and Westchester County police. All in a moment, there were a dozen cars in the meadow in front of us and the place was swarming with troopers and police.

One more chapter in that night of horror had to be played through, and it began with an officer of the troopers who stalked up to us and demanded, "Who in hell is running this show?" I told him that he could talk to me.

"Look," I said to him, "we've had a rough time here."

"You'll have a rougher time if you don't god damn well do as we say. Who are you anyway?"

I told him I was the chairman of the concert that never happened. He then told me to keep everyone where they were, and that if anyone tried to get away, there'd be trouble. I said that we had little children here, as he could see, and he replied that I was looking for trouble. I told him I had enough trouble.

In a way, that was the hardest part of the evening, not so much waiting in front of a dozen state troopers, their legs spread, fingering their guns and clubs — but being there after I learned what was behind all this tough talk. They let me walk around, and one of the Westchester police was willing to talk. Briefly, he told me that one of the mob, William Secor his name, had been knifed and had been taken to the hospital, and the rumor had just come through that he had died. If Secor was dead, every one of us who had held the road against the attack would face a murder charge. That was why we were being kept here this way — so that they could get a report from the hospital and if necessary pull us in on a murder rap.

(There was no knife among our men. Later, it was proved that Secor had been knifed by one of his mates in the drunken frenzy of their attack.)

Cars were coming back and forth now. The hollow was alive with action and with blue uniforms and with gray uniforms, and the fine jackbooted palace guards of Thomas E. Dewey were strutting all over the place, showing their slim waists and handsome profiles, and there was a conference taking place too among the big brass of the little army which had descended upon us. The local Westchester cop, the one with a core of something human left inside of him — a small-town cop from a small town nearby — nodded at me and I went over to him and he whispered that it was all right now. Secor was not going to die, and in fact he only had a small cut in his belly and they didn't know who cut him.

I went back and spread the news around, and we began to smile a little. There was a sudden change in the attitude of the state troopers; they became courteous, kind, obedient, cheerful, just as the book says they are, those fine gray guardians of the law and the people of the sovereign State of New York, and the big brass of them came over to me and put his hand on my shoulder, nice and warm and friendly, and said, "Look, Fast, what we want now is to get your people out of here, and we're going to get them out so that not a hair on anyone's head is harmed, and I guess you've had a tough night of it, but it's over now and you can just stop worrying. Now I want you to separate them into groups according to the town or place or resort they came from and my troopers will drive them home in our own cars."

It was past midnight when I reached home, put my car in the garage, and went into the house. Juliette was awake. The telephone had been ringing all evening with endless inquiries about me, where I was, whether I was alive or dead. Juliette didn't say much, only thank God that I was alive and how was Paul Robeson? The telephone calls had given her a good idea of what had happened, and I still did not know whether Paul was alive or dead. It turned out that his car had not been able to come within a mile of the picnic grounds, and that he was safe.

I have included the above, with some small changes and deletions, not only because it deeply affected my own life and my thinking, but also because it illustrates how easily, when terror is unleashed in a nation, it can take hold, and how thin the line is that separates constitutional government from tyranny and dictatorship. What happened that night and what happened at the second Peekskill incident was the result of a demented campaign of anti-Communism, led by such men as Senator Joseph McCarthy, Roy Cohn, Richard Nixon, and John Rankin. In the narrative above, insofar as my own knowledge extends, the only member of the Communist Party in that picnic hollow was Howard Fast, and if I had not been able to enter the hollow, the attempt at mass murder still would have taken place.

The incident happened in such isolation that I had the strange feeling the following day that the country and the world knew nothing about it. I was very wrong; it was headline news all over the world, and Bette, terrified, read an account in the *Paris Tribune*. Even Governor Dewey responded, asking District Attorney Fanelli of Westchester County to submit a full report. The response of Fanelli was so bland and incredible that it played like a scene from a film about Nazi Germany. Fanelli stated "that he didn't know anything about the disorders but was sure that the concert-goers — and not the veterans and hoodlums who attacked them — were responsible." This from *The New York Compass*. The press reports varied from straightforward accounts, very neutral, to gleeful approval. A few regretted that Howard Fast had survived. Sergeant Johnson of the New York State Police, said, "There was no need to be there in advance. We don't play into the hands of the commies. We went in when we found that a crime had been committed." The crime referred to was not the attempt to kill the concert goers but the cut in Secor's stomach.

A few days later, the concert was again attempted. This time, the arrangements were more carefully designed. Several thousand members of the Fur and Leather Workers' Union, the Teachers' Union, and District 65, a large local union, formed a ring, shoulder to shoulder, around the Hollow Brook Country Club picnic grounds, where the second Peekskill concert was held. Even though there was almost no time to prepare, over five thousand people came to the concert, and here Paul Robeson did sing. But before the second concert, I took Juliette and the children back to New York. I had had enough of the peaceful suburbs.

Like the first concert, the second concert ended in disaster. Discovering that we had planned carefully, that we had surrounded the picnic grounds with almost three thousand men, standing beside one another within arm's reach, the well-organized gang of hoodlums changed their plans accordingly. The road that led to the picnic grounds was almost a narrow country lane. All along this road, groups gathered piles of rock and waited. Farther along, where the road was crossed by highway bridges, they gathered tons of rocks and waited. Then, when the concert was finished, each car leaving the grounds ran a gauntlet of rocks. Car after car was smashed, windows shattered, cuts, bruises, skull fractures, splinters of glass embedded in eyes — all of this inflicted on the drivers and passengers to such an extent that every hospital in the vicinity was turned into an emergency trauma facility.

I doubt that Peekskill is much remembered, even by those who call themselves revisionists in the historical sense and who try to include in our history hundreds of happenings like the incidents at Peekskill, artfully omitted by the scholarly establishment. That was a strange year, 1949.

Bette returned from abroad with the bleak knowledge that one could not escape the current madness, even for a month. It followed you. How do you smile at each other and make love and pretend that your family is like any other? You walked down the street and nothing has changed, the same people, the same smiles, the same annoyance of some at others, the same indifference to each other, the same hurry and bustle. A dear friend of mine had been in Berlin in 1936, a few years after Hitler came to power, and he told me that he walked through the streets of Berlin and found nothing changed. Except that inside it was eating us up. I pretended, Bette pretended — but insofar as we knew at that moment, having no crystal ball, we were in a land hell-bent on repeating the story of Nazi Germany. It was not only that I was out front and on the way to becoming the establishment's number one symbolic threat, but we had two small children.

"Well, one day at a time," we said to each other.

There were still islands of support. A big trade union meeting to protest what had happened at Peekskill was scheduled in Springfield, Massachusetts, and I was asked to be the main speaker. That was in November of 1949. I went to Springfield and said my piece at a very large meeting indeed, and I thought to myself that if over a thousand people would come to hear this in a city as small as Springfield, there must be some hope. When I had finished speaking, two well-dressed young men standing backstage were introduced to me by a local trade union official. "They want you to go with them," he said. "They're all right."

"Why?"

"They want you to meet someone."

"Who?"

He shook his head. "It's all right. No names, but it's all right."

I am not trying to imitate a cheap film. It was a time when names were a frightening weapon. "Go with them," the trade union official said. "They're all right."

Under the circumstances, there was nothing else to do. Outside, a large, chauffeur-driven Cadillac waited. I got in with the two young men, who still had nothing to say, and I was driven to a house on the outskirts of Springfield, a large, rather splendid neo-Classical building. The two young men took me inside, where I was greeted by an impressive-looking man in his sixties, gray hair, a thoughtful, lined face, and a warm smile. "I'm so glad you agreed to come," he said. "Will you follow me."

The two young men left and I followed the older man into a rich-looking study, walnut-paneled walls, many books, everything in proper taste, a fine Persian rug on the floor, and leather armchairs. He indicated a Signer's chair by his desk for me to sit in, and he seated himself behind the desk and apologized for the way I had been brought to him.

"Are you frightened?" he asked. "I am," he continued before I could answer him. "These are frightening times, and I can speak with you only if you give me your word of honor that you will not reveal my name — if you trouble yourself to know the name. I shall not tell you my name."

I was testy. Since Peekskill, I had become increasingly testy. I was ready to say, Oh, fuck off. I've had enough bullshit to last me the rest of my life. Of course, I didn't say it. As in Shaw's play, I had become a middle-class gentleman as well as a Communist. I simply sighed and nodded.

"You see," he added, "sooner or later you'll come up against one of those damn committees again. If you don't know my name, you're much better off."

"You trust me a lot more than I trust myself," I said.

"I asked around," he said, and then he went on to explain why he had summoned me. He was an important cog in the Republican Party organization in Massachusetts, possibly the head of the party in that state. At that point, New England was suffering severe economic difficulties, a situation far worse than in other parts of the country. This man had arranged an appointment with President Truman — an attempt, as he put it, to convince Truman that New England was in economic crisis and had to be helped. Truman, in response to this plea, had assured the man from Springfield that something would be done. Truman explained that North Korean troops had made several incursions across the dividing line in the direction of Seoul. American troops were on the alert, and at the proper moment the American troops would counterattack, and that would mean war. Truman assured him that the war would bring prosperity to New England as well as to the rest of the country.

"It was a cold-blooded and awful thing," this Republican gentleman said. "I cannot countenance such an exchange, prosperity in exchange for God only knows how many lives of young Americans."

Not his exact words; I don't pretend to quote him precisely. I asked him how I figured in this, and he said that since I wrote for

The Daily Worker, we could print the story. I told him that without his name, the story was worthless, and he replied that his friend, the editor of the local Springfield paper, had said the same thing. I began to lose my temper, a practice that had brought me enough grief, deciding that in his mind we were a newspaper without principles and would therefore print such a story without naming its source. But then I realized that this man was totally sincere, tears welling into his eyes. He said something I can quote precisely: "Fast, we've lost everything, haven't we?" He went on to say that in his mind, as far as he could interpret what Truman had said, there was the thought that this might be the beginning of another world war.

He was an honorable, decent, frightened man. I took his story to John Gates of *The Daily Worker,* and Gates agreed with the editor of the Springfield paper. There was no way we could print the story without naming its source. He asked me the name of the man, and I replied that I had honored his wish and not asked his name. Gates had just been sentenced to prison as the trial of the Communist leaders came to its close. He was provoked by the whole thing and decided to let it lie. *The Daily Worker* was in no position to do investigative reporting in the neighborhood of the White House.

IT WAS CHRISTMAS, and finally that strange year of 1949 was drawing to a close. People in the arts — actors, writers, painters, dancers — are for the most part romantics. We are very aware of ourselves, and the ten or eleven hundred men and women in the Cultural Section of the Communist Party shared that awareness. We saw ourselves as a circle of awareness in a mostly indifferent population, and we felt a sense of identity with the early Christians; indeed, as we saw it, we practiced a sort of primitive Christianity in emphasizing brotherhood and sacrifice, and the fact that some of us were Jewish and some were not made no difference. The only place in my own lifetime where I experienced the same compassion for the poor and persecuted that I saw in the Communist Party was in the Fellowship of Reconciliation, a religious-pacifist organization of which I have been a member for the past thirty years.

Yet our government had turned all that we were into its opposite, and defined us as a set of murderous villains or puppets on strings held by Moscow. To us, Christmas was apart from any organized religion; it was an ingathering of love and faith. Most of us by far were of the generation of the thirties, the generation of the Depression and of war. We were now in our thirties or late twenties. Our children were three, four, five, and six and seven. We went from home to home on Christmas Day, loaded with gifts. We who were Jews were well aware of the Holocaust; we saw it as the ultimate horror and we were not disposed to secrete ourselves or make a wall around us. There are only three places in our society where I sensed no smell or whisper of anti-Semitism: in the Communist Party, in the theater, and in the Fellowship of Reconciliation.

I suppose we deceived ourselves; we had to. We could not accept that the American people had rejected us completely, whether out of fear, indifference, or belief in the enormous message of anti-Communism that was pouring out of the press, the radio, and the new medium of television. We had been turned into the focus of the greatest hate campaign in American history, and in all the United States, *not one major newspaper* printed a word in our defense.

So we drew together at Christmastime, thinking that we were the point-people and believing that millions silently stood behind us. The millions never materialized. And when Representative Vito Marcantonio, standing alone in Congress, cried out that "the defense of Communists is the defense of the first line of American democracy," his colleagues kept silent — very silent.

Meanwhile, that Christmas did bring us, from the Hungarian embassy in Washington, a case of the Imperial Tokay, made of grapes grown in the gardens of the Emperor Franz Josef — a golden brew that lingers in my memory and the likes of which Bette and I never tasted again. Neither of us likes sweet wine, but that was not sweet wine but liquid gold. The Russians also came bearing gifts. Two young men from the Russian consulate presented themselves at our house, bearing with them two kilos of the incredible green-gray Beluga caviar and six bottles of vodka — a princely Christmas gift if ever there was one. The two young diplomats, delighted to be in our home, meeting Howard Fast, of whom they had heard so much, seated themselves side by side on our couch. They were pink-cheeked, pleasant young men, clad appropriately in striped trousers and black jackets.

Rachel, now almost six years old, at the top of the stairs leading to her bedroom, heard the voices and realized that friendly guests had arrived. She decided to show her own sense of responsibility, stuffed three pieces of bubble gum into her mouth, and masticated frantically. Then she came downstairs, stationed herself in front of the two young Russian diplomats, a beautiful little girl with honey-colored hair. The Russians smiled broadly, ignoring the lump in her cheek, and Bette and I watched in horror as Rachel began to blow a bubble. But our horror was nothing compared to the horror of the two Russians as the bubble grew larger and larger and larger — indeed, the largest bubble gum bubble we had ever seen — and then exploded, leaving a film of bubble gum across my daughter's face. The Russians were very upset. How could this be — the daughter of Howard Fast chewing gum?

I said to them, "Listen to me. Someday this lunatic Cold War between my country and yours will end, and when that day comes, you will buy shiploads of bubble gum from us."

"Never!" they cried. "Never!"

I have lived to see that day, and while I have not yet heard of a bubble gum deal with the Soviet Union, I'm sure there's one in the offing. This chewing gum business with the Russians was a strange manifestation of the time. They knew as little of America as we knew of Russia; they put us down as vulgar barbarians, and chewing gum was their symbol of vulgarity. Ilya Ehrenburg, the Russian novelist and war correspondent, seized on chewing gum as the symbol of the gross American, and he used it frequently. When I was in Paris, Louis Aragon asked me to dine one evening with him and Ilya Ehrenburg. The temptation to do as I did was irresistible, and I hunted in Paris until I found a package of American chewing gum. Aragon took us to a restaurant on the Left Bank where he was well known and received like royalty, and where we were served one of the most wonderful meals I had ever eaten, along with bottles of fine wine. When this splendid meal and the good conversation — both men were fluent in English — that went with it were finished and Ehrenburg and Aragon lit cigarettes, I quite deliberately took the package of gum out of my pocket, opened it, and offered a piece to Ehrenburg. He could not have reacted with more horror had I laid a hot grenade on the table; Aragon, on the other hand, broke up with laughter. It took a while to convince Ehrenburg that it was a silly practical joke, and I'm not sure he ever forgave me for it.

The truth is that I simply did not believe we were going to prison. Bette and I still lived in peace with our children. I still received considerable income from the publication of my books abroad. We gave dinner parties; we loved to have people join us at dinner — although lately they were mostly other Communists. There were no troops of Brown Shirts prowling our streets, and while some people who had been close to us withdrew from us, it was never an act of hostility or accusation, only a gentle no, we're sorry, some other time. The thousands of people who were blacklisted, both for refusing to name names and for being unwilling to sign the proliferating loyalty oaths, were denied attention in the media, and thus the great mass of the population lived with perhaps some vague disquiet or uneasy delight in the victories over our tiny Communist Party by the government. Life went on, and the erosion of democracy and constitutional rights was slow and hardly noticed. Those "liberals" who had turned against the party kept cheering each step of the mini-terror as a victory of democracy over Communism — and life went on.

As a writer, I could not believe that the blacklist would stop at the film community; it had to spread to the publishers, and the first real warning I had came with a book called *The Fallen Angel*. Angus Cameron, a dear friend of ours and one of the few people we knew who was neither disturbed nor frightened by a relationship with Communists, had become vice president and editor in chief of Little, Brown and Company, an old and very distinguished Boston publisher. Two Boston publishing houses, Little, Brown and Houghton Mifflin, had for years had a reputation for both quality and integrity not quite equaled by any New York house. They were not simply publishers; they were part of the literary history of America. After Sam Sloan's death, his publishing house — which had published all my pre-terror best sellers — began to crumble, went into bankruptcy, and had its copyrights taken over by Little, Brown, and Angus Cameron suggested that I become a Little, Brown author.

The first book of mine that house published was *My Glorious Brothers*, the book about the Maccabees that I have already mentioned; it was reasonably successful. It was followed by a collection of short stories, called *Departure*, all the stories previously written, and then, in 1950, *The Proud and the Free*, the book about the mutiny of the Pennsylvania Line, which was written the year before. There is frequently a gap of anything from six months to a year and a half between contracting for a finished manuscript and the publication of the printed book, and that left me time during the first months of 1950 to write a book that was to be my defense against "future shock," to be published under a pseudonym. It was a sort of anti-fascist mystery, a form I had never attempted before. It was fun to do, and I called it *The Fallen Angel*. Angus Cameron liked the book immensely and agreed that it would be a good idea to establish a second personality, just in case everything took a turn for the worse. The blacklisted screenwriters were already discussing this procedure; but at Little, Brown, some employee, trying to gain points for himself as a 100 percent loyal American, told the FBI what I was planning. J. Edgar Hoover himself called the president of Little, Brown and suggested that a book by Fast under a pseudonym would not meet with his approval. So it goes; they could publish Fast, but not under a pseudonym. Since the book was in print and bound by then, they printed a new dust jacket, which informed the public that Howard Fast had taken the name of Walter Ericson for this type of fiction. They wanted one and all to know whose baleful words these were.

Meanwhile, as I said before, Bette and I did not expect that I or any of the others on the board of the Spanish Refugee Appeal would go to prison. Remember, three of them were physicians, one an esteemed head of a university department, others people of dignity, middle aged. I was the youngest of the group. Everyone I spoke to about it assured me that such people are not sent to prison — not as political prisoners in the United States of America.

The case was up before the Supreme Court, surrounded by scholarly briefs petitioning for a writ of certiorari, the right to argue the case before the highest court in the nation. In order to do so, one had to demonstrate that the case involved constitutional points of importance. Supreme Court decisions were usually made public on Mondays, and all during the first months of 1950, Bette and I stayed up late Monday evenings so that we could get the early edition of Tuesday's *New York Times*.

We could have saved ourselves the loss of sleep. On Monday the fifth of June, our lawyers telephoned to tell us that the Supreme Court had denied certiorari, and that I was to be in Washington two days later, Wednesday, June 7, to surrender and enter prison.

So at last, here it was. I remember that an hour or so after the telephone call, a friend stopped in with a petition for us to sign in the case of Owen Lattimore. Some weeks earlier, Lattimore, who was no more a Communist than was Harry Truman, had been denounced as a party member by Louis Budenz, a one-time member of the CP who was a ready hand at denouncing this one or that one if the price was right. It was an odd meeting of circumstances. We signed the petition and then told our friend to go. We had our own problems. Juliette, that wonderful woman who had seen me through the Peekskill affair, put her arms around us and told us that she was here and would be here. But summer was starting. What do we do with the kids? What do we tell them? Rachel, just past her sixth birthday, must not know that I was going to jail. She would not understand it and it might create trauma. As for Jonathan, he was just two, and he could do without much explanation. We decided to tell Rachel that I had been summoned to Paris for three months. She had heard me talk so much of my love for Paris and the joy of being there that she would accept the explanation. Mommy had to stay with the kids; Daddy is off to Paris. Good enough. But where do we go? New York, especially the Upper West Side, where we lived, was becoming a little hairy; I wouldn't rest easy with them there alone. Bette's folks had a house in Belmar, New Jersey, and a little cottage next to their house was usually for rent in the summer. Bette got in touch with her father immediately and pinned down the rental. Her father was a judicious but not judgmental man who loved her very much, and he and her mother were tolerant of what they saw as our madness. We were stubborn and independent, never accepting a penny from them, even though it was offered, and her father respected this. Among his friends were the circulation managers of the New York newspapers, *The Times, The Sun, The Post, The Journal,* and *The Mirror.* They were all tough men, streetwise, nonpolitical, and they said to me that a lot of good men do a little time for this thing or that thing. No judgment or blame.

There were a hundred things to do in the three days I had left: make sure that Bette had everything in hand, make sure that my one insurance policy was active, see that Bette had power of attorney, and try to anticipate contingencies. I had no certainty that I would be released from jail after three months — indeed, no certainty in those strange times that I would be released at all.

As a matter of fact, it was not three days, only Monday and Tuesday. Early Wednesday morning, with the children still sleeping, I slipped out of the house, kissed my wife, and took a cab to Pennsylvania Station and a train to Washington. I had been instructed to report to the U.S. Court House at eleven o'clock, and I made it just on time. I

met two of my fellow criminals on the train. The rest were already
in Washington. Our lawyers had worked out a final plea for clem-
ency, but Judge Keech refused to hear it.

"What now?" we asked our attorney.

"You go to jail."

We dutifully paraded down a flight of stairs to the basement, where
we were fingerprinted once again. We had been fingerprinted when
we were arrested, but the Justice Department likes fingerprints. Dr.
Louis Miller, the dear, gentle little man, had won the right to serve
his time in the federal holding prison in downtown Manhattan, so
he was separated from us and sent off. This was because he had two
patients who were critically ill, and he had to see them at least once
a week; and James V. Bennett, director of the Federal Bureau of
Prisons, a wise and humane man, made the adjustment possible. Dr.
Louis Miller was not only a good friend but our family physician for
years to come.

I hate fingerprinting; the dirt of the ink on one's hands is symbolic
to me, just as handcuffs are symbolic of men reduced to the condition
of animals. After we were fingerprinted, the women in our group
were separated. We had been handcuffed for the few minutes it took
us to get down to the basement. I was handcuffed to Lyman Richard
Bradley, whose nickname was Dick. From there on, whenever we
were handcuffed, I was handcuffed to Bradley, a matter of alphabet-
ical listing, for the names of our committee members ran this way:
Auslander, Barsky, Bradley, Fast. Auslander to Barsky; Bradley to
Fast. But I could not have asked for a more pleasant, erudite and
philosophical partner. Dick Bradley took the entire experience with
such scientific interest and unflagging curiosity, never relaxing a sweet
professorial manner, that I rarely complained about anything.

After the fingerprinting, we were locked in a bullpen, a cage about
twenty feet square. A dozen other prisoners were in there — some
new like us, others brought to court for trial or hearing and held in
the bullpen because they were considered violent. We spent about
two hours in this cage, smoking, talking, trying to anticipate what
prison would be like, questioning the other prisoners — discovering
for the first time that the average prison inmate is very little different
from the man outside the walls. The bullpen was a poor example of
a federal prison. It was mean and dirty. Federal prisons, I was to
learn, degrade one in a number of ways but not with dirt.

From the bullpen, we were taken to the district prison. Once again, the handcuffs and the marshals. Now the three women in our committee, who had been held elsewhere, joined us on the bus. They were seated in the rear, separated from us by a wire screen. When we reached the district prison, the women were taken away to the women's wing — and that was the last we saw of them until our terms were over.

I had imagined that the jail in the District of Columbia would be small, since it was not considered a penitentiary but a common jail; it turned out to be an enormous institution, red brick walls, armed guards, towering cell blocks — and tight, so incredibly tight that an adventurous mouse would have gone insane trying to escape. We were led through an electric gate, then another and another. Already, I could sense the stripping away of humanity and dignity. Prison does that to you; prison guards do that to you. They look through you, up you, and down you, but they never look at you as they would if they considered you human.

We entered a long corridor, and there I saw a sight that I recall most vividly, for all the years gone by. At the end of the corridor was a large room. There on long benches sat about a hundred men, black men and white men, all of them naked. They sat despondently, hunched over, heads bent, evoking pictures of the extermination camps of World War Two.

We entered the room, and there we were told to undress. We stripped down, made bundles of our clothes and possessions, and joined the men on the benches. The dignity we had clung to so desperately was now taken from us. Naked I sat, and naked were the men beside me, the doctors, lawyers, labor leaders, and the college professor. Naked we were processed, fingerprinted again, questioned, filed, indexed. Then showers, antiseptic soap, antiseptic footbaths. Then the faded blue uniforms, and we were ready for our cells.

An old Hollywood prison film gives a good sense of what this prison was like: five tiers of cells, the deep, narrow open well, the metal tables at the bottom of the well, the staircase at one end, the exercise walk above. Separated from the rest, I was put on the third tier of cell block one — C.B. 1, as the cons called it. My cell was five by seven, and I shared it with another prisoner, a poor frightened kid of eighteen who had first been caught when he was twelve and had already spent years of his young life in prisons and reformatories. He was a slender, blue-eyed, handsome kid with cornsilk hair, and he had been raped by fellow prisoners at least a hundred times. It took a while to win his confidence and get him to talk. He was in prison for "carnal knowledge," otherwise known as petting, charged by the father of the girl he had kissed. He had been there for fifty-eight days without indictment.

In that five-by-seven space were two beds, a toilet, sink, and a little table. No window, and the whole front of the cell was bars, the rest metal sheeting, and when the heavy electric door clanged shut behind me, I experienced a kind of hopeless cessation of the will to struggle. You can become used to a cell five by seven feet. I did. It becomes your world; you adjust to it, live in it, and somehow time begins to pass — or, as it is better put in prison terms, you begin to build time. This was our schedule: we woke at about six, made our beds, washed. Then the electric doors opened with a great clang, and we stepped onto the balcony. We marched to the end of the balcony, down the stairs, picked up tin trays, and walked along a sort of abbreviated cafeteria line where other prisoners slopped food into our trays. The food was not good, but some prisoners told me that it was much better than it was before we came — an acknowledgment that we might be heard by those outside.

My tray was piled high with food and bread, because I had received it in silence, saying neither more nor less, and when I had squeezed in between two old-timers, they whispered to me — no talking allowed at mealtime — that if I left food on my plate, it meant ten or fifteen days in the hole. I couldn't touch the food. The two cons solved the problem by dividing it between them and wolfing it down. After breakfast, we cleaned the cell. Then we had time for reading, if anything could be found for reading. The library allowed us one book a week, which arrived in a library cart pushed to the front of the cell. I chose the thickest binding on the cart; the book happened to be *The Forsyte Saga*. I finished it in three days, a remarkable book, and since in my letters to Bette I could include nothing about the prison, I filled the page with a brief critique of Galsworthy.

Eventually, lunch, and in the afternoon, an hour and a half of walking back and forth on the top tier. Time and more time. Then supper. A meal took ten minutes, no more, head bowed, a spoon to eat with, and then silence. Then back in the cell until lights-out at nine-thirty. This was a day, one day, any day, but even in that narrow world not without incident and interest for a writer. I remember in particular the Rubber Nose Gang. This was a group of five morons who had swept across the country, robbing eleven banks before they were caught. As a disguise, they wore the big rubber noses that kids used on Halloween, and they were passing their time in prison diagramming their next job — if and when they got out of jail. The prison grapevine had it that a group of professors had entered the prison, and the moment I appeared — since I wore glasses — they grabbed me. This was during the hour-and-a-half walk on the top tier. They showed me their diagrams for their next job and asked my opinion. Wonderful and weird. The diagrams came from the minds of slightly backward children, and how this group of imbeciles had managed to take eleven banks, I will never understand.

On June 8, my second day in prison, I wrote to Bette: "I have been thinking of you and the children since I came in here, and I've had plenty of time to think. Why is it, Bette, that we seem to find each other only when the going is tough? It should not be that way, and we'll try to make it different . . ."

Yet we did find each other whenever the going was tough, and that counted.

I spent nine days in that tiny cell with the kid whose life had been washed out before he had had a chance to grow and look around, whose soul had been crushed, and I spent nine nights listening to eight convicts, two rows beneath us, who had been sentenced to death, and who were being held in the district jail until they could be sent out to another prison for execution. I recommend the experience to those who believe in capital punishment! And I ate three meals a day with convicts who were thieves and hoodlums, and in the afternoons, on the top tier, I listened to them. I listened to a great deal. Lie awake most of the night in a tiny cell and listen to men pray to God that they don't want to die, and plead with God to give them another chance, and weep out their confessions with no priest to hear them, and beg God to understand the hate and bruises and mistakes and cruelties inflicted on them by others, so that their path to hell was laid out for them before they took their first step — and then you will learn of the human condition what can't be otherwise taught.

On the morning of the ninth day, I was given my clothes, told to dress and come to the front. The doors opened for me, and downstairs Dick Bradley and Ed Barsky joined me. I had seen neither of them nor anyone else from the committee since I had been put in the cell. We were given our possessions, handcuffed once again, and put into a car with two United States marshals.

It feels very strange and very good to see the outside world again after nine days in a cell. We didn't know where we were going, but it was change, motion, movement — and that was a tremendous lot. We were prisoners now. The handcuffs were not needed; we certainly had no intention of trying to escape from two heavily armed marshals; we were prisoners and we accepted the fact. We sat in the car and looked at the sunshine, the people walking around, so free and so thoughtless of that wonderful condition; the streets of Washington, the soft, gracious Virginia countryside. We rode in that car about three hundred miles, deeper and deeper into the wild and lonely mountains of West Virginia, until finally we came to the prison camp where Bradley and I were to serve the rest of our sentences — a place called Mill Point. There we said a sad goodbye to Ed Barsky, who was taken to Petersburg prison.

After the maddening, medieval closeness of the Washington jail, Mill Point prison was a blessing and a relief. It was still prison, but it was a prison that returned to us at least some of our dignity as human beings. There were no walls at Mill Point — only almost impenetrable walls of forest — no cells, no bars, no punishment holes, no crashing electric gates, no door ever locked except the door to the kitchen. I heard that Bennett, head of the federal prison system, sat down with a group of penologists and psychiatrists and had a number of discussions about prison, and that was when the notion arose that if you build a prison without walls or doors, no one can escape from it. So there were no walls at Mill Point, only a series of small white signs set around on about ten acres of land, and these signs said, simply, STAY INSIDE. Of course, it was not as open as all that. No one brought to Mill Point had more than two years to serve. Some convicts who had been sentenced to ten or fifteen years were permitted to finish their sentences at Mill Point, but mostly the white population was made of moonshiners from the mountains of Kentucky and West Virginia, and the blacks were short-end servers, mail fraud, assault, wife beating, petty larceny. Since the penalty for escape was five years more to serve, not at Mill Point but at a heavy-time jail, very few tried to escape. The jail had been in existence twelve years when I got there, established in 1938 by Roosevelt, who was fascinated by the notion of a prison without walls. During the twelve years, only eight men had escaped, and they were picked up by the warden calling the sheriff in each man's hometown.

It was a simpler time than today: no cocaine, a little grass here and there in the camp, but not much of it. No one was keen to break the rules and lose the two days a month for good behavior. In the ordinary course of things, people like Dick Bradley and me would have been sent to the federal prison at Danbury, Connecticut, where, for example, Congressman J. Parnell Thomas — one of those who had designated us for contempt — served his time after being run in by J. Edgar Hoover, whom Thomas had made the mistake of investigating, intending to blow Hoover's cover and tell the country that J. Edgar was a homosexual. Two years in jail cooled Mr. Thomas's ardor. But the government knew that if Bradley and I were interned in Danbury, there would be endless demonstrations and delegations and vigils, none of which they desired. Mill Point was far too isolated to be a point of political demonstration.

In fact, Bette went through a lot of difficulty coming down to visit me. She took a train from New York to a tiny station somewhere in West Virginia. There was no sleeping car on that run, and she arrived at the station after sitting up all night in an ancient railroad car. The station was a point at nowhere, no house, no activity as one might expect around any station, only a shed and a station man, sitting with his chair tilted back, chewing on a straw. When Bette asked about a taxi, he pointed to a small church spire down the road. There was no telephone at the station. Bette plodded down the road, a rutted dirt road, to a small mining town. There was a general store and in it half a dozen of the local population and a pool table. She summoned up her courage and announced loudly, "I have to get to the prison. Will anyone take me there?" Long silence. The men at the pool table went on playing pool. No women in the room. "For heaven's sake," Bette cried out after a while, "don't any of you have tongues or ears?" One of the men at the pool table said, "Cost you twenty dollars, lady." She paid it readily. The regular cab from the prison took her back to the station, about fifteen miles, for five dollars. My wife is not an aggressive woman; she is a gentle woman but with tremendous underlying strength. A great meeting was held in Madison Square Garden to protest our imprisonment, coincidentally with similar meetings in Paris and Italy. Bette had never spoken publicly in her entire life; her shyness made it impossible; yet she stood up in front of that great hall, every seat taken, and spoke her piece, calmly, certainly, and without any evidence of the terror that permeated her whole being.

Mill Point, as we in the prison put it, lay in the bowl of nowhere. It was deep in a federal forest, with mountains looming up on every side. We slept in army barracks, eighty-eight men to each barracks, two white barracks, two black barracks. The barracks were not always filled, and the prison population varied from three hundred to capacity. It was a fine-looking place, well kept, and the warden, Kenneth Thieman, was one of the kindest, most compassionate gentleman I have ever met in government service. How this remarkable, understanding man came to be a prison warden, I don't know, but fortunately for us he was there at the time. The news that Bette had spoken at the Madison Square Garden meeting came to me via *The New York Times,* and Thieman pointed it out to me before I received my copy of the paper. "You must have a wonderful wife," he said to me. I said it was a damn sight more than I deserved. Before coming to Mill Point, during the war years, Thieman had been the warden at Danbury prison, then holding several hundred Quakers and pacifists. His own son, age nineteen, had died in the war; and Thieman told me the hardest task he had ever faced was to be just and decent to conscientious objectors.

Mill Point was a work camp. Everyone worked. The lumber crew felled trees marked by the federal rangers for thinning. The prison ran the mill where the logs were cut into boards. Prisoners did the cooking, the laundry, and even the baking. There was a small but good prison library, and Dick Bradley was given the job of librarian, which had just been vacated. When Thieman asked me where I wanted to be put, explaining that I wouldn't last two days with the logging crews or at the mill, I replied angrily that since I was in prison, I'd just as soon break stone. Smiling, he told me that it was out of date. "We don't break stone anymore, but I'll tell you what I will do. If that's your natural bent, I can put you in the masonry gang. We're building a terrace and a fountain out there in the middle of the big lawn."

"Great!" I agreed. What I had come to fear most about prison was boredom, that enemy of all prisoners, and this would keep me in the open air and give me a chance to get in shape.

"Also," Thieman added, "I was talking to Mr. Bennett about you, and he asked me to stress that every convenience for writing will be put at your disposal. We have a typewriter for you, and paper will be furnished, and no restrictions will be placed on what you write. Of course, it will be after hours — I can show no favoritism on that score — and you will have to keep the manuscript until your release. Mr. Bennett is very eager for you to write about this place."

I made one of my silly romantic statements, something I would not have thought of saying after I got to know Thieman better. I resented his being so kind to me. The hell with you, I thought, I'm in prison — I don't want any goddamn favors from you; aloud, I said, "I can't write as a prisoner. I can't think as a prisoner."

Kenneth Thieman was very tolerant. He shrugged and nodded. "I can understand that. But if you change your mind, tell me." I did ask for the typewriter, but only for my letters. My rude answer to Thieman was self-serving. The truth was that I desperately wanted a time without writing. My happiest hours came when I was able to work with my hands, and it was years since I had had a chance to do so. I became an apprentice stone mason to an old black master mason.

Dick Bradley and I were given beds side by side. On Dick's right was a Kentucky moonshiner. On my left, Lemuel Ayers, car thief, robber, manslaughter convict, arms the size of my thighs, probably the most dangerous man in the prison and one who fell absolutely in love with Bradley and me. He called each of us Professor, as did most of the convicts. He was in the woods gang, a key man in the lumbering, and Dick Bradley and I had to tread gently and never evidence any sign of being mistreated, because Lemuel Ayers would have killed anyone who looked sidewise at us. The only man in the prison who hated us as Communists was the prisoner in charge of the garage, a huge, surly brute who snarled at us every time we passed him but who was deadly afraid of Ayers. Most of our barracks was given to Kentucky moonshiners, decent men who made whiskey and took it over the border to Ohio to sell it. In their infertile mountain valleys there was no other way to make a living.

They were deeply religious men, these Kentucky moonshiners, and in the evening, after supper, they would sit reading Scripture and discussing it. Bradley and I were both secular Bible students, Bradley from his Presbyterian childhood and I from historical and literary curiosity, regarding the King James version as the foundation of our language. Usually they turned to Dick, but one evening when he was at the library a hot discussion arose among the Kentucky men about the passage wherein Jesus says, "Suffer little children, and forbid them not to come unto me." They could make no sense of it until I explained that at the time the Bible was translated, *suffer* also meant to allow, to permit. That raised my status enormously. While some of the Kentucky men could read, most of them were illiterate, and after I had done my little exegesis, a group of them went to the warden and asked whether I could teach reading and writing to the illiterates. They had approached Dick first, but he was involved in writing and begged me to take over, and when I said I knew nothing about teaching illiterates, he protested that he knew nothing either.

At this point, I have to say a few words about anti-Semitism and the unique form it took in Mill Point. I was the only Jew in the prison until Albert Maltz and Edward Dmytryk came there. Maltz was Jewish but Dmytryk was not, and since no one ever asked me, I did not offer the information. But there was a fat, whimpering Tidewater criminal whose name was Kline. He was not Jewish, but the prison population decided that he was, and since they detested him, they always referred to him, in third person and to his face, as Jew Bastard. Kline came to Bradley, pleading that he wasn't no Jew bastard and wouldn't Dick speak to the point? Dick remained aloof. In the work areas, black and white prisoners labored together, but they lived in segregated barracks and had their meals in a segregated dining room. However, when it came to nightly softball — three games a week — segregation was dropped. Mill Point did it before the National League. There was one Irish Catholic in the prison, a car thief from Chicago whose name was Costello. He stood in as umpire behind the batter one night. He had a bad reputation and he was suspected of being a rat to the guards, so he should not have taken the job, but he took it and he called one wrong. A wild cry went up:

"Kill the fucken Jew bastard," and they would have killed him had not Bradley intervened. Why and how the prisoners had decided that Costello was a Jewish name, I don't know — perhaps because he came from Chicago. Such was anti-Semitism at Mill Point. Neither Maltz nor I was ever troubled, and whether they knew we were Jewish or not, I don't know.

There are brutal, demonic prisons, and many an evening Dick and I would sit and listen with horror to the stories the prisoners told of state penitentiaries. I worked on the masonry gang with a young black man who had been hung by his thumbs in a Virginia jail; by consensus, Virginia was the worst, a house of horror that made me swear I'd never set foot in Virginia again; all the southern states in terms of prisons were terrible. The black prisoners showed me the whip scars on their backs. But Mill Point was different. Mill Point, with its intelligent warden, was the most well-run institution I had ever seen, prison or otherwise, and the three months I spent in that place were less a punishment than an indignity. Often, Bradley and Maltz and I would discuss the irony of a government that could put us in prison and at the same time have so wise and compassionate a prison policy.

Here was my day: up at seven, wash, shave, breakfast. (Thieman was given forty-two cents a day to feed each man. But he managed. The food was not great but we never went hungry. There was always enough bread.) After breakfast, work. We had already cleaned our quarters and made up our beds. The masonry gang I worked with was all black but me. I made friends there. I was taught the work by this old black man who held that the mixing of cement was a mystical process. Perhaps he was right. Then lunch. Then work again. Finish at four o'clock, and then a very decent free period until supper at six. After supper, for some, softball, letter writing, sitting, and smoking, whatever — for me, my class of illiterates.

There was a fairly large room with folding chairs that was a sort of isolation room, usually empty. I was told to use this room, and to my amazement over twenty of the Kentucky mountain men showed up. I had a blackboard and chalk. What do I do? I took the simplest direction. A boy is a boy. You know a boy when you see him, but suppose you want to leave a message for your wife about the boy.

You can't draw a picture of him unless you're very gifted. But you can make a symbol. B O Y on the blackboard. Now let's take that apart, letter by letter, and then we'll put it together again.

I finished that evening with the alphabet in block letters. I was so excited that night I couldn't sleep, and I poured out my heart in a long letter to Bette.

I taught three sessions, and at the end of the third session, some of the men were able to print their names in block letters, and others were able to read and write a few simple words. Each one had printed the alphabet, and almost all of them had memorized it. They were no fools, these Kentucky men. They were sharp and bright and always hewed to the point. It was one of the most exciting things that had ever happened to me, and I felt the kind of exultation that I imagine many teachers have felt at one point or another.

And then Thieman came to me. "Fast, I'm afraid the teaching is finished."

"Why?"

"Orders from the Justice Department. No Communists are to do any work in the education department."

"Why? For God's sake, do they think I'm going to teach these men revolution? I'm teaching them to read and write, and they're learning."

"Those are the orders. I have no alternative."

Which was the end of my teaching in prison — something that hurt more than anything else in those months.

We could receive newspapers from the publisher and books from the publisher — not from a bookstore but only from the publisher. Bette got me a subscription to *The New York Times,* so each morning I had the paper, even though it was a day late. I read a review in the book section of a new translation of *Don Quixote* that was described as being absolutely brilliant. Dick agreed with me that he had never read a good translation of Cervantes. I believe the translator's name was Putnam. Dick could read anything. There in prison, I received a copy of Philip Foner's *History of the Fur and Leather Workers Union,* perhaps the most scholarly history of a trade union ever written. I managed forty of its five hundred pages. Dick sailed through the whole book. I wrote Bette to have the publisher send me *Don Quix-*

ote, and Dick and I waited eagerly for its appearance. When it came, I bowed to the professor, and Dick Bradley plunged right into it. Two days later, he surrendered, and said to me, "Howard, this never happened to me before, but I'm defeated. I cannot read this book. In fact, I am beginning to believe that no one ever finished an una- bridged edition of *Don Quixote*."

Now in the rest hours between the end of work and supper call, the prisoners would sit around and smoke and talk. Lemuel Ayers, the oversized, overmuscled thief and hoodlum, would sit on his bed — the bed next to mine — cross-legged, making wallets and such out of folded pieces of the plastic in which cigarette packages are wrapped. It's a prison art, and Ayers had done a lot of prison time. While doing this, he would listen carefully to everything Dick and I said. Ayers had a remarkable manner of speech; he managed in every sentence, regardless of how short it was, to insert *motherfucker* at least once, sometimes twice, and sometimes, in a burst of creativity, three times. When Dick Bradley gave up on *Don Quixote*, Ayers, who had been listening, said, "Professor, I'd motherfucken like to read that moth- erfucken book."

"Oh?" Dick and I looked at each other.

"Lem, do you read much?"

"Never read a motherfucken book. I read the motherfucken comic books."

"Well," I said, "don't you think you might start with something easier?"

"No, sir. I want to read that motherfucken book you and the pro- fessor been talking about."

Well, you didn't argue with Ayers, and we gave him the book. For the next three months, Ayers read the book, page by page. Whenever he hit a particularly fascinating passage — fascinating, that is, to Ayers — he would shout, "Shut up all you motherfuckers and listen to me!" And then he'd proceed to read the passage aloud.

What an astonishing business! I don't pretend to explain it; I sim- ply tell it.

Albert Maltz and Edward Dmytryk came to Mill Point after I had been there for two weeks. Maltz was a gentle, sensitive, and gifted novelist and screenwriter who was one of the ten Hollywood film workers sentenced to prison by the House Un-American Committee

for refusing to name names. Dmytryk was a successful director, as
different from Maltz as he could be. They were brought to Mill Point
while I was out on garbage detail. That was Saturday. On Saturday,
the whole prison population stopped work and cleaned and spruced
up the place, cutting grass, washing windows, and so forth. I volunteered for garbage detail because it meant riding the garbage truck
four miles out of the prison to the dump. There were few volunteers
because part of the job was picking up the sludge at the sawmill; the
smell was so horrible that few stomachs could accept it. It was about
three o'clock on a hot, sunny afternoon when I returned to the prison
and found that Maltz and Dmytryk had arrived; Thieman had mentioned that they were coming, and I was delighted to see them. I had
never met either before, so I introduced myself and said that if they
ran into any problems, come to me, seeing that I already knew the
ropes.

On Saturday, about twenty convicts were given lawn mowers and
put to work mowing the wide prison lawns, and since the two new
men were unassigned, they were given lawn mowers and told to mow.
They had been at it all morning, and both were sweating profusely.

The first thing Dmytryk said to me after we met was "How do
you turn someone in?"

"What?"

"You heard me. How do you turn someone in?"

"What the hell are you talking about?" I wanted to know.

"Forget it," Maltz said to him. "Eddie, forget it."

Dmytryk pointed to where two convicts sat in the shade of a great
oak tree, sprawled out, smoking, while their lawn mowers stood idle
beside them. "They been sitting there like that for hours while Albert
and I worked our asses off. The hell with that. I'm going to turn
them in."

It was a case of instant disgust, my first meeting with Dmytryk. I
said to him, very slowly and precisely, "If you turn them in, Dmytryk, you'll be dead tomorrow morning."

"Come off it!" He grinned and told me that he made the movies
where that happened. "Who's going to kill me?"

"The cons will decide that. But you'll be dead in the morning," I
assured him, beginning to wonder why I cared. Maltz and I talked
him out of it, but it was a proper introduction to Edward Dmytryk.

Shortly after his wife's first visit, he was released from prison and eventually resumed his work in Hollywood. So much for Dmytryk.

Now for good, dear Albert, who lived his life as a sort of Communist saint. There were many like Albert Maltz in the Communist Party, gentle, decent people of total morality. You didn't find them among the leadership, only in the rank and file. Albert Maltz was utterly true to himself. I was with him night and day for almost two months, and never once was there a false note — and at times this absolutely infuriated me, since I was no saint.

I have always worked the angles. I say that shamelessly. Whatever else I might be, I am a survivor. At age eight, when my mother died, I faced the question of whether to live or die, and I decided to live — but it has not always been easy. In small matters as well as large matters, I could never accept things the way they were, and in prison it was no different. Each prison barracks had attached to it a latrine of twelve toilets, two facing rows of six each, and no toilet seats. Prison was indignity enough, but I discovered that in the small prison hospital there were two toilets with seats. The hospital, four beds, was always empty. The only injuries I saw at Mill Point happened in the softball games. A convict was assigned the job of caring for the hospital, and in this case the convict was corruptible. I corrupted him each day with a candy bar — there was a small prison canteen — and in return I was privileged to read my morning *Times* on a wooden toilet seat. Not much, but in jail one is thankful for small victories. But three weeks after I arrived, the hospital convict told me he was due for release, and having heard that Albert Maltz would be arriving one day soon, I immediately began a somewhat Machiavellian scheme to replace him with Albert, assuring Mr. Thieman that Albert had always dreamed of being a doctor. He had. And in due time, Albert was made hospital orderly.

But when, on Albert's first day of practice, I came strolling up with my *New York Times,* Albert barred my way and wanted to know where I was bound. I told him. He told me that he had just sanitized the toilets. They were for the sick and only for the sick.

"But Albert, there are no sick," I pleaded.

"That doesn't change it. My God, Howard, we're friends, comrades. How could I explain extending such a privilege to you and no one else?" I couldn't argue with him. With someone else, yes, but not with Albert. He was the most principled person I ever knew, and principled people can be very difficult.

The masonry crew was by now devoted to me. It was by no means easy to get them to talk to a white man, much less trust him; but bit by bit, I won their confidence, and we submitted to Mr. Thieman some drawings and plans that I had sketched, and he approved them. The plans were for the fountain in the middle of the plaza or terrace that we were building. At that point, the crew began to believe that I could get Mr. Thieman to agree to anything, and they begged me to make a piece of sculpture to crown the fountain — like those they had seen in various public places. I had never made any sculpture, and this was before Bette did much sculpture, and I had only the vaguest notion of how one went about it, but I did go to Thieman and broach the idea to him. He was interested but wanted to know whether I could do it or whether I'd wing it.

"What material?"

"Concrete," I said.

"Well, we have plenty of that. What else would you need?"

"Fifty pounds of wax."

He thought about it, then decided that the institution could afford the wax, and asked me what kind of a figure I thought I could make. On his desk, he had a small replica of the *Pissing Prince of Essen,* that wonderful sculpture of a little boy, his clothes raised as he urinates. I pointed to it. Thieman burst into laughter, handed me the piece of bronze, and told me to go ahead. "But, remember," he said, "you work on Sundays or evenings. I can't give you any work time. That goes into the record."

The wax came. I recalled the lost-wax method and carved the little prince out of wax. The first Sunday I worked on it in the open machine shed, I had an audience of at least a hundred convicts, and they immediately baptized the prince *Little Motherfucker,* and this remained his name at least until I left. There was always a man or two from the masonry gang to help me, and we never lacked an audience of convicts. One Sunday morning, before work started, I read to the assembled work watchers a few paragraphs from the autobiography of Benvenuto Cellini — a fortunate find in the library — where he speaks of his final attempt to cast the bronze horse. The comparison was preposterous, but there we were, lost in the mountains of West

Virginia, encasing *Little Motherfucker* in a great mass of plaster of Paris, leaving only the bottom open, whence I intended to melt out the wax. Which I finally managed to do with the aid of welding torches manned by a couple of convict machine workers. Then we put a quarter-inch copper pipe through the bottom of the cast and out the lad's little penis. About eight inches was left out to be cut for a fountain spray later, and the emergence brought a roar of approval from the assembled convicts.

So much for *Little MF*. Whether he still stands on the fountain at Mill Point or whether there still is a Mill Point, I don't know. I suppose I could inquire and find out, but I prefer not to. That was four decades ago.

And then we heard that the United States was at war again; the forlorn tale told to me by the Republican leader in Springfield, Massachusetts, had come true. I was in prison and my country was at war. Albert, who was very formal about such things, told me that he was calling a meeting. With whom? Myself and Dick Bradley. I asked him about Dmytryk.

"I don't trust him."

I couldn't anticipate what secrets we had to conceal from Dmytryk, but I went along with Albert, and after supper, on a lovely summer evening, the three of us sat down on the grass, Dick good-naturedly falling in with Albert's desire.

Albert made the point that if the war in Korea spread into a general war against Communism, we ought to make plans to escape.

"Albert," I said, "I don't want to escape. I don't even want to think about escape."

Dick was also very doubtful that the war would spread beyond Korea. Albert was prepared to suffer and to endure and have vile things happen to us, a continuation of what had begun at Peekskill, but whereas at Peekskill I had fought against hoodlums, the *lumpen* dregs of the Hudson River towns, here I was dealing with two extraordinary men, James Bennett and Kenneth Thieman, both of them deeply troubled by what was happening to the country, both of them aware that the Hollywood Ten and our committee and others, like the head of the Civil Rights Congress, and the entire top leadership of the Communist Party were the first political prisoners in America in thirty years. They were bending over backward to

make certain that what had happened to political prisoners in Germany and Italy and Russia did not happen here, and Albert found
this hard to accept. After he was released from prison, he took his
family to Mexico, still convinced that the United States would move
toward fascism.

My sentence was coming to its close. I am trying to be very truthful about my prison sentence, and it is not easy. The whole world
saw me as a martyr, and passionate meetings crying out for my freedom took place all over the world. Pablo Neruda, that gracious good
man and great poet, wrote a poem to me. It follows in part:

To Howard Fast

I speak to you, Howard Fast. You, who are jailed.
I embrace you, my comrade; and I bid you good morning, my brother.
I saw Spain's doors close, and I saw a poet's head rolling in the shad-
    ows;
He who was Spain's light.
The bloody beasts closed in upon him,
and from that time Spain has known
darkness and night and blood and tears.
I am not of this country. I am from Chile.
My comrades are there, and my books and my house that
gazes upon the cold Pacific's gigantic waves.
They wish that I, too, were in a deep prison,
Or dead and forever silent . . .
Those of us who love you are in all lands.
We see in you the figure of the people.
We hear in your voice chords not to be muted.
We march towards peace with you and your people.
Your face is a banner that we see from your prison,
and we follow the steps of each jailer.

Now when Neruda wrote that poem he knew nothing of Mill
Point or Kenneth Thieman. There was no way he could have known,
and he saw me languishing in one of the torture chambers of Chile
or Nicaragua or Turkey — his models for prison. His praise is too
lavish by far, but consider the time. The war in Korea had begun,
and a great many people saw it as the beginning of World War Three,
the beginning of the great crusade into Communist China that had
been pushed for so long by elements of the media. We had a not

unreal fear that we would never be released from prison, and if that had been the case, it would have meant immediate transfer to Leavenworth or some such place. The point was not what kind of prison I was in, but that none of us should have been in prison at all. We had done nothing wrong, broken no law. We were framed in a crazy time of hysteria and thrown in jail senselessly. I include parts of Neruda's poem here because they reflect the mood of much of the world. Millions of copies of the poem were reprinted.

I had become a martyr, not because I sought martyrdom and not because I had suffered as a martyr, but because the people of the world — not all of them, but many, many millions of them — saw America as the atomic threat to all life on earth. It was around that time, perhaps before I went to jail or shortly afterward, that I had dinner with the Hungarian consul in New York, who said to me, "At this moment our country — Hungary — and the Soviet Union have no foreign policy. From day to day, we live with the terrible certainty that America will begin to throw its atomic bombs — and that will be the end of everything."

In 1950, the peace movement, led by Communists and very small compared with the great peace movement that ended the Vietnam War, was constantly accused of being a tool of the Soviet Union. In a way it was. And also a tool, if you would have it that way, of people of good will the world over. Peace was the only hope of mankind in the new atomic age, and when the Korean War began, the hope of peace crumbled. The government that put me and the other political prisoners in jail was a government bereft of all common sense. Having been put in prison, I had become a force for peace beyond any act or energy of my own.

Meanwhile, my sentence was coming to its end. I had suffered no deprivation in prison — except the deprivation of my freedom, my right to exist as a free person and go where I would. We have criticized the Soviet Union bitterly for its refusal to allow its citizens to go beyond its borders, but in that time of terror no left-wing American was allowed to have a passport. Mine was taken from me when I returned from Paris, nor would the government issue another one to me for ten years. I recall a great concert arranged for Paul Robeson in Canada. We still had an open border and no passport was required to visit Canada, but Paul, through some antique laws, was

denied the right to go there. The rationale of Washington was that if
we were permitted to go abroad, we would become a focus of anti-
American propaganda; but we became that focus in any case.

At Mill Point prison, I had finished *Little MF,* cast him in concrete,
and we put him on a concrete pedestal basin, with a copper line from
our water supply through his body and out his little penis, where
about eight inches of copper extruded. "We shall have to cut that
down and fix a small nozzle there," Mr. Thieman said, "and before
any of those Washington people come to inspect us."

"The prisoners won't like that."

"They'll live with it."

We scheduled the water test for directly after supper, while it was
still light, and the entire prison population gathered around the new
fountain. I bent up the copper tubing, gave the signal to turn on the
water, and then, as the stream of water emerged from the statue,
lifting high into the air, such a roar of applause went up from the
population of Mill Point as was never heard before. I would leave
Mill Point, but I would leave behind my concrete work as a reminder
that I had been there.

The night before the day of my release I slept poorly. I had stayed
up late, talking to Dick Bradley and Albert Maltz. Albert still had
some months to serve. Dmytryk had sold his time to the FBI for his
betrayal of us, although what he could have told them that would
have been worth their buying, I can't imagine. But since all the business of the FBI in those days was a combination of stupidity and
chicanery, there was no reason that they should not do business with
Dmytryk as well as anyone else.

Dick and Albert and I had become very close in those months at
Mill Point, although, curiously enough, I lost touch with Dick completely after his release and saw Albert again only briefly in Mexico.
But his home was in Los Angeles, and I did not often go to Los
Angeles in those days. Dick was going to meet one of the women on
our board, and in time they were married, but they were to meet at
a women's prison south of where we were. I had written to Bette,
suggesting that we spend a day or two together, just the two of us,
before we returned to the kids. I asked her to meet me at the Greenbrier Hotel in White Sulphur Springs, and to bring me some clean
shirts and underwear, an extra pair of flannels, and a sweater. I had

told Ken Thieman what I intended to do, and he asked me how I proposed to get to White Sulphur Springs. I thought I would take a taxi if I could find one.

"That will cost you a bundle," he said. "You know, you have seventy-two dollars coming to you."

"How's that?"

"We don't believe in slavery," the warden said. "This is a work prison, and people who work should be paid. We don't pay a lot, but we pay. Now if you'll take that seventy-two dollars and put it into the protein fund, I'll drive you to the Greenbrier. It's only thirty miles from here, and it'll be a good day off."

As I said, Thieman had forty-two cents a day to feed each prisoner, and while he could buy vegetables at a prison farm a few miles to the south of us, meat was a problem. The seventy-two dollars would be a welcome addition, and I agreed to his proposal.

As we sat talking that last night, Albert wondered why they should be so decent. "He doesn't see us as criminals," Dick said. "He's a decent man."

"He treats the criminals the same way."

Albert had become more firmly convinced that we would never be released; now he felt that he would never be released. He was a sweet, dear, and stubborn man, and that night, sleeping only fitfully, I thought a great deal about him and how hard the Communist way of life was for him and how comparatively easy for me. For endless hours, we had discussed the contradictions in the Communist Party, the stupidity and rigidity of our leadership, the no-strike position during the war — calling on the workers not to strike while their employers were wallowing in the enormous profits that the war brought them — the dreadful rumors about Stalin, what to believe and what not to believe.

Albert agonized, and he would say, "It doesn't seem to trouble you. How do you live with it?"

"It troubles me, but where do I go? Where do I find people willing to stand up to Truman and McCarthy and the FBI? Show me them. I'll join up in a minute. Meanwhile, I'm here. We're both here. We can't run, Albert."

The next morning, we embraced each other. One of the guards had brought me a bag with my clothes and wallet and watch and keys. Dick and I dressed and then we walked up the hill to the administration building. I turned to see Albert standing by the little hospital, which was his preserve and which he ruled so zealously. My eyes were clouded with tears.

At the railroad station in White Sulphur Springs, I shook hands with Kenneth Thieman and watched him drive away. I was never to see him again, and since he was a good deal older than I, the likelihood is that he, like so many of the people in these memoirs, is dead. I think of him fondly. I was perhaps an hour early for Bette's train, and when it finally arrived, it was a good moment indeed. She fell into my arms, and we held on to each other as if there were nothing else on earth. At the Greenbrier, we sat at lunch, staring at each other with a kind of desperation. It was not the time we had been apart; it was the feeling we had both entertained that with the Korean War in progress, we might never see each other again.

Yet here we were, together, able to hold each other in our arms and kiss and love and be loved. This was real, but in my imagination, the other thing, the other possibility, had also been lived out.

13

I DO NOT look back at prison as either a lark or as justified punishment. I have tried to tell the truth about it, and to give the federal prison system credit for its intelligent handling of one of the darker spots on our civilization. The forces in government that took me there, I recall with anger and disgust. The business of putting writers in jail is an ancient and obscene practice, one of the habits of the Soviet government that disgraced the name of socialism, and one that is still alive in China. It is of course normal behavior in any and all of the dirty little dictatorships that are sprinkled through the Third World, many of them our client states.

However, without that prison term, I never would have written *Spartacus,* a book I began to brood over during that time at Mill Point, where I began more deeply than ever before to comprehend the full agony and hopelessness of the underclass. Meanwhile, I had come home to my children and my wife and our small brownstone house on Ninety-fourth Street, and never had children or wife or home looked so beautiful. In our tiny Victorian parlor, Bette had put down woven black carpeting, full of red roses, and there the antique furniture that we had bought when we were kids — twenty-five dollars for a horsehair couch, ten dollars apiece for some handsome Federal chairs, everything bought in the thirties, when nothing cost much more than twenty-five cents — looked absolutely right. I saw all these things with new delight, and it came home to me forcefully that all I had ever desired was to write well and tell stories, and to raise a family and live as a normal person should.

But then there was the Communist Party U.S.A., and what happened next should help to explain the party and its share of paranoid stupidity. All my life, I have loved the theater, and I suppose that if there were a way to make a decent and reliable living out of the theater without being Neil Simon, I would have devoted most of my life to it. As it happened, I lived a sort of double life: as a novelist, I had a career and a profession and a reputation and the means of earning a middle-class living; as a playwright, I had my dreams and I wrote my plays and never earned much more than twenty cents from any of them except, I must confess, *Citizen Tom Paine,* a play of mine that ran for seven very profitable weeks in the Kennedy Center, long after I had left the Communist Party, and from another play I wrote during the Communist years that became a great hit in Australia and was never produced in America. But two out of twenty is not a great average, and the others came to life briefly in summer playhouses, regional theaters, and universities.

During the weeks before going to prison, I had written a play called *The Hammer.* It was a drama about a Jewish family during the war years, a hard-working father who keeps his head just above water, and his three sons. One son comes out of the army, badly wounded, badly scarred. Another son makes a fortune out of the war, and the youngest son provides his share of the drama by deciding to enlist. Not a very good play, a judgment apart from any modesty on my side. It was tendentious and preachy. However, a year before this — that is, before my release from prison — I had come together with two good friends, Herb Tank, a merchant seaman turned writer, and Barney Rubin, Spanish vet, machine gunner in World War Two, and perhaps the best-known columnist for *Stars and Stripes.* With the actor Frank Silvera and the writers Arnold Manoff and Alice Childress, we had formed New Playwrights. *The Hammer* was my contribution to the endeavor.

While I was in prison, Barney Rubin and Herb Tank were determined that when I got out, I should be greeted with a mounted production, with a first-night opening on the night of my release. However, I won a few days off for good behavior and was released earlier than expected, early enough to see the first run-through. New Playwrights was a left-wing theater operation, an off-Broadway effort, launched on a shoestring and with the cooperation of the Cultural Section of the party. Without the party, it could not have come into existence, and by the definition of the Un-American Committee at the time, it was a Communist-front organization. It had the use of the Czechoslovak House on East Seventy-second Street.

Barney telephoned the day I got home, greeted me enthusiastically, and told me that the first run-through would be for Bette and me. "Curtain at eight-thirty," he said. The author never knows how bad his play is until the first night, but I was very uneasy about this one, the more so for its being cast and rehearsed without my presence or participation, but what was done was done and you can't saw sawdust; and Bette and I decided that we would not criticize, no matter what, since this had been done with great good will.

We were greeted warmly by Barney and Herb. Half a dozen men and women from the Cultural Section completed the audience for the run-through. The play began. The father came onstage, Michael Lewin, small, slender, pale white skin, and orange hair. Nina Normani, playing Michael's wife, small, pale. The first son came onstage, James Earl Jones, six feet and two inches, barrel-chested, eighteen years old if my memory serves me, two hundred pounds of bone and muscle if an ounce, and a bass voice that shook the walls of the little theater.

"God help us," I said to Bette.

"I'm sure he's only a stand-in," Bette whispered back.

"No, no, no," I moaned softly. "He's not a stand-in. The gods hate me. The muse hates me. I'm doomed."

Time crept on, slowly, painfully. Understand me: Jimmy Jones, as we called him then, was a lovely, modest young man, his whole life and being in and of the theater. But he was also black and twice as tall as anyone else in the play.

At last the first act ended and the curtain came down, and I turned to Barney Rubin and said, "Jimmy was a stand-in, wasn't he?"

Barney shook his head. Lionel Berman, organizer of the Cultural Section, was there, and Barney nodded at him.

"Hello, Lionel."

Lionel, voice of the party, said, "What do you mean, 'stand-in'?"

"Well — I mean an actor's sick or something else, and someone else does the part for tonight."

"No. Jimmy's been cast for the part. Your reaction is a chauvinist reaction."

Bullshit, I thought.

"No," I said, restraining myself, remembering that this little commissar was the voice and power of the party, and that every friend I had in the world was in the party. "I'm not being a white chauvinist, Lionel. But Mike here weighs in at maybe a hundred and ten pounds, and he's as pale as anyone can be and he's Jewish, and for God's sake, tell me what genetic miracle could produce Jimmy Jones."

"You are missing the point completely," Berman said.

"All right. Tell me the point."

"The point is that the theater is not the film. The theater depends on the suspension of disbelief, and if the actor is good enough, that suspension of disbelief will allow him to do the role and the audience will go along with him. Think about Canada Lee."

The black actor Canada Lee had made a small triumph of his role in *The Duchess of Malfi*, but there he played a white man, his skin covered with white makeup, and people who saw him saw a white man. I slowly but emphatically explained the difference. "I like Jimmy," I said, "but if he plays this impossible role, he'll be made a fool of and the play will become a joke."

"The party does not agree with you," Berman said. He could perhaps be argued with. But how can you argue with the party? He informed me that the matter had been thoroughly discussed with V. J. Jerome, a silly man who was the official party cultural authority east of the Mississippi River.

"It's my play," I said, "and I will not have it."

Barney Rubin and Herb Tank listened in silence. Like me, they were not willing to break with the party. All the years of their young lives had been invested there, in war and peace. Like me, they had seen people brought up on charges for expulsion from the party, and then expelled, and then isolated, unable to go crawling to those who hated the party and frozen away from the friends of a lifetime. No, you don't break easily.

"Is that your position?" Berman asked me. "Because if it is, you'll be brought up on charges —"

I turned to Barney. "Is it your position? Did you and Herb agree to this?"

"We had to," Barney said.

And Herb Tank said, "Give it a chance. Who knows? What Lionel says about the suspension of disbelief is the whole sense of the theater. We can't do anything about it now. Jimmy wants to try to make it work. Give it a chance."

"And otherwise I'm brought up on charges of white chauvinism — is that it?"

Berman nodded, and I stood on the edge of a cliff I'd stand on again and again in the coming years. It was not alone being brought up on charges for expulsion; I was almost ready in my anger at what had happened to face that and let them expel me; but if I pulled the play, it would sink New Playwrights. They had sold theater parties to every left-wing group in the city; they had spent ticket money that there was no hope of repaying; Barney and Herb had worked like diggers, and there were the jobs and hopes of the seven cast members, the understudies, the director, and all the rest of the company.

"All right, I'll go along with it," I said hopelessly.

The house for the first night had been bought up by the Jewish Workmen's Circle, garment workers and their wives at a time when eighty percent of the garment workers in New York were Jewish, people in their fifties and sixties who liked me and were eager to see anything I had written. They were simple, hard-working people who loved the theater and had in their youth supported the Yiddish theater passionately. Now they waited to see what Howard Fast, just out of prison, had written. It came on. They were not critical. They were with the play, absorbed in it, until James Earl Jones walked onto the stage, towering over the rest of the cast, obviously black. Facing an audience, sensitive to a point of despair, as so many black actors are, yet locked into what he had been talked into, he was trying desperately to control the rich vibrancy of his voice.

Bette and I shrank in our seats, and all over the hall, the whispers of the Yiddish-speaking audience could be heard — "Vere is er?" (Who is he?) and "Fin vonent cumpt er?" (Where does he come from?) — and various expressions of confusion, disbelief, and annoyance as the audience came to understand that Jimmy Jones had been cast as the son of tiny Michael Lewin with his orange hair and pasty-white skin. If those petty commissars of culture had thought the matter through, they would have realized that putting James Earl Jones into that impossible position was the act of white chauvinism, not my attempt to stop it. But in a microscopic form, this incident was a total definition of the leadership of the Communist Party, here and, I believe, everywhere. For one thing, they were a leadership cut off from the rank and file, and, most important, they were absolutely rigid in their preference for theory over reality. They could not and would not conform to reality, and while in this case it was a small matter, in the larger arena of politics it was tragedy.

They had decided that an obviously black actor could convince an audience that he was white; their decision made it real because it fitted in with what they felt was "Marxist thinking." Stalin had decided that the German infantrymen would not fire on the Soviet workers because both were of the working class, and therefore he issued orders for the Soviet soldiers not to fire at the advancing Germans — who mowed down the Russian soldiers by the thousands. The American party leadership had decided in 1948 that it was theoretically time for a third party. They lured Henry Wallace in as their candidate and the election became a national disaster, revealing not the strength of liberal America but the weakness. The same with the wartime no-strike pledge. And again and again. I could fill pages with accounts of Communist Party decisions made in the face of clearly opposite reality. But it must be noted that this did not make Communism a more dangerous force to the establishment; it was an inner contradiction that drained the strength from Communism, which had been defined by Lenin as the correct path to socialism. Abused as it was by its leadership — so often petty and stupid — it became something else entirely.

But I am telling my own story here, and now we are at the final curtain of *The Hammer*. The curtain came down, as third act curtains do, and here and there in the audience were a few hand claps, a feeble whisper of applause. Between the acts, we had lost a third of the audience. Bette and I were in the shadows in the rear, hoping we would not be noticed. I had vague wishes that I could be back at Mill Point, far from this test of the human spirit, and Bette clung to me, whispering assurances that the world still existed.

Leaving the theater, we encountered the drama critic of *The New York Herald Tribune*, who said to me, "Fast, I admire the way you've stood up to the bastards, and I'm going to take this opportunity to help. I'm not going to review your play."

Blessings on him.

*

Slipping back into the life that I had left behind was harder than I had expected. Something changed in prison, a sense of the world that was different from my previous outlook. I write best about where I have been and what I have known, and in some very deep way, I was different. I had changed. I would never again have that wonderful feeling of overcoming that was so much a part of my makeup ten years before, and I would never again write the way I used to write, but possibly I could write a little better because I knew a little more. Everything was so precious now, the two children whom Bette and I had brought into the world, the house, the air we breathed, and the right to be with each other. The black and white of my world had crumbled; I could not find an enemy in Kenneth Thieman. In the prison library, of all places, I had found a book about Germany after the First World War, and there was a great deal about Rosa Luxemburg that I had not known. This small, crippled, and remarkable woman, born to a Jewish family in Poland, German by marriage, imprisoned during the First World War, released to become one of the leaders of the abortive German socialist revolution in 1918, was one of the great minds of the time. It was she who named the new organization of German socialists the Spartacists, who watched what was happening in Russia with both delight and despair, and who wrote, shortly before she was murdered by the Germans in 1919, "Freedom for the supporters of the government only, for the members of one party only — no matter how big its membership may be — is no freedom at all. Freedom is always freedom for the man who thinks differently. This contention does not spring from a fanatical love of abstract justice, but from the fact that everything which is enlightening, healthy, and purifying in political freedom derives from its independent character, and from the fact that freedom loses all its virtue when it becomes a privilege."

I discussed that with Maltz; I brooded over it; I discussed it with the soft-spoken eminently reasonable Dick Bradley, who agreed with her, and again with Albert Maltz, who felt that there could have been no Soviet Union if her ideas had won out. I didn't know precisely where I stood. I was still a member of the party. I was contentious as hell and I fought them tooth and nail, but I won my points.

"Yes, because you're Howard Fast," Maltz said. "When they expel you, who is left?"

"You are and a lot more."

Jail arguments. When you sit with a cigarette on the wooden steps of a barracks and the sun is setting, you talk and talk. I wanted to write about that abortive revolution in Germany, but it was too soon after the Holocaust and I would not go to Germany, yet there in prison I began to think of Spartacus the slave and why Rosa had chosen him. I read every scrap and thread of information about Spartacus that I could find in that small prison library. I read whatever there was about Rome — precious little. I had been reading in ancient history for years, so I had a foundation there; but it was not until I got home that I began to read, from cover to cover — I had read much of it before — the wonderful two-volume history of the ancient working people, titled *The Ancient Lowly,* originally written in 1888 and, in the edition I have, republished in 1907 by Charles H. Kerr and Company in Chicago. The two books amount to a thousand-page history of slavery in ancient times, and they were a gift to me when I finished my course at the party training school. I read Hy Gordon's inscription today, forty-three years later, with great pride, and this I would rather have said of me than all the critical praise my life as a Communist denied me:

To Howard

From the school commission, teaching staff and student body of the
    national training school,
For exemplifying the best type of revolutionary working-class intellec-
    tual and showing exceptional solicitude for fellow students

Hy Gordon

There, in these two books, I found the story of Spartacus — and became convinced that there was a way to tell it so that it could at least approximate the truth. The truth of history is always lost; indeed, the truth of each day we live through is almost beyond recognition, and that old adage that the rich man's patriotism is the poor man's treason applies to most of our living; and the best a historical novelist can do is to find a sense of the time he writes about and convey it to the reader.

My own problems were manifold. There was ancient Rome — how much could I read to give me a valid sense of it? My pickup education included no Latin. The poet Walter Lowenfels, a close friend, had a sister who taught Latin in a New York high school; I became her endured nuisance, demanding an instantaneous knowledge of Latin. Morning, noon, and night, I lived in ancient Rome. And finally I began to write, change, rewrite. But not quite the way it sounds, nor had I returned from prison to the quiet life of a scholar and a writer. The mini-terror continued, and there was no way out of it for me. There was always the picket line and the demonstration. Milton Wolf, a tall, handsome man, a Spanish Civil War vet and a much-decorated infantryman in World War Two, was obsessed by the need to oppose Franco. Hardly a month went by without Wolf and a picket line.

I'd get a call in the middle of a page. "This is Milt. We're picketing." It could be the Spanish consulate or a hotel where a Franco representative was staying. Milt Wolf would load a truck with picket signs, have us waiting at the spot, drive up, and hand out the signs. We'd be in motion before the cops knew what had happened. One day, we picketed the White House. The day before, Puerto Rican nationalists had attempted to assassinate President Truman. Our picket line, protesting the Rosenberg decision, was scheduled for five A.M. on an icy cold winter morning. We should have called it off, but we were too stubborn to do so. I was suffering from a godawful cold, but after three hours of picketing, back and forth in front of the machine gun guard posts that had been set up the night before, I found that my cold had disappeared. I told myself again and again that I was writing a very important book; Bette told me that I was writing a very important book. I tried to explain that I couldn't say no. The Rosenbergs had been sentenced to death by Judge Irving R. Kaufman. These were simple things they asked of me. How could I say no?

Strangely enough, with all the books and articles written about the Rosenbergs, no one ever questioned why the important atomic physicists of the time were not brought in as witnesses. Those I spoke to privately said that the whole trial was a ghastly black joke, that there was no conceivable way that a drawing by David Greenglass — the only real testimony at the trial — could have had anything to do with the Soviet development of the bomb. The Communist Party here was reluctant to take up the defense, but Julie Trupin and I forced the issue. I wrote to de Jouvenel in Paris, and he put the case to the

leadership of the French Communist Party, and they agreed to spear-
head a worldwide movement in defense of the Rosenbergs. Julie Trupin and I actually began the defense movement here in the United
States, and once under way, it steamrollered well apart from ourselves, but only to what was left of the uncowed liberals. The terror
was not slackening — indeed, the Rosenberg case had been orchestrated to an anti-Communist frenzy that matched the exuberant hysteria of the Nazi horror. The Un-American Committee was still at
work. Dashiell Hammett refused to name names, and become an
informer, and was sentenced to six months in prison.

I knew Emanuel Bloch, the defense lawyer, and at the very beginning of the case, five years earlier, I had asked him to have lunch
with me. His position was that neither evidence nor skill could help;
the handwriting was on the wall, and the Rosenbergs were going to
be sent down, and nothing could be done about it. He made the
point that in a city with the largest metropolitan Jewish population
in the world, no Jew was on the jury. It was a matter of very clever
and muted anti-Semitism, with a cowardly Jew on the bench, doing
the will of Harry Truman. And with not one shred of evidence in the
hands of the government that could connect espionage with the Rosenbergs. That is quite true. The whole case rested on David Greenglass having copied a drawing that had to do with the mechanism
that triggered the bomb. By his word, spoken to save his hide and
part of the deal the government made with him, he had passed on
the evidence to Julius Rosenberg, his brother-in-law. There was bitterness between Greenglass and Rosenberg, and Greenglass chose
Rosenberg for the fall guy. On Ethel, Julius's wife, there was nothing.

I had made the luncheon appointment with Manny Bloch because
I wanted to tell him the story of my meeting with Frédéric Joliot-
Curie. At that time, five years ago now, we had talked at length
about the bomb; his wife, Irène Curie, had joined in the conversation, and both of them had stressed that there were no secrets to be
either hidden or revealed, and since both were deeply concerned with
atomic power — Joliot-Curie being then the head of the French atom
bomb project — they spoke with authority. No one knew more about
the Russian endeavor than Joliot-Curie, and I felt that if he could
testify in the case, it might influence things.

Manny's reply was that they would never allow him into America, and even if by some miracle he were to testify, his testimony would be utterly trashed. A week before this, a Cornell professor, intimately involved in the Manhattan Project, had expressed the same opinion of the case against the Rosenbergs. Dining at our home, this Cornell professor said the case was so transparently weak that no person with even a smattering of scientific knowledge could believe it. When I asked him whether he would testify for the Rosenbergs, he shook his head and told me he was not that eager to spend five years in prison. The government had been parading J. Robert Oppenheimer as its witness against the Rosenbergs, but Oppenheimer never testified, and my friend, the Cornell scientist, told me that Oppenheimer said he could degrade himself only so much, what with the government's threats against him, but he could not degrade himself so low as to mouth the government's inventions of evidence against the Rosenbergs. Dr. Harold C. Urey, another announced government witness, never testified, nor did Lieutenant General Leslie Groves, who had been the head man in the atom bomb project.

The Rosenberg case absorbed me, fascinated me, intrigued me. I was living in a moment of awful drama in a demented world that appeared to be aching to blow itself into extinction. A war was in progress that threatened to engulf us in a war with China; and within this gigantic drama, the Rosenbergs were the strange focus. I wanted desperately for them not to die, and Manny Bloch wanted the same thing, so desperately that it killed him. He died of a heart attack during his defense of the Rosenbergs.

The terror continued. Twenty-one additional Communist leaders were indicted for conspiring to overthrow the government by force and violence, a charge as far from reality as a charge of conspiring to go to the moon. And then it began to get too dangerous — too close to Armageddon. The American forces in Korea penetrated too close to the Chinese border, and a Chinese army of 300,000 crossed the border and inflicted a bloody defeat on the Americans. I say the Americans, but of course the forces were purported to be a United Nations army, although there were only token representations from other nations. In the face of all this, MacArthur, the commanding officer in Korea, began to talk about an all-out war against China, and this sent a chill of fear through Mr. Truman. He acted quickly, stripped General MacArthur of all his commands in the East, and ordered him to return to the United States immediately. Nevertheless, in New York City, where he was scheduled to be on April 21, a great triumphal parade was planned for him.

Irv Goff had lunch with me. He was the incredible, romantic young man who had led a guerrilla band behind the Franco lines during the Spanish Civil War, who had been an infantryman in World War Two, and who had been together with me in Communist training school. We had long talks about Spain, which resulted in my stories of the Spanish Civil War in my book *Departure and Other Stories*, published in 1949. I had great respect and fondness for Irv, even though a few years earlier he had involved me in a rather loony adventure. We wanted to do something for the people arrested and imprisoned either because they would not name names or because they were involved in the Communist leadership. I wrote an impassioned speech against a police state, against war, and then I recorded it at a friendly studio. We rented a room, Irv and I and Julie Trupin, in the old Astor Hotel on the twelfth floor, if I remember correctly, and we brought into the room a record player and a loudspeaker with good amplification. We had a timer to start the record. After we had set up the mechanism, we opened the window, set the loudspeaker on a chair facing the open window and Broadway, closed the door behind us, and broke the key in the lock. Then we went down to the street and waited on the east side of Broadway.

It was quite extraordinary. Everyone in the area heard the voice denouncing the drive toward war. The record was eighteen minutes long, and the message finished and started all over again and finished and began to play a third time and almost finished its third playing before they got into the room and stopped it. From this distance, it may seem a childish caper, but remember that except for a handful of left-wing periodicals, with a combined circulation of perhaps 200,000, the vast apparatus of the media was closed to our ideas — closed to any and all arguments for peace. We felt that it was not enough to face imprisonment, blacklist, and slander; we had to be heard, and if we were not heard, there would be no voice for what we felt was best in America.

Now, on April 16, 1951, Irv Goff laid out his plan simply and directly. Truman had fired MacArthur, but MacArthur would be coming to New York in five days as a conquering hero, and the dead were in Korea, and the living were still fighting there. Someone had to challenge him. Could I write something denouncing his mad scheme to fight China and spelling out what he had cost the American people in human lives?

I said that I could do it, but to what end? We'd print it in *The Daily Worker* and it wouldn't make one damn bit of difference. Goff had something else in mind, and he said that he had talked the people in the party into it and that they were willing to put up $2500 for costs. He reminded me of the incident at the Astor Hotel.

MacArthur would be staying at the Waldorf, Goff told me, and as far as he could find out, the parade honoring him would go up Park Avenue. His scheme was to have me make a record, much as we had done at the Astor, rent a room on the Park Avenue side of the hotel, put into it a really powerful set of amplifiers and huge speakers, and blast the message out full strength. He said he had a sound engineer already involved, he knew the kind of equipment we needed, and he had the money to pay for it.

I loved the idea, but at the same time I felt it was impossible. The place would be loaded with Secret Service and Justice Department men. (Actually there were more than fifty men assigned to guard General MacArthur, aside from the hotel security and the city police, who had assigned special details of plainclothesmen to the Waldorf.) I told him that it was a beautiful idea that would get us either shot or in the slammer. He said that I should leave the execution to him. He reminded me that he had blown up a train in Spain a mile from Franco's headquarters, and that in Italy, in World War Two, he had seen and then destroyed Colonel Donovan's secret files condemning Goff and two other Communists to "accidental" death, once their mission with the Italian guerrillas was over. "Don't worry about the security," he told me. "Those guys are not smart. Smart guys don't become guards."

He told me what he wanted of me. First, an absolutely unshakable man to rent the room, someone beyond reproach and not to be recognized. That would be, I said, a man named Sam Schachner, a bond salesman in his late fifties. He lived in Jersey and he looked the part. The second thing Goff needed was a handsome Wasp actor, strong, sympathetic, Ivy League. I knew the actors in the party, and one came to mind immediately, John ———. I can't use his name because he's still working, an aging character actor very much in demand.

Then the plan went into effect. I wrote the words. I recruited Sam Schachner, who was as excited as a kid. John joined the forces, quiet, unflappable, and brave beyond reason. The room was rented. The equipment was packed in suitcases, nine different suitcases, so that none would be too heavy to lift. Irv and John carried the heaviest one in through the side street entrance, from where they could go directly into the elevators. The big loudspeakers were folded. Hundreds of pounds of equipment were brought into that room, and by April 21, the timer had been set and the project was ready to go. And on the day of the parade, on April 21, we waited on Park Avenue for the great voice to sound off and denounce MacArthur. It never happened. We had overlooked one very important factor: at that time, almost forty years ago, the Waldorf used direct current.

The party people said, OK, you screwed up, but we paid for the sound equipment with the hard-earned dollars of party members. We want that equipment back.

This time, we had to add a locksmith to the crew, since Goff had broken the key in the lock, but the equipment was brought out, every last bit of it, by Sam Schachner and John and Goff. My face was too well known to the city cops for me to be in and out of the hotel, but the other three men took the stuff past a small army of guards, and to this day no one knew what had happened. So much for the FBI and the Secret Service.

At home, I worked on *Spartacus* and tried to convince Bette that I was not succumbing to some childish insanity. It was the lowest low point of our marriage. It's not a healthy thing to fight in desperation against all odds; it bends your sense of judgment and gives too much importance to one thing and too little to another. It's a condition that films much better than it plays in real life, and as you and the people who believe as you do are increasingly isolated, desperation increases. Not a totally valid comparison by any means, but I began to understand what it meant to be an anti-fascist in Hitler's Germany, and how his opponents must have been torn to shreds emotionally. In some profound manner, the organization I had been willing to pledge my life to was wrong. It was not a secret society, but neither was it an open society. It was not simply that the Communist Party was isolated; its very structure had doomed it to this isolation, and in the situation that existed in 1950 and 1951, this isolation led to the beginning of our destruction. There were millions of Americans who believed that there must be no war, but we lost them. It was no wonder that Bette and I had to fight like tigers to keep a marriage together; we had lost any hope of the future.

The Rosenbergs were a symbol. If two people in these United States could be so deliberately framed and put to death, then we were no longer a nation of law. Julie Trupin felt the same way. Trupin and I were very close, we worked well together, we were equally involved with children and family, and we were both of us being torn to shreds. He put it to me this way: "They must not die. We both understand that. It would be something this nation could not digest, worse than the Sacco and Vanzetti case. Somehow, we must stop it."

That was a very tall order; both he and I had dealt with the basic corruption of our government. Since there was an active and well recognized and not only tolerated but respected fix functioning in New York City, we reasoned that there had to be a much larger fix in Washington. Julie knew a lawyer who worked for a firm that had as their clients some of the most important lobbyists in the city, and since we all functioned under the belief — somewhat paranoid — that the FBI had tapped every radical telephone in America, we dealt very little on the telephone; instead, we caught an early train to Washington, where we bought lunch for said lawyer. What followed was absolutely fascinating. He told us that the biggest and best fix in the city was at the White House (this was before we had introduced the name of the Rosenbergs) and then went on to explain, with a good deal of admiration, that Harry Truman was totally honest and dependable, that when he was senator, his price was $3000, that when he was Vice President, his price was $3000, and when he became President, his price was still $3000 — and he always delivered. There are enough men still alive who know that I am writing the truth. I am not trying to trash the memory of Harry Truman. I am telling what I know, and in what follows, I am also telling what I heard and what I believe to be the truth.

When Julie's friend heard that it was the Rosenberg case, he became very alarmed and could not wait to finish lunch and get away from us. The thought of going to Truman was, of course, laughable, but he did give us the name of a certain senator, one of the handful of men in Congress who had dared to speak out against the shadow dictatorship of J. Edgar Hoover.

He said that the senator could be reached and talked to, but his fix was infrequent. We went to the senator's office and spoke to his assistant. This man explained that the senator would not see us, that his name must never be linked to this matter, that if there was money involved, it would have to be paid to this assistant and in a manner to be detailed at a later time. The senator was a decent man, but the process was as sleazy as any other fix. We would have our answer tomorrow. In the course of this, we were told that Truman was putting enormous pressure on Judge Kaufman to sentence the Rosenbergs to death. The story around Washington was that Truman had Kaufman in a position where he could not refuse, and even though Kaufman pleaded for Truman to find a non-Jew to pronounce the sentence, because if he, Kaufman, pronounced it he would become a pariah among his people, Truman had refused to budge an inch. Truman's shameful anti-Semitism has been amply detailed elsewhere, but this story has never been told. A week later, while I was sitting in the waiting room of my dentist, Dr. Irving Naidorf, Judge Kaufman came out of his office, wiping the tears away. Naidorf, by no means a liberal, told me that Kaufman had asked him what he should do in the face of Truman's threats. Shocked, Naidorf reminded Kaufman that he, Naidorf, was only a dentist. Why didn't he go to his rabbi, if he had one. Kaufman replied that he had gone to his rabbi, who said that in this, Kaufman must make his own choice. There is no indication in any of the numerous books written about the Rosenberg case of Judge Irving Kaufman's agony; nor do I wish to make his sentence of death less cruel and self-serving than it has been taken to be. In a crazy defense of his despicable surrender to Truman's spite, Judge Irving Kaufman justified himself by saying, in his final statement to the condemned Rosenbergs: "Indeed, by your betrayal you undoubtedly have altered the course of history to the disadvantage of our country . . ."

Suppose the charges against the Rosenbergs were true? What was Kaufman saying — that they had prevented an atomic attack against the Soviet cities? The plan bruited about by everyone in 1948 was that Truman planned to take out eight Russian cities with the bomb. But if this lunatic idea had any foundation in truth, then the Rosenbergs could have been credited with saving the lives of thirty-five million people, the estimated casualties of such an attack. But even Truman could not have been that insane — at least I hope so — and, as I have written, Frédéric Joliot-Curie had assured me that the Russians had the bomb. I believe he told me the truth.

Now let me go back to our visit to the senator's office. I had to return to New York the same day. Neither Julie nor I met the senator, but when Julie returned to New York the following day, he told me that he had these assurances: the request and the money, $5000, must come from the Rosenberg defense group, from the lawyers. The money would be paid as a legal fee, and though nothing could be guaranteed, the senator felt he could persuade Truman to relent.

This was, of course, before Kaufman pronounced sentence. Manny Bloch had died of a heart attack — he lived for the case, and it finally destroyed him — and a new defense was functioning. The French Committee to Defend the Rosenbergs had sent one of their lawyers to join the defense here in America — she was tall, amazingly beautiful, and bright, but no expert in American law — and she was one of the people Julie Trupin took the senator's offer to. Julie told the defense team that he and I would raise the $5000, but that made no difference. They indignantly rejected our interference and snorted at our opinion that the death sentence had already been decided on and would be pronounced; they said that the mass movement gathered behind them would win the Rosenbergs' freedom without anyone paying off "some bastard" in Washington.

Another example of the gross misjudgment of the left about the willingness of the American people to support them. It was simply not to be. Two years later, the civil rights leader Bill Patterson and I led the final delegation to the gates of Sing Sing prison, a mute display on the day of the Rosenbergs' execution.

14

I CONTINUED TO WORK on *Spartacus*. It was not easy, and what made it very difficult was that I was denied a passport and could not go to Italy. There were dozens of situations as the story progressed that I wanted to check out personally, and years later I prowled through the ruins of Pompeii again and again, seeing what I should have seen when I wrote *Spartacus*. The denial of a passport was inflicted on thousands of left-wingers, a curious commentary on our bitter criticism of the Soviet Union for the same practice. I studied Latin furiously. I spent hours with classical encyclopedias and I used whatever knowledge I could pluck out of others. I had, in one instance, Varinia — the wife of Spartacus — sing a lullaby to her baby, and I prodded Louis Untermeyer to give me the proper meter for the period. He told me to use the six-stress rhythm used in the ancient epics, but because it happened to be the same meter that Longfellow had used for *Evangeline,* a reviewer snottily condemned me for my ignorance, which in fact showed his ignorance. Somehow, the book was written, the story put down on paper, and for a second time, I told the story of a slave. The first time, it was the account of Gideon Jackson in *Freedom Road,* and now it was *Spartacus.* Strangely, both books sold millions of copies in the Third World and there has never been a year of my life since then when I have not had a request for a reprinting of *Spartacus.*

I finished the manuscript, read it and reread it, and then sent it off with whatever corrections I felt necessary to Angus Cameron of Little, Brown, which had published two of my novels and a book of short stories. That was at the beginning of June 1951, and a few weeks later Angus sent me the following report, part of which follows:

> I haven't the slightest doubt but that if this novel had any other name on it than that of Howard Fast, it would become a best seller. It is endlessly engaging, most ingeniously put together, and, all in all, an entertaining and meaningful novel about Spartacus and the slave revolt he led. As a character, the slave leader never enters the story directly and the skill of the novel lies in the author's ability to make him not only a real man to the reader and to the other characters in the story but the epitome of the underdog with the courage to struggle for the truth in any society and at any time ...
>
> The novel has suspense, excellent characterizations, a feeling of the times, and a profound comment on those times and, indeed, on any time of crisis. Fast, however, does not draw any analogies. As I say, without his name attached to it I am sure it would sell as a fine novel of the end of the Republic.
>
> It is a novel we can publish with pride and with the gamble that it will do better than *The Proud and the Free*. This novel has more motion, more variety, more sex (a plenty of that both pure and profane), better drawn and more varied characters, and more maturity and meaningful comment.
>
> This is a fine novel.

This above is a portion of the in-house report Angus Cameron sent to me. I quote it because it bears directly upon what followed — a story of a book and its fate, unprecedented in all the literary history of this country. With the above report, Angus sent me a personal letter. Here is the first paragraph.

> Dear Howard:
> After I had written this report, I decided that I would send it along to you unedited. It tells briefly what I think of the book. It does not attempt to say all the things I feel about it and it does not do justice, really, to my admiration for the skillful technique of the telling. It shows the sure hand of a real artist, for the form you have selected is

a difficult kind which, once it falters, is fatal to the illusion, but it never falters. You have told this on many levels and yet managed to find a unity in the telling of Spartacus' life.

I find it hard to relate my feelings at that time. For a writer to receive a report like the above under any conditions would be overwhelming; but to receive this report in the crazy atmosphere of fear and terror covering my world was just short of miraculous. Bette and I celebrated in proper fashion, certain that this would break through the sneering, hate-filled reviews that had become the book reviewers' obeisance to the ravings of Senator McCarthy and the stylish hatred of Communism.

And of course the courage of Angus Cameron, a man who was not a Communist but was firm enough in his American values to be disgusted by what was going around and to have none of it. That was like new wine and should have been an inspiration to the entire publishing world.

Unfortunately, it was not, and Cameron stood almost alone. For a week or so, Bette and I bathed in appreciation and hope; and then Angus telephoned and said he was coming to New York and would I have lunch with him, and the following day he told me an incredible story. J. Edgar Hoover had sent his personal emissary, a federal agent, to Boston, where he met with the president of Little, Brown. He told him that he was not to publish any more books by Howard Fast, that these were the express instructions of J. Edgar Hoover, and that if he continued to publish Howard Fast, action would be taken against his company. The details of the action were not specified.

An editorial meeting followed, during which Angus pointed out that this was a blow at the most basic constitutional freedom, the First Amendment, that it was utterly disgraceful, and that there was no precedent to this in all American history — an appointed member of the federal government instructing a publisher not to publish a book under threat of dire consequences. I have no details of the debate that followed, except that it was hot and heavy, as Angus indicated, and that the majority of the editorial board sided with the president. Finally, Angus said that his basic self-respect, his ability to live with himself, led him to this conclusion. Either they published *Spartacus*, or he would have to resign as vice president and editor in chief. They refused to undertake publication, and thereupon Angus resigned; he was without a job and I without a publisher.

Under ordinary circumstances, this would have been a newsbreak of national importance; under the conditions that prevailed in July of 1951, *The Daily Worker* was one of the few papers that took notice of what had happened.

Of course, this was an awful blow to Angus Cameron. In ordinary times it would have been different; an editor of Angus's intellect, skill, and experience, for years the successful editor in chief at Little, Brown, a man respected and honored throughout the industry, would not have gone a single day without work, but because of the fear that had blanketed both the publishing and the film industries, no one would hire him, and it was years before he could once again find work in a publishing house.

I believed that my own position was better, and I had to deal with a lot of guilt over what I felt was Angus's sacrifice. He made it easier by telling me that he had done it not for me but for himself and his own need to live with himself. But I had other publishers to go to, and while I would miss the guidance and help of Angus as my editor, there were publishers aplenty, and one or another would be delighted to have my book. Or so I thought.

I chose Viking Press for my first approach and sent them the manuscript. A week passed. They sent it back with a polite note that it did not fit into their publishing schedule. Well, that could be. Why not? Probably they had their season filled.

I then sent it to Scribner's. They sent it back with a note saying that they were glad to have had a chance to see it, but it was not for them.

Harper was my next choice. Harper sent it back with a note informing me that they accepted only manuscripts from literary agents. This was almost twenty years after the publication of my first novel. I was already one of the most widely read serious writers on earth, with my books translated into eighty-two languages. But Harper read only books submitted by literary agents.

This was before the time of multiple submissions. One submitted a manuscript to one publisher at a time. The summer was going by and I had no publisher. The next on my list was Alfred A. Knopf, for whose publishing house I had long had great respect. And the courageous Mr. Knopf sent the manuscript back unopened with a note attached to it saying that he would not dirty his hands by opening a manuscript sent to him by Howard Fast. I do not know whether he sent a carbon copy of the letter to J. Edgar Hoover.

It becomes repetitive and increasingly disgusting. The next submission was to Simon and Schuster. They had published *Conceived in Liberty*, one of my earliest books. They had granted me an advance of $1200 to write *The Last Frontier*. When I decided to give the manuscript to Sam Sloan at Duell, Sloan and Pearce, I had paid back the advance in full. They then sent me a letter of surprise and delight, and begged me to return to them if I changed my mind about Sam Sloan. Now they returned the manuscript of *Spartacus* without a word, with not even a printed rejection slip. Careful people.

All this increased my understanding. I would never again fulminate against the German people for not defying Adolf Hitler. He, at least, had firing squads and concentration camps. Here, it was simply the threat of J. Edgar Hoover and his FBI, for the story of what had happened at Little, Brown was all over the industry, and no "brave" publisher wanted to be Horatius, standing at the bridge.

By now, I was determined to see how deeply this cowardice had pervaded the publishing industry, and I made my sixth submission to Doubleday. And here, indeed, something very different happened: I received a call a week or so after my submission to Doubleday from a man named George Hecht. He was the president of the Doubleday chain of bookstores and here is what he said to me on the telephone. I put it down for the record.

"Mr. Fast," George Hecht said, "I have just experienced a sickening two hours with a group of yellow-bellied crumbs who constitute the editorial board of Doubleday. They spent an hour talking about how great your *Spartacus* is and how they have no hope of seeing another book like it, and then they spent the second hour talking about why they were not going to publish it. The hell with that lousy bunch of cowards. I've read the book, and I tell you this right now. Publish the book yourself, and I hereby give you an order for six hundred copies for the bookstores. If you ask around, they'll tell you what my word is worth. So publish it yourself and God bless you."

To this day, I have never met George Hecht. I don't know whether he lives or has passed on. We made several appointments, but they had to be broken. But his word was good and he kept it. I salute him. He was a man of courage and dignity at a time when courage was in very short supply.

"Publish it yourself . . . " Fine. Swim around Manhattan Island; it had been done, but was I a candidate? With all the books I had written, I had never inquired into the process of publication. I wrote the book; a publisher published it. I knew the steps: the manuscript was pored over by an editor; he made suggestions and pointed out blunders, gross or otherwise. Then it was returned to the writer, who was to brood over the suggested changes. Then back to the editor, who reviewed the writer's changes; then to the copy editor, who was supposed to pick up and rectify misspellings, gross errors of grammar, and errors of fact, date, and place. Then it went back to the writer again, to agree or disagree with the copy editor. Then back to the copy editor for final adjustments, and then to the typesetter, the printer at his Linotype machine. (That was still in the days of Linotype.) Then the type was set and proofs were drawn. The proofs were read again by a proofreader, then sent to the author for a final reading, then cast and sent to the printer and then to the binder.

Well, I had an order for six hundred books and I might as well set about making them. I rented Post Office Box 171, at the Planetarium Station. Now I had an address. But the basic problem was that we were broke. Bette and I had enough to pay the mortgage and keep food on the table, but there was nothing put away that would enable me to start a publishing business. Friends reminded me of Mark Twain's awful fate when he became his own publisher, but I had no alternative. Certainly I was not going to continue the wretched process of sending my manuscript to one terrified publisher after another. Bette and I discussed it at length. I had meanwhile heard from two British publishers who were eager to publish the book, but I felt that having it published first in England would be a degrading surrender, and Bette agreed with me. I was constantly surprised by the strength of purpose of this slender woman I had married. The book must be published here, in the United States. Suppose we sent a letter to a group of people, telling them of the circumstances and asking them to subscribe to the book in advance? The general price of a novel at that time varied between three and six dollars. My last novel before *Spartacus, The Proud and the Free,* had been priced at three dollars. We decided that we would offer the novel — a third longer than *The Proud and the Free* — at three dollars for the regular edition and five dollars for a special autographed edition, bound in excellent cloth and with gold lettering on the spine, hoping that people who were avid readers of mine might go for the special edition. I had already spoken to Mel Freedman, one of the executive salesmen at the American Book Company, and had gotten prices from him, and I felt that at three and five dollars, I might make out without debt.

I went out on a limb with whatever savings we had. We painted the basement of our house and turned it into a storeroom and shipping room for the books — providing that we had books to ship. I engaged Charles Humboldt, a fine editor who had been on the staff of *The New Masses,* to do editorial and copy reading, and an old friend, Bert Clark, one of the industry's most gifted book designers, to lay out the pages and design the book. I could in no way pay them what their going rate would have been; they did it out of their feeling for Bette and me, as did that splendid black artist Charles White, who drew the picture for the dust jacket, a drawing I still have and treasure. We stretched our small store of money desperately. I wrote the letter. I bought names from *The Nation, The New Republic,* and *The New Masses* — and then the orders began to come in. First a handful, then more and more, and then word got around beyond the mailings, and the orders poured in. I had paid orders for over three thousand books, and suddenly I was in the publishing business. And not only was I in the publishing business, but as impossible as it might have been considered a few weeks earlier, I was paying my own way.

Bette and I and a secretary worked long hours, and bit by bit everything fell into place. The book was edited, copy edited, printed, and bound, and one astonishing morning cartons of books began to arrive at 43 West Ninety-fourth Street. I asked Mel Freedman to have six hundred books shipped from the bindery to the Doubleday bookstore warehouse. This was done, the books were paid for promptly, and not one copy was ever returned. Morris Sorkin and Philip Foner, the historian, owned a small, left-of-center publishing house called Citadel. I suppose my own arrogance had kept me from submitting the manuscript to them; certainly they would have published it. But I was insistent that it be published by a major publisher.

Now Morris Sorkin got in touch with me and asked me what I intended to do about sales to bookstores. I replied that I didn't know, and so far, the only bookstores that were carrying the book were the Doubleday stores. He told me that they had salesmen in the major book territories, and if I so desired, and for a reasonable charge, his salesmen would sell *Spartacus*.

I was absolutely overwhelmed by the runaway success of *Spartacus*. I took the production out of my home and rented an office. Bette drew a sketch for a full-page advertisement in *The New York Times Book Review*. I tried a couple of advertising agencies, but neither of them wanted anything to do with me, whereupon I took the layout down to *The Times,* where I had an appointment to see the censor. I never knew that they had a censor of advertising at *The Times,* but here he was, an elderly gentleman who studied my sketch thoughtfully. "Doesn't appear to be anything demonic in it," he said. "What about the book? Anything about the overthrow of the government by force and violence?"

"Not this government. Ancient Rome."

"We'll take a chance on that."

The full-page advertisement ran in the Sunday *Times Book Review*. It cost somewhere around $5000, reducing my bank account to practically nothing. But *Spartacus* was still selling. For the most part, the reviewers ignored it, but here and there a reviewer took it seriously. In the small-circulation publications of the left, the book was praised to the skies, but the mass-circulation, important papers of America brushed it off, saying that no publisher could be blamed for refusing a book by a red like Howard Fast. I had become a notorious symbol of the Communist Party. The film people had been totally blacklisted. Albert Maltz, Dalton Trumbo, Ring Lardner, and a dozen other talented screenwriters were no longer working; no films of theirs appeared, except those which were written under other names, so in a sense they were beyond attack; but the book reviewers had their day, and almost every one of them went on record to show that their hatred of Communism and of Howard Fast was second to none. In time, *Spartacus* would be praised and millions of copies would be sold, but that was years in the future.

Meanwhile, I had no right to complain about sales. I had ordered a first printing of five thousand copies, and then I ordered a second printing and then a third and a fourth printing. My having broken through in this manner became an increasing irritation to the media, and the book was treated with petulant nastiness, particularly by *The New York Times*. In the issue of February 3, 1952, a certain Melville Heath recalled *The Unvanquished*, which I wrote at age twenty-five. Of *Spartacus* he wrote, "It is a far cry from such notable books as *The Unvanquished*, a dreary proof that polemics and fiction cannot mix." Then this curious Mr. Heath (I have no idea who he was) went on to say, "Every schoolboy knows by now that Roman civilization began to suffer from dry rot long before the advent of the Caesars. That same schoolboy can understand how and why the serfdom that cemented a power-drunk empire would also spell its eventual doom."

It would be a safe bet to say that before the appearance of my book and the film that Kirk Douglas made from it ten years later, not one schoolboy in ten thousand had ever heard of Spartacus. I don't know where Mr. Heath met his schoolboys, but they were a rare lot. The review went on to sneer and castigate and brush me off — a pattern for every book I published from then on.

All told, I printed fifty thousand copies of *Spartacus*, of which forty-eight thousand were sold within three months of publication by the Citadel salesmen and my direct-mail effort. I plowed back almost all of my profits into advertising, yet it was not a losing proposition. I had about $2000 in the company bank account. Of course, I had not taken anything for myself; we were surviving decently enough on my foreign royalties. The appearance of the book in Great Britain was greeted with enthusiasm and quite a few outright raves. I received about six hundred letters from England and Ireland and over four thousand letters from American readers — an experience I never had either before or since, and from what I learned, almost unheard-of in American letters. I discovered through the years — often from the children of those who had bought the book — that reading it became an act of defiance by people who loathed the climate of the time. I do think that, considering that so many bookstores and chain stores — Doubleday exempted, of course — would not carry the book, forty-eight thousand copies was a respectable sale indeed.

Curiously enough, at forty-eight thousand, the sales slowed almost to nothing, just a few books a week, but the returns were very light, and I never reached a point where I had to remainder *Spartacus*.

Eventually, all but some twenty copies of my edition were sold, and today, so many years later, I still have half a dozen copies of my edition. I have tried to calculate how many editions of *Spartacus* have been printed since then, and worldwide the figure is almost a hundred. As to how many were printed in Third World countries without license, I could not even guess. When the blacklist vanished, it was reprinted in America in hard cover by Crown Publishers, and many hundreds of thousands more were printed as paperbacks. It must be said that the right to publish was maintained through those years, and that J. Edgar Hoover and his troops were unable to destroy the gift of the First Amendment to the Constitution. Not that they didn't try.

The next ploy of Mr. Hoover was directed against Signet Books, a man by the name of Kurt Enoch, and Howard Fast. I sometimes wonder what J. Edgar Hoover would have done without Howard Fast. Of course, as we estimated at the time, there were at least twelve hundred FBI agents who were dues-paying members of the Communist Party, unearthing nonexistent secrets and plots to overthrow the government, yet in all the years I was a member, they came up with not a single secret, not even enough for one of them to take the stand and bear witness during all the trials of Communist Party leadership. Since I had no secrets to hide, J. Edgar could concentrate on my work. Two of my books, *The Unvanquished* and *Conceived in Liberty,* had been reissued in paperback by Signet Books, which was owned by Kurt Enoch. Both were books about Colonial times, and both were written years before I joined the Communist Party.

I first met Kurt Enoch in 1941 at a literary affair of some kind. He was a refugee from Hitler's Germany, and I was absolutely fascinated by his story. He had owned a publishing house in pre-Hitler Germany; his imprint had been Albatross. Not only had he published books in German; he also published a list of books in English, to be sold to travelers and students on the continent. The Nazis took over his publishing house and made bonfires of the books he had published, and he barely escaped with his life. Since arriving in America, he had painfully and slowly put together a library of some of his Albatross publications. But, as he explained to me, these books were hard to come by, and when I mentioned that I had an Albatross book, he immediately offered to buy it from me at whatever price I asked for. I said I was only too pleased for him to have it as a gift, and the following day I sent it to him. He thanked me warmly.

Kurt Enoch prospered, and some years later, he was the president of Signet Books, a large and successful publisher of paperbacks at a time when a paperback cost twenty-five cents. He had followed my career, and when he requested permission to reprint *Conceived in Liberty* and *The Unvanquished*, I was delighted to grant it. He knew that I had a large following, and he felt that he could safely print and sell half a million copies of each title — a very large printing for the times. By the time *Spartacus* had been published, he had sold an enormous number of the two titles. (I must note that, though *Spartacus* is dated December 1951, I did not receive books until January 1952. The rush of sales took place in the following three months.)

It must have gotten through to J. Edgar Hoover that, while he had knocked the props from under me at Little, Brown and Company, here was a publisher flooding the market with thousands of copies of Fast books, and he promptly sent one of his agents to Signet with instructions that Mr. Kurt Enoch should sell no more of Howard Fast's books and that those books he had in stock were not to be sold. When Enoch asked what he was to do with the books in stock, the federal agent said that he was to destroy them. (It may be that I am taking total credit when it should be shared. Mr. Hoover also sent instructions that all books by Eric Ambler were to be destroyed. Mr. Hoover apparently had the notion that Eric Ambler was a Communist, and that the only thing to do with commie books was to burn them.)

An editor working for Kurt Enoch telephoned to tell me the gist of the conversation between Kurt Enoch and the FBI man who ran J. Edgar Hoover's errands. I then called Kurt Enoch to ask whether all I had heard was true. All true, he told me.

"But, Kurt," I begged him, "you can't do this!"

"What else can I do?" he asked. "It's the second time. Would you have advised me to stop the Nazis from burning my books? You can't stop the Nazis. There's no place for me to go."

"This little bastard," I argued, "is not Hitler and this is not Germany. It's bad, but it's not Germany and you have to fight it."

"You don't understand," he said, his voice breaking. "None of you understands."

I said then that if he went on to destroy the books, to put them through a shredder, which was what he planned, I would have to give the whole story to the press. He was in tears. He said that I could give it to the press, that no one would print it. He was almost right. I put together a press release and we sent it out. Both *The Compass* — the left-of-center New York daily that was trying desperately to exist — and *The Daily Worker* carried the story, *The Daily Worker* adding the information that Signet had just published *One Lonely Night* by Mickey Spillane, in which there was a gleeful mass killing of Communists by Mike Hammer. However, I am sure Enoch never read the book by Spillane, and after the news stories appeared, Enoch called me in utter despair. "What will I do?" he begged me. "What can I do now?"

I told him that I could get him off the hook, providing he did not destroy the books, and he countered with the news that Hoover had threatened to send men to his company to do an inventory. "Let me buy the books," I said, "and you can then put out a news release that you destroyed no books. That will save your reputation, and when Hoover discovers that you have no more of my books, he'll leave you alone. Believe me. The news release puts the heat on him as well as on you."

Enoch agreed, and when I explained that I had very small funds, he sold me the 130,000 books that remained for $300, which was only a token price. But then I discovered that his warehouse was in Chicago, and that bringing the books from Chicago to New York would require an expenditure of $800 for a trailer truck — and what was I to do with 130,000 books when they arrived?

Bette's father, who distributed newspapers over part of New Jersey, Hudson County, and Essex County, had a large garage and a sizable fleet of trucks. He and my mother-in-law were conservative folk, yet they never questioned what we were doing, and when I was in prison, they bent over backward to be kind and caring toward Bette and our two children. Now I told him my problem, and he said that he had a large storage room beneath his garage that I could use. In return, I said that if he could put some of the books in any of his many outlets, I would like whatever money that came in to be applied against the rental of space. He brushed that aside, but he did put out a great many books to be sold at ten cents each and at that price they sold.

So much for that situation. Then a letter arrived from Little, Brown, explaining that since they had taken over Duell, Sloan and Pearce when it went bankrupt, they had plates for all of my books back to *The Last Frontier*. They also had three thousand or so copies of all my titles. They wanted to be rid of every bit of evidence that connected them to Howard Fast, and they would be happy to sell me the plates and all the contractual rights to these books for $4,683.31. This covered plates and thirteen titles. The plates alone were worth more than that, and the residual rights to these books in due time came to over a million dollars — and all this for $4,683 to get them off the hook and, figuratively speaking, J. Edgar Hoover out of their editorial chambers.

Did I respond? I certainly did. Bette and I cashed in a few bonds we owned, borrowed on our insurance, took some loans and somehow scraped together $4,683. The plates were at the American Book Company, if I remember correctly, and I worked out a way to leave them there for the time being. The books were shipped to the tiny office I had rented. And there I was, with cartons of books piled high around me, books I could not sell, a publishing company on the edge of bankruptcy, enough cash to pay the next month's rent, and after that? Well, I could keep it alive as long as my foreign royalties continued to come in — I did, for six years — and in the process learn something about small business in a world of big business. I did learn here what I had never learned in the party — that being a small businessman can be as self-destructive as being a member of the Communist Party. I incorporated and became the Blue Heron Press. The name rose from the caustic suggestion of a friend that I call it the Red Herring Press, and while that was colorful, it did not strike me as a fruitful aid to selling books. I was a rotten businessman; I had no talent for it, and I never spent more than a couple of hours a day with the Blue Heron Press. I hired a lady to run it, and somehow it survived.

I reissued four of my old books, published two new novels, *The Passion of Sacco and Vanzetti* and *Silas Timberman,* as well as a book of my short stories. I covered my costs, if not my office expenses, because I still had a large reading public who would pay to read anything I wrote. To Bette and me, this was our great personal struggle to maintain our dignity and pride. She got a job as a designer of women's clothes; I wrote my novels, wrote a column for *The Daily*

Worker, and ran my publishing company. When Shirley Graham came
to me and asked me whether I would reprint W. E. B. Du Bois's
classic work, *The Souls of Black Folk,* which no other publisher would
touch, I agreed — again, a no-profit-net-loss project, but a very beautiful book that made me quite proud. The results were similar when
I published a book of Edward Biberman's working-class paintings,
and even worse when Walter Lowenfels, one of those soft-spoken
Communists, beseeched me to publish a book of his poems. My venture into free enterprise was teaching me only the dark side of capitalism, but I will say that J. Edgar Hoover sent none of his agents to
knock on my door and instruct me not to publish books by Howard
Fast. To that extent I had beaten the little bastard, and whatever it
cost, it was my small victory.

There is an addendum to the story of *Spartacus.* A few weeks after
its publication, John Howard Lawson, the party's cultural chief on
the West Coast, attacked it bitterly. Lawson's small battle with Fast
began when *The Daily Worker* asked me to do a regular column. I
said I would agree only if the column bore the title "I Write As I
Please." At first my request was turned down flat, but the editors
wanted the column and finally agreed. But when Lawson, out in Los
Angeles, saw my first column, he reacted like a bull to the red cape.
He felt that the title was a violation of party discipline, and he argued
his point hotly — that no person could belong to the party and write
what he pleased to write. Suppose he attacked the party itself? Would
The Daily Worker, a Communist paper, print what he wrote? Would
any newspaper in America give a hired hand the privilege of writing
as he pleased? My position was precisely that — that no other newspaper would print what I wrote, and if there was any validity to *The
Daily Worker* and its Communist position, it was that this paper
must give a writer the freedom denied him elsewhere.

Of course, my position was extreme. Week after week, month after
month, I was desperately attempting to validate my having joined
the party. A man's life is not to be separated from his work; I was a
writer; whatever else I proposed or attempted, in the deepest sense
that a man can define his life, I was a writer, my mind was a writer's
mind, and my eyes saw what a writer sees. I had already been sav-
aged by the party's rigid, mindless leadership. Betty Gannet, a stern
watchdog of the party line as she saw it, had brought me up on

charges for expulsion because in *The Proud and the Free* I had used
the Colonial term *nigra* for black. Again and again, I was brought
up on similar charges, and I suppose what saved me was that every
other novelist with any sort of national name had left the party. If
they dumped me, that would have been a very considerable public
relations injury.

Why didn't I let it happen and be done with it? I heard an old red
say, "I know why I joined the party and I know why I left the party,
but why I spent the twenty years in between in the party, I just don't
know." One day I would face the necessity of leaving — but not yet.

A last word about *Spartacus*. The book had been praised in *The
Daily Worker* and in what remained of the left-wing, non-party press
in America, but at the same time the ending was seized on by *The
Daily Worker* for the scene in which a Roman politician manages to
facilitate the freeing of the dead Spartacus' wife. This is what *The
Worker* printed: "What is intended here? Is this Goethe's idealistic
vision of the Eternal Woman, leading us all, oppressor and oppressed, upward and on? . . . Can we imagine a Nazi pleading for
the love of a Russian woman? . . . We get something very close to
sexual reconciliation of the classes . . . The incursion is felt here of
the destructive influence of Freudian mystifications concerning the
erotic as against the social basis of character." And so forth and so
on, such utter nonsense that it chilled my blood. It made no difference to me that this came after at least two thousand words of praise.
It was the same old thing, the unwillingness to let a novel be a novel,
to let a story be a story, to allow a writer to see things as he saw
them and not as a party cultural commissar desired him to see them.
John Howard Lawson not only agreed with this strange *Daily Worker*
review, but charged that my scenes of gladitorial combat and other
warlike incidents in the book proved an anti-human lust for brutal-
ity — sufficient to bring me up on charges for expulsion from the
party. His effort came to nothing, but reached a point of puritanical
lunacy that caused certain people to put up signs in their homes:
THERE WILL BE NO DISCUSSION OF SPARTACUS HERE TO-
NIGHT.

15

SUMMER CAME. Bette finished her season of designing and could get away for a month, and I wanted desperately to forget the class struggle, Blue Heron Press, and the endless inanities that constituted ideological and cultural theory in Communist Party circles. I wanted to be with Bette and my kids. Julie Trupin said, "Come to the Fur Workers' resort. They'll welcome you with open arms." The resort was on White Lake, one of the loveliest lakes in Sullivan County, the only resort on the lake — or so it was then. It had been built and was then operated by the Fur and Leather Workers' Union, then under the leadership of the almost mythical labor leader Ben Gold, the man who had been one of the organizers of the union and who led the struggle in the thirties to free the union from the mob. It was a labor battle in which no quarter was given or asked. Mob gunmen murdered fur workers. In return, when the killers entered the shops, the fur workers cut them to pieces with their fur-cutting knives and then threw them out the windows — from the fifth, the tenth, or the twentieth floor. The mob lost and left the union strictly alone, and under Gold's leadership, the Fur and Leather Workers gained a well-deserved reputation for incorruptibility.

The resort on White Lake was the union's rest home for the workers — inexpensive cottages that were airy and clean, good food, and surroundings of great beauty. Julie Trupin had done a good deal of legal work for the union, and as he said, we were welcomed with open arms. Much of my support came from the left-wing unions —

which, of course, were under the most savage attack from the federal
government and the anti-communist union leaders. It was a good,
restful month, but some very odd things came from it.

When I was in prison, I had begun to experience a syndrome known
as cluster headache. It is a form of headache related to migraine, but
much more painful. Some physicians hold that it is the most intense
pain known to medicine, and whether or not this is so, the pain of
cluster, as anyone who has experienced it knows, is beyond description. When I went to the White Lake resort with my family, I was
still in the last stages of a series of attacks. When the attacks began
in prison, I had no medicine, only a cold water faucet. They continued about two weeks, then tapered off. Six months later, when I was
back home, they began again, lasted for some two weeks, then tapered off. After that, each set of attacks was longer, and this last set
occupied the first week at the resort before disappearing. Each attack
would begin at three or four in the morning, last an hour or so, and
then vanish. At White Lake, Julie Trupin, sleepless and walking in
the moonlight at three o'clock in the morning, saw me sitting on the
front steps of our little cottage in pain so severe that I could hardly
talk and explain. He brought me ice, which provided some relief and
was an act of ingenuity and great kindness, considering the hour.
The following afternoon we talked about my affliction, and Julie
exhibited some surprising insight.

He suggested that perhaps part of the syndrome came from endless
frustration. For years now, I had fought battle after battle, and almost every battle had ended in defeat. We might have compared
ourselves to the men and women of the French Resistance, but we
were not in an occupied country, and the bitter truth was that only
a comparative handful of people gave two damns about our fate and
whether we lived or died. "We have to change that," Julie said. "We
have to give you a chance to hit back."

"And how do we do that?"

"I want to think about it. Maybe I'll come up with something."

There was an element of truth in what Julie Trupin proposed.
Frustration and depression tended to start up the syndrome. But here
after a week or so, I had stopped being depressed. No meetings,
thank God, no speeches, no subpoenas being served. The kids were
happy. Bette could draw peacefully and find time to paint. I swam in
the lake with the kids, took them out in a canoe for hours, played

games. I was surrounded by decent, loving factory workers, men and women, watching over me, delighted with any opportunity to chat. The kitchen staff went out of their way to cook delicacies for our family. Nighttime, there was dancing and entertainment, just as in any Sullivan County hotel at the time. Since even a single drink would explode my head, I drank only ginger ale, but the worker-guests, thinking it was liquor, appointed a committee to beg me, since they valued me so, to stop drinking. Jack Foner, who worked for the union, and his wife were there, and we became close friends, and their son, Eric, later to be a distinguished professor of history at Columbia, played with our son, Jonathan, each of them six years old, and Les Pine and his wife, Ellie, and the ballad singer Martha Schlamme provided entertainment each night. It was a quiet, lovely summer month in which nothing happened except that Julie Trupin came up with an idea to ease my suffering.

Seeking me out about a week after the incident I mentioned, Julie said, "I've been thinking about it, and I got it."

"What?"

"A way to hit back at those bastards."

I waited. Neither of us was a man of violence, and the notion of striking back in a society so subdued and indifferent as this time in our lives was hopeful but hardly realistic.

"Tell me," I said.

"You're going to Congress," Julie said triumphantly. "Do you remember what Marcantonio used to say — that one man could make himself heard and felt if he had enough guts? No more headaches. You fight back."

I told him he had gone out of his mind, that I could not be elected dog catcher of White Lake, that I hated politics, I loathed politics, that I had promised H. L. Mencken that I would join him in his contempt for all political parties, and right now I hated the Communist Party as much as the others, remaining in it only because I was a goddamn hero and there was nowhere else to go in a country ruled by a nutty haberdasher, a crazy senator, and a demented chief of police. But Julie went on talking and laying out facts and being convincing, because when he tried he was the most convincing man you could find, and bit by bit, I began to succumb to this obviously impossible idea.

He had been very busy. He had talked to Ben Gold, and Gold said

he would back me with whatever the union could do. He had talked
to the people at the American Labor Party — an organization at this
moment at its lowest point — and the leaders were delighted and
would give me the designation (assuredly, there were no other con-
tenders) and would back me all the way, for whatever that was worth.
And everyone he had spoken to (meaning Communists and those few
brave non-Communist souls who still admired Communists) had been
excited and ready to help.

"And my head is in the noose. Where do they hang me?"

Julie replied that it was the Twenty-third Congressional District in
the South Bronx, the area known today as Fort Apache. The Twenty-
third was then a district of working people, in the clothing industries,
in the fur trade, in furniture, in upholstery, and municipal work. The
district was divided ethnically into three parts: the largest, the Jewish
section, was in the eastern half of the district; the Irish and the Hispanic-black area was in the western half. As a clincher, he told me
that Corliss Lamont had already accepted the designation of the
American Labor Party for United States senator.

The Progressive Party, which had been organized four years before
and had run Henry A. Wallace as its presidential candidate, was
making its last real attempt at a third position in American politics.
For the 1952 election, it chose Vincent Hallinan as its presidential
candidate, and in New York State he was represented on the American Labor Party line. Carlotta Bass, a black woman of experience
and intelligence, was chosen as the vice presidential candidate. Hallinan, a tall, handsome Irishman, a cousin of Eamon de Valera, and
a wealthy San Francisco lawyer, was no Communist, but he had
stood firmly against what was happening in America, and I think he
accepted the designation not because he had the vaguest notion that
the Progressives could win but because he felt that it was a statement
he must make.

On the other hand, my friend Julie Trupin convinced me that we
had a chance of winning. He said that he would give up his legal
practice for the two months of campaigning, be my campaign manager, stay with me through every contingency that might arise, and
this would be night and day. I must say he did. I could have asked
no more of anyone. And never being very good at knowing how and
when to say no, I finally agreed to become the candidate for the
Twenty-third Congressional District.

Having made this decision, I immediately contracted a political disease called *candidatitus*, which, freely translated, means having a conviction that you can win when common sense, statistics, and history tell you that it is totally impossible. I was neither the first nor the last to be infected. Instead of enjoying the last week of the summer and desiring it to go on indefinitely, I found myself counting the days until we could begin our campaign. I must say that Trupin, a sober, level-headed lawyer, felt the same way, and soon we were the center of a group of eager and excited young men and women who had begun to dream the same dream. Even Bette came to believe that I had a chance of winning — an admission of love but a mark against her usual good sense.

The Republican Party barely existed in the Twenty-third; the enemy was the Democratic candidate, Isidore Dollinger, a standard inhouse congressman who was rolled into office every two years by the Democratic machine, a loyal, mindless, idea-less, faithful party hack who did absolutely nothing to rock the boat and who could be depended on to vote as instructed no matter what the situation might be. Julie's idea was to force Dollinger to debate. He felt that if we could get him to debate even once or twice, he could be utterly demolished. But the local Democratic machine was not run by fools, and, as we later learned, Dollinger was instructed to leave the district, to go to a hotel in the Catskills, and not return until after Election Day. In all the campaign, Dollinger never appeared, not even for a moment. I ran not against a man, but against a designation, a category.

I told Julie that money would have to be found and that I could not throw myself into campaigning and fund raising at the same time. I was sick to death of fund raising, and I had no aptitude for it. He said he'd be responsible. In essence, Julie Trupin financed the campaign, not out of his own pocket, but with the money from the American Labor Party, a fund-raising committee he set up, certain wealthy individuals who gave very quietly, affairs he promoted, and even some small sum from the Communist Party. The party, however, did not run our campaign. We ran it. We rented headquarters in the Hunts Point Palace, on Southern Boulevard, near 161st Street in the Bronx. We rented a sound truck for three hours a night and ten hours on Saturdays as our main means of reaching the people of the district. Dan Sheppard, Consuelo Marcial, Jose Semprit, Belle

Bailynson, Herb Randall, and Marion Gonzalez, all of them candidates for the New York State Assembly or Senate, shared the sound truck and its costs with me. They were on intermittent schedules, but I was on the truck every night it functioned, and on one memorable night, I shared it with Corliss Lamont.

I had met Corliss Lamont a few times before the evening he shared the sound truck with me. His father, Thomas Lamont, was a partner in J. P. Morgan and Company and immensely wealthy, his charitable gifts alone running into many millions; and his son, Corliss, was born with the proverbial silver (indeed gold) spoon in his mouth. For all of his own wealth and upper-class background and education, Corliss Lamont gravitated toward the left and was close to the Communist Party. Whether he actually belonged to the party, I don't know, but he stood by all of us, in our battering by the government, as firm as a rock, unshaken and devoted to common sense, peace, and the humanistic point of view. That night, he asked me to join him at an early dinner, after which we would go up to the Bronx together.

He lived then in one of the old apartment houses on Riverside Drive in the Columbia University area. It was a big, roomy apartment, and there were only the two of us at dinner in the large dining room. The dinner went very well, good food served by a butler, and Corliss's bright and energetic conversation — a tonic in its enthusiasm for the future — delighted me. I am sure that he knew far better than I did that our campaigns were symbolic at best, but he looked at things with a kind of sprightly optimism that I did not share, but that was so refreshing that it could not be denied. He spoke of the vast sums the regular party candidates — Republicans and Democrats — were spending, and said that our campaigns' being run on pennies was a reaffirmation of democracy. Then something happened that I am sure Corliss Lamont neither noticed nor recalls to this day, yet it impressed me so deeply that I used it in several of my novels. It marked the almost unbridgeable gap between the rich and the poor — showing that, despite all good will, it is almost impossible for the rich man to think as the poor man does.

It was a small incident. The butler brought us dessert. It consisted of a gallon brick of ice cream sitting in a venerable and beautiful tureen. Hardly pausing in what he was saying, Corliss spooned out a portion of ice cream for each of us, barely scarring the big gallon brick, and then went on talking. He was a fine conversationalist, and when he brought up a point or a position, he did not drop it naked, but went on into a historical and social definition. As of this moment, the issue was the parade of the independent party through the past of America, its goals, its successes, its failures. Meanwhile, the room being warm, the great brick of ice cream began to melt. Melted ice cream is almost impossible to reconstitute. It melts and it is wasted, and sitting at the table, watching the ice cream melt, I became increasingly nervous. Why didn't the silly butler return to put the damn ice cream in the freezer? Why didn't Corliss call him? Why couldn't Corliss understand that a whole gallon of what every kid in America since Dolly Madison venerated and dreamed of was being destroyed right under his nose? Finally, I could tolerate it no longer, and I said, very tentatively, "Corliss, the ice cream is melting."

"Oh, yes," he replied absently, and then returned to the subject he was discussing. He went on speaking and the ice cream became a pool of liquid.

I became irritated at this, at the indifference to wasted food by a man so thoughtful as Lamont. The plan that evening was for him, in his car, to follow me up to the Bronx, and when I got into my car — rented for the campaign — I was determined to lose Corliss and let him find his own way to campaign headquarters at Hunts Point. I am a good driver, and this night I became a fantastic driver, breaking every rule to get rid of Corliss, but no matter what I did, I could not lose him. My respect for this man grew. He drove like a racing driver, and when we reached headquarters, he never even mentioned my driving, perhaps because he did not wish to hurt the feelings of someone who drove dementedly but might otherwise be fairly sane.

Going out on the sound truck with him was an experience. He was a little fellow, and when they hooted him and threw things at him in the Irish sector — normal nightly behavior — he snapped back at them, hopping up and down in his anger at their bad manners until he simply awed them to silence and made them listen to him. In the Hispanic-black sector, he spoke about how he was going to get after the postal service so that "once again a man can experience the delight of opening his correspondence with the morning coffee." His exact words — and the crowd, most of whom hadn't the faintest notion of what the word *correspondence* meant, stared at this strange man in open-mouthed wonder, their own correspondence being either eviction notices or bills they could not pay. No matter. At the next stop, they dropped bottles from the adjacent rooftops. This had happened several times before, and it required very cool nerves to stand there and shout back. I had warned Corliss about it, but he took it in his stride. It was quite an evening. Whatever I might have felt about Corliss Lamont's innocence in terms of poverty, his cool nerves and absolute unflappability made up for it.

The campaign itself got off to a bad start. The cops broke up our first street meeting, pushing us around and threatening us because we had no permit. Julie Trupin, angered and annoyed, insisted that we needed no permit and assured me that he would fix it. The following day, he folded a twenty-dollar bill into an envelope, sealed it, but wrote nothing on it, and told me that we'd be off to see the captain at the local police station. The captain sat behind his desk, not even nodding at us; he looked at us with contempt and told us coldly that in his precinct the law was the law, and that was that. Julie, remaining calm and polite, said that we felt we had to come to him and at least introduce ourselves, and we'd be dropping in again. While saying this, he unobtrusively laid the envelope on the corner of the desk. Then we left.

This was pre-inflation, but still, twenty dollars was only twenty dollars. We had both learned that corruption, like any other business, must keep its prices low and meet the competition. When we reached our headquarters, we were told that the captain had called and would like us to return his call. Julie spoke to him, and the captain said words to the effect of "Trupin, I want you to know that if you run into any trouble, just call me. Send me a schedule of your street meetings, and I'll have a good man at every one of them."

The captain was as good as his word, and every week someone dropped an unmarked envelope onto his desk. We had no trouble at our street meetings after that. However, one evening at our headquarters, about a dozen very tough Hispanic and Italian kids appeared and waited for me to show up. I had been warned that the local Democratic club would be getting together some of their boys to take care of me, and I suppose that if Julie had been there, he would have called the cops. But Julie was not there, and I could either turn away from my headquarters, afraid to enter, or face this —

and if I did not face it now, I would have to face it sooner or later. I was a fair to middling street fighter at one time, but by now I was old enough and wise enough to know that for me to get into a physical fight would be an act of sheer lunacy.

They were waiting, about ten or twelve of them, large, hard-muscled ghetto kids. At the back of our offices, there was a staircase that led to a row of meeting rooms on the second floor of the building. With a great show of authority, I walked straight through the boys and started up the staircase, telling them, loudly and firmly, "If you're going to beat me up, come upstairs where no one can bother you or stop you!" And after a moment of shock at the unusual — which is always a stopper — they did just that. They followed me up the stairs into a big meeting room, set up with chairs to hold about sixty people.

"Now listen to me," I said to them, still very firm and authoritative, "I know why you're here, and you're free to beat the hell out of me, and no one will call the cops; but before you beat me up because I'm a Communist, will you give me ten minutes to tell you why I'm a Communist?"

No one moved, no one said yes, no one said no. It was all too unexpected. I wasn't running away. I gave no evidence of being frightened, and curiously enough, I wasn't. I had an absolute belief that I could talk them out of it. I came from the same place they had come from. I knew their habitat, their thoughts, their hatreds, their dreams, and I talked to them. An hour later I was still talking, and no one had moved. I talked about my mother's death, my childhood, my life on the street, my own hopes and dreams, and no one moved. I saw Julie Trupin and a couple of strong-armed fur workers appear in the doorway, and I shook my head at them, and they sat down in the back row. Other election workers came in and sat down. A Puerto Rican stood up and asked whether he could ask me a question. Then the questions came, one after another, and I was thinking to myself, My God, I did it. I broke through, and it may not be my party or my lifetime, but one day the human race will talk instead of killing, and will understand.

Bit by bit, that meeting room filled up, candidates, party workers — everyone who came into the Hunts Point headquarters that night and asked for Julie or me was directed upstairs. I think that anyone who was there that night and who is still alive will remember the occasion. I think it was one of the wonderful moments of my existence. It was eight o'clock when I had walked into my headquarters and faced the gang, and now it was almost eleven. Needless to say, they did not beat me up, and when they were leaving, their leader, a big Puerto Rican, asked me what they could do to help my campaign. We always needed volunteers to hand out leaflets and stuff envelopes, and since I had been narrowly missed by the milk bottles dropped from the roofs of tenements five and six stories high, I thought it would be helpful to have someone patrol the roofs when our sound truck parked. "It's done," he said, and there was never a night after that until Election Day when we didn't have two or three of them turn up, to give out leaflets or to patrol the roofs.

When they left and I was alone downstairs in the office with Julie Trupin, I said to him that no matter what else happened, tonight had paid off.

Three or four times, I took either Rachel or Jonathan along with me on the sound truck. Jonathan was four and a half, Rachel four years older, and I doubt that either of them remembers it too well. I wanted them to see democracy in practice, for whatever I might say about the condition of the country at the time — and truthfully — elections were not interfered with. We presented a wonderful program, but we did not win votes. Strangely, my overall election slogan, "Cease-fire in Korea," was matched by Eisenhower, who pledged that he would go to Korea and stop the fighting, a pledge that elected him and that he kept. On the other hand, Adlai Stevenson's timidity in the face of a population that was sick and tired of Mr. Truman's senseless, bloody war lost him the election.

I had worked out a statistical pamphlet that was the basis of my campaign; we printed it and handed it out by the thousands. On it were two cost sheets, printed side by side:

One Day of War [remember, all of this before inflation]:	*One Day of Peace* (if the same money were invested):
Overall Cost: $177,000,000	Overall Cost: $177,000,000
Which buys:	Which buys:
21 coffins	10 schools
1000 yards of dressing	5 hospitals
400 pints of blood plasma	100 playgrounds
100 guns	4 parks

2 tanks
1,000,000 bullets
10,000 dog tags
3000 shells
3 planes
and other associated war materials
Net daily profit to munition makers:
  $65,000,000
Net daily cost to people (October 8,
  1952):
21 boys killed
79 wounded
6 missing
2 injured
Also: 3 hours out of every 8 hours work
  per worker

10 recreation centers
5 housing projects (25,000 families)
2 medical schools
2 universities
10 churches
10 libraries
Net daily profit to munitions makers:
  $00.00
Net daily profit to the people:
healthy children
education
a good life
happiness
security

The rest of the pamphlet contained my short statement of purpose: "I call for a cease-fire immediately on the present line of battle in Korea, with a civilian commission to decide the remaining armament questions thereafter. I ask you to cast your vote for me as a vote for peace and for life, for the future of our land, our city, and our children."

There was my position and my program. We printed, as I said, tens of thousands of these leaflets. Now and then I would hand them out myself at subway stations when people were coming home from work, at churches and synagogues, in stores; and again and again, when people read them, they responded with "That says it!" "That's the way it is!" And even when they just glanced at it, they nodded. No one tore the leaflets up and no one rejected them. At the same time, I spoke night after night on the sound truck. We also made a deal with the radio station WMCA for ten fifteen-minute radio talks, at a cost of $128 for each. All told, the campaign cost no more than $10,000 as against the millions of dollars spent on congressional campaigns today, yet I think I reached most of the voters in the district.

Isidore Dollinger reached none of them. He made no speeches, never set foot in the district, nor did the local Democratic Party print up literature. How do people vote? One of the major shortcomings of the Communist Party — and finally a fatal one — was that it put pragmatic experience aside and substituted theoretical conclusions. The Twenty-third C.D. in the Bronx was almost entirely a working-class neighborhood. The Korean War was fought, for the most part, by the children of the working class; the costs were on the back of the working class. I was a candidate of the American Labor Party. I offered the voters a platform with which they could not disagree. Why didn't they vote for me, as the party theoreticians said they would?

I could say they responded to fear; that would be patently untrue. In the voting booth, an American is alone with his mind and his soul. No one threatens him. Even at that point in history, no one — not J. Edgar Hoover, not Senator McCarthy — no one dared threaten the American worker in the voting booth. In November 1952, they were at the point of hating the Korean War. The fiction that it was a war in our interests had worn too thin. I was everywhere in that district. I met little hostility; in most places, none. Well, perhaps I can explain by telling of one small incident.

It was the morning of Election Day. Here was the bottom line, the moment of truth. We had our volunteer watchers at all the polls. We had labored day and night; we had done all that we could do. Early in the morning, I picked up Julie Trupin and we drove to the South Bronx. We were going to visit the polls. We started in the Jewish neighborhood. We went into our first polling place, and even as we entered a woman came out of one of the voting booths, and recognized me. She was a stout, motherly Jewish woman in her forties, almost a clone of the Molly Goldberg stereotype on television. She threw her arms around me in a great, warm hug and cried out, "Howard Fast! What a beautiful experience to meet you here! I love you. You're my hero!"

"And of course you voted for me?" I said shyly.

"No, no," she responded, without even pausing to think about her answer. "I'm a Democrat. I voted the Democratic line."

Certainly that doesn't explain everything. For weeks, the newspapers had been trashing us, calling us tools of Moscow, subversives, evil plotters planning to sell our country, traitors, tools of North Korea — and all the other rubbish that was the meat and potatoes of the so-called free press of the United States. It's not easy to pull the lever for a guy who's the skulking — we were always skulking, never walking or skipping or running — henchman of Josef Stalin.

We walked out of that first polling station full of knowledge, and

I asked Julie Trupin why a man has to work his butt off to gain a little knowledge.

Anyway, I did poll almost two thousand votes.

Isidore Dollinger came in with forty thousand plus.

The Republican vote? I don't remember whether they counted it.

Until I went to prison, I luxuriated in a good, athletic body that had provided me with an apparently inexhaustible amount of energy. I had little illness, and I never gave a second thought to the state of my health. The Fasts were a rugged lot, and I had no cause for complaint. But in prison, I had developed a severe sinus infection, and with no doctor available, a fellow inmate had held open my sinuses with a tongue depressor and a full half inch of brown pus flowed into the pan he held under my nose. That healed quickly, but it was after the primitive treatment that the incidence of cluster became more frequent and intolerable. The pain of such a headache is so acute that the slightest sound is merciless, the slightest movement unbearable, and to speak is an effort almost beyond human endurance. This agony appears in a curve, starting slowly, rising in intensity for about twenty minutes to a point of ultimate horror, and then slowly disappearing. While it continues, you cannot lie down — which increases the pain — but must sit motionless until it is gone. You cannot moan or cry out, because the very act of doing so is painful. The pain can only be endured.

It is called cluster because the attack, if uninhibited, will occur again and again in a period of a few hours. It has also been called the suicide syndrome. However, I have never had inclinations toward suicide; life, for all of its inconveniences and pain, is a most wonderful thing, and I cherish it. For two years I went from doctor to doctor, attempting to get a proper diagnosis. I was examined, tested, x-rayed, tapped on my joints, but no one could tell me what I suffered from. Several doctors pronounced it Horton's histamine headache, out of that fine medical necessity that begs for a name for a disease, even if it is not understood. One doctor suggested a headache medicine, Cafergot, and that was somewhat helpful, but nothing to write home about. My poor wife and children watched me go into these paralyzing phases of pain, and suffered along with me. When possible, I hid myself in bathrooms; when it took me on the street, I crept into churches, where I could sit in a pew in the half light and not be bothered or touched or spoken to by anyone; and in these long hours of pain and silence, I felt a deep change taking hold of me.

The only way I could deal with the pain was to separate myself from it, to be a thing outside the pain, watching it, as if the pain were a thing in itself and I a separate thing in myself. I told myself I was strong, I had a will, and no pain would ever destroy me. I told myself that the pain was physical, but that my being was beyond the physical and could not be damaged by the pain. I don't know whether the doctors are right when they say there is no pain worse than cluster, but if there is, God help those who experience it.

Yet perhaps what happened to me was more important than the pain, and perhaps worth the pain — which, though controlled to a degree, would remain with me for the rest of my life. In effect, what I was doing to survive the pain was a form of meditation, a form very close to Zen meditation. It consisted of stopping my mind, of stilling my thoughts, of separating myself from the pain and observing it. All human beings deal with pain, but the experience of constant and extreme pain is a soul-searing thing; and to deal with it and to remain alive and creative requires deep insight and determination, and eventually this led me to Buddhism and to meditation.

But that would be years later. My effort now was to discover what my illness was, and that came about through a Dr. Yost, at Columbia Presbyterian Hospital. He was a neurologist, and after a thorough neurological examination, he said, "You have a syndrome we don't understand too well. It's called cluster headache."

I asked him whether there was any hope, any cure, any hopeful prognosis. He didn't think so, other than the Cafergot I was already taking, but he suggested, almost in passing, that I try oxygen. The logic of oxygen treatment was interesting. A pilot who drank too much the night before would come into the cockpit with a splitting headache, and he would notice that after he put on his oxygen mask, the headache would disappear. It's one thing to get such advice; it's quite another thing to go out and find the oxygen. I put it off. If I was lucky, the pain would go into recession, sometimes for as long as a week. Then the day came when I could not break the pain, and from two in the afternoon until two in the morning, each headache was followed by another until the crescendo of pain was utterly unbearable. I whispered to Bette to please find oxygen somewhere, and at two in the morning, she called Dr. Louis Miller, who had been in prison with me. Louis was the ultimate doctor; he was a person of healing, and he would go anywhere at any time if he was needed. He had a vast, empirical knowledge of illness and a reputation for diagnosis. My children adored him, and when they were ill, they would have no other doctor. He was our dear friend as well as our physician, and he had told us about the small tank of oxygen that he carried in the trunk of his car. He boasted that he had thirty notches on his gun, thirty lives that had been saved because he carried that tank of oxygen in his car. On that night when we called him, he came in with the oxygen tank in his arms, put the mask on my face, started the flow, and in ten minutes a miracle of sorts took place: the pain died away. I think he saved my life that night.

After that, I tried always to have access to oxygen. It was not easy when we traveled, yet it made life possible and I spared no effort to spread the word whenever I met a fellow sufferer. Yet strangely enough, as of this writing, very few physicians can either diagnose cluster properly or are aware of the oxygen treatment, even though Dr. Lee Kudrow, who runs the West Coast Clinic for Headache, has written of this and uses oxygen constantly.

Nothing in a long and eventful life has had an effect on me as deep and profound as this awful disease. I have lived with it on almost a daily basis for close to forty years, and I am resigned to the fact that there will probably not be a cure for it in my lifetime; at the same time, facing it has restructured my entire being and enlarged my life. It has given me an understanding of life beyond anything I had, a sense of compassion beyond what I had known, and it reinforced my pacifism. It also fixed the bonds of love between Bette and me more firmly than ever. She suffered with me. It was never easy for her and often much harder than it was for me. In spite of this illness, I have managed to live a fairly normal and creative life, and to this day, few people I know realize that I live with this syndrome. When it appears, I am always able to find a place of refuge, so what is unthinkable becomes acceptable.

We needed money, and we decided to sell our small house on Ninety-fourth Street. The French Communists asked whether we could spare some clothes for their very poor, and we decided to take up a collection. I had too many clothes anyway. I piled most of what I had on an overcoat, buttoned it, and Bette and I carried the buttoned overcoat, the size of a man's body, outside and hailed a cab. We rode the cab downtown, and I gave the driver a fifty-cent tip. He sneered at it, and wanted to know what kind of a phony I was to offer him fifty cents. Since the whole ride at that time cost under two dollars, I told him I thought it was a pretty good tip.

"For carrying a stiff through the city!"

We opened the overcoat. Not a very important incident, but a comment on the cool of a city cabby.

We moved into a small ground-floor apartment and gave away most of the furniture from the house. I organized a left-wing book club, the Liberty Book Club, and then I left it to Angus Cameron to run. I didn't want a book club; I didn't want the publishing house that I was saddled with. I wanted desperately to make my children feel that they were like anyone else, but that was impossible. I would start to write a new book, and then stare for hours at a typewriter that refused to type. I managed to write *The Passion of Sacco and Vanzetti,* which I tore out of my flesh, word by word. People have criticized me for writing too much, as if there were a limit to what one should write and how much; there are no markers for the endless hours when I could write nothing at all. It was easier to write for *The Daily Worker.* There, I had only to look at the world around me and the story would come. But the circulation of *The Worker* had dropped well below thirty thousand. I had the sensation that we were a candle, slowly dying. On Tuesday, December 23, 1952, William Patterson asked me to lead a delegation with him to Sing Sing prison, to the gates, where the Rosenbergs sat, condemned to death. "It will be on to Christmastime," he said. "I want to kneel in front of the gates and remember that I am a Christian."

Bill Patterson was an extraordinary man, a close friend and a dedicated Communist. He was one of the black men — few in those days — who had opened all the doors with college and law school degrees and good looks, and he could have been a millionaire token black, but chose his own road, to be a civil rights leader in the days when the civil rights struggle had just begun, led — indeed, undertaken from scratch — by the Communists, in particular the black Communists. Together with Bill Patterson, I put together a book

about the murder of blacks in the United States: *Genocide, U.S.A.*
we called it. It was a tremendous project, and when I first voiced the
idea to Bill, he saw it immediately, formed a research group, and
worked tirelessly to produce it.

The trip to Sing Sing prison was something organized in a few
hours, yet we managed to have eight hundred people at Grand Central: Bessie Mitchell, Karen Morley — both of them civil rights fighters and Karen a fine and beautiful actress, blacklisted — Rosalie
McGee, Aubrey Grossman, and of course Bill Patterson and I. There
were dozens of bouquets of flowers in our party, and a pouring rain
when we arrived in Ossining.

We formed on the station, standing in the rain, and then moved
out of the station and down onto Hunter Street. There we were met
by a small army of police and by a battery of newspaper people and
photographers. There were many rumors that a second Peekskill would
come out of this; but in the pelting downpour there was no sign of
anyone but ourselves, the police, and the press.

Patterson conferred with the police. Formerly, arrangements had
been made for our delegation to march directly to the gates of the
prison. But now the police told us that we would be permitted to go
only to a point some three blocks from the prison gates.

Which we did. We stood on a little hillock, close together in the
pouring rain, and then Bill Patterson, his voice low and deep, began
to sing, "Mine eyes have seen the glory of the coming of the Lord;
He is trampling out the vintage where the grapes of wrath are stored
. . ." And we joined in, and in the wind and the icy rain, our voices
came low and heavy, filled with sorrow. Then Bill talked to the police
again, and in the face of that song, they agreed that five of us could
go to the prison gates, and five of us went, our arms filled with rain-
soaked bouquets of flowers, which we made into a great pile at the
prison gates; and then Bill Patterson knelt and a woman's voice behind me said, "Our Father who art in heaven . . . thy kingdom come,
thy will be done . . ."

I would return to Sing Sing a few months later, on the nineteenth
of June, the day the Rosenbergs were executed, but when I think
about the case, I remember most the huddled group in the winter
rain, singing "The Battle Hymn of the Republic."

Eisenhower was President, but nothing was very different; if anything, the national hysteria increased. Anti-Communist pictures poured out of Hollywood. Television appeared to subsist on anti-Communism. Alger Hiss, whose name I had never heard until his trial began, and who seemed to me as unlikely and improbably a Communist as the President himself, was imprisoned in a case so ridiculous that it might have come straight from the pages of *Alice in Wonderland*. Now anti-Communism had become a vast ferry, with room aboard for everyone. Day by day, more and more people cut off their contacts and relationships with Bette and me.

The International Committee, headed by Louis Aragon, awarded me the Stalin International Peace Prize. This consisted of a beautiful leather-bound diploma case, a gold medal, and $25,000, which reversed our slide to poverty. The medal, if anyone is interested, resides with the Numismatic Society of the United States, to which I presented it soon after receiving it; and considering the hundreds of thousands of my books printed in the Soviet Union, for which no royalties had ever been paid, the $25,000 aroused no guilts for undeserved gratuities. The only other American to receive the prize was Paul Robeson. He deserved it.

Only the Hearst newspapers reviled my gift of "Moscow gold," and speaking of the Hearst organization, there was a delicious incident that happened in the mid-forties, when my pink color was just turning into a red flush. The editor of *Harper's Bazaar*, Carmel Snow, asked me to write a piece for the magazine. The issue was printed, but when one of the top New York officers of the Hearst organization saw the article, "Tolerance," he exploded, I was told, with words to this effect: "My God, do you know what the old man [William Randolph Hearst] will do when he sees a story by a notorious red? He'll have the head of every one of us."

No use that Carmel Snow pleaded ignorance of the depth of my color; the old man would not hear that for a moment. Yet there was no way they could destroy the hundreds of thousands of magazines already printed. What then to do? Solution: they printed two copies of *Harper's Bazaar* without my story. The old man, out at San Simeon, received two copies of each of his publications. Those two of *Harper's Bazaar*, bowdlerized of Fast, kept the peace.

But now, aside from the Hearst papers, little was made of the peace prize, the story in *The New York Times* being straightforward reporting. The Soviets not only gave me the peace prize, but they turned to me again and again to unravel some of their total ignorance and bewilderment concerning the United States and what went on here, and in most of these instances, their ignorance and delusions passed belief. I'll mention some of them, but first I want to stress that when Bette and I embarked on this business of being reds, we decided that our safety lay in having no secrets. We did nothing secretively unless it was to protect another person. We were out in the open. The FBI knew when we brushed our teeth and when we bought a pair of shoes. They tapped our telephone, followed us, photographed us, attended my speeches, went to classes I taught, and even tried to get into our parties. It was commonly said that J. Edgar Hoover had planted over twelve hundred agents in a Communist Party that had dwindled to hardly more than ten times that number.

But to return to the Russians. Example: They decided to send David Oistrakh, their great Jewish violinist, to New York to play at a concert in Carnegie Hall, where Wilhelm Furtwängler, associated with the Nazis, would conduct. The Jewish War Veterans decided that they would picket Carnegie Hall. It was Julie Trupin who suggested to me that we stop Oistrakh. At this point, Julie's lack of respect for the leadership of the Communist Party equaled mine. The plan was simple. I walked into the Soviet consulate in New York, where I was reasonably well known, since Bette and I were invited to all of their diplomatic functions, and told them that the National Committee of our party had decided that it would be an error for Mr. Oistrakh to take part in a concert with Furtwängler. The next day, *The New York Times* announced, from Moscow, that Mr. Oistrakh had canceled his trip to New York because he had a severe cold. Carnegie Hall was picketed, but without the humiliation of a Jewish Soviet artist playing with a pro-Nazi conductor.

Yet the fact of myself, alone, being the only one in the party in America able and willing to talk to the Soviets was in itself patently ridiculous. It would have been far better if our party had some communication with the Russians, instead of this dread of being connected with them in any way.

The Russians were as ignorant of America as Washington was ignorant of them. I had friends with the news agency Tass; one of them came to us one day and told us that *Pravda* wanted a story about the southern states. Was it possible to do a story about the South without being lynched? They believed that in the South, any-one the locals disapproved of was hanged.

Is this credible? That this should be their understanding of Amer-ica? I am not exaggerating. The year: 1953; and these Russian news-papermen actually believed that they could not visit the South with-out being lynched.

I told the Tass correspondent that he should start with *The Rich-mond Times*. He intended to travel with two other correspondents. I said that when they walked into the offices of the Richmond paper, the editors would greet them with pleasure and courtesy, feed them, make a great thing of them — probably get them together with the mayor and other worthies. I told them that wherever they went in the South, they would be greeted graciously and wined and dined to distraction, and that the great danger would be overeating, because southern food is very good indeed. They could go from newspaper to newspaper — a very good journey.

Instead, they rented a bulletproof Cadillac. Took an ice chest and a portable toilet. Drove through all the southern states, stopping only to buy gas and food. Such was their understanding of our country and our culture.

Another time, a second-rank diplomat came to me from the Soviet embassy in Washington. He spoke to me as follows: "Comrade Fast, we come to you because you write of this country with such under-standing. In our country, our agronomists are valued above all other scientists. Our existence depends on them. They are precious to us. We have been watching your corn-pig culture, and we want desper-ately to study it and introduce it to Russia. We want to send seven of our top agronomists here to study it. But we cannot risk their lives. We cannot send them to their deaths."

It took a while for me to get his meaning. The State Department had already agreed to the visit of the agronomists. What he feared was that the seven agronomists would be torn limb from limb by the bloodthirsty Americans.

"I'm alive," I pointed out to him.

"But you are here in New York."

"And last week I spoke in Detroit, and I spoke in Cleveland and in Philadelphia the week before, and no one tore me to pieces. For the people of my country, Communists exist in the newspapers, in television, in film — but in real life? It's true that there's fear, but that's different. Please believe me, your agronomists will be welcomed with open arms. In Illinois and Indiana and Ohio and Iowa, they will be welcomed, fed, feted — there will be picnics and celebrations wherever they go."

"But how can that be?" he asked. "We read your papers. We see what your government does to you and other Communists. You can't be right."

Nevertheless, I was right. I argued, pleaded, took the responsibility on my own back, and of course I was right. Readers who remember the incident will recall the affection that greeted the agronomists wherever they went, the picnics and barbecues.

When *Pravda* came out — the article was translated in *The New York Times* — with a nutty attack on baseball, I told Eugene Litescu, the chief of Tass, that he was completely out of line — that there was one sacred, utterly honest thing in America, and that was baseball and to all of us it was like a religion. I don't know why I took all this on myself, part ego I suppose, but in much larger part a hope that I could do something to ease the state of lunacy. I talked to them; they talked to me; but it appeared during those crazy years that no one else talked to anyone except in the guise of diplomacy. When the Soviets refused a visa to Eleanor Roosevelt, a woman I adored and believed to be one of the strongest bastions of American democracy and decency, I went to the Soviet consulate in a rage and did not withhold my anger when I spoke to the consul general.

There is an interesting aspect to this ignorance of America. The time of which I am writing was only about thirty years after the Russian revolution (which is regarded as having occurred in 1917, but which did not finish as a fact of state power until the mid-twenties); most of the Russian leadership was woefully ignorant, insular, isolated, and without a proper education. The same might be said of much of the leadership of the party in America. They were steeped in the works of Marx and Engels and Lenin, and these books were used almost in the manner of the ancient books of the alchemists. Example: Marxism-Leninism is the key. The key to what? To all things, we were taught — and this was nonsense. Marxism was a brilliant analysis of the class system and social industrialization during the nineteenth century. Its philosophical system of dialectical materialism was pertinent to a developing factory system based on mechanical invention — to a point where Russian scientists, with whom I spoke at social gatherings here in America, admitted that they had had to rid themselves of dialectical-materialist thinking (including the Russian denunciation of Albert Einstein and his theories) in order to make the atom bomb.

And if one asks a very proper question, namely, how could such a society or party survive, the answer lies in the mindless hostility of the non-Communist countries. An army exists because it sets aside reality: the human need for freedom, the human taboo against murder, compassion, pity, brotherhood; and it calls the result discipline. What horrors are laid to discipline — yet what achievements are the result of discipline! A great many things in life contain profound contradictions.

Yet if one recalls that the rank and file of the Communist Party, like the rank and file of all exuberant organizations, was recruited from the young, one can begin to understand their awe of this new way of thinking called Marxism-Leninism. It was a way of ignorant, narrow-minded men pretending to great wisdom and understanding, perhaps not too different from the pretensions of the men who populate Washington, D.C. And of course the proof of the pudding was that a handful of Russian Marxists, through the magic of Marxism-Leninism, had taken Russia, the most backward of all European states, turned it into the first socialist country, built it into a "workers' paradise," and through the magic of Marxism-Leninism, destroyed Hitler's armies and Nazism as well.

But it didn't happen quite that way.

On January 13, 1953, newspapers carried the story of nine Soviet doctors who had conspired to murder Soviet leaders. Quoting a Soviet radio report, the news story went on to say that the doctors were accused of killing Politburo member Andrei Zhdanov in 1948 and Alexander S. Scherbakov, the administrative chief of the Soviet army, in 1945. The killings were carried out through incorrect diagnosis and wrong medicine. They were halted in their plan to kill Stalin, according to the story.

The day after this appeared, I received a telephone call from Dr. Jacob Auslander, who asked me to lunch with him. Dr. Auslander, then in his fifties, had been sentenced to prison as one of the board of the Spanish Refugee Appeal, but had served his time in a different prison from mine. I had seen him on occasion since the trial, but not often. I had great respect for him. Born in Vienna, he had come to the United States in the twenties and had taken his medical training in the Midwest. He was a courtly, soft-spoken man and, on this occasion, very upset. We had barely seated ourselves when he asked me what I thought of the story about the nine Soviet doctors. I said I was very disturbed by it.

"It's a lie," he said flatly. "A frameup of the worst kind. Did you know that all the nine doctors are Jewish — that they are accused of being a part of a Zionist plot?"

"I heard something like that."

"Do you believe it?" he asked me.

"I don't know what to think. It sounds impossible — nine doctors, all of them Jewish, and that they could do this in 1945 and be discovered now, eight years later. No, it makes no sense."

"It's not true," he insisted, growing more emotional as he spoke. "Doctors could not do this kind of thing — one doctor, maybe, maybe — but nine doctors. No. It's impossible."

I thought of my own mission in Paris, where, speaking for the Jewish Section of the Communist Party of the United States, I had delivered a formal accusation of anti-Semitism in the highest reaches of the Soviet government and party. I had spoken to no one but my wife and Chaim Suller and Paul Novick of what had happened there. Now I told Dr. Auslander of my talk with Fadeev.

"Oh, my God — why haven't you written of this?"

"Because the party asked me not to." I had no idea as to whether Dr. Auslander was a party member or not. I simply took it for granted that, because he stood so firm and went to prison before he would agree to naming names, he was a Communist. I never asked him nor did I ask him now.

"Because the party asked you not to? My God, Howard, what are you saying to me?"

"You know I'm a Communist. I can't write about this unless they agree. I spoke to Fadeev as a disciplined party member —"

"Discipline! Discipline! Listen to yourself. There's something so awful going on there that I'm afraid to contemplate it. Nine Jewish doctors in a plot to murder Communist leaders? I'm a doctor. I'm Jewish. I've taken an oath. If Adolf Hitler himself were under my knife, I could not take his life. Don't you see that something infernal is going on over there?"

Did I see it? Because I knew at first hand that all the lies and slanders spoken about our party in the United States were just that, lies and slanders, I had been absolutely unwilling to believe the endless torrent of anti-Soviet propaganda. I knew what our party in the United States was — we were brave, uncorruptible, and led by stupid, rigid men whose orders we accepted without demurral. But we had never committed a crime; the jailing of the leadership was a frame; and we gave of whatever we had with charity and compassion. Rigidity, insensitivity, stupidity — we were guilty of all these. But cruelty, harm to other human beings — never, and in all the years of our existence, we had fought to organize working people, to build trade unions, to increase wages, to prevent evictions of the poor — and in Spain we had fought and died to stop the fascists.

"Always," Auslander said painfully, "we accepted what the Russians said as the truth. It wasn't the truth. Maybe what was said here about the Soviets by those who hated us was the truth."

"I can't accept that."

"Because we can't accept any wrong or evil about them, because they made socialism here on earth, and for that we forgive them everything and make miracle men out of them. Let me tell you something, Howard, and maybe some of the cobwebs will blow away. In 1933, Louis Miller, who is our friend and my colleague, began sending medical journals and texts to the Soviet Union. He sent them to a hospital in Moscow, where he knew the director. Month after month, for fourteen years, Louis sent the leading journals and every book and pamphlet that marked an important advance in our profession. Do you know how much money this cost Louis? Do you know how much labor? The postage alone ran to thousands of dollars. And finally, Louis went to Moscow after the war, and his friend in the hospital had to answer for this material. With tears in his eyes, he took Louis to a room where the fourteen years of journals lay, unopened, in piles. They could not find anyone to translate from English to Russian. Do you understand? We created a great race of people overnight out of peasants and uneducated workingmen, and a party where the leadership holds educated and creative people in contempt — we created these brilliant people in our minds, and they don't exist. The whole damn party is a fraud — a fraud we have perpetrated on ourselves, and now they imitate Hitler. They have found nine Jewish doctors to crucify."

Of course the above is not word for word what was said, but it repeats the essence of our conversation. At home that evening, I told Bette the gist of Auslander's words and thinking. She asked me what I thought.

"I don't know."

"Has Stalin become insane?"

"Maybe he was always insane. I think most people who rule are insane. Read Plutarch's *Lives*. They're all insane. Napoleon was insane — at least according to Tolstoy. Hitler was insane —"

"What does that prove?"

"I don't know. For years, I've been telling myself that Stalin means nothing, that Gene Dennis means nothing — that we fight for a belief that's separate from all of them."

"You don't have to be a Communist to do that."

"I love the people I know who are Communists. They're decent, brave people."

"Sure," Bette said bitterly. "We've cut ourselves off from everyone else. We don't talk to other people."

"Are you telling me to leave the party?"

"What would be the use? You wouldn't leave, would you?"

She was right. I couldn't leave. I was a goddamn hero. The foremost poet in the Spanish-speaking world had written an ode to me. I was Howard Fast, heroic and unblemished and all the other bullshit that goes with being a hero, and all over the world my name was known and my books were read, and that's a heavy lot for a kid from the streets whose mother had told him when he was eight, as she lay dying, "Be a good boy, Howard." A little bit of insight is harder to come by than fluency in classical Greek; and day after day, as I sat locked and silent for an hour each day, wrapped in the unbearable pain of cluster headache, I began to understand the man called Fast, at least a beginning, and I began to understand a good many other things as well.

What an unfortunate creature God put together that can learn only through unbearable pain.

And then, two months later, Josef Stalin died. Ashes to ashes and dust to dust, and thank God that no man lives forever.

16

IN TELLING THIS STORY, I have tried not to be overjudgmental. Not to be judgmental would, for me, be impossible; but I had become a Communist as an innocent. That's neither an apology nor an evasion, but an explanation. Among all the party people I had worked with, not one of them had experienced the essence and degradation of poverty to the extent that I had. I was street-wise, survival-wise, full of street smarts and tricks and all the dirty, necessary ploys of the poor, without which they could not survive. By the time I was thirteen, I knew about cops and whores and how to use my feet in a fight and how to hit a newsstand running and come away with the three cents on the papers and how to play scully for pennies and how to cheat at it, and how to shoot craps and other odds and ends of survival; but this was the world of the damned, and there were those who put their lives on the line to do away forever with the world of the damned. When I found the Communist Party, I joined the company of the good.

No good guys, no bad guys, just shit and confusion, and the only validity is not to hurt another human being. It is complex and confusing to be a human being; to be a priest is even more complex and confusing, and we were, as I have said, priests of the brotherhood of man. That made it even more confusing, believe me, for the brotherhood we dreamed of was nowhere connected to earth, and when you lose your connection with reality, nothing works very well.

I returned to Chaim Suller and Paul Novick, with Auslander's words hanging like a rock around my neck, and Novick said, "Howard, what good would it do to accuse the Soviet Union of anti-Semitism before the whole world?"

"Because if it's true, the world should know. It's important. Anti-Semitism is the meat of hate and murder, not of socialism."

"But Russia is a socialist country — the only socialist country. That's more important."

"And then we have socialist anti-Semitism."

I think it was Suller who said that I was looking for perfection, and that that was a romantic fault of mine. I was moralistic in those years, a sin that I overcame, but not the kind of sin that the Communist leadership put me down for. Morality could become picky, picky, picky. Theater people, artists, and literary people are plagued with morality, and they pick at things. Those good party people could never wholly swallow Stalin's pact with Hitler, and Lionel Berman would respond to this kind of confusion with a story about Pete. Pete was a Communist leader in Chicago, a big, heavy workingman, an Italian, and a very direct theoretician, and when the comrades came to him, bewildered by Stalin's pact and his advance into the Baltic countries and Poland, Pete spread out a map of the world and said, "You look on that map — one red spot in the whole damn world, one red spot — and when that spot becomes bigger, it's all right with Pete."

It was not as simple as that or as all right as that. With the leadership of the party in prison, a black man became the head of the party and instituted an even crazier tyranny, based on combating "white chauvinism," than had existed before. Previously, the white chauvinist business had been mystical at best. Any black member of the party could accuse any white member of chauvinism and have him up on charges. As a result, we lost loyal and decent white members, and even what I have written above would be grounds for bringing me up for expulsion were I a member of the party today.

Now a lovely black lady came to Bette and me and told us that this man had made advances, and when she brushed them off, he intimated that either she went along with his desire for sex, or he'd have her up for expulsion.

"The hell with him!" I told her. "Just stay away from him. Forget he exists."

"He calls me. He instructs me to meet him."

"Don't. Just stay away from him."

She loved the party. In the party she had found whites who treated her as if she were white or as if they were black. She found love and equality outside the ghetto. She also found bastards. Throw a loop around any dozen people in a church, a factory, a garden party, or a police station, and you find the good and the bad. And when you find that a priest can be a selfish bastard and a rabbi a lecher and a judge a cold-blooded murderer, and that a father who beats his children half to death is a pillar of a church and a lousy, grasping fool is the president of a synagogue — and in your Communist Party, the same lechers and mindless jerks and egotistical power-hungry bastards, then something washes out of you and you are cold and empty inside.

I knew the feeling. Like this woman, I had found the children of God, but I was better equipped to deal with it. The people of good will are still people, but I don't know if they ever were again to this lady who sat in my living room, crying her heart out. I told this incident to Lionel Berman, and he said, "Well, it happens. It happens outside the party and it happens inside."

I was naïve. I couldn't go along with Berman's "Well, it happens." It shouldn't happen, and when a leader of an organization, Communist Party or otherwise, tells a member that she must go to bed with him or else, there is something deep down rotten. There was no truth in the government's charge that we were subject to the Soviet Union, that we planned to overthrow the government by force and violence; but there were other things that the J. Edgar Hoovers and the Joseph McCarthys couldn't dream up or understand — for they were infected with the same rot. *Stated most briefly, it was the rot of people who possess power.*

In June of 1954, Bette and I and our two kids took off for Mexico. We would have preferred Europe, but we were denied passports (a neat trick the government learned from the Russians) and thereby barred from Europe. At this point, we had lived through ten years of being Communist Party members in the United States. Our nerves were stretched thin; we lived in constant apprehension, and if the particular threat was not defined, it was still there. The main leaders of the Communist Party were in prison. The party was shrinking as the government's campaign against us took its toll, and aside from writing more or less regularly for *The Daily Worker,* my party efforts fell off. I tried to go on writing as my own publisher, but it was almost impossible. The publisher-writer relationship is a very important one. It's part of the cement that binds a writer to his readers, and it is by no means the same thing to be your own publisher — aside from the fact that the more one publishes, of my writing or others, the more money is lost.

Then the strange business of Michols and Feffer arose. Michols was an eminent Soviet actor, a Jew, and Colonel Itzhak Feffer, also Jewish, was an officer in the Red Army who had fought gallantly through the defense of Russia during the Nazi invasion and was a Hero of the Soviet Union, the highest Soviet honor, and a very handsome and striking man. They had both visited America some years before, mainly to reassure American Jews that the stories of anti-Semitism in the Soviet Union were without foundation. A homely story went around at that time. Feffer had relatives here who had done well, and they offered to set him up in some small retail business. He laughed at them — he, a colonel in the Red Army, to give up everything to live under capitalism.

Then, in 1954, a woman friend, a Communist not known as a Communist, had gone to the Soviet Union as a tourist and had spoken to a number of Jews there; she was told that Michols had died in an accident and that Feffer had been executed. Very vague stuff, and there was no more than this to be found out. I don't know whether I believed it, but at the time it was very disturbing. Just as the unceasing witch hunt here at home was endlessly disturbing. It was part and parcel of what was happening to the party here, and I began to realize that as much as the FBI was destroying the party, the party was destroying itself. More and more people, loyal party members, were being driven out of the party with charges of white chauvinism, and the reputation of Petis Perry, the interim head of the party, was not a pleasant one. And to cap things off, I received an anonymous letter from someone who said he worked at the Justice Department in Washington and they had a black man in the party who could have anyone they wanted to be rid of expelled from the party. The writer asked me to destroy the letter, which I did. When I discussed the matter with people in the party whom I trusted, they shrugged it off.

Thus, we went to Mexico with the feeling that if we could only get away for a while, we could unravel our brains and think clearly. The sale of our brownstone, for $18,000, gave us a financial foothold, even though our share, after mortgage and costs, was only about $8000. Bette and I had been to Mexico in 1939, and we had only the warmest memories of a land I loved deeply. At this point, the cluster syndrome had taken a tremendous toll of my strength, and I needed desperately to rest and to forget for a while that my phone was tapped and that across the street, some idiot FBI man was waiting to tail me.

We went via Air France, and it was a long, nerve-wracking flight in a crowded, propellor-driven aircraft, an unending roar of the engines. The children were wonderful, and Jonathan, then a bright, endearing six-year-old, charmed everyone in the plane, while Rachel reveled in being told over and over how beautiful she was. Indeed, she was, with her long honey-colored hair and ten-year-old pink-cheeked health. How often during that trip I reflected on our being a sort of central-casting American family.

We stayed overnight at a hotel on Cinco de Mayo Street, and the next morning we piled into a cab and drove to Cuernavaca. A dear friend of mine, Maxim Lieber, had been one of the most important and best literary agents in New York. But under special attack — he was the agent of a number of Communist writers, European as well as native — he had panicked and, with his wife, Minna, and his two children, had gone to Mexico. He was kind enough to have made the arrangements for us to stay at an excellent Mexican apartment hotel. The peso was then twelve to the dollar, but it was before the inflation at home and in Mexico, and for an American, the prices were ridiculously cheap. We had two bedrooms, living room, kitchen, and a balcony. The balcony looked out on a towering range of purple mountains, and each afternoon the clouds would gather around these high peaks, like a loose, blowing veil on some great lady, and then explode into thunder and lightning. It was a beautiful place, dramatic yet peaceful and strangely apart from the world, and that suited us. Bette and I felt that we had had enough excitement to last us a good while. The hotel provided us with an Indian cook, a small, good-natured lady by the name of Raquel, and during the time we lived at the Hotel Latino Americana, Raquel fed us a lengthy menu of strange and delicious Mexican food of endless variety. Each evening, just before dinner, she would run down to the street and buy hot, newly made tortillas. Our dinners soon became justly famous among the Communists who had taken refuge there.

For the most part, the Communists who had fled the States to take refuge in Mexico were from the West Coast. Because the witch hunt had taken such a devastating toll of the film industry, the mood of Communists and other left-inclined people was desperate and despairing. Those punished, imprisoned, denied the right ever to work again — as they saw it — were part of a single industry, unlike in the East, where persecuted leftists were spread among a variety of industries and locations. By their thinking, fascism had already become a fixture in American government, and even though the mass of the population were not yet aware of the fact, it would permeate the American system until we became an American copy of Hitler's Germany. Wasn't Henry Luce already proclaiming the "American Century," and wasn't that similar to Hitler's call for Germany to rule the world?

It was a condition of despair that I could not agree with, although Albert Maltz had accepted it and taken a house in Mexico City, where we would see him later. There were too many deep roots of freedom and human rights in the United States to allow for such an easy drift into fascism. I thought it was by no means inevitable, but the little colony of exiles were glad to have us among them to buttress their opinion, as they saw it, even though I insisted that we were there only for the few months before the kids' school began.

Thirty-six years ago, Cuernavaca was a small, delightful town — with its gardens and its fine *zócalo* and its old Palace of Cortés, now a museum, and on its walls the murals by Diego Rivera, depicting the conquest of Mexico. We went many times to see the murals, and we were specially intrigued by the number of peons, very poor men and women who seemed to have made their way from every corner of the land to look at the splendid paintings.

It was a quiet life. We became close friends with a German doctor, Ernesto Aman, who had fought with the Fifteenth Battalion of the International Brigades in Spain, and there too was the writer John

Penn and his wife, and a handful of others. Not a great social life but enough for us. The hotel had a large, well-kept swimming pool, where the children played for hours. We made a trip with Ernst to a lost city on a mountaintop about thirty kilometers from Cuernavaca, a wonderful place still unexcavated and far off the tourists' path. A Mexican boy from the valley below became a guide for a few pesos. He knew every corner of this ancient city, and he spoke fluent English. He worked on and off with an American group of archaeologists who, together with a Mexican group, had begun the excavation. He told us proudly that his ancestors had built this city, and that one day he would go to the university and become an archaeologist and complete the excavation.

That was so many years ago. I wonder whether he ever did become the archaeologist he dreamed of being. There were only twenty-seven million people in Mexico then; the population has increased threefold since, and I doubt that the country is still as wild and mysterious and enchanting as it was then. The great Mexican artist Siqueiros came from Mexico City to visit us. We had never met him, but of course we knew his work and reputation, and he had heard that we were in Cuernavaca. He was a tall, handsome, elegant man, and he came with his wife and several members of his family. Jonathan could be made happy with a piece of paper and a crayon. He drew constantly, and one of his recent creations was a dinosaur. He had started the drawing on one sheet of paper, and since he had miscalculated the size of the beast, he required a second sheet of paper to complete the drawing. Bette stuck both sheets on the wall, where Siqueiros saw them, admired the drawing, and said to Jon, "Oh, how many times I wished I could build another wall to complete a painting."

It was absolutely marvelous to be in a place where we could live and function like normal human beings, where there was no one waiting across the street to follow us, where a day or a week went by without news of another political jailing, another life ruined, and some new editorial calling for the destruction of Howard Fast. We walked the streets as free people, and those who knew us did not have to pretend not to see us.

Yet this was not life, not any kind of life for us. I couldn't write and Bette couldn't paint. Days drifted by without meaning. Our children found children to play with, but we were left wallowing in a misty nonexistence and facing the strange contradiction that here, in this backward, beautiful land, a Communist could walk as a free man, while in the great giant to the north, the stream of anti-Communist lies and slanders and hatred never ceased, and Communists were persecuted and imprisoned. We could not make a life here as other American Communists, writers, artists, film people, had done. We were bored to distraction. We had planned to spend three months in Cuernavaca; at the end of two months, we had all of it that we could tolerate, and we decided that Mexico City might be less boring.

Max Lieber, who had been spending some time with us in Cuernavaca to help us settle in, had an apartment in Mexico City on the edge of Chapultepec Park, and he found a smaller furnished apartment in the same building that we could take for a month. It was a fairly new building in one of the better neighborhoods, with all of Chapultepec Park spread out in front of our windows, an endlessly diverting place with playing fields, museums, fine restaurants — all of it sweeping up to Chapultepec Heights, where the Mexicans had made their last stand against an invading American army, and where, at the time we were there, a building on the heights housed a huge map that showed Texas, New Mexico, Arizona, California, and Nevada as part of Mexico.

Although Jon could no longer spend four or five hours a day in the swimming pool, there were other things for the kids, and when word got around that we were living there, an endless stream of visitors came to see us. Someone suggested a trip to the Pyramid of the Sun, where the working archaeologists went out of their way to greet us. They presented Jon with a handful of shards that, they explained, were three thousand years old. With both kids, I climbed to the top of the great pyramid while Bette stood below and watched and prayed, and if nothing else came out of the months in Mexico, Bette and I found in each other an enduring love that was not broken or strained for the next thirty-six years.

That much Mexico gave us, for which I will be everlastingly grateful. After ten years of being reviled as a common criminal, here I was sought out and honored and admired. A message from Diego Rivera asked Bette and me to lunch at his home. We explained that we had no one to leave the children with, and we were told to bring them along. It was a wonderful few hours we spent with this man, a great artist who was the soul of Mexico. His wife had very recently died; the house was draped in mourning; and he told Rachel that she must never fear death. I can't imagine what she made of it, that big, strange, remarkable man, who, she had been told, was a very great artist, sitting in the filtered light of the room, surrounded by his large collection of clay Aztec grave dogs. He told us, the children listening open-mouthed, that each person who dies must be buried with one of these dogs, for only they know the way across the river of the underworld to the paradise beyond — and then he smiled and assured them that it was only an old Indian folk tale. "But, you see, I am an old Indian," he explained. "My roots are deep under the land."

He had recently completed a set of murals for the new luxury hotel of Mexico City, the Prado, murals that protested the rape of the Mexican people; and when he finished, the hotel owners had covered his work with a big screen, lest the rich American tourists see it and be offended. "An artist must offend," he said, and asked me whether I understood that. I understood it. He had painted the flag of Guatemala on the door of his house some weeks before, when the CIA overthrew the democratically elected government so that they could put a United States–approved dictator in power. "It is such a small gesture," he said. "But it is always the same. Mexico is too far from God and too close to the United States."

He insisted on walking with us from his studio, in a neighborhood of small, tight streets, to the main avenue, where we could hail a cab. Rachel, fascinated by him, held his hand as we walked, and in that rather poor neighborhood every person we met — workingman, street sweeper, women cooking tortillas, women shopping, shopkeepers — everyone paused to bow: "Greetings, maestro." *Maestro* is the Spanish word for teacher, but that and much more applied to Diego Rivera. There was for us love and compassion and respect there in Mexico, yet neither Bette nor I was of the stuff that makes an exile or an expatriate, and the more we were away, the more we longed to be home. We went to Oaxaca in the south to look at the ruins, traveling with a beautiful Mexican lady who was the daughter of a man remembered as the "Christian general," the owner of a great hacienda who had divided up his land among the peons and joined forces with the revolutionaries under Zapata. She was a wonderful guide, a bright, delightful companion.

Back in Mexico City, a mind-shattering surprise awaited us; it was a letter from Julie Trupin, informing us that Congress had passed the Communist Control Act, a measure long discussed but so inhuman and vicious that it went beyond any enactment of the past. It did away with the First Amendment of the Constitution, and legally turned America into a police state. To the date of this writing, the Communist Control Act of 1954 has never been used, but it remains in the United States Criminal Code, lying there like an obscene and rotting memory of the past. But in 1954 we were not gifted with prescience. We felt that the law had been enacted for use, and its use meant the end of life as we knew it — indeed, as every person of good will in the United States knew it; for this was a law that could put every liberal in America in prison for twenty years.

Let me spell out its provisions. There are fourteen definitions of the persons who come under its jurisdiction and who may, on the basis of those definitions, be put in prison for up to twenty years. In other words, anyone defined by the following paragraphs is presumed guilty and can be arrested and put on trial. (Note that I say "presumed guilty," as opposed to "innocent until proven guilty," which is basic to criminal law in the United States, because the legislation instructs the jury so widely in terms of evidence as to create an unbreakable net of guilt.)

In determining membership or participation in the Communist Party or in any other organization defined in this act, or knowledge of the purpose or objective of such party or organization, the jury, under instructions from the court, shall consider evidence, if presented, as to whether the accused person

1. Has been listed to his knowledge as a member in any book or in any of the lists, records, correspondence, or any other document of the organization;
2. Has made financial contribution to the organization in dues, assessments, loans, or in any other form;
3. Has made himself subject to the discipline of the organization in any form whatsoever;

4. Has executed orders, plans, or directives of any kind of the organization;

5. Has acted as an agent, courier, messenger, correspondent, organizer, or in any other capacity in behalf of the organization;

6. Has conferred with officers or other members of the organization in behalf of any plan or enterprise of the organization;

7. Has been accepted to his knowledge as an officer or member of the organization or as one to be called upon for services by other officers or members of the organization;

8. Has written, spoken, or in any other way communicated by signal, semaphore, sign, or in any other form of communication, orders, directives, or plans of the organization;

9. Has prepared documents, pamphlets, leaflets, books, or any other type of publication in behalf of the objectives and purposes of the organization;

10. Has mailed, shipped, circulated, distributed, delivered, or in any other way sent or delivered to others material or propaganda of any kind in behalf of the organization;

11. Has advised, counseled, or in any other way imparted information, suggestions, recommendations to officers or members of the organization or to anyone else in behalf of the objectives of the organization;

12. Has indicated by word, action, conduct, writing, or in any other way a willingness to carry out in any manner and to any degree the plans, designs, objectives, or purposes of the organization;

13. Has in any other way participated in the activities, planning, actions, objectives, or purposes of the organization;

14. The enumeration of the above subjects of evidence of membership or participation in the Communist Party, or any other organization as above defined, shall not limit the inquiry into and consideration of any other subject of evidence of membership and participation as herein stated.

This absolutely incredible law is still part of the criminal code of the United States. There is no law extant in any country in the entire world as all-embracing and as terrifying. Under this law, any teacher, labor leader, charitable worker, historian, could be imprisoned. The point Bette made to me, as her first reaction, was this: if a charity worker were engaged in a clothing collection, working with a Communist, and we contributed clothing, that charity worker might well be put away for twenty years. That was the demonic ultimate of this law; the clear and present danger to us was that, as members of the Communist Party, we could be arrested soon if not immediately, and while there was a possibility that we might win a legal battle, nothing that had happened until this time made us in any way optimistic. No Communist had won a court battle.

And then, what would happen to our children? Since they were the focus of our lives, our own fate was secondary.

Or do we leave the country and flee with them to Europe? We had no passports; but there was the possibility of taking Air Canada to Canada and then to England, where we could claim our rights as political refugees. My books had been published in England for many years and were still published there, and I didn't think the country would deny us refuge. And since I had not yet been arrested and charged under the new law, there would be small chance of extradition.

Now I know well enough that any lawyer reading this will snort at the ridiculous law and say that it was absolutely unconstitutional and could not stand up for a moment. Well enough to say this in 1990. In 1954, the situation was totally different, and such had been our experience during the last ten years that we had no reason to believe that the new law would not become functional. We knew that under Truman seven very large internment camps had been built — hidden from media notice, since Hitler and the Holocaust were still too fresh in memory — but certainly known to the cowardly Congress that had passed this law.

What do we do? For hours, we discussed this. The Israeli ambassador, hearing of the new situation, invited us to meet with him. He was a tall, handsome gentleman with a pronounced English accent, and he told us that if we were fearful of returning to the United States under the new law, we would be welcomed in Israel, and the Israeli government would happily issue passports to us and arrange for safe passage. My novel about the Maccabees had been translated into Hebrew six years before this, and according to the ambassador, it was a book that every literate citizen of Israel had read and I would be greeted in Israel as a hero, Communist or not.

There was a left-socialist organization in Mexico City, made up of young Mexican Jews who were preparing to go to Kibbutz Meggido in the north of Israel — a Spanish-speaking kibbutz already established — and through them we had hired a young woman as a baby sitter when Bette and I had to go out of an evening. Hearing of our family's plight, the young leader of the group came to us with an idea. They had located an old freighter in Vera Cruz, and it could be bought for $10,000. If we could contribute and help them raise the money, they would refit it and we could all sail to Israel. We thanked them and said, "Bless you, but no."

It seemed that everyone in Mexico City knew about the Fast family and their predicament. Siqueiros got in touch with me and told me that he had been discussing our situation with both the French ambassador and the president of Mexico. The president said that we could consider Mexico our home for as long as we desired to remain there and that we would be excused from the six-month period of a temporary resident. Such a resident had to return to the border every six months and establish re-entry, and this raised the possibility of his being arrested as he crossed over the border. The French ambassador said that France would welcome us and that Air France would make arrangements to take us there without our touching American territory.

It was all most gratifying to learn that to a good part of the world I was not a common criminal, as I was now defined in my own land, but a creative person respected and valued. I knew that many film people had fled to England, where they were now working; but the more these offers came to us, the more intolerable was the thought of living out our lives and raising our children in a foreign land, and so for the moment we made no move. There were still two weeks before the children's schools opened.

The Soviet ambassador sent us an invitation to a children's party at the embassy. We dressed both kids in their best and went off to the garden party. There were lots of kids there, and our children had a fine time of it. At one point, the ambassador asked me to step into his office. "About this new law," he said; "what does it mean? Does it mean that the United States is now a fascist country?" His English was quite good.

I did not know how to respond to that. Out of the country, one loses all perspective, and if one thinks like a refugee, one must constantly exaggerate the evil of the oppressor to justify existence as a refugee. I was not a refugee; I detested the thought of being a refugee.

"If you should decide to come to Russia, we will make it possible. You will find a place where you can live in peace and where you can go on with your writing." Or more or less those words. They were very kind, he and his wife, but I had no desire to live in the Soviet Union. I had done nothing wrong. I had enriched the culture of my country; I had written of its birth and agony; and this was good and valuable teaching for the millions who had read my books. I had never committed a crime that was recognized by civilized people as a crime.

I thanked him, and told him that I had no desire to live anywhere but in the United States of America. If I had to live part of the rest of my life in prison, so be it. But I wouldn't be alone, and sooner or later this madness would end. This sounds a good deal more coura-geous than the truth of it — the truth being that both Bette and I were heartsick, but the longer we lived in Mexico, the more we be-came convinced that it would be impossible for us to live out our lives there.

We talked and we talked, and finally we came to a decision. We would go home but we would have to change our life styles and our place of residence so that our children could be protected. Bette's mother and father, now living in Teaneck, New Jersey, were in their early sixties, but both of them were energetic and vital, with good years ahead of them. We had always maintained amiable relations with them, and they loved our children. Politically, they were as na-ïve as most Americans; they were a world apart from us, but while they did not comprehend our lives or beliefs, they were almost never overtly critical.

Bette telephoned her mother from our apartment in Mexico City. We were determined to find a house near theirs so that whatever happened to us, they could care for our children. As it happened, there was a small, attractive house for sale just around the corner, and when Bette's mother heard that we might be living only a block away, where she could see her grandchildren each day, she was so delighted that she did not even inquire as to what events had changed our minds about a suburb we had disliked intensely — a feeling not specific to Teaneck, but applying to any and all of the near New York suburbs. She described the house, and, listening with my ear close to Bette's, I nodded.

"Buy it," Bette said.

"But don't you want to see it?"

We both of us had a vague memory of the house. "I don't have to see it," Bette said. "We remember it. Put down a deposit and we'll reimburse you."

"Don't worry about that. Are you sure you want the house?"

"Absolutely."

"What did she say about the price?" I asked Bette.

"I never asked her. But how would she know?"

It turned out that the price was $32,500, and since we had most of the money from the sale of our West Side brownstone, the price was no problem.

Our time in Mexico was almost finished, but before we left we had dinner with Albert Maltz. He had taken a small house in the San Angel neighborhood and had installed his family there. At the time I met him in prison, Albert Maltz had been serving a six-month sentence. Prison had had a much deeper and more destructive effect on Albert than on me. He was a very sensitive person, and I suppose he could not bear the thought of years in prison. I had a great affection for him, and it broke my heart to see his resignation and misery. Not only had he given up the struggle and decided on a more or less permanent residence in Mexico (a decision he reversed in due time and returned to the States), but his marriage and family situation were not good. We had seen him several times before this final dinner; he had an adopted son who had a pet monkey, and together they frightened my children, not without reason; the son appeared to be completely out of Albert's control.

Albert was working on a new book, and he was giving pages to everyone who visited him, asking for an opinion — the result of his own distraction and misery. He offered pages to me, but I would not accept them and begged him to stop showing his work. "Wait for an editor to see it. These people know nothing. They want to say they advised you, and you don't need advice, not from me and not from anyone else. You're an old pro, and you're a fine writer."

Just Albert alone at that last dinner with us, and it was not a happy occasion. I felt as I had in prison — here was a man my heart went out to, and I was leaving him.

"Come home with us," I begged him. "You're a writer. You can't remain here and write well. This is an alien place to us, no matter how kind and generous they are. We have no roots here and we don't have our language. Our lives are our language."

"Have you read the Communist Control Act?"

"Of course I read it."

"I missed too much," Albert said. "I have to live. I have to find love. I have books I must write. I can't face the rest of my life in prison."

"They may never use this stupid law. It's crazy. This law makes half of the United States criminal. And even if they use it, people will have to fight back. This isn't Germany."

"They do it differently," Albert said forlornly. "We'll have our own native kind of Black Shirt."

He was wrong. I embraced him. I never saw him again.

We went home. We went by train, the unpleasant trip down to Mexico still fresh in our memories; and I wanted the kids to see the exciting country north to the border, the dramatic mountains of the Sierra Madre Oriental. Diego Rivera had given us a print, which he inscribed, and I was wondering whether customs would make some sort of fuss over it; but at the border, customs was a sweet lady who poked her head into our compartment, smiled at my children and my wife with pleasure, and said, "Well, I certainly don't have to look at your luggage."

Of course! How could this beautiful blond lady and her two children do anything wrong? Such is judgment. As for the Communist Control Act, no one north of the border ever mentioned it — except lefties — and no one seemed to know that it existed; as if, having passed this obscene bill, Congress in its shame pretended that it did not exist.

Yet until the day I die, I will ponder the mentality of an American Congress that subscribed to this infamous document.

17

IT WAS MY OWN TIME of total despair. Bit by bit, knowledge of the tyranny of Josef Stalin and the men around him was coming out of the Soviet Union. The death of Stalin had opened floodgates that would never again be closed. Living in Teaneck, I had my only contact with the party now through *The Daily Worker*. After years of writing intermittently for *The Worker*, I had finally agreed to become a permanent staff member and was doing my regular column of commentary. For all my battles through the years with the editors and their policies, I loved and revered the paper. It was a newspaper of courage and independence unmatched on the American scene, and for all the ten thousand and more accusations against us that we merely echoed the Soviet line, we were independent.

We had no connection with the Russians; we asked nothing from them and received nothing from them. But now we inherited their guilt and criminal cruelty, and because we were Communists, their sins became our sins. We had defended them for years, and we had nursed our own awful illusions about them. We deified them; we gave them virtues they in no way possessed; and while the knowledge of their shortcomings came to me early on, it was in no way so easy for others. We had greeted them as the harbingers of the brotherhood of man.

But under Stalin, it did not work. I could make a long and convincing argument that Stalin was insane, but that would explain nothing. During my last months in the party, I read two books with great excitement; one was *The Lives of the Twelve Caesars* by Suetonius, in the Robert Graves translation, and the other was Plutarch's

Lives. Each book bore a relationship to the life and actions of Stalin. Both books forced upon me the notion that all of the subjects of these two books were madmen. I went on to read Freud and others on paranoia, and I came to the conclusion, which many will disagree with, that most of the people who rule nations, sects, trade unions, Communist Parties (with some few exceptions), and a hundred other types of organization are clinically insane; that the drive for power originates at least in part from a paranoid personality.

But as I said, this does not explain sufficiently the horrible and unbelievable cruelties of Stalin. Part of the blame must inhere to the manner of organization that gave him the passport to power. If there had been in America, through those postwar years, one other organization that had the guts and integrity to stand up to the terror, and the willingness to face down J. Edgar Hoover and McCarthy, the Communist Party would not have lasted ten minutes.

But this was not Russia, and the people who made up the membership of the Communist Party of the United States were not Russians, and we on *The Daily Worker* were not working for *Pravda.* The truth was coming out, and, bit by bit, we printed it.

Meanwhile, we lived a very quiet life, Bette and I and our children. So often I had cursed the political innocence of the American people; now I blessed it. No one in the local schools, except a very few knowledgeable teachers, connected Rachel Fast or Jonathan Fast with the notorious Howard Fast — if, indeed, they had any notion of Howard Fast other than a name on a library shelf.

The almost absolute unwillingness of the media, large and small, print and voice, to deal with the persecution of the left gave us a security I had not anticipated; and living in a quiet suburb was an interesting change from the daily excitement and violence of the past ten years. Bette found a very decent job in New York as a designer of women's clothes; she was so skilled and creative that she was allowed to dictate her own hours. I still attended to my moribund publishing business, and one or the other of us was always home in Teaneck when the children returned from school. We could never conquer our fear for the children, and not without cause. Children of other Communists had been molested and threatened, and in those years I always slept with a baseball bat under my bed. Thankful I am that I never had to use it.

However, I was depressed and unhappy. Denying a man the right to continue in a creative effort he has spent his life to perfect is an awful thing, and in this deep misery I was one with the hundreds and hundreds of teachers, actors, musicians, novelists, screenwriters, playwrights, and artists who had been hounded out of their professions, not to mention the thousands of workers blacklisted into semi-starvation. I had proven Mark Twain's dictum that the man who becomes his own publisher has an idiot for a writer, and, like him, I had lost every cent I put into the venture. I became increasingly miserable.

The Communist Party leaders who had been imprisoned in 1950 now came out of jail, and John Gates, the best of them, the most innovative and independent, resumed his job as executive editor of *The Daily Worker*. It was under him that I joined the staff; a new life began for *The Worker,* and at the same time, a split in the leadership of the party between Gates and William Z. Foster, now seventy-five.

Since this is not a history of the Communist Party, I will not go into great detail concerning this split in the leadership; the origins of it were long in making and long in coming. William Z. Foster, Ben Davis, and Gene Dennis stood by the rigid doctrines of the Leninist pattern of organization, a party governed by theory that was neither pragmatic nor relevant to the American situation, a party of unbreakable discipline taking its cues from the Soviet party and rejecting every criticism of the Soviet Union. The opposition to this, led by John Gates, held that the Russians made grave errors, for which they must be criticized, that the rigid Leninist form was neither right for America nor helpful in the struggle of the American left, that it isolated the party, and was now bringing the party to its final moment of self-destruction. This, of course, is the briefest definition of what was happening.

Chaim Suller returned from the Soviet Union and sought me out in private to tell me a horrendous story of the persecution, not only of Jews, but of others — executions without trial, whipping, torture — all of this under the benign rule of Josef Stalin. Writing in *The Worker,* I began to deal with these matters, but Suller, for one, would not be quoted. The *Worker* staff defended me; the hatred of the leadership around Dennis and Foster for Howard Fast increased. They would have happily expelled me had I been alone, but the staff of *The Worker* was moving along the same road.

The Russians I knew put a strange face on things. Eugene Litescu, from Tass, had lunch with me in New York. He had just come back from Russia, and he said that for the first time in his life he had walked on a street in Moscow without fear.

"But this is something you never mentioned," I said.

"It's my country."

They gave a party at the consulate — the last party with the Soviets that we were ever invited to. I mentioned Suller and his story. A diplomat I knew said to me, indignantly, "Do you think Stalin killed only Jews?" His response so horrified me that I could say nothing in reply.

At a meeting of the staff at *The Daily Worker*, Joe Clark, the *Worker* Moscow correspondent during the early fifties, told John Gates that if he, Gates, had been found in Moscow with a copy of *The New York Times* in his possession, he would have been subject to ten years' imprisonment. East balanced West, but Gates, in the free and democratic United States, had served a sentence of five years for committing no crime whatsoever. I asked them, "Is there anyone here who can believe that he would not be sentenced to death if the Foster group had the power to do it?"

I had a note from Sean O'Casey: "Don't be taken in by the bastards!" — meaning those who attacked Russia. To be a revolutionary in Ireland is more simple.

No, no way. The taking of a human life is the ultimate, inexcusable human evil. I learned that from World War Two. I learned that when I was in the Washington, D.C., jail, listening to the condemned men weeping in the night and pleading for life. I think I became a pacifist there. I am a pacifist still. Sean O'Casey might pursue his dreams of brotherhood through hell; I could not. Years before, I had brought charges of anti-Semitism against the representative of the Communist Party of the Soviet Union, and the charges had been brushed away. Now we learned, at *The Worker*, that in 1948 all the Yiddish-language institutions and publications had been done away with, Yiddish-language poets put to death — a senseless crusade against the Jews, not in Germany but in the Soviet Union.

At *The Daily Worker*, we fought back. We accused the Soviets. We demanded explanations. For the first time in the life of the Communist Party of the United States, we challenged the Russians for the truth, we challenged the disgraceful executions that had taken place in Czechoslovakia and Hungary. We demanded explanations and openness. John Gates pulled no punches, printed the hundreds of letters that poured in from our readers, the bitterness of those who had given the best and most fruitful years of their lives to an organization that still clung to the tail of the Soviet Union.

Then, at that moment when we were fighting to make the paper a vehicle of truth and independence, the federal government stepped in and seized all the assets of *The Worker* — the editorial offices, all the premises — charging that we had not paid back taxes. Nobody knew better than the staff of the paper how ridiculous these charges were. Our annual deficit had never been below $200,000 a year, and again and again the paper was in a desperate crisis for funds. How many flying expeditions we had made to every corner of the metropolitan area to scrape together enough money to keep the paper alive for another few issues! In all my years with the paper, I had never taken a dollar for pay or expenses, but I was the only one on the staff who could afford to do that. The others were professional newspapermen who depended on their weekly wages to keep their families going; and again and again, they had missed paychecks because there was no money.

And now, after destroying thousands of people who believed in socialism, and jailing hundreds of others, and making life a living hell for people of good will all over the country, the idiots in the Treasury Department had thought up this new gimmick — closing the paper down for nonpayment of taxes.

They didn't quite succeed in closing us down, and the stupid move backfired. Every major newspaper in America cried out that this was a direct assault on freedom of the press and the First Amendment. Treasury agents seized our typewriters and files and office furniture, all of it worth about twenty cents. They slapped a lien on us that stated that *The Daily Worker* owed $46,049 in taxes and penalties for three years, from 1951 through 1953. When major newspapers charged Washington with this idiocy, the Internal Revenue offices in Washington backed down and claimed that the raid had been undertaken without their knowledge, at the behest of Donald R. Moysey, a Treasury official. Moysey, no great intellect, had thought that the raids would increase his importance politically. The opposite was true.

At *The Worker*, we put out the paper and stayed to our record of never missing a day of publication. Actually, the paper was printed by an independent publishing company in the same building. We found desks and typewriters where we could, and the next morning, our headline read OUR OFFICE SEIZED — HERE WE ARE. In all truth, I must say that the American press, which slandered us and lied about us day in and day out, saw to it that as a newspaper we were not attacked or closed down, and once, in a crisis when we had no newsprint, *The New York Times* gave us newsprint out of its own stock.

This did not halt us in our single-minded purpose, at *The Worker,* to re-create the paper as an independent vehicle, yet events were moving too quickly for us to adjust. It was in April of 1956 that I received an invitation to an evening at the Polish consulate in New York from Juliusz Katz-Suchy.

Katz-Suchy was then the leading representative of Poland in America. He had been the permanent representative of Poland to the United Nations, and at that time, when the United Nations was still meeting at Lake Success, I met him and talked to him about the anti-Communist drive in the United States. "How would you like to tell that story to the whole world?" he had asked me. I said I would be delighted to, and he told me to come out to Lake Success the following day at four o'clock and meet him in the delegates' lounge. My *Worker* press pass let me in. A session had just finished, and the delegates' lounge was packed with people. I found Katz-Suchy. He shook hands and led me to a narrow table against one wall. "If you have the guts for it," he said, "here are the delegates of the world. Get up on that table and talk to them." I did as he said, and when I called out, in a very large voice, the conversation in the lounge came to a stop, and for the next half hour I spoke without interruption — a full half hour before a guard appeared and politely asked me to get off the table and leave.

I was never punished in any way for this act, and though there were American delegates in the room, they did not attempt to stop me, nor did any newspaper take note of it, and I really do not know what good it did except to win me the friendship and admiration, I suppose, of Juliusz Katz-Suchy. That had been many years before. I had since met him at various Polish functions. But for each such function, there had been an embossed invitation with the gold lettering of the consulate. Now it was simply a handwritten note, and Bette and I supposed that it would be a small affair with just a few guests. It turned out to include only five diplomats from the Polish mission, including Katz-Suchy; Bette and I were the only outsiders present.

In the years since then, Bette and I have talked a great deal about that evening. There is no way I can recall precisely what was said there, but it was a recital, by the various men and the one woman present, of the horrors that Stalin had inflicted, not only on Poland but on the Polish Communist Party, three thousand members of which he had put to death. Every person in that room with us that evening was a member of the Communist Party of Poland, and as the evening wore on, all of them began to cry out of the well of emotion stirred up, including Katz-Suchy; and at the end of that ghastly evening Katz-Suchy declared, almost wildly, "There will never be a split between the Polish people and the Polish Communist Party! We are united forever in a holy hatred of Stalin and Russia!"

Ah, well — that was thirty-four years ago. Things change and things are forgotten, and new generations look at things differently. Perhaps it is best that it be thus; otherwise the whole world would exist in a mesh of hatred that could never be untangled. But for us, then, in 1956, it was an endless unrolling of horror.

And next, there was the secret speech by Nikita Khrushchev. This was the shattering and terrible analysis of Stalin and his crimes and the crimes of those who acted at his behest, and it was delivered during the sessions of the Twentieth Congress of the Communist Party of the Soviet Union. The congress met for eleven days, from February 14 to February 24, 1956. On the day Khrushchev delivered his speech, the most stringent efforts at secrecy were maintained. No members of the press were allowed in, and besides the Soviet delegates, only a few very trusted delegates from other countries were admitted. One of the Hungarian delegates proved to be a little less than "very trusted," and in due time he got in touch with the State Department — exactly how, I don't know — and after a proper price was arrived at, sold his copy of the secret speech to the State Department. They analyzed it, checked it out in every way possible, and decided that the Hungarian copy was valid. They then — and it took some months to arrive at this point — passed it on to *The New York*

Times. This was in the first week of June 1956. The day the editors of *The Times* received it and studied it, they got in touch with John Gates.

"We have it," the *Times* people told him. "We are convinced, as is the State Department, that it is genuine, with no word of it changed, and that this is a precise translation. If you want it, we will send you a copy, and if you wish to print it, you can do so on the day we print our copy."

At *The Worker,* we wanted it. John Gates read it, and the staff members read it, all twenty thousand bone-chilling words, and then we discussed it. The only good and positive thing you could say about the Soviet leadership at this point was that they had the courage and integrity to create this document. At least, one could argue that post-Nazi Germany had produced no such document and lacked the will and the courage to do so.

And Khrushchev, no fool, knew that in the end there are no secrets, and that this secret speech would cease to be secret and would shake the Communist world as nothing had ever shaken it before. That is precisely what happened, and in that part of the Communist world where *The New York Daily Worker* was printed, in the offices of this small and gallant newspaper that for thirty-two years had never missed an issue, had fought big business and reaction and anti-unionism, had fought for the poor and the oppressed — though it had slavishly supported every action of the Soviet Union — it shook us violently.

There is no use in trying to sum up the contents of the speech; it is an awful and terrifying list of infamies, murders, tortures, and betrayals. Yet in one part of it, Khrushchev said, "We cannot say that these were the deeds of a giddy despot. He [Stalin] considered that these things should be done in the interests of the party, of the working masses, in the name of the defense of the revolution's gains. In this lies the whole tragedy." What a sad, awful commentary! When I first read those twenty thousand words of horror and infamy, I exploded with rage — as did so many of the others on the staff of *The Worker.* Today, I look back on it with great sorrow, but with some understanding of the forces that created the situation and some knowledge of what an awful price mankind pays for a small step forward, for a little knowledge.

We printed the entire text of the secret speech in *The Worker*. We were the only Communist newspaper in the world to do so, and we did it in the face of the opposition of the Foster group. They still held the Communist Party — or what was left of it — in thrall, and they did not go along with the paper. In the end, some months later, they would win, and the life of *The Daily Worker* would come to an end.

All things come to an end. Being a part of this brave and decent newspaper had been an important act of my life. Now, on June 13, 1956, a couple of days after the appearance of the secret speech, I wrote my last column for *The Daily Worker*.

It was written out of torment; it should have said more and it should have said less. Who was I to make judgments, to prescribe the future? I was waking from a dream into a world where a handful of compassionate souls had cried out for justice since man began to make a society. When I brought the column into the offices of *The Worker*, I waited for Johnny Gates to read it and then pass it around to others. I asked him whether he would print it.

"Of course," he said.

"It's the last one," I told him.

Others on the staff argued with me, but they didn't plead. We had been through too much, and I think Johnny and they knew how I felt.

"And the party? What about the party?"

"That too. It's over."

They wanted to know whether I intended to make some public announcement, and I said that I would not. I desired no more publicity, no more of the endless parade of slanted, vicious stories about Howard Fast. For me, it seemed that everything was over. I had stopped writing and, in a sense, I had stopped living. Now I desired only to rest, to think, to try to put my world together as much as I could, to be with my wife and children.

In his book *The Story of an American Communist* (1958), Gates talks of that leave-taking:

One of those most shaken was Howard Fast, the only literary figure of note left in the Communist Party. He was a controversial figure not only in the country generally but in the party too. A fabulously suc-

cessful author before becoming known as a communist, he had been
boycotted for his political beliefs. In the communist movement he was
both idolized and cordially disliked. His forte was the popular historical novel, although he was not noted for his depth of characterization
or historical scholarship. Fast had made money but he had also lost it
because of his adherence to his principles, and he had gone to jail for
his beliefs. Fast had stuck out his neck more than most; he had received the Stalin Prize and defended everything communist and attacked everything capitalist in the most extravagant terms. It was to
be expected that he would react to the Khrushchev revelations in a
highly emotional manner, and I know of no one who went through a
greater moral anguish and torture.

I told Dennis and other party leaders of Fast's deep personal crisis
and I implored them to talk to him, but outside of some of us on the
Daily Worker, not a single party leader thought it important enough
to talk to the one writer of national, even worldwide reputation still
in the party. Later, when he announced his withdrawal and told his
story, party leaders leaped on him like a pack of wolves and began
that particular brand of character assassination which the communist
movement has always reserved for defectors from its ranks.

However, at this point I was absolutely indifferent to what the
leaders of the party thought of me — or for that matter what the
great American media thought of me. Bette and I had moved to Teaneck to provide a haven for our children in case we were both arrested under the Communist Control Act, but now it proved a refuge
for us. The telephone number most people had was that of my small
office in New York where the Blue Heron Press, moribund, still paid
the rent, mostly out of my pocket. I subscribed to an answering service — being unable to afford a secretary — and let whatever calls
there were pile up, coming into the city no more than once or twice
a week. Time passed; I lived very quietly, doing almost nothing. That
summer we sent the children to summer camp. Bette and I took a
long auto trip and ended up spending two weeks at a resort in the
Adirondacks, our first vacation of this sort in almost ten years. We
swam and canoed during the day and at night listened to a quartet
play classical music. The summer left us almost broke.

Then, in October of 1956, a very curious thing happened. The
cultural attaché at the Soviet embassy sent me a letter, advising me
that the Soviet Union intended, in February of 1957, to send me

almost $600,000 for past royalties. Could it be that they did not
know I had left the party? Or was this a grandiose bribe for me to
remain in the party? After all, they had printed a bibliography of my
books, printed in the millions in eighty-two languages in almost every
country on earth.

I think the first person we would have turned to was Julie Trupin,
but he was in the hospital, dying of cancer of the brain. A few other
people close to me said words to the effect that I had earned the
money. It was mine and I should let them send it, but Bette disagreed,
and I became convinced that she was right. If I took that money, I
would be silenced and obligated, and I had decided that I would
never again be silenced or obligated or disciplined. And again, how
did I know that my books had earned this money? Where were the
royalty statements? We licked our lips at the thought of that avalanche of money pouring into our almost empty bank account, and
then, as I recall it, we burst into laughter. What a gesture! Six hundred
thousand dollars down the drain. The letter had also informed me
that they had just printed 300,000 copies of a new edition of *Spartacus.* (Whether that edition continued to be sold, I never knew.) I
wrote to the embassy that I had resigned from the Communist Party,
and that I intended in the future to write about the Soviet Union as I
pleased. The "royalty payments" were never sent. If they had been,
they would have been returned; but long before the date promised,
my resignation from the Communist Party became public knowledge.

Fortune magazine was preparing an article about the Communist
movement in America, and they telephoned to ask whether I would
be interviewed. I told them that I was no longer a member of the
party but that I would be willing to be interviewed. Nevertheless,
when the *Fortune* article appeared in January 1957, it carried the
news that I had left the party. On the day of its appearance, Harry
Schwartz, an editor of *The New York Times,* called me and demanded to know whether the *Fortune* piece was right.

I said it was. Then he said, didn't I know that this was a story of
world importance? I said that had not really occurred to me, with all
that was happening in the world, and that I actually did not give a
damn. He argued me into giving him a short statement, and the following day it appeared on the front page of *The New York Times.*
For what it was worth, the world knew.

18

BILL FOSTER, for years the general secretary of the Communist Party of the United States, told me once that according to his calculations, during the thirty years (at the time) of the party's existence in America, more than 600,000 men and women had signed party cards and had become members of the party — most of them leaving after various lengths of time. The membership of the party at the end of World War Two had been, along with that of the Young Communist League, close to 100,000. When I left the party, the membership had dropped to about twenty thousand. It was said that more than half of that membership resigned when I did, and by the end of 1957, the Communist Party of the United States had for all practical purposes ceased to exist.

The Daily Worker published its last issue on January 13, 1958, precisely thirty-four years after its first issue had appeared. I doubt whether there was a day during those decades when the paper was not in debt. It was always understaffed, and its staff was always underpaid. It never compromised with the truth as it saw the truth; and while it was at times rigid and believing of whatever the Soviet Union put forth, it was so only because of its blind faith in the socialist cause. It is a part of the history of this country, and like the party that supported it, it preached love for its native land. It had once boasted a daily circulation of close to 100,000. Its final run was five thousand copies.

When my public statement of departure appeared in *The New*

York Times on the first day of February 1957, it was the end of part of my life; and even as my resignation drew forth a chorus of rage and slander from the leadership of the Communist Party here in America, a leadership with no party left to lead — so did it provoke a river of slander and hate from Russia, mostly from the pages of *The Literary Gazette*. The same Russian critics who had once hailed me as the most important novelist in the capitalist world now trashed me soundly, their display of irritation commensurate with what I had received from their western colleagues during the preceding twelve years. From that date on, no more books by Howard Fast were published or reprinted in the Soviet Union.

Only four years before this writing, a Soviet journalist interviewing me in New York City said to me, "Fast, we do not burn books, like the Nazis. We do not destroy books. You must not think that we have destroyed your books. My wife is a schoolteacher. She asks her students to read your books. You must remember that your books are in homes in the Soviet Union. They are read by a new generation."

And so it goes. What am I to say at the end of these long memoirs? Do I regret those years in the Communist Party? But regret is a meaningless word. Would I do it over again? That is equally meaningless. No human being is given a second time around. It is a time gone by, and most of us who played our roles during that time are dead. We were not a long-lived generation, and we gave of our lives and our strength unsparingly. In the party, I found ambition, rigidity, narrowness, and hatred; I also found love and dedication and high courage and integrity — and some of the noblest human beings I have ever known. I could not finish these memoirs without saying that, even knowing the sneers such a statement will evoke. Be damned to all of that! A man who will traduce those who stood with him in battle is not worth much.

I have tried to tell a truthful story here, but when one writes of the past, one writes of a fluid situation, changed already in the memory of those who lived through it and fated to endless change in the future as each generation rewrites history. Also, there is so much that I left out — as one must, or write endlessly — that this is at best only a small part of the story of the times — indeed only part of my own story. I could write a book of equal length dealing only with the remarkable woman I married and of our struggle to remain married and raise a family during those years.

I was forty-two years old when I left the Communist Party. I had joined it as one of the most praised and honored writers in the United States. I resigned from it as a man whose past had been totally obscured, who had been barred from publishing, who had been slandered and reviled as no other writer in American history. I suppose that in itself is a distinction of sorts. In 1957, when my action became clear to the Russians, they joined in this litany of hatred and slander — after which they consigned me to nonexistence.

Well, I have lived to see a new America and a new Soviet Union, and the real possibility of peace, not only between these two superpowers, but among all the nations of Europe. Our desperate struggle for peace had perhaps some small effect, as did our struggle for the rights of the poor and the working people of America.

Some years after I left the Communist Party, Bette and I, having been given passports — as the era of terror and lunacy began to fade — went off to Europe. We decided to cross on the old *Queen Mary,* a gracious and beautiful ship; it was a time when a good many people went to Europe by ship. Since I had just sold a book to film, we were able to afford first class, so we were seated for meals at a table with a physician, a fascinating gentleman whose name, unfortunately, I have forgotten. This doctor appeared to know everyone of importance in the world, and while he dropped names like snow in winter, we were to discover that he did know a very large number of people. At breakfast on the third day out, he told us that several United Nations delegations were aboard ship, that the Nigerian ambassador to the United Nations was giving a cocktail party for the Soviet delegation, and that, having heard that we were on board, the ambassador had requested our table companion to bring us to the party.

That was nice but impossible. I told him so. I pointed out that in the Soviet Union, I no longer existed. I had been wiped out of the human race. Correspondents had told me that my name, which had been a household word in Russia, had ceased to appear, even with a scurrilous epithet attached to it.

"This is not a Russian party. This is a Nigerian party. The Nigerian ambassador has read *Freedom Road.* He is very excited that you and your wife are aboard. He insists. If you do not come, it will be a breach of courtesy. As for the Soviets — they'll behave, I assure you."

He made his point, and Bette and I dressed for dinner and presented ourselves to the Nigerian ambassador, a tall, handsome man and one of those unflappable hosts. He introduced us to the Soviet ambassador to the United Nations and to the Soviet ambassador to Washington, and both responded with icy politeness. While the Nigerians crowded around to speak warmly to us, the Russian delegation avoided us. We had been to many Soviet parties in the past — parties where we were overwhelmed with kindness — but this was different and exactly what we had expected.

In fact, it was almost funny, as if the scene had been put together as a TV situation comedy. While the sitting room of the Nigerian suite was commodious, it was nevertheless aboard ship, and with thirty or so people in the place, it was quite crowded. There was no avoiding us, and the Soviet delegates and their wives fell into foolish smiles and head nodding, while the Nigerians leaned just a little bit backward in their efforts to be pleasant to us. I suppose the doctor at our table, who knew a good deal about my life in the time of terror and blacklisting, had given the Nigerians some background material — and so our presence turned into a small political event.

Each evening after dinner, Bette and I walked for a half hour or so on the deck. The transatlantic crossings in those days were not considered cruises or holidays on water. They were transportation, a comfortable way to go to Europe and return from Europe, in a time less frantic than today, and one of the great pleasures of this five-day period was to walk the deck, specially after dinner. The deck of the *Queen Mary* was long, providing a good walk in each lap, and as Bette and I walked, Ambassador Federenko appeared at my side, tapped me on the shoulder, apologized to Bette, and asked her whether she would permit me to walk with him and have a private talk. Graciously, Bette said that she had walked enough and that she would meet me later in the main lounge.

We walked and talked for almost an hour. Federenko began by apologizing for the cold reception at the cocktail party. His English was perfect. "We were taken by surprise," he said.

I accepted his apology, and he went on to tell me that he had sought me out because he considered me an honest man. I thanked him, and then he said that he hoped I could tell him what had happened to the Communist Party of the United States.

"You mean to tell me you don't know — even at this late date?"

"No, we don't. We read what you wrote and what John Gates wrote and it's not enough. It simply doesn't explain what is basic. In Germany, Hitler destroyed the party by murdering its membership. But that didn't happen to you."

"No," I agreed, "that didn't happen to us. You see, Mr. Federenko, we have a folk tale in America about a man called Jesse Pyme. We call Jesse the fool killer, and when someone dies as a result of his own foolishness, we say that Jesse Pyme got him. Well, that's what happened to us. Jesse Pyme got us."

That didn't satisfy him, and we talked and talked — to what Bette, sitting alone in the lounge, felt was eternity. He was a bright, intuitive man, a man without rigidity, and when I spelled out the nature of American society, he was able to accept what I said — and was, I may say, absolutely horrified by my story of the Tass team of reporters who had surveyed our southland from a bulletproof limousine.

Before becoming a diplomat, he had been a professor of Chinese at Moscow University, and when he had finished picking my brain for whatever he could find there of prime causes and social mores, I said to him, "I must get back to my wife before she decides that I have been lost overboard. You've thrown a lot of questions at me. Will you answer one question of mine?"

"If I can."

"Then tell me, Ambassador Federenko, when your country, united with China, could have kept the peace forever, why did you split?"

His answer is fixed in my memory for as long as I shall live. "Fast," he said to me, "why should you imagine that the people who rule my country are less stupid than the people who rule yours?"

As good a place as any to end these memoirs.

Index

Communist Party of France, 213, 278

Communist Party of India, 116–18, 127, 130–32

Communist Party of Poland, 349

Communist Party of the Soviet Union, 206–7, 217–19, 325, 346

Compass, The, 297

Conceived in Liberty, 20, 71, 80, 195, 290, 295, 296

Congress of Industrial Organizations, 77

Conway, Robert, 208–9, 211

Coronet, 96–97, 120

Cousins, Norman, 193

Cowan, Louis G., 21–26, 93

Crichton, Kyle, 95

Curie. *See* Joliot-Curie

Curley, Mayor James, 173

Daily Mirror, 201

Daily Worker, 130, 134, 141, 164–65, 197, 209–10, 214–16, 241, 289, 299, 300, 316, 330, 343, 345–48, 354

Davis, Ben, 345

Davis, Elmer, 5, 6–9, 11, 13, 18, 21, 154–55

Debs, Eugene V., 86, 87

Dennis, Gene, 117–18, 130–31, 345

Departure, 245

Derma, Joe, 186

Dewey, Thomas E., 91, 237

Dial Press, 19, 62

Dmytryk, Edward, 182, 256, 259, 260–61, 266

Dodd, Mead and Company, 19, 62

Dollinger, Isidore, 305, 311, 313

Doubleday, 290–91

Dreiser, Theodore, 77, 139

Dubinsky, David, 185

Du Bois, W. E. B., 77, 84, 156, 183, 299

Duell, Charles, 75

Duell, Jo Pringle-Smith, 75–76

Duell, Sloan and Pearce, 20, 43, 73, 290, 298

Dunlop, Helen, 10

Dystel, Oscar, 96–97

Egypt, 104–8

Ehrenberg, Ilya, 244

Eisenhower, Dwight, 310

Elks magazine, 69

Enoch, Kurt, 295–97

Fadeev, Alexander, 217–19, 323

Fadiman, Clifton, 133

Fallen Angel, The, 245–46

Farmer-Labor Party, 189

Farrell, James T., 52, 53, 71

Fast, Arthur, 29

Fast, Barbara, 157

Fast, Barney, 28–31, 37, 38, 40, 55, 63–64, 73–74

Fast, Bette (Cohen), 2, 10, 17, 66–67, 68–70, 129, 140, 156, 170, 172, 174, 222–24, 238–39, 253–54, 297, 298, 315, 344; in Signal Corps, 3, 16, 76; as Communist Party member, 83, 88, 133, 172

Fast, Edward, 28, 34–35

Fast, Howard: family background and early years, 2, 28–54; at Office of War Information, 4–15, 17–26; education, 32, 38–39, 44–46, 48–49, 51; House Un-American Activities